Microsoft® ASP.NET 2.0
Step By Step

George Shepherd

PUBLISHED BY
Microsoft Press
A Division of Microsoft Corporation
One Microsoft Way
Redmond, Washington 98052-6399

Library of Congress Control Number: 2005933911

Printed and bound in the United States of America.

2 3 4 5 6 7 8 9 QWT 8 7 6 5

Distributed in Canada by H.B. Fenn and Company Ltd. A CIP catalogue record for this book is available from the British Library.

Microsoft Press books are available through booksellers and distributors worldwide. For further information about international editions, contact your local Microsoft Corporation office or contact Microsoft Press International directly at fax (425) 936-7329. Visit our Web site at www.microsoft.com/mspress. Send comments to [For Resource Kits: rkinput@microsoft.com.; For Training Kits: tkinput@microsoft.com.; For all other titles: mspinput@microsoft.com.]

Microsoft, ActiveX, BizTalk, FrontPage, Hotmail, Microsoft Press, MSN, SharePoint, Verdana, Visual Basic, Visual Studio, Windows, Windows NT, and Windows Server are either registered trademarks or trademarks of Microsoft Corporation in the United States and/or other countries. Other product and company names mentioned herein may be the trademarks of their respective owners.

The example companies, organizations, products, domain names, e-mail addresses, logos, people, places, and events depicted herein are fictitious. No association with any real company, organization, product, domain name, e-mail address, logo, person, place, or event is intended or should be inferred.

This book expresses the author's views and opinions out any express, statutory, or implied warranties. Neither the authors, Microsoft Corporation, nor its resellers, or distributors will be held liable for any damages caused or alleged to be caused either directly or indirectly by this book.

Acquisitions Editor: Ben Ryan
Project Editor: Kathleen Atkins
Editorial and Production: Custom Editorial Productions, Inc.

Body Part No. X11-50498

Dedicated to

Ted Gregory Daston Shepherd

Contents at a Glance

Table of Contents

Introduction

This book will help you figure out how to write Web applications using Microsoft's most current version of its HTTP request processing framework—ASP.NET 2.0. Web development has come a long way since the earliest sites began popping up in the early 1990s. The world of Web development offers several different choices as far as development tools go. Over the past few years, ASP.NET has evolved to become one of the most consistent, stable, and feature-rich frameworks available for managing HTTP requests.

ASP.NET together with Visual Studio include a number of features to make your life as a Web developer easier. For example, Visual Studio starts you off with several very useful project templates from which to develop your site. Visual Studio also supports a number of development modes, including using Internet Information Services directly to test your site during development, using a built-in Web server, or developing your site over an FTP connection. The debugger in Visual Studio lets you run the site and step through the critical areas of your code to find problems. The Visual Studio designer enables effective user interface development, allowing you to drop control elements onto a canvas to see how they appear visually. These are but a few of the features built into the ASP.NET framework when paired with Visual Studio.

While ASP.NET and Visual Studio offer excellent tools for writing Web applications, Web development on the Microsoft platform hasn't always been this way. The road to ASP.NET 2.0 has been nearly a decade in the making.

The Road to ASP.NET 2.0

Until about 1993, there were very few Web servers in the world. Most of these earliest Web servers lived at universities or other research centers. In the early 1990s, the number of Web sites available began to increase dramatically. If you used the Web back in the early 1990s, chances are you probably came across little more than some HTML pages put together by the earliest Web site pioneers or some photo collections represented by links to GIF or JPEG files. Back then, there was no Google, no Yahoo, and certainly no MSN Search. The only way you could get to someone's site was if you either knew the site's Uniform Resource Locator (URL) or were referred to it through someone else's page.

Typing a URL like this:

```
http://www.somesite.com
```

into a browser's navigation window sent your request through a maze of routers, finally appearing at a server somewhere. The earliest Web servers lived on UNIX boxes. They performed the simple job of loading the HTML file and sending it back to the requestor (perhaps a browser such as Mosaic).

The advent of the Common Gateway Interface (CGI) introduced a standard way to interface with browsers to produce interactive Web applications. While a Web server that serves up plain, static HTML documents is useful in certain contexts (for example, a hyperlinked dictionary), more complex applications require a conversation between the user and end server.

That's where CGI comes in. With the help of HTML tags representing standard GUI controls, CGI applications can respond to requests dynamically. That is, CGI applications vary their output depending upon the state within the request and the application, paving the way for widely interactive applications. For example, a CGI application can examine an incoming request and determine the user is looking for a certain piece of information (perhaps a product code). The CGI application can perform a database lookup for the product and shoot some HTML that describes the product back to the client.

When it became clear that the Web was an important aspect of information technology, Microsoft entered the fray by introducing the Internet Services API (ISAPI) and a program to listen for HTTP requests: Internet Information Services (IIS). While the first UNIX Web servers started a new process to handle each HTTP new request (in keeping with the classical UNIX model), that model is very expensive. The Microsoft Web strategy is based on DLLs. It's much faster to load a DLL to respond to an HTTP request than it is to start a whole new process.

When programming to the Microsoft platform, IIS listens to port 80 for HTTP requests. IIS handles some requests directly, while delegating other requests to specific ISAPI extension DLLs to execute the request. In other cases, IIS will map a file extension to a specific ISAPI DLL. A number of ISAPI DLLs come preinstalled with Windows. However, IIS is extensible, and you may map different extensions to any ISAPI DLL—even one you wrote. To make a Web site work using IIS and ISAPI, developers employ ISAPI DLLs. These DLLs intercept the request, decompose it, and respond by sending back something to the client (usually some HTML).

While the IIS/ISAPI platform represents a very flexible and functional way to create Web applications, it's not without its downside. Specifically, ISAPI DLLs are traditionally written in C++ and are subject to the pitfalls of C++ programming (including such foibles as de-referencing bad pointers, forgetting to free memory, and traditionally lengthy development cycles). The other problem with ISAPI DLLs is that it's becoming increasingly more difficult to find C++ programmers. Enter Active Server Pages, or classic ASP.

Classic ASP

In an effort to make Web development more accessible on the Microsoft platform, Microsoft introduced Active Server Pages (ASP). The idea behind classic ASP is that a single ISAPI DLL named ASP.DLL interprets files with the extension ASP (for example, MYSITE.asp). ASP files include some HTML and perhaps some script code to be executed on the server. The ASP ISAPI DLL executes the script code as necessary and sends the HTML contained in the ASP file back to the client. The script code usually calls COM objects that do the dirty work (for example, looking up items in a database and tailoring the output based upon its findings) while the look and feel of the page is defined by the HTML in the ASP file.

While ASP opened the doors to a whole host of new programmers by catering to a much more widely used programming language (Visual Basic and VBScript), it wasn't the silver bullet. Among the downsides of classic ASP are:

- Mixing of user interface code and programming logic

- Performance issues due to *IDispatch*

- Inconsistent means of managing state (session state and application state)

- An ad-hoc security model

This isn't an exhaustive list by any means, but it highlights the most important issues with classic ASP. That's why ASP.NET exists.

ASP.NET 1.0 and 1.1

Microsoft's .NET framework introduces a whole new way of programming the Microsoft platform. Microsoft developers are primarily concerned with threads and memory (that's basically the API programming model). This model carried over to all areas of development, including Web development, placing a heavy burden upon programmers.

.NET is built upon the notion of managed types. Developers writing classic Windows code (and Web code) wrote classes using C++ or Visual Basic. In many ways, types are similar to the notion of the C++ class in that types are units of state with functionality attached to them. However, the similarity ends there. Whereas it was incumbent upon the developer to manage instances of classes, types are managed completely by the .NET runtime services—the Common Language Runtime (CLR). Because the CLR takes over managing memory and threads, developers are much more at liberty to concentrate on the actual application (rather than chasing down errant pointers, memory leaks, and unexplained crashes).

ASP.NET introduces runtime services and a well-engineered class library for greatly enhancing Web development. In a way, classic ASP was sort of "taped onto" the IIS/ISAPI architecture without any real organic thought as to how early design decisions would affect developers later on. Well, now it's later on and classic ASP.NET's warts have become fairly obvious.

ASP.NET is built from the ground up to be an extensible, feature-rich way to handle HTTP requests. ASP.NET leverages IIS in that requests for ASP.NET services are mapped to an ISAPI DLL. The DLL is named ASPNET_ISAPI.DLL. From there, processing is passed into a worker process provided by ASP.NET (ASPNET_WP.EXE in IIS 5 or W3WP.EXE in IIS 6). The fundamental request processing is handled by managed types within the worker process. Control

xviii   Introduction

passes between a number of classes plugged into the pipeline—some provided by Microsoft and/or third parties, and some provided by the developer. What's more, ASP.NET is built from the ground up to be a comprehensive framework for writing Web applications. All the parts of the framework execute together to handle requests. By contrast, classic ASP.NET script code had no structure to it, and code logic within applications tended to be ad hoc.

ASP.NET 1.0 and 1.1 provided a significant number of features, including:

- An object-oriented framework for defining applications
- Separation of user interface declarations (HTML) and application logic
- Compiled code for executing application logic
- Configurable session state management
- Built-in data caching
- Built-in content caching
- A well-defined UI componentization architecture
- High-level components for managing data formatting (grids, lists, text boxes)
- Built-in program tracing and diagnostics
- Built-in user input validation
- An easy-to-use custom authentication mechanism
- Solid integration with ADO.NET (the .NET database story)
- Excellent support for Web Services
- Zero reliance on the Component Object Model
- An extensible pipeline with many places in which a request can be intercepted

ASP.NET 1.0 set the stage for many developers both moving into Web development and moving to the Microsoft Platform.

ASP.NET 2.0

Which brings us to ASP.NET 2.0. ASP.NET 2.0 builds upon ASP.NET 1.0 and 1.1 by providing a number of new features in addition to what already existed with ASP.NET 1.0. These features include

- Master Pages and Skins
- Declarative databinding
- Provider pattern model
- New cache features

- Membership controls
- Personalization controls
- Support for Web Parts
- Programmable configuration
- Administration tools
- New compilation model

All the features of ASP.NET 1.0/1.1 are still there. However, these new features make ASP.NET an even more compelling platform for creating Web sites. We'll visit all these features as we tour ASP.NET 2.0.

A Word About the .NET Runtime

ASP.NET 2.0 is built upon Microsoft's Common Language Runtime. In its earliest days, programming Windows involved interacting with the operating system at a very intimate level. For example, getting a Window to show up on a screen took many lines of C code. In addition, Windows included a rudimentary component technology—raw Dynamic Link Libraries. Dynamic Link Libraries (DLLs) represent a necessary technology to enable composing systems dynamically—that is, to assemble applications from several disparate *binary* components. However, DLLs by themselves are not sufficient for composing systems reliably—primarily because it's very difficult to manage multiple versions of a component (a DLL).

During the mid 90's, the Component Object Model (COM) emerged as a way to help manage multiple versions of a component. By stipulating strict rules about how clients and components may interact, COM represented a technology sufficient for composing applications from different binary components. However, COM faced a few dead ends which became apparent as developers began building larger systems.

First, COM relied on humans following rules to get things to interoperate. For example, COM stipulates a rule that once a programmatic interface is published, it must never change. Changing a published COM interface after clients begin coding against it will almost certainly bring a system to its knees. In addition, COM relied on sometimes obtuse rules as far as managing resources. However, the *coup de grace* for COM was probably the disparate type systems involved. That is, COM represented many data types differently for three separate classes of developers: C++ developers, Visual Basic developers, and scripting developers. The different data type systems made it extremely inconvenient to build systems built from different languages. It could be done, but developers had to be very wary when making calls across such component boundaries.

.NET and the Common Language Runtime (the CLR) were developed to solve the dead ends appearing in COM near the end of the last century. When you choose to buy into the .NET runtime, it's like putting your code in a nice hotel room when it runs. For example, the .NET runtime loads and manages your code as it runs. Pure memory leaks are a thing of the past because the runtime collects garbage when necessary. The problem of overrunning array boundaries disappears because the .NET runtime keeps careful watch over memory and knows when anything is out of place. In addition, the .NET runtime includes a new security model making it more difficult to hack into .NET-based software. Finally, the .NET runtime introduces a new packaging and deployment model, .NET Assemblies, which helps enforce versioning components.

ASP.NET is founded on the .NET runtime. As we'll see in the following chapters, ASP.NET runs completely under the auspices of the CLR. After IIS hands an HTTP request off to ASP.NET, it runs through the ASP.NET pipeline. The request may be intercepted at various places along the way, and you have ample opportunity to interrogate the request and modify the response before it finally leaves the ASP.NET runtime. Gone is the COM layer between the HTTP request processing machinery and a business's domain objects. Domain objects running under .NET can be linked into the request processing pipeline for high performance and tight security. In addition, because all .NET components agree upon the data types being passed between them, there are no more bizarre data conversions (as there used to be in classic ASP).

In the process of building ASP.NET applications you will be developing .NET assemblies—most of the time implicitly, but sometimes explicitly. While you'll be focusing on ASP.NET as a Web application framework, you'll develop a strong familiarity with the .NET runtime as well. Very often, the classes you use in an ASP.NET application are the same or very similar to those you'd use in a console application, a Windows application, or even a component library.

Using This Book

The purpose of this book is to weave the story of ASP.NET 2.0 development for you. Each section presents a specific ASP.NET feature in a digestible format *with* examples. The step-wise instructions should yield working results for you immediately. You'll find most of the main features within ASP.NET illustrated here with succinct, easily duplicated examples. I made the examples rich to illustrate the feature without being overbearing. In addition to showing off ASP.NET features by example, you'll find practical applications of each feature so you can take these techniques into the real world.

Who Is This Book For?

This book is targeted to several developers:

- **Those starting out completely new with ASP.NET**   The text includes enough back story to explain the Web development saga even if you've developed only desktop applications.

- **Those migrating from either ASP.NET 1.x or even classic ASP**   The text explains how ASP.NET 2.0 is different from ASP.NET 1.x. The text also includes references explaining differences between ASP.NET and classic ASP.

- **Those wanting to consume ASP.NET how-to knowledge in digestible pieces**   Most chapters stand independently. You don't have to read the chapters in any particular order to find the book valuable. Each chapter stands more or less on its own (with the exception of the first chapter detailing the fundamentals of Web applications—you may want to read it first if you've never ventured beyond desktop application development). You may find it useful to study the chapters about server-side controls together (Chapters 3, 4, and 5), but it's not completely necessary to do so.

Organization of This Book

This book is organized so that each chapter may be read independently, for the most part. With the exception of Chapter 1 about Web application essentials and the three server-side control chapters—Chapters 3, 4, and 5—which make sense to tackle together, each chapter serves as a self-contained block of information about a particular ASP.NET feature.

Getting Started

If you've gotten this far, you're probably ready to begin writing some code. Before beginning, make sure that Visual Studio 2005 is installed on your machine. As long as you've installed the development environment, you can be sure the .NET runtime support is installed as well.

The first few examples will require nothing but a text editor and a working installation of Internet Information Services. To start, we'll begin with some basic examples to illustrate ASP.NET's object-oriented nature and compilation model. In addition to letting you see exactly how ASP.NET works when handling a request, this is a good time to lay out ASP.NET's architecture from a high level. We'll progress to Web form programming and soon begin using Visual Studio to write code (which makes things much easier!).

After learning the fundamentals of Web form development, we'll break apart the rest of ASP.NET, using examples to understand ASP.NET's features such as server-side controls, content caching, writing custom handlers, caching output and data, and debugging and diagnostics, all the way to ASP.NET's support for Web Services.

Finding Your Best Starting Point in This Book

This book is designed to help you build skills in a number of essential areas. You can use this book whether you are new to Web programming or you are switching from another Web development platform. Use the following table to find your best starting point in this book.

If you are	Follow these steps
New	
To Web development	1. Install the code samples.
	2. Work through the examples in Chapters 1 and 2 sequentially. They will ground you in the ways of Web development. They will also familiarize you with ASP.NET and Visual Studio.
	3. Complete the rest of the book as your requirements dictate.
New	
To ASP.NET and Visual Studio	1. Install the code samples.
	2. Work through the examples in Chapter 2. They provide a foundation for working with ASP.NET and Visual Studio.
	3. Complete the rest of the book as your requirements dictate.
Migrating	
From ASP.NET 1.x or from classic ASP	1. Install the code samples.
	2. Skim the first two chapters to get an overview of Web development on the Microsoft platform and Visual Studio 2005.
	3. Concentrate on Chapters 3 through 20 as necessary. You may already be familiar with some topics and may only need to see how a particular feature differs between ASP.NET 1.x and ASP.NET 2.0. In other cases, you may need to explore a feature that's completely new for ASP.NET 2.0.
Referencing	
The book after working through the exercises	1. Use the Index or the Table of Contents to find information about particular subjects.
	2. Read the Quick Reference sections at the end of each chapter to find a brief review of the syntax and techniques presented in the chapter.

Conventions and Features in This Book

This book presents information using conventions designed to make the information readable and easy to follow. Before you start the book, read the following list, which explains conventions you'll see throughout the book and points out helpful features in the book that you might want to use.

Conventions

- Each chapter includes a summary of objectives near the beginning.
- Each exercise is a series of tasks. Each task is presented as a series of steps to be followed sequentially.
- Notes labeled "Tip" provide additional information or alternative methods for completing a step successfully.

- Text that you type appears in bold, like so:

```
class foo
{
    System.Console.WriteLine("HelloWorld");
}
```

- The directions often include alternate ways of accomplishing a single result. For example, adding a new item to a Visual Studio project may be done from either the main menu, or by right mouse clicking in the Solution Explorer.

- Most of the examples in this book are written using C#. However a few chapters have examples in both C# and Visual Basic so you may see how the same programming idioms are expressed in different languages.

Other Features

- Some text includes sidebars and notes to provide more in-depth information about the particular topic. The sidebars might contain background information, design tips, or features related to the information being discussed. They may also inform you about how a particular feature may differ in this version of ASP.NET.

- Each chapter ends with a Conclusion and a Quick Reference section. The Quick Reference section contains concise reminders of how to perform the tasks you learned in the chapter.

System Requirements

You'll need the following hardware and software to complete the practice exercises in this book:

> **Note**   The Visual Studio 2005 software is *not* included with this book! The CD-ROM packaged in the back of this book contains the codes samples needed to complete the exercises. The Visual Studio 2005 software must be purchased separately.

- Microsoft Windows XP Professional with Service Pack 2, Microsoft Windows Server 2003 with Service Pack 1, or Microsoft Windows 2000 with Service Pack 4

- Microsoft Internet Information Services (IIS) (included with Windows)

- Microsoft Visual Studio 2005 Standard Edition or Microsoft Visual Studio 2005 Professional Edition

- Microsoft SQL Server 2005 Express Edition (included with Visual Studio 2005) or Microsoft SQL Server 2005

- 600 MHz Pentium or compatible processor (1 GHz Pentium recommended)

- 192 MB RAM (256 MB or more recommended)

- Video (800 × 600 or higher resolution) monitor with at least 256 colors (1024 × 768 High Color 16-bit recommended)

- CD-ROM or DVD-ROM drive

- Microsoft Mouse or compatible pointing device

You will also need to have Administrator access to your computer to configure SQL Server 2005 Express Edition.

Using Microsoft Access

Chapter 13 on databinding and Chapter 14 on application data caching both use Microsoft Access. If you want to look at the databases and modify them, you need to have installed Microsoft Access on your machine. If you have Microsoft Office, you probably already have it. There is nothing special you need to do to set it up, and there is nothing special you need to do to use the databases within the ASP.NET applications.

Code Samples

The companion CD inside this book contains the code samples, written in C#, that you'll use as you perform the exercises in the book. By using the code samples, you won't waste time creating files that aren't relevant to the exercise. The files and the step-by-step instructions in the lessons also let you learn by doing, which is an easy and effective way to acquire and remember new skills.

Note If you prefer to use code samples written in Visual Basic, you can download a Visual Basic version of the code samples. See the "Installing the Visual Basic Code Samples" section for more information.

Installing the C# Code Samples

Follow these steps to install the C# code samples on your computer so that you can use them with the exercises in this book.

Note The code sample installer modifies IIS, so you must have Administrator permissions on your computer to install the code samples.

1. Remove the companion CD from the package inside this book and insert it into your CD-ROM drive.

Note An end user license agreement should open automatically. If this agreement does not appear, open My Computer on the desktop or Start menu, double-click the icon for your CD-ROM drive, and then double-click StartCD.exe.

2. Review the end user license agreement. If you accept the terms, select the accept option and then click Next.

    A menu will appear with options related to the book.

3. Click Install Code Samples.

4. Follow the instructions that appear.

Note If IIS is not installed and running, a message will appear indicating that the installer cannot connect to IIS. You can choose to ignore the message and install the code sample files, however, the code samples that require IIS will not run properly.

The code samples will be installed to the following location on your computer: C:\Microsoft Press\ASP.NET 2.0 Step by Step\

The installer will create a virtual directory named aspnet2sbs under the Default Web Site. Below the aspnet2sbs virtual directory, various Web applications are created. To view these settings, open the Internet Information Services console.

Installing the Visual Basic Code Samples

Follow these steps to download and install the Visual Basic code samples on your computer so that you use them with the exercises in this book.

> **Note**   The code sample installer modifies IIS, so you must have Administrator permissions on your computer to install the code samples.

1. Download the Visual Basic code samples installer from the book's online companion content page:
    http://www.microsoft.com/mspress/companion/0-7356-2201-9/

2. Run the installer.

3. Follow the instructions that appear.

> **Note**   If IIS is not installed and running, a message will appear indicating that the installer can not connect to IIS. You can choose to ignore the message and install the code sample files, however, the code samples that require IIS will not run properly.

The code samples will be installed to the following location on your computer: C:\Microsoft Press\ASP.NET 2.0 Step by Step\

The installer will create a virtual directory named aspnet2sbs under the Default Web Site. Below the aspnet2sbs virtual directory, various Web applications are created. To view these settings, open the Internet Information Services console.

Using the Code Samples

Each chapter in this book explains when and how to use any code samples for that chapter. When it's time to use a code sample, the book will list the instructions for how to open the files. Many chapters begin projects completely from scratch so you can grok the whole development process. Some examples borrow bits of code from previous examples.

Here's a comprehensive list of the code sample projects.

Project	Description
Chapter 1	
HelloWorld.asp, Selectnoform.asp, Selectfeature.htm, Selectfeature2.htm, Selectfeature.asp	Several Web resources illustrating different examples of raw HTTP requests.
WebRequestor	A simple application that issues a raw HTTP Request.
Chapter 2	
HelloWorld, HelloWorld2, HelloWorld3, HelloWorld4, HelloWorld5, partial1.cs, partial2.cs	Web resources illustrating ASP.NET's compilation models and partial classes.
Chapter 3	
BunchOfControls.htm, BunchOf-Controls.asp, BunchOfControls.aspx	Web resources illustrating rendering control tags.
ControlORama	Visual Studio-based project illustrating Visual Studio and server-side controls.
Chapter 4	
ControlORama	Illustrates creating and using rendered server-side controls.
Chapter 5	
ControlORama	Illustrates creating and using composite server-side controls and *User* controls.
Chapter 6	
ControlPotpourri	Illustrates control validation, the *TreeView*, and the *MultiView* / *View* controls.
Chapter 7	
UseWebParts	Illustrates using Web Parts within a Web application.
Chapter 8	
MasterPageSite	Illustrates developing a common look and feel throughout multiple pages within a single Web application using Master Pages, Themes, and Skins.
Chapter 9	
ConfigORama	Illustrates configuration within ASP.NET. Shows how to manage the Web.Config file, how to add new configuration elements and how to retrieve those configuration elements.
Chapter 10	
SecureSite	Illustrates Forms Authentication and authorization within a Web site.
Login.aspx, OptionalLogin.aspx, Web.Config, Web.ConfigForceAuthentication, Web.ConfigForOptionalLogin	Web resources for illustrating Forms Authentication at the very barest level.

Project	Description
Chapter 11	
DataBindORama	Illustrates databinding to several different controls, including the *GridView*. Also illustrates loading and saving datasets as XML and XML schema.
Chapter 12	
MaketPersonal	Illustrates the new ASP.NET 2.0 personalization features.
Chapter 13	
SessionState	Illustrates using session state within a Web application.
Chapter 14	
UseDataCaching	Illustrates caching data to increase performance.
Chapter 15	
OutputCaching	Illustrates caching output to increase performance.
Chapter 16	
DebugORama	Illustrates debugging and tracing Web applications.
Chapter 17	
UseApplication	Illustrates using the global application object and HTTP modules as a rendezvous point for the application. Illustrates storing globally scoped data and handling application-wide events. Includes an equivalent example module in Visual Basic.
Chapter 18	
CustomHandlers	Illustrates custom HTTP handlers, both as separate assemblies and as ASHX files. Includes code in C# and Visual Basic.
Chapter 19	
WebServiceORama	Illustrates a Web service that serves up random quotes.
QuoteServiceVB	Illustrates a Web service using Visual Basic that serves up random quotes.
Chapter 20	
DeployThis	Illustrates how to make an installation package to deploy a Web site.

All these projects are available as complete solutions for the practice exercises (in case you need any inspiration).

Uninstalling the Code Samples

Follow these steps to remove the code samples from your computer.

1. In Control Panel, open Add Or Remove Programs.

2. From the list of Currently Installed Programs, select Microsoft ASP.NET 2.0 Step by Step.

3. Click Remove.

4. Follow the instructions that appear to remove the code samples.

Prerelease Software

This book was reviewed and tested against the August 2005 Community Technical Preview (CTP) of Visual Studio 2005. The August CTP was the last preview before the final release of Visual Studio 2005. This book is expected to be fully compatible with the final release of Visual Studio 2005. If there are any changes or corrections for this book, they will be collected and added to a Microsoft Knowledge Base article. See the "Support for This Book" section in this Introduction for more information.

Online Companion Content

The online companion content page has content, code samples, and links related to this book, including a link to the Microsoft Press Technology Updates Web page. (As technologies related to this book are updated, links to additional information will be added to the Microsoft Press Technology Updates Web page. Visit the page periodically for updates on Visual Studio 2005 and other technologies.) The online companion content page for this book can be found at:

http://www.microsoft.com/mspress/companion/0-7356-2201-9/

Support for This Book

Every effort has been made to ensure the accuracy of this book and the contents of the companion CD. As corrections or changes are collected, they will be added to a Microsoft Knowledge Base article. To view the list of known corrections for this book, visit the following article:

http://support.microsoft.com/kb/905042/

Microsoft Press provides support for books and companion CDs at the following Web site:

http://www.microsoft.com/learning/support/books/

Questions and Comments

If you have comments, questions, or ideas regarding the book or the companion CD, or questions that are not answered by visiting the sites above, please send them to Microsoft Press via e-mail to

mspinput@microsoft.com

Or via postal mail to

Microsoft Press

Attn: Step by Step Series Editor

One Microsoft Way

Redmond, WA 98052-6399

Please note that Microsoft software product support is not offered through the above addresses.

Acknowledgments

I got a great Father's Day card from my 14 year old son this year. When I opened it up, I saw that he wrote the greeting in HTML!

```
<html>
   <head>
      <title>
         Father's Day Card
      </title>
   </head>
<body>
   Happy Father's Day!!!
</body>
</html>
```

After wiping away the tears, seeing Ted's card reinforced for me the increasing importance of Web-based applications. The Web permeates our social infrastructure. Whether you're a business person wanting to increase the visibility of your business, an avid reader trying to find an out-of-print book, a student fetching homework assignments from a school Web site, or any other producer or consumer of information, you touch the Internet.

This book is all about building Web applications using the most recent edition of Microsoft's modern HTTP-handling framework—ASP.NET 2.0. After spending some time with it (and comparing it to other approaches), I imagine you'll find it to be well-engineered, robust, and rich enough to handle most of what you can throw at it. And for those odd HTTP requests you need to handle, ASP.NET has enough hooks that you'll almost certainly be able to deal with them.

Publishing a book is a huge effort. My name's on the lower right-hand corner of the cover as the author, but I did only some of the work. I have many so people to thank for helping get this book out.

Thank you, Claudette Moore for hooking me up with Microsoft Press again. Claudette has acted as my agent for all my work with Microsoft Press, handling the business issues associated with this work.

Thank you, Kathleen Atkins for managing the project. This project was a major effort for me—and I know you had several other projects going at the same time.

Thank you, Sally Stickney for helping with the project management as well. Sally and I worked together 6 years ago on another Microsoft Press project.

Thank you, Ericka McIntyre and the staff at Custom Editorial Productions for editing my work and making it appear that I can actually write coherent sentences. You all did a wonderful job on the editing, production, and layout.

Thank you, Jawaharlal Puvvala for providing the technical objective eye for the work.

Thank you, Robert Lyon for getting all my sample code into a usable format.

Thank you, Ben Ryan for accepting the book proposal and hiring me to create it.

Thank you, Christine Shooter for your love and support as I worked away on the project over the summer. You're always a welcome sight after hours staring at the computer screen.

Thanks to my evil Java twin, Pat Shepherd and his family, Michelle Belfie and Bronson for the best trip to the Grand Canyon ever this summer. It was a welcome break in the middle of this project.

Ted Shepherd, thank you for the Father's Day HTML card. You're the best son ever. You write the coolest games on a TI-83 calculator. I can't wait to see what you can do with C#.

Thank you, George Robbins Shepherd and Betsy Shepherd. As my parents you guided me and encouraged me to always do my best. I miss you both dearly.

Thank you, Sandy Daston for your support and guidance in my writing career. Your help lets me see the red marks *before* I write the sentence.

Thank you, Jeff Duntemann for buying and publishing my first piece ever for *PC Tech Journal*.

Thank you, JD Hildebrand for buying my second writing piece ever, and for the opportunity to work with you all at Oakley Publishing.

Thank you Joshua Trupin, Stephen Taub, and the staff at *Microsoft Developer Network* magazine. You produce an excellent magazine and I'm proud to be able to contribute.

Thank you Mark Peot, Mark Anderson, Craig Anderson, Barry Ahrens, Bina Thakkar, Mario Aguilar, Thomas Hawkins, and Rich Tarquini, and Jennifer Grater at Rockwell Scientific. You're all such a great group of people to work with.

Thank you to the folks at DevelopMentor for being an excellent group of technical colleagues and a great place for learning new technology.

Finally, thank you Reader for going through this book and spending time learning ASP.NET 2.0. May you continue to explore ASP.NET and always find new and interesting ways to handle HTTP requests.

George Shepherd
Chapel Hill, NC
August 2005

Chapter 1
Web Application Basics

After completing this chapter, you will be able to

- Interpret HTTP requests

- Use the .NET Framework to make HTTP requests without a browser

- Interpret HTML

- Work with IIS

- Produce dynamic Web content without using ASP.NET yet

This chapter covers the fundamentals of building a Web-based application. Unlike the development of most desktop applications, in which most of the parts are available locally (as components on the user's hard disk drive), developing a Web application requires getting software parts to work over a widely distributed network using a disconnected protocol. The technologies underlying ASP.NET have been around for a long time. Of course ASP.NET makes use of this technology underneath, while making it very approachable at the same time.

Although ASP.NET makes developing Web applications far easier than ever before, you must have a solid understanding of how the plumbing is actually working during the development of an ASP.NET application. A good example of such a time might be when you're tracking down a stray HTTP request or trying to figure out why a section of your page is appearing in the wrong font within a client's browser. Another such time might occur while you're writing a custom control for a Web page. Custom controls often require that the rendering code be written manually. That is, you must carefully ensure that the HTML tags emitted by your control occur in exactly the right order. For that, you need to understand HTML.

This chapter covers three things necessary to allow you to work with ASP.NET:

- How HTTP requests work
- How HTML works
- How HTTP requests are handled on the Microsoft platform (IIS)

Understanding these three technologies underlying ASP.NET frames the rest of the system. As you study ASP.NET these pieces will undoubtedly fall into place.

HTTP Requests

The communication mechanism by which Web browsers talk to Web sites is named the HyperText Transfer Protocol (HTTP). The World Wide Web as we know it today began as a research project at CERN in Switzerland. In those days, the notion of hypertext—documents linked together arbitrarily—was becoming increasingly popular. Applications such as Hyper-card from Apple Computer Inc. introduced hypertext applications to a wider audience. Now, if documents could be linked over a network, that would revolutionize publishing. That's the reason for the HyperText Transfer Protocol, which lies on top of TCP/IP as an application layer.

In its original form, HTTP was meant to transfer hypertext documents. That is, it was originally intended simply to link documents together without consideration for anything like the Web-based user interfaces that are the staple of modern Web sites. The earliest versions of HTTP supported a single GET request to fetch the named resource. It then became the server's job to send the file as a stream of text. After the response arrived at the client's browser, the connection terminated. The earliest versions of HTTP supported only transfer of text streams and did not support any other sort of data transfer.

The first formal specification for HTTP found itself in version 1.0 and was published in the mid-1990s. HTTP 1.0 added support for more complex messaging beyond a simple text transfer protocol. HTTP grew to support different media (specified by the Multipurpose Internet Mail Extensions). The current version of HTTP is version 1.1.

As a connection protocol, HTTP is built around several basic commands. The most important ones we'll see in developing ASP.NET applications are GET, HEAD, and POST.

GET retrieves the information identified by the Uniform Resource Identifier (URI) specified by the request. The HEAD command retrieves only the header information identified by the Uniform Resource Identifier specified by the request (that is, it does not return a message body). You use the POST method to make a request to the server that may cause side effects. You make most initial contacts to a page using a GET command, and you handle subsequent interactions with POST commands.

HTTP Requests from a Browser

As an example, look at the request that is sent from a browser to fetch the helloworld.htm resource from the virtual directory ASPNETStepByStep running on localhost. Listing 1-1 shows the text of the request that is sent to the server. If you would like to see the data going back and forth, there are several TCP monitors available. In addition, you may use TELNET to send GET Requests to the server. Just look for some online. Most are very easy to use.

To send an HTTP request to a server using TELNET, follow these steps:

1. Open the Visual Studio command prompt to connect to your own PC over port 80.

2. At the prompt, type the following:

   ```
   C:\>TELNET localhost 80
   ```

3. After the TELNET client connects, type the following GET command (assuming you have a virtual directory named ASPNETStepByStep on you machine, containing a file named HelloWorld.HTM):

   ```
   C:/> GET /ASPNETStepByStep/helloworld.htm
   ```

4. You should see the file's contents returned to the command line.

Listing 1-1

```
GET /ASPNETStepByStep/helloworld.htm HTTP/1.1
Accept: image/gif, image/x-xbitmap, image/jpeg, image/pjpeg,
application/vnd.ms-powerpoint, application/vnd.ms-excel,
application/msword, application/x-shockwave-flash, */*
Accept-Language: en-us
Accept-Encoding: gzip, deflate
User-Agent: Mozilla/4.0 (compatible; MSIE 6.0; Windows NT 5.1; SV1; .NET CLR 1.1.4322; .NET CLR
2.0.50215)
Host: localhost:80
Connection: Keep-Alive
```

When a browser wants to make an HTTP request, it needs to cook up the HTTP request including the URI along with other information. The header information in the request includes details about the operating environment of the browser and some other information that is often useful to the server. When the server receives this request, it returns the requested resource as a text stream. The browser then parses it and formats the contents. Listing 1-2 shows the response provided by the server when asked for the HelloWorld.htm file. Normally, you don't see all the header information when viewing the resource through a browser. A good TCP tracing utility will show it to you. When we look at ASP.NET's tracing facilities later on, this header information will be visible.

Listing 1-2

```
HTTP/1.1 200 OK
Server: Microsoft-IIS/5.1
X-Powered-By: ASP.NET
Date: Wed, 01 Jun 2005 23:44:04 GMT
Content-Type: text/html
Accept-Ranges: bytes
Last-Modified: Sun, 22 May 2005 21:54:20 GMT
ETag: "04e9ace185fc51:bb6"
Content-Length: 130
```

```
<html>
   <body>
      <h1> Hello World </h1>
      Nothing really showing here yet, except some HTML...
   </body>
</html>
```

The first line indicates the protocol and the return code. The rest of the response (until the first *<html>* tag) is information about the time of the request, the last time the file was modified, and what kind of content is provided. This information will be useful later when we examine such issues as page caching and detecting browser capabilities. The content following the response header information is literally the HTML file sent back by the server.

Making HTTP Requests Without a Browser

In addition to being a framework for building Web applications, the .NET development environment includes classes for making HTTP requests in the raw. The WebRequest class includes a member named *GetResponse* that will send a request to the address specified by the Uniform Resource Locater. To get a flavor as to how to make direct requests to a Web server without a browser, try compiling and then running this short program that fetches the home page for *Microsoft.com*.

Build a Simple HTTP Requestor

1. Start Visual Studio.NET. Select **New | Project** from the main menu. In the New Project dialog box, select a Console application and name it **WebRequestorApp,** as shown below.

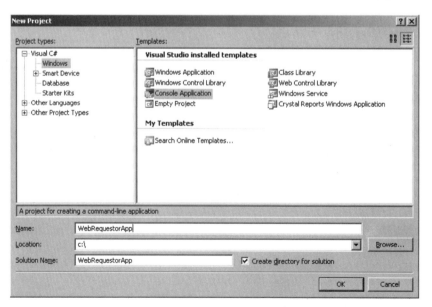

Visual Studio will generate a blank Console program for you.

2. Add the code necessary to make a Web request to the program. Visual Studio places the entry point of the Console application into a file named Program.cs. (This file is the code that shows up in the code window by default.) The code for making a Web request is shown in bold in the following lines of code:

```
using System;
using System.Collections.Generic;
using System.Text;
using System.Net;
using System.IO;

namespace WebRequestorApp
{
    class Program
    {
        static void Main(string[] args)
        {
            WebRequest req =
                WebRequest.Create
                    ("http://www.microsoft.com");
            WebResponse resp = req.GetResponse();

            StreamReader reader =
                new StreamReader(resp.GetResponseStream(),
                    Encoding.ASCII);
            Console.WriteLine(reader.ReadToEnd());
        }
    }
}
```

3. Run the application. You may do this by choosing **Debug | Start Without Debugging** from the main menu. Visual Studio will start up a Console for you and run the program. After a couple of moments, you'll see the following HTML spewed to your screen.

Of course, the HTML isn't meant for human consumption. That's what a browser is for. However, this example does show the fundamentals of making a Web request—and you can see exactly what comes back in the response.

In this case, the request sent to the server is much smaller. WebRequest.GetResponse doesn't include as much information in the request—just the requisite GET followed by the URI, host information, and connection type:

```
GET /ASPNETStepByStep/helloworld.htm HTTP/1.1
Host: localhost:80
Connection: Keep-Alive
```

The fundamental jobs of most browsers are (1) to package a request and send it to the server represented in the URI and (2) to receive the response from the server and render it in a useful way. The response usually comes back as a text stream marked up using HTML tags.

HyperText Markup Language (HTML)

In the course of looking at ASP.NET, we'll see quite a bit of HTML. Most of it will be generated by the ASP.NET server-side controls. However, it's important to understand HTML because you may want to write your own server-side control from scratch, and at times you may need to tweak or debug the output of your ASP.NET application.

Most HTTP requests result in a stream of text coming back to the caller. The world has pretty much agreed that HTML is the language for formatting documents, and most browsers understand HTML.

The first release of HTML worth using was version 2.0. Version 3.2 included many new features, such as tables, applets, text flow around images, and superscripts and subscripts, while providing backwards compatibility with the existing HTML 2.0 Standard.

The bottom line is that given a competent browser and well-structured HTML, you had the beginnings of a user interface development technology. And because HTML was understood by browsers running on a variety of platforms, the door was open for implementing a worldwide interactive computing platform. The other key that made this happen (besides a mature version of HTML) was the ability of servers to adapt their output to accommodate the requests of specific users at runtime.

For example, the HTML stream shown in Listing 1-3 will render an HTML page containing a button and a combo box filled with options. (This file is named SelectNoForm.htm in the collection of examples for this chapter.)

Listing 1-3

```
<html>
 <body>
   <h2>Hello there. What's your favorite .NET feature?</h2>
   <select name='Feature'>
    <option> Type-Safety</option>
    <option> Garbage collection</option>
    <option> Multiple syntaxes</option>
```

```
    <option> Code Access Security</option>
    <option> Simpler threading</option>
    <option> Versioning purgatory</option>
  </select>
  </br>
  <input type=submit name='Lookup' value='Lookup'></input>
  </br>
 </body>
</html>
```

See Figure 1-1 for an example of how the page looks when rendered by the browser.

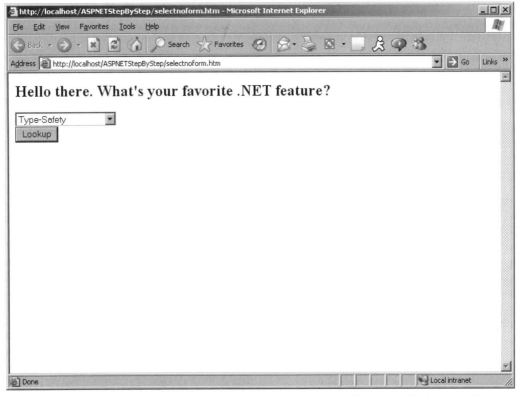

Figure 1-1 A simple HTML page showing a selection tag (rendered here as a Windows combo box) and a Submission button.

> **Note** We'll actually surf to an HTML file in subsequent chapters. Getting to that point is a bit involved, so for now, you can trust that the HTML will render in this fashion.

This is a static page. Even though it has a combo box and a button, they don't do anything worthwhile. You can pull down the combo box and work with it inside the browser. You can push the button, but all the action happens locally. That's because the server on the other end needs to support dynamic content.

Dynamic Content

The earliest Web sites were built primarily using static HTML pages. That is, you could surf to some page somewhere and read the HTML document living there. While at that time being able to do this was pretty amazing, HTML eventually evolved to be capable of much more than simply formatting text.

For example, HTML includes tags such as *<select></select>* that most browsers interpret as a combo box. Various attributes applied to the *<input></input>* tag causes browsers to draw text boxes and buttons.

HTML Forms

HTML includes a *<form></form>* tag for notifying the browser that a section of HTML includes tags representing controls. This is how you specify a Web document will be handling input from the end user (not just output).

The *<form>* tag usually sandwiches a set of tags specifying controls. Listing 1-4 shows the feature selection page, but with the form tag added (the file name is SelectFeature2.htm in the accompanying examples):

Listing 1-4

```
<html>
<body>
<form action="http://localhost/HttpHandlers/selectfeature.htm"
    method="get">
<h2>Hello there. What's your favorite .NET feature?</h2>
<select name='Feature'>
<option> Type-Safety</option>
<option> Garbage collection</option>
<option> Multiple syntaxes</option>
<option> Code Access Security</option>
<option> Simpler threading</option>
<option> Versioning purgatory</option>
</select>
</br>
<input type=submit name='Lookup' value='Lookup'></input>
</br>
</form>
</body>
</html>
```

The form tag includes several attributes that you may set to control how the page behaves. In the above example, notice the *<form>* tag sets the *ACTION* attribute, which points back to the server that will receive the form's contents. In its absence, the current document URL will be used.

The other attribute used in the Listing 1-4 is the *method* attribute. The *method* attribute specifies the HTTP method used when submitting the form. The method employed in the example is GET because the software on the server doesn't understand POST yet. GET causes the form contents to be appended to the URL. POST causes the form contents to be sent to the server in a data body.

Adding the form tag to the body of the document gets us part of the way to having a workable HTTP application. Now we need a little more support on the server end. When you click the Lookup button, the browser will actually force another round-trip back to the server (though it will only perform an HTTP GET command to refetch the document).

At this point, a normal HTTP GET command will only return the document. For a truly interactive environment, the server on the other end needs to modify the content as requests go back and forth between the browser and the server.

For example, imagine the user does an initial GET for the resource, then selects a features from the combo box and clicks the Submit button. For an interactive application to work, the browser will need to make a second round-trip to the server with a new request. The server will need to examine the request coming from the browser and figure out what to do about it.

Common Gateway Interface

The earliest Web servers supporting "dynamic Web content" did so through the Common Gateway Interface (CGI). CGI was the earliest standard for building Web servers. CGI programs execute in real time and change their output based on the state of the application and the requests coming in. Each request coming into a Web server running CGI runs a separate instance of a program to respond. The application can run any sort of operation, including looking up data in a database, accepting credit card numbers, and sending out formatted information.

The Microsoft Platform as a Web Server

On the Microsoft platform, it's too expensive to start up a new process for each request (à la CGI). Microsoft's solution is to have a single daemon process watch port 80 and load DLLs to handle separate requests when the content needs to change. Microsoft's standard Web platform is based on the Internet Information Services (IIS).

Internet Information Services

All Web application environments work fundamentally the same way. No matter what hardware/software platform you use, some piece of software is required on the server to watch port 80 for incoming HTTP requests. When a request arrives, it's the server's job to somehow respond to the request in a meaningful way. On the Microsoft platform, Internet Information Services is the watchdog intercepting HTTP requests from port 80—the normal inbound port for HTTP requests. Internet servers use other ports as well. For example, HTTPS (Secure HTTP) happens over port 443. However, right now we're mostly interested in normal Internet traffic over port 80.

When a browser makes a call to a server running on the Microsoft platform, IIS intercepts that request and searches for the resource identified by the URL. IIS divides its directory space into manageable chunks called virtual directories. For example, imagine someone tries to get to a resource on your server using this URL:

http://www.aspnetstepbystep.com/examples/showfeatures.htm

The domain "aspnetstepbystep" is fictitious and used here for illustration. However, if there were a server registered using this name, the URL would identify the entire resource. Within this URL, *http://www.aspnetstepbystep.com* identifies the server and will direct the request through a maze of routers. Once the request reaches the server, the server will look for the *showfeatures.htm* resource in some directory-type entity named *examples*. If the server is running IIS, *examples* refers to a virtual directory.

IIS divides its working space into multiple *virtual directories*. Each virtual directory typically refers to a single application. That way, IIS can serve multiple applications. Each virtual directory includes various configuration properties, including such things as security options, error handling redirections, and application isolation options (among others). The configuration parameters also include mappings between file extensions and ISAPI DLLs.

Internet Services Application Programming Interface DLLs

On the Microsoft platform, creating a process space is an expensive proposition (in terms of system resources and clock cycles). Imagine trying to write a server that responds to each request by starting a separate program. The poor server would be bogged down very quickly, and your e-commerce site would stop making money.

Microsoft's architecture prefers using DLLs to respond to requests. DLLs are relatively inexpensive to load, and running code within a DLL executes very quickly. The DLLs handling Web requests are named *ISAPI DLLs* (ISAPI stands for Internet Services Application Programming Interface).

While we won't dive all the way into the inner workings of ISAPI DLLs, we'll take a cursory look at their architecture so you can see how they relate to ASP.NET.

ISAPI DLLs handling normal HTTP requests define an entry point named *HttpExtensionProc*. Although ISAPI extension DLLs define more entry points than *HttpExtentsionProc*, it is by far the most important method in an ISAPI DLL. The important point to realize about ISAPI extension DLLs is that they all implement this singular function when responding to HTTP requests. However, they may all respond differently.

- The *HttpExtensionProc* method takes a single parameter—an EXTENSION_CONTROL_BLOCK structure. EXTENSION_CONTROL_BLOCK includes the entire context of a request. We don't need to see the whole structure here. However, we will see the managed equivalent in ASP.NET when we look at the *HttpContext* class.

Upon receiving a request, IIS packages the information into the EXTENSION_CONTROL_BLOCK. IIS then passes the structure into the ISAPI DLL through the *HttpExtensionProc* entry point. The ISAPI extnsion DLL is responsible for parsing the incoming request and doing something with it. The ISAPI extension DLL is completely at liberty to do whatever it wants to with the request. For example, the client might make a request that includes parameters in the query string (perhaps the client is looking for a customer lookup or something similar). The ISAPI extensio DLL uses those query string parameters to create a database query specific to the site. If the site is a commerce site, the database query might be for the current inventory. After processing the request, the ISAPI DLL streams any results back to the client.

You may have had some experience working with classic ASP, in which case much of this structure will appear familiar to you. For example, calling *Write* through ASP's intrinsic *Response* object eventually ends up executing the method pointed to by *WriteClient*.

We've explored the inner structure of an ISAPI DLL. Let's see how these DLLs fit into IIS.

Internet Information Services

The user interface to IIS is available through the Control Panel. To get a feel for how to administer IIS 5.1, let's take a short tour. It's important to have some facility with IIS because ASP.NET relies on it to service Web requests. IIS 5.x and 6.0 work similarly as far as dividing the server's application space into virtual directories. IIS 6.0 includes many other features such as application isolation and recycling, which is out of the scope of this discussion.

Running IIS

1. **Run IIS.**   To get to IIS, first go to **Administrative Tools**. On Windows XP Professional, you can do this through the Control Panel. Run Internet Information Services and you should see the IIS user interface on your screen:

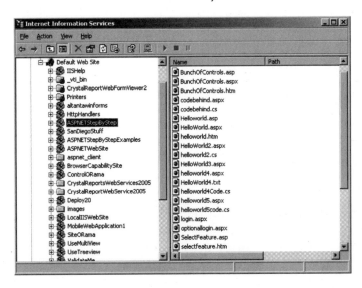

2. **View configuration for a specific virtual directory.**   On the left-hand side of the screen is an expandable tree showing the Web sites and virtual directories available through IIS on your machine. To find out more details about how the directory is configured, right-click on the directory and select **Properties** from the context menu. You'll see the Properties dialog box:

As you can see, the Properties dialog box is fairly extensive, covering all aspects of how the directory is accessed from the outside world. We won't spend a lot of time here because ASP.NET takes care of most of these issues (rather than leaving them up to IIS).

3. **View file mappings for a virtual directory.**   Click the **Configuration** button to see the file mappings. IIS responds by showing you another dialog box listing the file mappings for the directory:

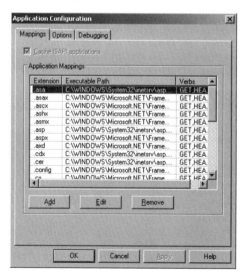

These mappings tell IIS which DLL should handle the request. Static file types such as HTM are transmitted directly back to the client. However, dynamic pages whose contents can change between posts require further processing, so they are assigned to specific ISAPI DLLs. There's not a lot of variety in the kinds of DLLs listed above. In fact, most of the file types in this directory are handled by a file named ASPNET_ISAPI.DLL. We'll talk about that DLL in much greater detail soon. Notice the other DLL in the list: ASP.DLL. This is the DLL for handling classic Active Server Pages requests.

Classic ASP

Microsoft originally developed Active Server Pages to encourage a larger number of developers than just those using C++ to undertake Web development. When IIS came out, it was certainly a feasible environment for developing Web sites on the Microsoft platform. In fact, you can still see some sites today deployed as pure ISAPI DLL sites; just look in the query strings going between the browser and the server for clues. For example, you might see a file name such as ACMEISAPI.DLL embedded within the query string.

However, writing an entire site using ISAPI DLLs can be daunting. Writing ISAPI DLLs in C or C++ gives you complete control over how your site will perform and makes the site work. However, along with that control comes an equal amount of responsibility, because developing software using C or C++ presents numerous challenges.

So in delivering ASP, Microsoft provided a single IASPI DLL named ASP.DLL. ASP Web developers write their code into files tagged with the extension .asp (for example, foo.asp). ASP files often contain a mixture of static HTML and executable sections (usually written in a scripting language) that emit output at runtime. For example, the code in Listing 1-5 shows an ASP program that spits out the HelloWorld page, which contains both static HTML and text generated at runtime. (The file name is HelloWorld.asp in the accompanying examples.)

Listing 1-5

```
<%@ Language="javascript" %>
<html><body><form>

    <h3>Hello world!!! This is an ASP page.</h3>

    <% Response.Write("This content was generated ");%>
    <% Response.Write("as part of an execution block");%>
  </form>
</body></html>
```

The code shown in Listing 1-5 renders the following page. IIS watched port 80 for requests. When a request for the file Helloworld.asp came through, IIS saw the .asp file extension and asked ASP.DLL to handle the request (that's how the file mapping was set up). ASP.DLL simply rendered the static HTML as the string "Hello world!!! This is an ASP page." Then when

ASP.DLL encountered the funny-looking execution tags (<% and %>), it executed those blocks by running them through a JavaScript parser. Figure 1-2 shows how the page renders in Internet Explorer.

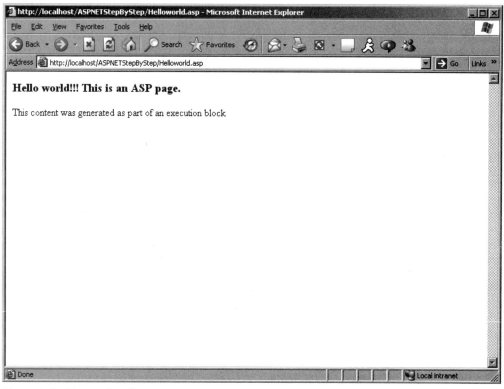

Figure 1-2   The results of a request made to the ASP program from Listing 1-5.

This book is about developing ASP.NET software, so we'll focus most of the attention there. However, before leaving the topic of classic ASP, Listing 1-6 shows the SelectFeature.htm page rewritten as a classic ASP page. Looking at this simple ASP application presents some of the core issues in Web development and illustrates why Microsoft rewrote its Web server technology as ASP.NET. (The accompanying file name is SelectFeature.asp.)

Listing 1-6

```
<%@ Language="javascript" %>
<html><body><form>

    <h2>HelloWorld<h2>

  <h3>What's your favorite .NET feature?</h3>
  <select name='Feature'>
     <option> Type-Safety</option>
     <option> Garbage collection</option>
     <option> Multiple syntaxes</option>
```

```
      <option> Code Access Security</option>
      <option> Simpler threading</option>
      <option> Versioning purgatory</option>
    </select>
    </br>
    <input type=submit name="Submit" value="Submit"></input>
    <p>
        Hi, you selected <%=Request("Feature") %>
    </p>
  </form>
</body></html>
```

Much of the text in SelectFeature.asp looks very similar to SelectFeature.htm, doesn't it? The differences lie mainly in the first line (that now specifies a syntax for executable blocks) and the executable block marked by <% and %>. The rest of the static HTML renders a selection control within a form.

Take note of the executable blocks and how the blocks use the *Response* object (managed by the ASP infrastructure) to push text out to the browser. The executable block examines the *Feature* control (specified by the *<select>* tag) and prints out the value selected by the user.

Figure 1-3 shows how SelectFeature.asp renders in Internet Explorer.

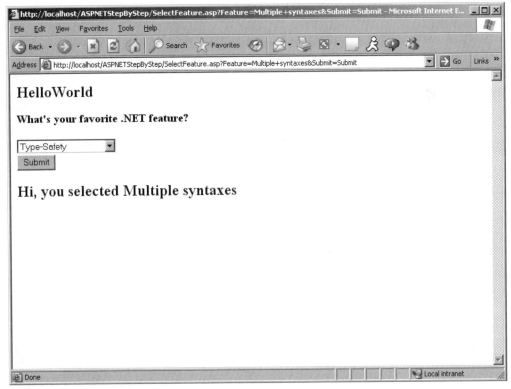

Figure 1-3   The code from Listing 1-6 as viewed using Internet Explorer.

The screen in Figure 1-3 may look a bit odd because the drop-down list box shows "Type-Safety" while the rendered text shows "Multiple syntaxes." Without doing anything extra, the drop-down list box will always re-render with the first element as the selected element. We'll see how ASP.NET fixes this later when we look at server-side controls. That's enough background information to help you understand the core issues associated with developing Web applications.

Web Development Issues

In the end, developing Web applications forces you to deal with two significant issues, which are managing UI using HTML over a disconnected protocol and managing the state of your application. These fundamental activities separate Web development from other types of application development.

In many ways, the programming model has gone back to the model that dominated the mid-1970s, when large mainframes served output to terminals connected directly to them. Users would submit jobs to the mainframe and get output to their terminals. So, what's changed here? First, the terminal is a lot fancier—it's a powerful PC running a browser that interprets HTML. The end point to which the browser connects is a Web server (or perhaps a server farm). Finally, the connection protocol used by the client and the server is indirect (and a request can quite literally cross the globe before the user sees a result).

In Web application development, the program's primary job is to receive requests from "out there" and to provide meaningful responses to the requestors. That often means generating complex HTML that renders in a form humans can read on the client's browser. That can be fairly involved, for example, in a modern commercial Web site supporting commerce. Customers will undoubtedly ask about current pricing, request inventory levels, and perhaps even order items or services from the Web site. The process of "generating meaningful HTML for the client" suddenly means doing things such as making database accesses, authenticating the identity of the client, and keeping track of the client's order. Imagine doing all this from scratch!

While frameworks such as classic ASP go a long way toward making Web development more approachable, many features are still left for developers to create on their own (mostly related to the two issues mentioned at the beginning of this section). For example, building a secure but manageable Web site in classic ASP usually meant writing your own security subsystem (or buying one). Managing the state of the UI emitted by your Web site was often a tedious chore as well.

ASP.NET

All of this brings us to ASP.NET. A common theme you'll see throughout this book is that ASP.NET takes features usually implemented (over and over again) by developers and rolls them into the ASP.NET framework.

ASP.NET 2.0 takes ASP.NET 1.1 to the next level and pushes even more commonly implemented features into the framework. An example of how ASP.NET 2.0 improves upon

ASP.NET 1.1 is the authentication and authorization services provided by ASP.NET 1.1; ASP.NET 1.1 included a reasonable and easy-to-manage authentication model. However, developers were often left with the task of rolling their own authentication systems into their Web sites. ASP.NET 2.0 adds an authorization subsystem. We'll cover ASP.NET Forms Authentication and other security features in depth during chapter 10.

In the following chapters, we'll cover the most important ASP.NET features. By the end of the last chapter, you'll be well equipped to develop a Web site based on ASP.NET.

Chapter 1 Quick Reference

To	Do This
Start Internet Information Services console	Go to the Control Panel
	Select administrative tools
	Select Internet Information Services
Create a new virtual directory	Open the IIS Console
	Open the Web Sites node
	Open the Default Web Site node
	Right mouse click on the Default Web Site node
	Select New Virtual Directory
	Follow the wizard
Surf to a resource from IIS	Right mouse click on the resource
	Select Browse
See what file types are supported in IIS	Right mouse click on the Virtual directory
	Select Properties
	Press the Configure button

Chapter 2
ASP.NET Application Fundamentals

After completing this chapter, you will be able to

- Create an IIS Virtual Directory
- Develop an HTML page into an ASP.NET application
- Mix HTML with executable code and work with server side script blocks
- Locate and view the assembly compiled by ASP.NET using your ASPX file
- Work with code-behind and code-beside execution models

This chapter covers the fundamentals involved in building an ASP.NET application. From a syntactical point of view, writing .NET code is similar to writing the classic ASP code that you may have seen during the late dot-com era. Many of the key symbols remain the same, and even some of the syntax survives. However, the entire underlying execution model changed dramatically between classic ASP and ASP.NET. Whereas executing classic ASP pages was primarily an exercise in rendering HTML, interpreting script code, and calling Component Object Model code, ASP.NET introduces an entirely new object-oriented execution model. ASP.NET execution centers around CLR classes that implement an interface named *IHttpHandler*. ASP.NET includes a number of classes that already implement *IHttpHandler*, and you may actually write your own implementation from scratch.

We'll examine the ASP.NET execution model and show what's new in ASP.NET 2.0. We'll take a bottom-up approach, showing how the simplest ASP.NET page executes. Along the way we'll introduce various ASP.NET programming techniques including code behind. We'll see how ASP.NET's compilation model works. Finally, we'll observe how ASP.NET's Web Form architecture operates and how it's all nicely wrapped up by Visual Studio 2005.

19

Let's start by studying a simple page to discover how we can evolve it using ASP.NET's programming techniques.

The Canonical Hello World Application

Nearly all programming texts start by using the technology at hand to present the classic string "Hello World" to the end user. This time, our job is to send the statement "Hello World" to the awaiting browser.

To see how ASP works, we'll take the simplest Web page and develop it as an ASP.NET Web application. All the files for this example are loaded into a specific virtual directory. We'll examine each iteration along the way to see what ASP.NET is doing.

Building the HelloWorld Web Application

1. **Create a directory to hold the Web application files.**   Using either a command shell or Windows Explorer, create a new folder to hold the Web application files. While the name of the directory is unimportant to IIS, call it something meaningful. I used c:\aspnetstepbystepexamples.

2. **Map a virtual directory to hold the files.**   To start, we need a virtual directory in which to hold the source code. As we saw earlier when examining the Web Application architecture imposed by the Windows platform, IIS divides the applications on your server using virtual directories. There's nothing really magic about this scheme—it's mostly simply a mapping between requests coming in over port 80 and some real directory on your machine. Virtual directories show IIS where to find the code you want to execute in your application.

    Run the **Control Panel**, and then go to **Administrative Tools** and start **Information Services**. Expand the nodes in the tree on the left-hand side to expose the Default Web Site node under the Web Sites node, as shown in the following illustration:

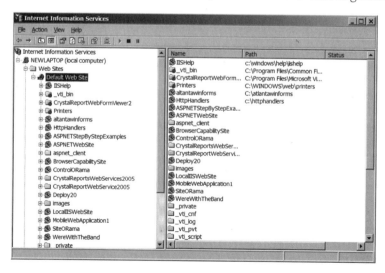

Then right-click on the Default Web Site node and select **New Virtual directory** from the context menu. IIS will run the Virtual Directory Creation Wizard. The second page asks you to provide a name for the virtual directory:

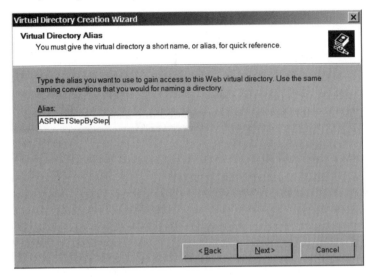

Call the Web site ASPNETStepByStep. This is the name by which your Web application will be known to the world. For example, when someone surfs to your Web site, they'll use the following URL:

http://www.mysite.com/ASPNETStepByStep

The name "mysite.com" is a fictitious site, only here for illustration. The wizard will ask you to provide a physical path for the virtual directory. Either browse to the physical directory you just created, or type the name of the directory.

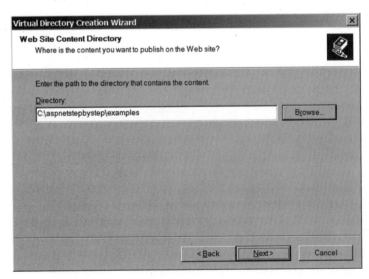

Finish paging through the Wizard, accepting the defaults.

3. **Start with a simple HTML page.**   The easiest way to implement HelloWorld as a Web application is to store some text in an HTML file and browse to it.

   Start Visual Studio and select **File | New | File**. Select **HTML** as the file type.

   Type the following text and save it in a file named HelloWorld.htm within your new physical directory (that's been mapped to a virtual directory).

   ```html
   <html>
       <body>
           <h1> Hello World </h1>
           Nothing really showing here yet, except some HTML...
       </body>
   </html>
   ```

4. **Browse to the page.**   Browse to the page by selecting the file from within IIS. The browser will send an HTTP request to the server. On the Microsoft platform, IIS will see the HTM file extension and simply return the contents of the file to the browser. Because the text is marked using standard HTML tags, the browser understands it and displays it correctly.

   Here's how the file appears to the end browser:

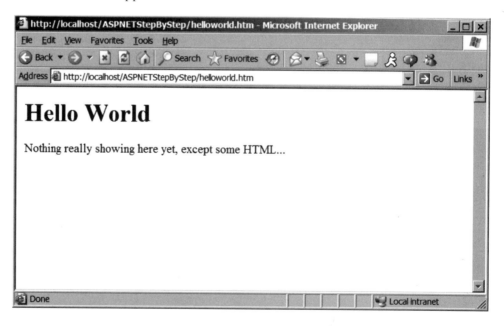

5. **Convert the HTML file to an ASP.NET application.**   Turning this file into an ASP.NET application involves two small steps: adding a single line to the top of the file (the *Page* directive), and renaming the file to HelloWorld.aspx. This text represents an

implementation of HelloWorld that works within the ASP.NET framework (be sure to save the file as HelloWorld.aspx):

```
<%@ Page Language="C#" %>
<html>
   <body>
      <h1> Hello World </h1>
      Nothing really showing here yet, except some HTML...
   </body>
</html>
```

When you fire up your browser and surf to this file within the virtual directory on your computer, you'll see the following in your browser. Be sure to browse the file—don't just open it. Browsing using the full URL activates HTTP whereas simply opening the file will show the literal text within Hello.aspx.

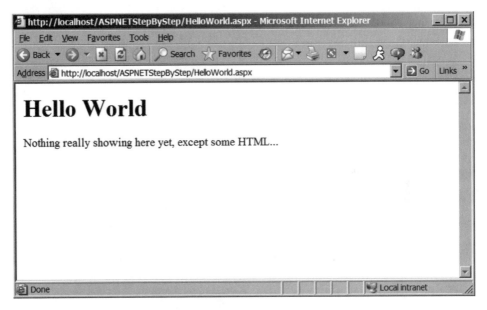

Admittedly, this is a small feat. However, if you get this far, it means you have IIS installed correctly on your machine, and the ASP.NET file types are registered correctly with IIS.

6. **View the HTML source that the browser is interpreting**.   While this content is showing in your browser, use the **View | Source** menu to show the text being processed by the browser. It should look like this:

```
<html>
   <body>
      <h1> Hello World </h1>
      Nothing really showing here yet, except some HTML...
   </body>
</html>
```

Notice this text is almost identical to the text in Hello.aspx (without the *Page* directive: *<%@ Page Language="C#" Debug="true" %>*). In this case you can see the page-processing logic is fairly simple. That is, the ASP.NET runtime is simply spitting out the text within the file

---

A Note about Application Pools

IIS 6.0 supports a feature named application pooling. One of the primary purposes behind application pooling is to support application isolation. For example, imagine you wanted to isolate the Web applications running in the same computer from other software managed by IIS. By creating a separate application pool for each Web application, you tell IIS to run the application in its own worker process. If anything bad happens in one application pool, the other applications will continue to run unaffected.

Application pooling also lets you govern the security aspects of a Web application. Some applications may need a higher degree of security while others may not.

IIS 5.0 runs the ASP.NET worker process as LocalSystem. LocalSystem has system administrator privileges. This has interesting implications because the account can access virtually any resource on the server. IIS 6.0 allows you to set the identity of the worker process to be the same as that of the application pool level. Application pools operate under the NetworkService account by default—which does not have as much access right as localSystem.

The *Page* directive appearing at the top of the code is used by the ASP.NET runtime as it compiles the code. The *Page* directive shown above is fairly simple—it tells the runtime to compile this code and base it on the *Page* class and to treat any code syntax it encounters as C# code. ASP.NET supports integrating ASPX files with assemblies, which we'll see shortly. In subsequent examples, we'll see how ASP.NET compiles code on the fly and stores the assemblies in a temporary directory. There's no C# code in HelloWorld.aspx, so let's add some.

Mixing HTML with Executable Code

Classic ASP had an interesting way of marking code segments within a page. ASP always supported the classic script tag (*<script> </script>*) where anything found between the script tags was treated as executable code. However, in classic ASP, the script blocks were sent to the browser and it became the browser's job to run the script. In addition to client-side script blocks, a classic ASP Web page could define script blocks to be interpreted on the server. These methods often performed tasks such as database lookups. Causing code to execute on the server involved marking executable segments with angle braces and percent signs like this:

```
<% ExecuteMe() %>
```

ASP.NET also supports server-side code execution. To write code that executes inline, simply mark it with the <% %> tags. When ASP.NET parses the file to manufacture the runtime class representing the page (more on that shortly), it will insert whatever code it finds between the execution tags as executable code. The only requirement is that the code between the execution tags is valid C# (because that's the language specified in the *Page* directive).

Adding Executable Code Inline

1. **Add executable code to the Web application.**   Create a new blank text file from within Visual Studio. Type the following code into the text file and save it as HelloWorld2.aspx.

```
<%@ Page Language="C#" Debug="true" %>
<html>
    <body>
        <h1>Hello World!!!</h1>
        <%
            // This block will execute in the Render_Control method
            Response.Write("Check out the family tree: <br> <br>");
            Response.Write(this.GetType().ToString());
            Response.Write(" which derives from: <br> ");
            Response.Write(this.GetType().BaseType.ToString());
            Response.Write(" which derives from: <br> ");
            Response.Write(this.GetType().BaseType.BaseType.ToString());
            Response.Write(" which derives from: <br> ");
            Response.Write(
              this.GetType().BaseType.BaseType.BaseType.ToString());
            Response.Write(" which derives from: <br> ");
            Response.Write(
              this.GetType().BaseType.BaseType.BaseType.BaseType.ToString());
        %>
    </body>
</html>
```

This code is almost exactly identical to code you'd see in a classic ASP application—including references to the *Response* object. In classic ASP, the *Response* object was one of those intrinsic objects, perennially available to the page's execution block. The *Response* object in classic ASP was a *COM* object that hung off the thread managed by the ASP ISAPI DLL. Notice that ASP.NET also has a *Response* object. However, this one is part of the *HttpContext* managed by the ASP.NET pipeline.

2. **Browse to the ASP.NET page. Surf to the Web page using Internet Explorer**.   The
    page should look like this in the browser:

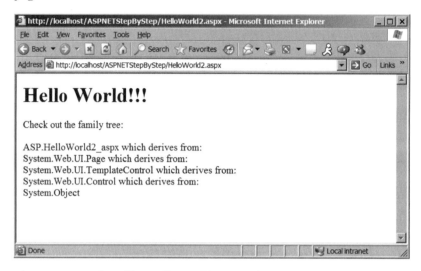

The output produced by HelloWorld2.aspx shows a very important aspect of ASP.NET's
execution model. Before moving on, take a look at the inline code listed in the previous
exercise and compare it to the output appearing in the browser. Notice the code
includes statements like:

```
Response.Write(this.GetType().BaseType.ToString());
```

Of course, the C# *this* keyword specifies an instance of a class. The code that's executing
is clearly part of a member function of a class instance. The output shown by the
browser indicates the class rendering the HTML to the browser is named
ASP.HelloWorld2_aspx, and it derives from a class named *System.Web.UI.Page*. We'll
learn more about this later in the chapter.

Server-Side Executable Blocks

ASP.NET also supports server-side code blocks (not just inline execution tags). ASP.NET adds a
new *runat* attribute to the script tag that tells ASP.NET to execute the code block at the server end.

Adding Executable Code via a Script Block

1. **Add an executable script block to the page**.   Create a new text file in Visual Studio.
    Type the following code into some code that separates rendering from the rest of the
    page using a script block that runs at the server. Save the file as HelloWorld3.aspx in
    your virtual directory.

```
<%@ Page Language="C#" Debug="true" %>
<script runat="server">
    void ShowLineage()
```

```
    {
        Response.Write("Check out the family tree: <br> <br>");
        Response.Write(this.GetType().ToString());
        Response.Write(" which derives from: <br> ");
        Response.Write(this.GetType().BaseType.ToString());
        Response.Write(" which derives from: <br> ");
        Response.Write(this.GetType().BaseType.BaseType.ToString());
        Response.Write(" which derives from: <br> ");
        Response.Write(
          this.GetType().BaseType.BaseType.BaseType.ToString());
        Response.Write(" which derives from: <br> ");
        Response.Write(
          this.GetType().BaseType.BaseType.BaseType.BaseType.ToString());
    }
</script>
<html>
    <body>
        <h1>Hello World!!!</h1>
        <%
            // This block will execute in the Render_Control method
            ShowLineage();
        %>
    </body>
</html>
```

As with the inline execution blocks, the most important criteria for the contents of the script block is that its syntax matches that of the language specified in the *Page* directive. The example above specifies a single method named *ShowLineage()*, which is called from within the page.

2. **Surf to the page.** Notice the output of HelloWorld2.aspx and HelloWorld3.aspx is identical.

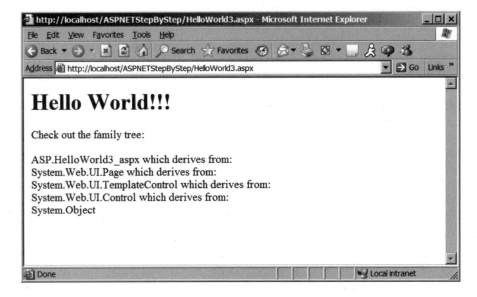

Marking the *ShowLineage()* method using the *runat=server* attribute causes ASP.NET to execute the code at the server. But while classic ASP interprets the script block using the designated script language, ASP.NET has an entirely different execution model—the whole page is actually compiled into a class that runs under the Common Language Runtime (CLR). Here's how the ASP.NET compilation model works.

A Trip Through the ASP.NET Architecture

The trip an HTTP request takes from the browser to the server and back is routed through myriad paths. Once a request ends up at the server, it winds its way through the ASP.NET pipeline. The best way to understand the path of an HTTP request through ASP.NET is to follow the entire path of a request as it originates in the browser and is intercepted by Internet Information Services and your Web application.

First Stop: Port 80

After an end user hits the *Return* key after typing in a URL, the browser sends an HTTP GET request to the target site. The request travels through a series of routers until it finally hits your Web server and is picked up on port 80. If your system has software listening to port 80, then the software can handle the request. On the Microsoft platform, the software most often listening to port 80 is Internet Information Services (IIS). For the time being, ASP.NET works with two flavors of IIS: version 5.0 and version 6.0.

If you're using IIS 5.0 to run your Web site, IIS watches your server's port 80 for incoming Web requests. IIS maintains a mapping between file extensions and Internet Services API (ISAPI) DLLs capable of interpreting the request. When a request comes in, IIS reads the file name named in the request and routes the request to the appropriate ISAPI DLL. If you're using IIS 6.0 to run your Web site, then a kernel-level driver named HTTP.SYS watches port 80 and picks up requests, routing the request to the appropriate ISAPI DLL.

You can see the list of file mappings between file extensions and ISAPI DLLs by running the IIS Console. Run IIS from the Control Panel Administrative Tools node. Open the Web Sites node, select Default Web Site, and right-click on one of the Web sites you see. Select Properties on the Directory tab, and select Configuration. The Mappings tab will show the relationship between file name extensions (as they come in through the HTTP request) and ISAPI DLLs.

All ISAPI DLLs include three well-defined entry points, the most important of which is named *HttpExtensionProc*. When a request comes into IIS and IIS understands the file extension appearing in the request, IIS wraps all the context information about the request into a structure named EXTENSION_CONTROL_BLOCK (that is, things like the originating URL, the content of the request, and so forth). IIS blindly calls the associated DLL's *HttpExtensionProc* method, passing in a pointer to the EXTENSION_CONTROL_BLOCK.

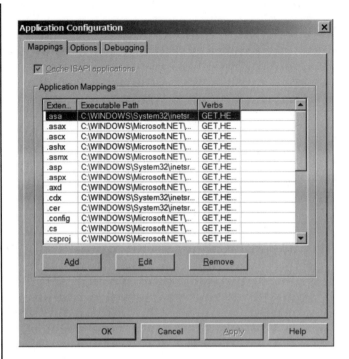

While much of ASP.NET is represented as Microsoft's managed library for handling HTTP requests, to IIS it's really just another ISAPI extension. When configured to run ASP.NET applications, IIS recognizes several distinguished file extensions and routes requests that include those extensions to ASP.NET's ISAPI DLL: aspnet_isapi.dll. If you look at the ISAPI DLL associated with ASP.NET's file extensions (for example: .aspx, .asax, .asmx, .ashx), you'll see they all point to a DLL named aspnet_isapi.dll.

aspnet_isapi.dll

The DLL named aspnet_isapi.dll is ASP.NET's ISAPI DLL. If you use a DLL spying tool such as DUMPBIN.EXE (a command line tool available along with the other Visual Studio .NET development tools) to show aspnet_isapi.dll's exported functions it shows that it contains the requisite exports (especially *HttpExtensionProc*). You'll also see that the DLL includes many other exports. However, right now the most important thing to realize is that it's simply another ISAPI DLL to which IIS directs requests.

If the page to which you're surfing happens to be named using one of ASP.NET's extensions (for example, .ashx, .aspx, .asax, among others), IIS directs the request to asp_isapi.dll.

IIS 5.0 versus IIS 6.0

If your server is using IIS 5.0 to process Web requests, then IIS picks up the request on Port 80 and forwards the request to asp_isapi.dll. asp_isapi.dll then forwards the request through a named pipe to the ASP.NET worker process: asp_wp.exe. At that point, ASP.NET pushes the request through the pipeline. We'll look at that process in much more detail shortly.

If your application is running on IIS 6.*x*, then your request is picked up using the HTTP.SYS driver and is piped directly to the ASP.NET worker process (which has the aspnet_isapi.dll loaded). HTTP.SYS is a kernel-level driver, lying close to the operating system. By routing the request directly to the ASP.NET worker process, ASP.NET bypasses the overhead of an extra out-of-process call and automatically enforces application isolation.

HTTP.SYS is where all incoming HTTP requests first hit the Web server. In addition to mandating connections, the HTTP service is also responsible for bandwidth throttling and text-based logging. Within HTTP.SYS, each application pool has its own request queue. HTTP.SYS listens for all HTTP requests and redirects them to the correct queue. Because HTTP.SYS is a kernel-level driver, responding to an HTTP request requires no more transitions to user mode. In addition to improving performance, separating HTTP listening in a separate driver increases reliability. The HTTP service will continue, even if the code responding to the request crashes in user mode. HTTP.SYS will accept requests continually.

The Worker Process

The ASP.NET worker process (w3wp.exe when using IIS 6.*x* and asp-net_wp.exe when using IIS 5.0) manages the ASP.NET pipeline (the route through which requests flow within ASP.NET). It acts as a surrogate process to host the goings on in ASP.NET. All ASP.NET software components—including the *HttpApplication* object, the *HttpModules*, and the *HttpHandler* invoked by each request—run within an instance of this surrogate process.

Once IIS intercepts the request and maps it to aspnet_isapi.dll, the request follows a very specific path through the pipeline. We'll look at each part of the pipeline in more detail in coming sections. The outline of the requests path is this:

1. The request lands in IIS.
2. IIS routes the request to aspnet_isapi.dll.
    - **2.1.** If IIS 5 is running, IIS asp_isapi.dll routes the request through a pipe to aspnet_wp.exe.
    - **2.2.** If IIS 6 is running, the request is already in the worker process.
3. ASP.NET packages the request context into an instance of *HttpContext*.
4. ASP.NET pipes the request through an instance of an *HttpApplication* object (or an *HttpApplication*-derived object).

5. If the application object is interested in receiving any of the request preprocessing events, *HttpApplication* fires the events to the application object. Any *HttpModules* that have subscribed to these events will receive the notifications as well.

6. Runtime instantiates a handler and handles the request.

Figure 2-1 shows how IIS version 5.0 and ASP.NET work together to handle HTTP requests. Figure 2-2 shows how IIS version 6.0 works with ASP.NET to handle requests.

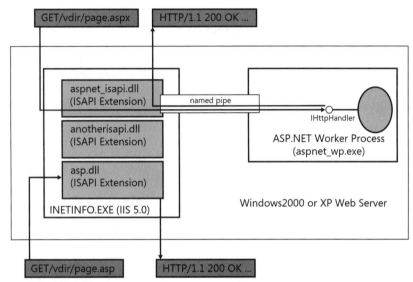

Figure 2-1   IIS 5.0 working in concert with ASP.NET.

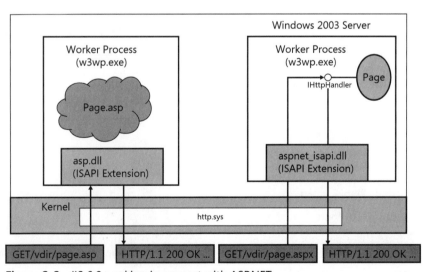

Figure 2-2   IIS 6.0 working in concert with ASP.NET.

Throughout the forthcoming chapters, we'll follow a request through the ASP.NET pipeline. You can plug into the ASP.NET pipeline at a number of distinct points to deal with various aspects of handling the requests. For example, if you'd like to do any preprocessing, you can either override event handlers in the *HttpApplication* class, or you may write HTTP modules and plug them into the pipeline. While the *System.Web.UI.Page* class provides as much functionality as you'll ever need for building Web-based user interfaces, the pipeline is flexible enough that you can easily write your own custom handlers.

The ASP.NET Compilation Model

One of the most important improvements Microsoft has made to the ASP development environment is to build the Web request handling framework out of classes. Pushing request processing into a class-based architecture allows for a Web-handling framework that's compiled. When ASP.NET pages are first accessed, they are compiled into assemblies.

This is advantageous because subsequent access loads the page directly from the assembly. Whereas classic ASP interpreted the same script code over and over, ASP.NET applications are compiled into .NET assemblies and ultimately perform better and are safer.

In addition, compiling the Web request framework allows for more robust and consistent debugging. Whenever you run an ASP.NET application from Visual Studio, you can debug it as though it were a normal desktop application.

ASP.NET compiles .aspx files automatically. To get an .aspx page to compile, you simply need to surf to the .aspx file containing the code. When you do so, ASP.NET compiles the page into a class. However, you won't see that class anywhere near your virtual directory. ASP.NET copies the resulting assemblies to a temporary directory.

Microsoft Visual Studio.Net has always included a tool named ILDASM that uses reflection to reverse compile an assembly so you may view its contents. The result is an easily negotiated tree view you may use to drill down to the contents of the assembly. Right now, that's the important thing. (If you want to peer any more deeply into the assembly and see the actual Intermediate Language, ILDASM will show you that as well.)

Viewing the ASP.NET Assemblies

Here's how to view the assemblies generated by ASP.NET.

1. To run ILDASM, open the Visual Studio .NET 2005 command prompt and type **ILDASM**.

2. Select **File | Open**.

3. To find the assembly compiled by the ASP.NET runtime, go to C:\WINDOWS\Microsoft.NET\Framework\v2.0.50110\Temporary ASP.NET Files\aspnetstepbystep\>. You'll see some oddly named directories underneath. The subdirectory is named v2.0.50110 at the time of this writing. The final subdirectory

may be slightly different. Poke around until you unearth some DLL files. Depending upon how many times you've run the application, you may see several files. Open one of them. You'll see something similar to Figure 2-3.

Figure 2-3   ILDASM showing the contents of the assembly generated by ASP.NET after surfing to HelloWorld3.aspx.

ASP.NET has used this temporary directory strategy since version 1.0. The reason ASP.NET copies these files to a temporary directory is to solve a long-standing problem that plagued classic ASP. Classic ASP Web sites often depended upon COM objects to do complex operations such as database lookups and transactions. When you deploy a classic ASP site and clients begin hitting it, those files become locked. Of course, that's not really a problem—until you decide to upgrade or modify part of the Web site.

Classic ASP locked files during execution, meaning you couldn't copy new files into the virtual directory without shutting down the Web site. For many enterprises, this is a bad option. Because ASP.NET copies the files and the components to the temporary directory and *runs them from there*, they're not locked. When it is time to update a component, simply copy the new assembly into the virtual directory. You can do that because it's not locked.

Coding Options

In addition to supporting inline code (that is, including executable code directly inside a server-side script block), ASP.NET 2.0 offers two other distinct options for managing code: ASP.NET 1.x code behind, and ASP.NET 2.0 code beside. ASP.NET supports code behind for backwards compatibility. Code beside is the style employed by Visual Studio 2005. Let's look at these.

ASP.NET 1.x Style

ASP.NET 2.0 continues to support ASP.NET 1.1 style code behind. Using the code-behind directives in the ASPX file, you provide the code to run behind the page in a separate class and use the *Page* directive to tell ASP.NET which class to apply to the page. Then you tell ASP.NET the name of the file containing the source code for the class.

```
using System.Web;
public class HelloWorld4Code : System.Web.UI.Page
{
public void ShowLineage()
  {
        Response.Write("Check out the family tree: <br> <br>");
        Response.Write(this.GetType().ToString());
        Response.Write(" which derives from: <br> ");
        Response.Write(this.GetType().BaseType.ToString());
        Response.Write(" which derives from: <br> ");
        Response.Write(this.GetType().BaseType.BaseType.ToString());
        Response.Write(" which derives from: <br> ");
        Response.Write(
          this.GetType().BaseType.BaseType.BaseType.ToString());
        Response.Write(" which derives from: <br> ");
        Response.Write(
          this.GetType().BaseType.BaseType.BaseType.BaseType.ToString());
    }
}
<%@ Page Language="C#" Inherits="HelloWorld4Code"
    src="HelloWorld4Code.cs" Debug="true" %>
<html>
    <body>
        <h1>Hello World!!!</h1>
        <%
            // This block will execute in the Render_Control method.
            this.ShowLineage();
        %>
    </body>
</html>
```

With the ASP.NET 1.x style of code behind, ASP.NET sees the *src* keyword in the directives and compiles that file. ASP.NET reads the *inherits* keyword to figure out how to base the class that runs the page. In the example above, ASP.NET uses the *HelloWorld4Code* class to drive the page.

By using the SRC directive, you tell the ASP.NET runtime to compile the file named by the SRC directive. The ASP.NET runtime will compile it into the temporary directory. Alternatively, you may also precompile the file into an assembly containing the *HelloWorld4Code* class. For this to work, the precompiled assembly must appear in the bin directory of your virtual directory. If you precompile the page class and put the assembly in the bin directory, you don't even need to mention the source code file. In the absence of a SRC directive, the ASP.NET runtime will search the assemblies in the bin directory looking for the class specified in the INHERITS directive.

ASP.NET 2.x Style

The other coding option for ASP.NET is new for version 2.0. This model is sometimes referred to as code beside.

```
<%@ Page Language="C#" CodeFile="HelloWorld5code.cs"
    Inherits="HelloWorld5Code" %>
<html>
    <body>
        <h1>Hello World!!!</h1>
        <%
            // This block will execute in the Render_Control method
            ShowLineage();
        %>
    </body>
</html>

using System.Web;
public partial class HelloWorld5Code : System.Web.UI.Page
{
    public void ShowLineage()
    {
        Response.Write("Check out the family tree: <br> <br>");
        Response.Write(this.GetType().ToString());
        Response.Write(" which derives from: <br> ");
        Response.Write(this.GetType().BaseType.ToString());
        Response.Write(" which derives from: <br> ");
        Response.Write(this.GetType().BaseType.BaseType.ToString());
        Response.Write(" which derives from: <br> ");
        Response.Write(
        this.GetType().BaseType.BaseType.BaseType.ToString());
        Response.Write(" which derives from: <br> ");
        Response.Write(
        this.GetType().BaseType.BaseType.BaseType.BaseType.ToString());
    }
}
```

In this case, ASP.NET looks to the *CodeFile* directive to figure out what code to compile. ASP.NET expects to find a partial class to implement the page's logic. Partial classes let you split the definition of a type (*class, struct,* or *interface*) between multiple source files, with a portion of the class definition living in each file. Compiling the source code files generates the entire class. This is especially useful when working with generated code, such as that generated by Visual Studio. You can augment a class without going back and changing the original code. Visual Studio.NET 2005 prefers the code-beside/partial class code representation.

The following short listings, Listing 2-1 and Listing 2-2, show two files that implement a singular class named *SplitMe*.

Listing 2-1   Partial1.cs

```
using System;
// partial1.cs
using System;
```

```
public partial class SplitMe
{
    public static void Main()
    {
        SplitMe splitMe = new SplitMe();
        splitMe.Method1();
        splitMe.Method2();
    }

    public void Method2()
    {
        Console.WriteLine("SplitMe Method2");
    }
}
```

Listing 2-2   Partial2.cs

```
// partial2.cs
using System;

public partial class SplitMe
{
    public static void Main()
    {
        SplitMe splitMe = new SplitMe();
        splitMe.Method1();
        splitMe.Method2();
    }

    public void Method2()
    {
        Console.WriteLine("SplitMe Method2");
    }
}
```

To compile the previous example, you may use the following command line:

```
csc /t:exe partial1.cs partial2.cs
```

This will generate an executable file named Partial2.exe.

After working with ASP.NET source code in the raw, it's time to look at how Visual Studio and ASP.NET work together. Visual Studio.NET 2005 brings many new features for creating and developing Web applications.

The ASP.NET Pipeline

As soon as ASP.NET 1.0 was released, it offered a huge improvement over classic ASP by introducing well-defined pipelines. Classic ASP was patched together from several disparate components (IIS, the Web Application Manager, and the ASP ISAPI DLL). The *Request* and *Response* objects were *COM* objects hanging off the threads owned by IIS. If you wanted to do any processing outside the context of ASP, you needed to write an ISAPI filter. If you wanted to write code to execute during processing, it had to occur within a *COM* object implementing IDispatch (severely limiting the available types of data you could use and negatively affecting performance). If you wanted to write any request-handling code (outside the context of ASP), you had to write a separate ISAPI DLL. The HTTP pipeline includes the facilities to do these things, but in a much more manageable way.

In ASP.NET, your application has the opportunity to perform preprocessing and post processing within *HttpModules*. Your application also has the opportunity to process application-wide events using the *HttpApplication* object. Because of ASP.NET's object model, the need for separate scripting objects disappears. The endpoint of all requests is an implementation of *IHttpHandler*. ASP.NET already includes some useful implementations of *IHttpHandler* (that is, *System.Web.UI.Page* and *System.Web.Services.WebService*). However, you may easily write your own (as we'll see later).

Request Path

Once a request comes into the *AppDomain* managed by the ASP.NET runtime, ASP.NET uses the *HttpWorkerRequest* class to store the request information. Following that, the runtime wraps the request's information in a class named *HttpContext*. The *HttpContext* class includes all the information you'd ever want to know about a request, including references to the current request's *HttpRequest* and *HttpResponse* objects. The runtime produces an instance of *HttpApplication* (if one is not already available) and then fires a number of application-wide events (such as *BeginRequest* and *AuthenticateRequest*). These events are also pumped through any *HttpModules* attached to the pipeline. Finally, ASP.NET figures out what kind of handler is required to handle the request, creates one, and asks the handler to process the request. After the handler deals with the request, ASP.NET fires a number of post-processing events (like *EndRequest*) through the *HttpApplication* object and the *HttpModules*.

The following figure illustrates the structure of the ASP.NET pipeline inside the ASP.NET worker process:

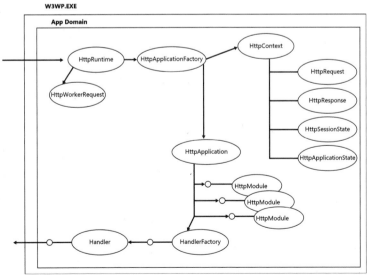

Figure 2-4   Main components of the HTTP pipeline within ASP.NET.

While some of the parts within the pipeline are unavailable to you as a developer, several parts are available directly and provide a useful means of managing your request as it goes through the pipeline. The most important parts of the pipeline that you can touch include the *HttpApplication*, the *HttpContext*, the *HttpModule*, and the *HttpHandler*.

Following are some details about these critical sections within the HTTP request path.

The HttpApplication

At this point, you understand the nature of a Web application as being very different from that of a normal desktop application. The code that you're writing is responsible for spitting some HTML response back to a client. In many ways, the model hearkens back to the terminal-mainframe model prevalent during the mid-1970s. In ASP.NET, the endpoint of a request is an implementation of *IHttpHandler*.

HTTP handlers live for a very short period of time. They stick around long enough to handle a request, and then they disappear. For very simple applications, this model might be just fine. However, imagine the requirements of even a modest commercial-grade application. If all you had to work with was these ephemeral handlers, you'd have no way to achieve application-wide functionality. For example, imagine you wanted to cache data to avoid round-trips to the database. You'd need to store that data in a place where all the HTTP handlers could get to it.

The *HttpApplication* class exists for that purpose—to act as a rendezvous point for your request processing. During the lifetime of a Web application, the *HttpApplication* objects serve as places to hold application-wide data and handle application-side events.

The HttpContext

The *HttpContext* class acts a central location in which you can access parts of the current request as it travels through the pipeline. In fact, every aspect of the current request is available through *HttpContext*. Even though the *HttpContext* components are really just references to other parts of the pipeline, having them available in a single place makes it much easier to manage the request.

Here is an abbreviated listing of *HttpContext*, showing the parts you'll be using most frequently in developing Web applications. The members are exposed as properties.

```
class HttpContext
{
    public static HttpContext Current…;
    public HttpRequest Request…;
    public HttpResponse Response…;
    public HttpSessionState Session…;
    public HttpServerUtility Server…;
    public Application HttpApplicationState…;
    public ApplicationInstance HttpApplication…;
    public IDictionary Items…;
    public IPrincipal User…;
```

```
    public IHttpHandler CurrentHandler…;
    public Cache Cache…;
    …
}
```

The static *Current* property gives you a means of getting to the current request at any time. Many times, the *HttpContext* is passed as a method parameter (as in the *method IHttp-Handler.RequestProcess(HttpContext ctx)*; however, there may be times when you need the context even though it hasn't been passed as a parameter. The *Current* property lets you grab the current process out of thin air. For example, this is how you might use *Http-Context.Current:*

```
Public void DealWithRequest()
{
    HttpContext thisRequest = HttpContext.Current;
    thisRequest.Response.Write("<h3> Hello World</h3>");
}
```

The other properties within *HttpContext* include such nuggets as

- a reference to the context's *Response* object (so you can send output to the client)

- a reference to the *Request* object (so you can find information about the request itself)

- a reference to the central application itself (so you can get to the application state)

- a reference to a per-request dictionary (for storing items for the duration of a request)

- a reference to the application-wide cache (to store data and avoid round-trips to the database)

We'll be seeing a lot more of the context—especially within the context of a custom *HttpHandler.*

HttpModules

While the *Application* object is suitable for handling application-wide events and data on a small scale, sometimes application-wide tasks need a little heavier machinery. *HttpModules* serve that purpose.

ASP.NET includes a number of predefined *HttpModules*. For example, session state, authentication, and authorization are handled via *HttpModules*. Writing *HttpModules* is pretty straightforward, and is a great way to handle complex application-wide operations. For example, if you wanted to write your own authentication scheme, using *HTTPModules* is a good way to do it. We'll see *HTTPModules* up close later.

HttpHandlers

The last stop a request makes in the pipeline is an *HttpHandler*. Any class implementing the interface *IHttpHandler* qualifies as a handler. When a request finally reaches the end of the pipeline, ASP.NET consults the configuration file to see if the particular file extension is mapped to an *HttpHandler*. If it is, the ASP.NET loads the handler and calls the handler's *IHttpHandler.ProcessRequest* method to execute the request.

ASP.NET includes several *HTTPHandlers* already, including *System.Web.UI.Page* and *System.Web.Services.WebService*. We'll use these as we move forward. In addition, we'll also learn how to write an *HTTPHandler* completely from scratch.

Visual Studio and ASP.NET

Visual Studio .NET 2005 expands your options for locating your Web sites during development. The Visual Studio .NET 2005 wizards define four separate Web site projects: local IIS Web sites, file system Web sites, FTP Web sites, and remote Web sites.

Kinds of Web Sites

Here's a rundown of the different types of Web sites available using the project wizard. Each is useful for a particular scenario, and having these options makes it much easier to develop and deploy an ASP.NET application with Visual Studio 2005 than with earlier versions.

Local IIS Web Sites

Creating a local IIS Web site is much like creating a Web site using the older versions of Visual Studio.NET specifying a local virtual directory. This option creates sites that run using IIS installed on your local computer. Local IIS Web sites store the pages and folders in the IIS default directory structure (that is, \Inetpub\wwwroot). By default, Visual Studio creates a virtual directory under IIS. However, you may create a virtual directory ahead of time and store the code for your Web site in any folder. The virtual directory just needs to point to that location.

One reason to create a local Web site is to test your application against a local version of IIS, for example, if you need to test such features as application pooling, ISAPI filters, or HTTP-based authentication. Even though a site is accessible from other computers, it's often much easier to test these aspects of your application when you can see it interact with IIS on your computer. To create a local Web site, you need to have administrative rights. For most developers, this is not an issue.

File System Web Sites

File system Web sites live in any folder you specify. The folder may be on your local computer or on another computer sharing that folder. File system Web sites do *not* require IIS running on your computer. Instead, you run pages by using the Visual Studio Web server.

> ## Visual Studio Web Server
>
> One of the issues plaguing Web developers using earlier versions of Visual Studio was the fact that it used IIS to serve up pages. That meant that developers needed to have IIS fully enabled on their machines to be able to develop effectively. This created a possible security compromise. Visual Studio 2005 now includes its own built-in Web server. This lets you develop Web applications effectively even if you don't have IIS installed on your development machine.

File system Web sites are useful for testing your site locally but independently of IIS. The most common approach is to create, develop, and test a file system Web site and then when it is time to expose your site, to simply create an IIS virtual directory and point it to the pages in the file system Web site.

Because file system Web sites employ the Visual Studio Web server rather than IIS, you may develop your Web site on your computer even when logged on as a user without administrative rights.

This scenario is only useful for developing and testing those features of your site that you develop. Because IIS is out of the picture, you won't be able to work with (or have to deal with) such IIS features as ISAPI filters, application pooling, or authentication.

FTP Web Sites

In addition to creating HTTP-based sites, you may use Visual Studio to manage Web sites available through an FTP server. For example, if you use a remote hosting company to host your Web site, an FTP offers a convenient way to move files back and forth between your development location and the hosting location.

Visual Studio connects to any FTP server for which you have reading and writing privileges. You then use Visual Studio to manage the content on the remote FTP server.

You might use this option to test the Web site on the live server where it will actually be deployed.

Remote Web Sites

The final option for developing and managing Web sites through Visual Studio is to use the remote Web sites option. Remote Web sites use IIS on another computer that is accessible over a local area network. Visual Studio 2003 also supported an option very like this one. In addition to running IIS, the remote computer must have IIS installed and needs to have FrontPage 2002 Server Extensions installed. Pages and folders on a remote site become stored under the default IIS folder on the remote computer.

This option is useful if you decide you want to test the Web site on its actual deployment server. In addition, the entire development team can work on the site simultaneously. The downside of this approach is that debugging and configuring a Web site remotely is tricky.

Hello World and Visual Studio

To get started, let's use Visual Studio to generate the HelloWorld Web application.

1. **Create a new Web site.**   To create a new Web site, select the following menu combination: **File | New | Web Site**. Visual Studio will display a dialog box like this one:

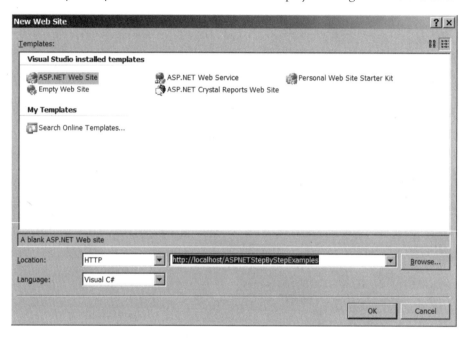

    Give the Web site a useful name like ASPNETStepByStepExamples.

    Notice that several different kinds of sites are showing in the dialog box. Choose **Empty Web Site** for this example.

    Choosing Empty Web Site causes Visual Studio to generate an ASP.NET solution file within a directory named Visual Studio 2005\Projects in your normal Documents directory. Visual Studio will also create a new directory within your inetpub\wwwroot directory and map it as an IIS virtual directory. However, the virtual directory will be devoid of any files.

    Selecting **ASP.NET Web Site** causes Visual Studio to generate a directory structure similar to the one generated by ASP.NET Web Site. However, Visual Studio will throw in a default Web form and source code to go with (default .aspx and default.aspx.cs). You'll also get an AppData directory that may contain data pertinent to your site (for example, user names will be contained here).

2. **Choose the language syntax.**   At this point, you have the option of choosing a syntax to use within your code. Choose among Visual Basic, C#, and J#. For this example, choose C#.

3. **Create a local Web site.**   For this example, select **HTTP** from the location combo box to run this Web site locally on your machine. Visual Studio's default option is to create a Web site on your local machine. Clients trying to access your Web site will have their requests directed through IIS. This is the best option to choose when learning ASP.NET because it gives you the chance to work with your Web site as an entire system, and you can use tracing and debugging on your local machine.

4. **Add a HelloWorld page.**   To add the HelloWorld page to the new site, select **Website |**
Add New Item... to reach the Add New Item dialog box:

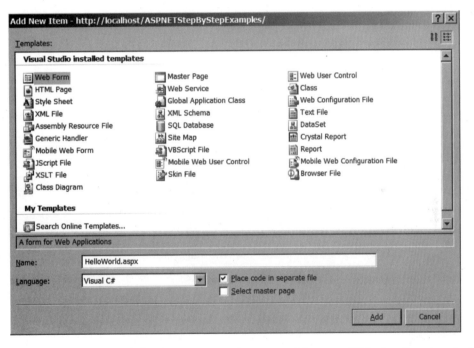

This dialog box lists all the various pieces you may add to your Web site. Topping the list is an item named Web Form. Select this option, and then type **Helloworld.aspx** into the Name text box. Leave the other defaults the same.

Visual Studio will immediately confront you with the pure ASP.NET code from the Helloworld.aspx file.

Notice that the code generated by Visual Studio includes directives near the top connecting Helloworld.aspx to the accompanying source file Helloworld.aspx.cs (with the *Code-File* and *Inherits* directives). Following the directives is some initial HTML produced by Visual Studio.

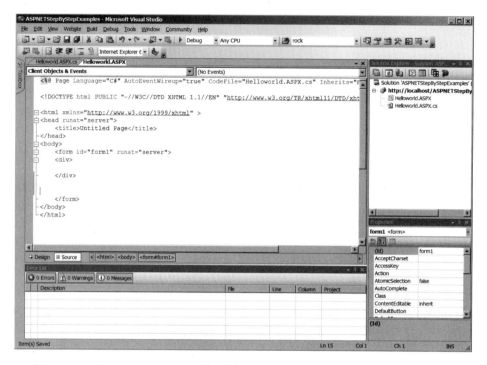

At this point, take a moment to explore the layout of Visual Studio. Along the top of the window, you'll see a number of toolbar buttons and menu options. We'll visit most of them throughout the course of this text. Directly beneath the code window, you'll see two tabs labeled Design and Source (the Source tab is selected by default). If you select the Design tab, you'll see what the page will look like in a browser. Right now, the page has no visible tags, so the design view is blank.

To the right of the Source window, you'll see the Solution Explorer, which lists the components of your application that Visual Studio is currently displaying. Along the top of the Solution Explorer, you'll find a number of buttons. By hovering your cursor over the buttons, you can see what they do. The following figure shows how each button functions.

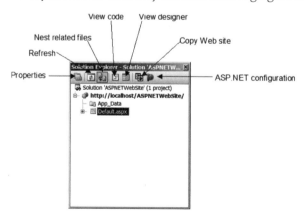

5. **Write some code into the page.**   Select the View code button from the Solution Explorer. This will show the C# code in the Source code window, like so:

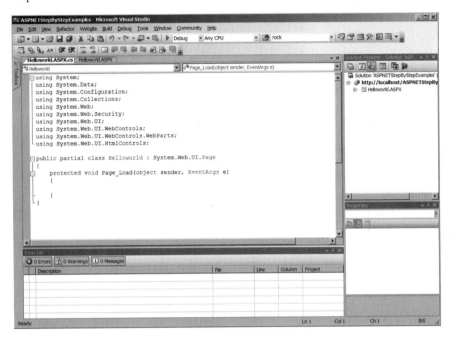

Add code to show the page's lineage (it's the same code from HelloWorld5 shown above). Add the *ShowLineage* method to the Helloworld.aspx.cs file.

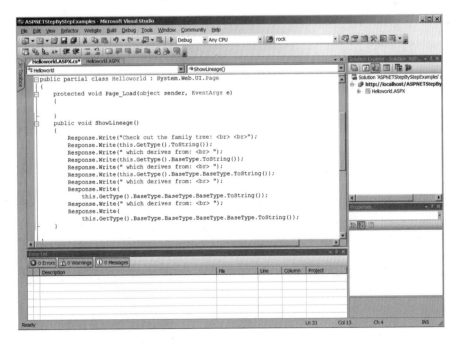

```
public void ShowLineage()
    {
        Response.Write("Check out the family tree: <br> <br>");
        Response.Write(this.GetType().ToString());
        Response.Write(" which derives from: <br> ");
        Response.Write(this.GetType().BaseType.ToString());
        Response.Write(" which derives from: <br> ");
        Response.Write(this.GetType().BaseType.BaseType.ToString());
        Response.Write(" which derives from: <br> ");
        Response.Write(
           this.GetType().BaseType.BaseType.BaseType.ToString());
        Response.Write(" which derives from: <br> ");
        Response.Write(
           this.GetType().BaseType.BaseType.BaseType.BaseType.ToString());
    }
```

6. **Call the ShowLineage method from the ASPX file.**   Select **View Designer** from the Solution Explorer, and then select the **Source** tab near the bottom of the screen.

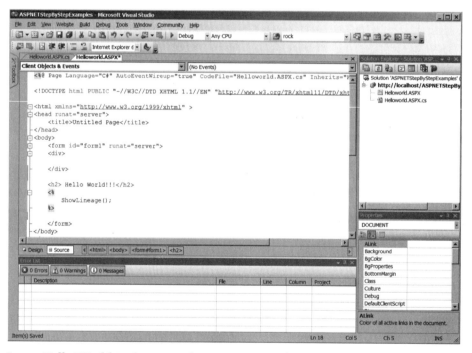

Insert **Hello World** in the page. Then insert a set of execution markers (<% and %>) and insert the call like this:

```
<h2> Hello World!!!</h2>
<%
ShowLineage();
%>
```

7. **Now build the project and run the Web site from Visual Studio.**   To build the application, select **Build | Solution** from the main menu. If the source code has any errors, they'll appear in the Errors window in the bottom window.

To run the application, select **Debug | Start Without Debugging**.   Visual Studio will start up a copy of an Internet browser (Microsoft Internet Explorer by default) and browse the page. You should see a page like this:

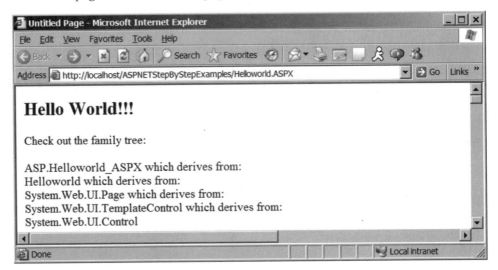

When you run this application, Visual Studio invokes the Visual Studio Web Server. The files are compiled and moved to the temporary ASP.NET directory. Alternatively, you may precompile the site by selecting **Build | Publish** from the main menu to pre-compile the code. The precompiled code will land in a subdirectory off your project named PrecompiledWeb. We'll look more closely at the various deexecution and deployment options later on.

Conclusion

We've just seen how ASP.NET works from a high level. When a client surfs to an ASPX file on your server, the request is pushed through IIS running on your server. IIS maps individual file extensions to specific ISAPI DLLs. When IIS sees the .aspx extension in the request, that ISAPI DLL is aspnet_isapi.dll. The request ends up within the ASP.NET worker process, which instantiates an HTTP handler to fulfill the request.

In the case of an ASPX file, ASP.NET instantiates a class derived from *System.Web.UI.Page* (which implements *IHttpHandler*). ASPX files are usually paired with source code files containing the source code for the page. The ASPX file behaves mainly as the presentation layer while the accompanying *Page* class contributes the logic behind the presentation layer.

Next up—all about *System.Web.UI.Page* and how Web forms work.

Chapter 2 Quick Reference

To	Do This
Create an FTP Web site	Select **File | New | Web site** from the main menu. Select FTP from the Locations combo box
	This option is useful for creating sites that will be eventually be deployed by sending the bits to the real host over FTP
Create an HTTP Web site	Select **File | New | Web site** from the main menu. Select HTTP from the Locations combo box
	This option is useful for creating sites that use IIS as the Web server throughout the whole development cycle
Create a File System Web site	Select **File | New | Web site** from the main menu. Select File system from the Locations combo box
	This option creates sites that use Visual Studio's built-in Web server. That way, you may develop your own site even if you don't have IIS available on your machine

Chapter 3

The Page Rendering Model

After completing this chapter, you will be able to

- Work directly with server-side control tags

- Create a Web site with Visual Studio

- Work with Web forms and server-side controls using Visual Studio

- Work with post-back events using Visual Studio

This chapter covers the heart of ASP.NET's Web Forms rendering model: controls. As we'll see here, *System.Web.UI.Page* works by partitioning the rendering process into small components known as server-side controls.

The entire tour of the ASP.NET control model will look at the fundamental control architecture. We'll start by looking at the HTML required to render controls in the browser. We'll take a very quick look at the classic ASP approach to displaying controls (and some of the problems there). This will lay the groundwork for following chapters in which we'll look at how controls can provide custom rendering, user controls, some of the standard UI controls, and the new ASP.NET 2.0 controls. We'll start with the ASP.NET rendering model.

Rendering Controls as Tags

As we saw when looking at Web forms, developing a Web-based UI is all about getting the right tags out to the browser. For example, imagine you wanted to have your application's UI appear as shown in Figure 3-1 in the client's browser.

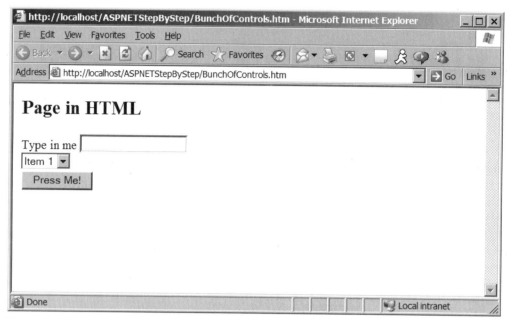

Figure 3-1   Some HTML tags rendered as controls in Internet Explorer.

Getting this to appear on a client's browser means populating an HTML stream with the correct tags so the browser represents the screen using controls. Listing 3-1 shows some HTML that does the job. If you would like to run this page, the file is named "BunchOfControls.htm." You'll find it in the sample code for this chapter. To run the page, take the file and save it in a virtual directory and browser to it.

Listing 3-1

```
<h2> Page in HTML </h2>
<form method="post" action="BunchOfControls.htm" id="Form1">
    <span>Type in me</span>
    <input name="textinfo" type="text" id="textinfo" />
    <BR>
    <select name="selectitems" id="ddl">
    <option value="Item 1">Item 1</option>
    <option value="Item 2">Item 2</option>
    <option value="Item 3">Item 3</option>
    <option value="Item 4">Item 4</option>

    </select>
    <BR>
    <input type="submit" name="pressme" value="Press Me!" id="pressme" />
</form>
```

Of course, using controls on a page usually implies dynamic content, so conjuring up this HTML should happen in a programmatic way. Classic ASP has facilities for rendering dynamic content. However, classic ASP generally relies on raw HTML for rendering its content. That means writing a page like the BunchOfControls.htm page shown above might look something like Listing 3-2 in classic ASP. Figure 3-2 shows how the ASP page renders in Internet Explorer.

Listing 3-2

```
<%@ Language="javascript" %>
<h2> Page in Classic ASP </h2>
<form>

    <span>Type in me</span>
    <input name="textinfo" type="text" id="textinfo" />
    <BR>
    <select name="selectitems" id="ddl">
    <option value="Item 1">Item 1</option>
    <option value="Item 2">Item 2</option>
    <option value="Item 3">Item 3</option>
    <option value="Item 4">Item 4</option>

</select>
    <BR>
    <input type="submit" name="pressme" value="Press Me!" id="pressme" />
<p>
    <% if (Request("textinfo") != "") { %>
        This was in the text box: <%=Request("textinfo") %> <br>
        And this was in the selection control: <%=Request("selectitems") %>
    <% } %>
</p>

</form>
```

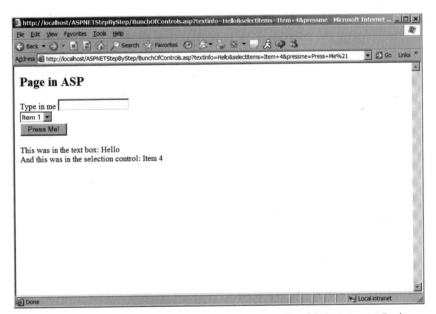

Figure 3-2   The ASP page from Listing 3-2 appears like this in Internet Explorer.

When you select an item from the selection control, notice that the page responds by telling you what you selected. This demonstrates ASP's support for dynamic content.

Notice that even though classic ASP offers a way to decide your page's content at runtime, you still have to create much of it using raw HTML. Also, the state of the controls is always reset between posts (we'll look at that when we examine View State a bit later). ASP.NET adds a layer of indirection between the raw HTML and the rendered page—that layer of indirection is ASP.NET's server-side controls. Server-side controls eliminate much of the tedium necessary to develop a Web-based UI in classic ASP.

Packaging UI as Components

Being able to assemble the UI from component parts is one of the most-cited benefits of producing components. Regular Windows programming originally employed VBXs (Visual Basic Controls) to build UIs. Of course, that was over a decade ago. Throughout the mid- and late 1990s and early 2000s, ActiveX controls represented the GUI componentization technology of the day. Windows Forms controls are the current standard for modular GUIs if you're writing a rich client application.

In the late 1990s, ActiveX controls also emerged as a way to render a Web-based GUI as components. The idea was that by using an ActiveX control in your page, the control would be downloaded as users surfed to the page. During the mid-1990s Java applets also gained some popularity as a way to package GUI components for distribution over the Web. However, both of these techniques depend on some fairly extensive infrastructure on the client machine (the Component Object Model infrastructure to support ActiveX and a Java Virtual Machine to support Java applets). When you're developing a Web site, you may not be able to count on a specific infrastructure's being available on the client machine to support your GUI. To support the greatest number of clients, represent your GUI using only HTML. That means all GUI componentization needs to happen on the server side.

As we saw earlier, ASP.NET introduces an entirely new model for managing Web pages. The infrastructure within ASP.NET includes a well-defined pipeline through which a request flows. When a request ends up at the server, ASP.NET instantiates a handler (an implementation of *IHttpHandler*) to deal with the request. As we'll see in a later chapter, the handling architecture is extraordinarily flexible. You may write any code you wish to handle the request. The *System.Web.UI.Page* class implements *IHttpHandler* by introducing an object-oriented approach to rendering. That is, every element you see on a Web page emitted by an ASP.NET page is somehow generated by a *server-side control*. Let's see how this works.

The Page Using ASP.NET

Try turning the previous Web page into an ASP.NET application.

1.   Create a file named **BunchOfControls.aspx**.

2. Add the source code in Listing 3-3 to the file.

    Listing 3-3

    ```
    <%@ Page Language=C# %>

    <script runat="server">
      protected void Page_Load(object sender, EventArgs ea)
      {
          ddl.Items.Add("Item 1");
          ddl.Items.Add("Item 2");
          ddl.Items.Add("Item 3");
          ddl.Items.Add("Item 4");
      }
    </script >
    <h2> Page in ASP.NET </h2>
    <form id="Form1" runat="server" >
        <asp:Label Text="Type in me" runat="server" />
        <asp:TextBox id="textinfo" runat="server" />
        <BR>
        <asp:DropDownList id="ddl" runat="server" />
        <BR>
        <asp:Button id="pressme" Text="Press Me!" runat="server" />
    </form>
    ```

3. Save the file in a virtual directory (either create one or use the one from the previous chapter).

Many of the same elements seen in the classic ASP page also appear here. There's a top level *Page* directive. The *Language* directive is new for ASP.NET, stipulating that any code encountered by the ASP.NET runtime should be interpreted as C# code. There's a server-side script block that handles the *Page_Load* event. Following the script block is an HTML *<form>* tag. Notice the *<form>* tag has an attribute named *runat*, and the attribute is set to *server*. The *runat=server* attribute tells the ASP.NET runtime to generate a server-side control to handle that aspect of the page.

By including the *runat=server* attribute in the control tag, the ASP.NET runtime implicitly creates an instance of the control in memory. The resulting assembly includes a member variable of the same type and name as the control listed on the page. Notice the ASP.NET code specifies the *DropDownList* named *ddl* to run at the server. To access the control programmatically, the code block (expressed inline in this case) simply needs to refer to the *DropDownList* as *ddl*. The example above accesses the member variable to add items to the drop-down list.

To access the control using code behind, you'd explicitly declare the *DropDownList* variable as *ddl*. This is required because ASP.NET derives the code-beside class from *System.Web.UI.Page*. Visual Studio will do this for you automatically, as we'll see shortly.

Further down the ASP.NET code, you'll see each of the other elements (the label, the text box, the selection control, and the Submit button) are also represented as server-side controls. The job of each of these controls is to add a little bit of HTML to the response. Each time you add a server-side control to the page, ASP.NET adds an instance of the control to a control tree the page maintains in memory. The control tree will show that every single element is encapsulated by one of these server-side controls—even the title text that seems to be floating near the top of the page.

The Page's Rendering Model

To get a good idea as to how ASP.NET's *Page* model works, we'll run the page again, but we'll turn on the tracing mechanism. We'll examine tracing in more detail when we look at ASP.NET's diagnostic features. For now, you simply need to know that ASP.NET will dump the entire context of a request and a response if you set the page's *Trace* attribute to true. Here's the page directive with tracing turned on:

```
<%@ Page Language=C#  trace=true %>
```

Figure 3-3 shows what the page looks like with tracing turned on.

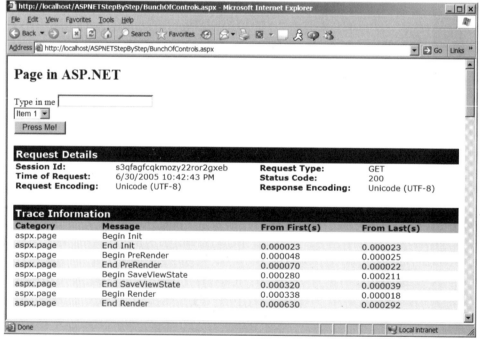

Figure 3-3   The ASPX file from Listing 3-3 rendered in Internet Explorer.

If you look at the raw text of the response (by selecting **View | Source** from the Internet Explorer menu), you see that ASP.NET responds with pretty straightforward run-of-the-mill HTML. There's a bit extra near the top—the hidden __*VIEWSTATE* field—which we'll cover a bit later. After that, the rest is familiar HTML describing a form. Listing 3-4 shows the raw HTML emitted by the ASP.NET code from Listing 3-3.

Listing 3-4

```
<h2> Page in ASP.NET </h2>
<form method="post" action="BunchOfControls.aspx" id="Form1">
<div>
<input type="hidden" name="__VIEWSTATE" id="__VIEWSTATE" value="/
wEPDwUJODQ1ODEzNjQ4D2QWAmYPZBYCAgUPD2QPFgRmAgECAgIDFgQQBQZJdGVtIDEFBkl0ZW0gMWcQBQZJdGVtIDIFB
kl0ZW0gMmcQBQZJdGVtIDMFBkl0ZW0gM2cQBQZJdGVtIDQFBkl0ZW0gNGdkZBIoyTUHSvKe61yeF4ReR/9OQFst" />
</div>

  <span>Type in me</span>
  <input name="textinfo" type="text" id="textinfo" />
  <BR>
  <select name="ddl" id="ddl">
  <option value="Item 1">Item 1</option>
  <option value="Item 2">Item 2</option>
  <option value="Item 3">Item 3</option>
  <option value="Item 4">Item 4</option>

</select>
  <BR>
  <input type="submit" name="pressme" value="Press Me!" id="pressme" />
</form>
```

You don't see any of the *runat=server* attributes anywhere in the rendered page. That's because the *runat=server* attributes are there to instruct ASP.NET how to construct the page's control tree.

The Page's Control Tree

After turning the page's *Trace* property to true, the ASP.NET will spew a ton of information your way in the form of a page trace. If you scroll down just a bit, you can see that part of ASP.NET's page trace includes the page's control tree. Figure 3-4 shows what the previous page's trace looks like with the focus on the control tree.

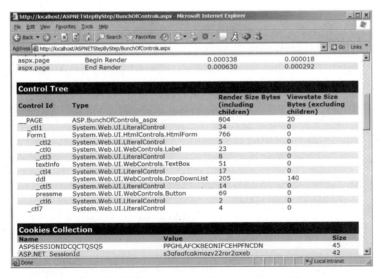

Figure 3-4   The ASP.NET page's control tree shown in the page trace.

The first line in the page's control tree trace is an item named *__Page*. This is in fact the *System.Web.UI.Page* object running in memory. Beneath that are a whole host of other items. You'll recognize some of their names as they were named in the ASP.NET source code. Notice the *Form1, textinfo,* and *pressme* items. Those names came from the tags in the original ASPX file.

What's happening here is that ASP.NET is breaking down the page rendering architecture into small, easily managed pieces. Every item in the list above derives from the *System.Web.UI.Control* class. Every time the *System.Web.UI.Page* needs to render the page, it simply walks the control tree, asking each control to render itself. For example, when the ASP.NET runtime asks the *TextBox* server-side control to render itself, the *TextBox* control adds the following HTML to the output stream heading for the browser:

```
<input name="textinfo" type="text" id="textinfo" />
```

This works similarly for the other controls. For example, the *DropDownList* is responsible for emitting the select and option tags (the option tags represent the collection of items held by the *DropDownList* control).

```
<select name="ddl" id="ddl">
    <option value="Item 1">Item 1</option>
    <option value="Item 2">Item 2</option>
    <option value="Item 3">Item 3</option>
    <option value="Item 4">Item 4</option>
</select>
```

Now that you see how these tags work, let's see how to manage them in Visual Studio.

Adding Controls Using Visual Studio

Visual Studio (in concert with ASP.NET) is very good at fooling you as to the real nature of Web-based development. As you saw from earlier chapters, Web-based development hearkens back to the old terminal–mainframe days of the mid-1970s. However, this time the terminal is a sophisticated browser, the computing platform is a Web server (or perhaps a Web farm), and the audience is worldwide. When a client browser makes a round-trip to the server, it's really getting only a snapshot of the state of the server. That's because Web user interfaces are built using a markup language over a disconnected protocol.

When you build Web applications in Visual Studio, it's almost as if you're developing a desktop application. With Visual Studio, you don't have to spend all your time typing ASP code. The designer is a great environment for designing a Web-based UI visually.

Building a Page with Visual Studio

To see how this works, let's develop a simple page that uses server-side controls. The page will look roughly like the ones we've seen so far.

1. **Create a Web site to experiment with controls.**   Use Visual Studio to create a new Web site. Call the Web site **ControlORama**.

2. **Use the Designer.**   Visual Studio starts you off in default ASPX. In Designer mode, switch to the Design view as shown here.

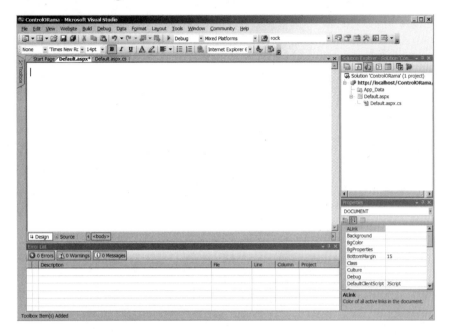

The ASP.NET code generated by Visual Studio includes an HTML *<div>* tag in the body of the page. If you simply start typing some text into the Design view, you'll see some text at the top of the page. The following figure illustrates the Design view.

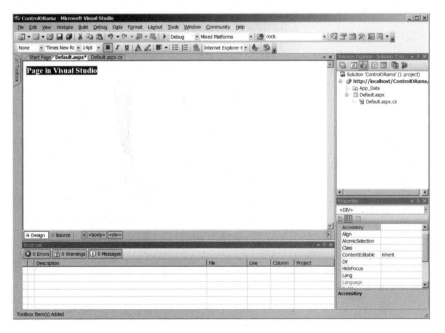

To edit the format of the text on the page, you need to view the page's properties. Highlight the text, right-click the text, and select **Properties** from the local menu. Then highlight the **Style** property in the Property dialog box. You'll see a small button appear in the *Property* field with an ellipsis (...). Click the button to reveal the Style Builder dialog box. The Style Builder sets the attributes for the *<div>* tag where you can set the font face and style. The following figure shows the Style Builder dialog box.

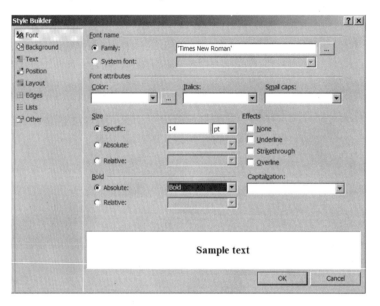

3.   **Open the Control toolbox.**   Next add a label to the page. Move the cursor to the Toolbox tab on the far left-hand side of Visual Studio. This will highlight the toolbox on the left as shown in the following graphic:

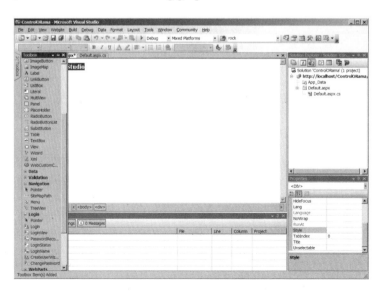

4. **Add a label to the page.**   Grab a label and drop it onto the page as shown in the following graphic:

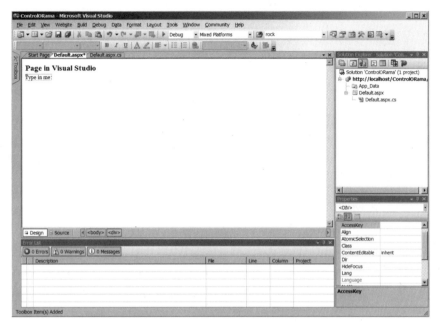

5. **Edit the content of the label.**   To edit the content of the label, you need to view the control's properties. If the properties aren't showing, right-click on the label and select **Properties** from the shortcut menu.The following graphic illustrates the property window.

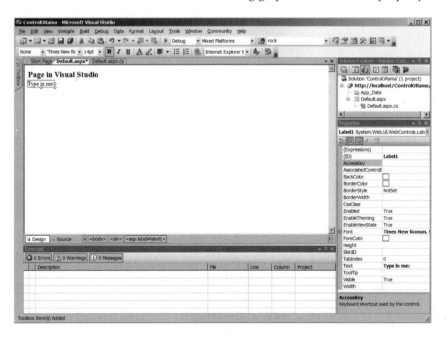

You can now manipulate the appearance of the label to your liking. The example label here uses a small Times New Roman font and the text in the label is *Type in me:*.

6. **Add a text box.**   Next, pick up a text box from the toolbox and drop it next to the label.

7. **Add a drop-down list.**   Next, add a *DropDownList* box by picking it up off the toolbox and dropping it onto the page. The following graphic illustrates the drop-down list as it appears in the designer. Notice the local menu for editing the data source and for adding items.

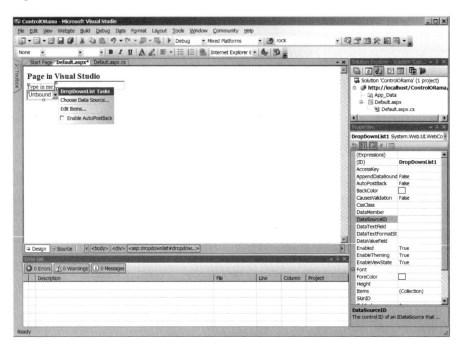

As soon as you drop the control onto the page, Visual Studio prompts you with the opportunity to add items to the *DropDownList*. Select **Edit Items** from the local menu. You'll see the ListItem Collection Editor dialog box as shown in the following graphic:

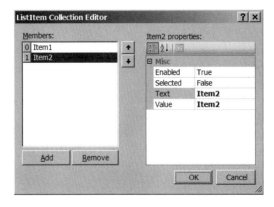

Each time you click the Add button, the ListItem Collection Editor adds a new item to the *DropDownList* item collection. You can edit the display name (the Text property). You may add a corresponding value to associate with the text as well. For example, in an inventory-tracking application, you might include a product name as the Text property and an enterprise-specific product code in the value field. You can retrieve either or both aspects of the item at runtime.

Add several of these items to the *DropDownList*.

8. **Add a button to the page.** Do this by picking one up from the toolbox and dropping it on the page. The following graphic shows the controls in place.

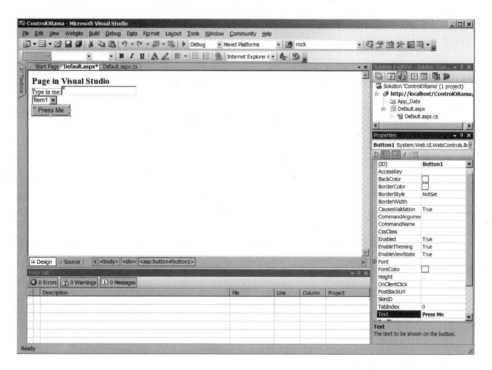

Add some meaningful text to the button by modifying its Text property.

Before moving on, take a minute to look at the source code generated by Visual Studio. In adding a *Label* control, a *TextBox* control, a *DropDownList* control, and a *Button* control, Visual Studio has added four new member variables to your code. The contents of the ASPX file (within the form tag) looks something like Listing 3-5 now.

Listing 3-5

```
<form id="form1" runat="server">
<div>
    Page in Visual Studio<br />
    <asp:Label ID="Label1" runat="server"
      Text="Type in me:"
      Font-Bold="False" Font-Names="Times New Roman" Font-
```

```
      Size="Small">
    </asp:Label><asp:TextBox
    ID="TextBox1" runat="server"></asp:TextBox>
    <br />
    <asp:DropDownList ID="DropDownList1" runat="server">
        <asp:ListItem>Item 1</asp:ListItem>
        <asp:ListItem>Item 2</asp:ListItem>
        <asp:ListItem>Item 3</asp:ListItem>
        <asp:ListItem>Item 4</asp:ListItem>
    </asp:DropDownList><br />
    <asp:Button ID="Button1"
    runat="server" OnClick="Button1_Click"
    Text="Press Me" />
  </div>
</form>
```

Notice each ASP.NET tag that runs at the server is given an ID attribute. This is the identifier by which the control will be known at runtime. We'll make user of that shortly.

9. **Add an event handler for the button.**   Finally, to make the button do something, you need to add an event handler to the page so it will respond when the button is clicked. The easiest way to do that is to double-click on the button in Design mode. Visual Studio will generate a handler function for the button press, and then show that code in the Source code view. At this point, you can add some code to respond to the button press. The following graphic illustrates the button handling event as it appears in the code editor.

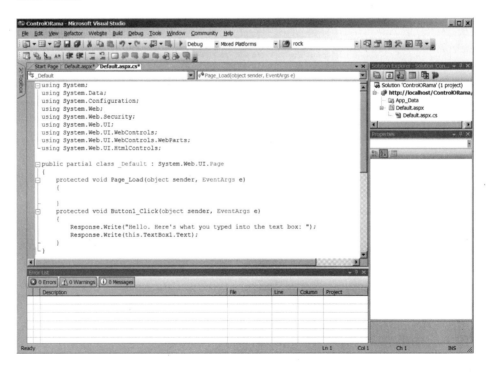

The code shown above responds to the button press by sending some text to the output stream via the *Response* object. The text coming through *Response.Write* will be the first text the client browser will see, and so will appear at the top of the page.

Notice that the response code uses the *TextBox1* member variable in the page's class, showing that the controls are available programmatically at runtime. Here's how the page appears to the client browser:

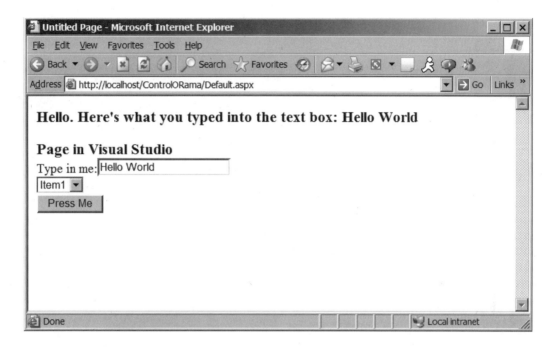

To test the controls on the page, browse to the page by selecting **Debug | Start Without Debugging** from the main menu.

Layout Considerations

You may have noticed when building the last page that the layout of the page flowed. That is, every time you dropped a control onto the page, the designer forced it up against the placement of the previous control. If you've worked with earlier versions of Visual Studio, you'll notice this is different default behavior. Visual Studio 2003 started off with absolute positioning for elements on a page (which is what you're used to if you've done rich client or standard Windows development).

To change the layout options for a Web page in Visual Studio 2005, select **Layout | Position | Auto position Options**... to get the layout options for the page. The following graphic shows the positioning options dialog box.

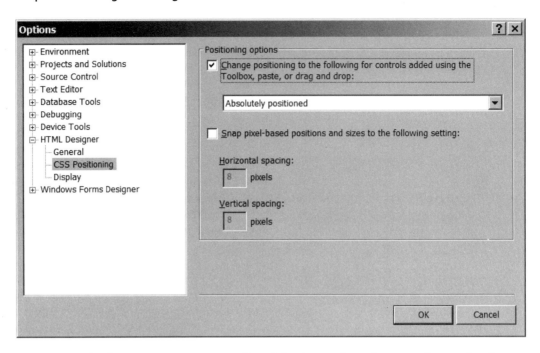

Turning on absolute positioning causes Visual Studio to place the controls exactly where you want them instead of your being confined to a flow layout. With absolute positioning turned on, Visual Studio adds positioning attributes to the controls as it places them on the Web form.

Conclusion

The *System.Web.UI.Page* class includes a collection of server-side controls. Everything that ever makes its way out to the client browser was somehow generated by a server-side control. Even literal text on the page was rendered using a *LiteralControl*. When the ASP.NET runtime compiles a page, it scans the ASPX file for any tag that says *runat=server* and adds a member variable representing that control to the page's control tree. Nothing escapes being packaged as a control—when ASP.NET finds literal text on the page, ASP.NET packages that as a literal control. When it comes time for the page to render, ASP.NET walks the control list and asks each control in the list to render itself.

Visual Studio 2005 includes a useful designer that lets you drag and drop controls onto a page. This development environment lets you feel as though you're developing normal applications for a single machine, even though the UI is represented as HTML over HTTP.

We'll take a look at writing a custom control in the next chapter.

Chapter 3 Quick Reference

To	Do This
Switch between ASPX Source code mode and Designer mode	The Design and Source tabs appear near the bottom left-hand side of the editor window
Add a server-side control to a page	Show the toolbox if it's not already showing by selecting **View | Toolbox** from the main menu
	Click on the control from the toolbar
	Drag the control onto the page
Change the properties of controls on a page	Make sure the page editor is in Designer mode
	Highlight the control whose property you want to change
	Select the property to edit in the property window
Turn tracing on	In Source code editing mode, edit the Page directive to include the phrase trace=true
	OR
	Select the Document element from the combo box near the top of Properties window
	Edit the Trace property to be true
Change the size of a server-side control	Click on the control once to highlight it
	Click on one of the handles appearing on the border of the control. Hold the mouse button down and drag the mouse until the control is the correct size
Add a handler for a control's default event	Double-click on the control for which you want to handle the event
Add a handler for a control event (other than the default event)	Press the events button (the lightning bolt) in the properties dialog box
	Choose the event you want to add
	Double-click in the right-hand pane immediately next to the property in the properties dialog to have Visual Studio invent a handler name for you
	OR
	Type a name for the handler
	Visual Studio will add a handler for you
Change the layout characteristics of a page	Select Layout from the main menu
	Choose from Absolute, Static, Relative, or more detailed options from the Auto Position Options dialog box

Chapter 4
Custom Rendered Controls

After completing this chapter, you will be able to

- Add a new project to the existing project within a Visual Studio solution file
- Create a server-side control that renders custom HTML
- Add a server-side control to the Visual Studio toolbox
- Place a server-side control on a Web form
- Manage events within the control
- Use ASP.NET to detect differences in client browsers and apply that information

In Chapter 3, we saw the fundamental architecture behind the ASP.NET rendering model. *System.Web.UI.Page* manages a list of server-side controls, and it's the job of each server-side control to render a particular portion of the page. ASP.NET broadly classifies server-side controls into two categories:

- Rendering controls (controls that completely manage the rendering process)
- Composite controls (multiple server-side controls bundled into a single unit)

This chapter focuses on the first type: custom rendered controls. We'll see how the control works once it's part of a Web page. Along the way we'll cover topics such as how controls manage events and how they detect the differences in client browsers.

Let's start by looking at the heart of the ASP.NET server-side control architecture—the *System.Web.UI.Control* class.

The Control Class

ASP.NET server-side controls derive from a class named *System.Web.UI.Control*. In fact, the *Control* class is the core of almost every *User Interface* element within ASP.NET. Even *System.Web.UI.Page* is derived from the *Control* class. Listing 4-1 shows a small sampling of the *System.Web.UI.Page* class.

Listing 4-1

```
public class Control : IComponent, IParserAccessor, ...
{
  public virtual void ApplyStyleSheetSkin();
  protected virtual void CreateChildControls();
  protected virtual void Render(HtmlTextWriter);
  public virtual void RenderControl(HtmlTextWriter);
  protected internal virtual void RenderChildren(HtmlTextWriter);

  public virtual bool Visible {get; set;}
  public virtual bool EnableViewState {get; set;}
  public virtual string SkinID {get; set;}
  public virtual string UniqueID {get;}
  public virtual ControlCollection Controls {get;}

  public virtual Page Page {get; set;}
  public virtual Control Parent {get;}
  protected virtual HttpContext Context {get;}

  public event EventHandler Init;
  public event EventHandler Load;
  public event EventHandler PreRender;
  public event EventHandler Unload;

  internal virtual void OnInit();
  internal virtual void OnLoad();
  internal virtual void OnPreRender();
  internal virtual void OnUnload();

  //...
}
```

The code in Listing 4-1 shows a small cross section of the functionality available within *System.Web.UI.Control*. However, it's enough to get an understanding of the class's importance within ASP.NET Web forms. Remember from the last chapter that ASP.NET Web forms manage a list of controls as part of their internal structure. As you add controls to a Web page, they're placed within the list. When it comes time for a page to render its content back to the client, *System.Web.UI.Page* walks the list of controls and asks each one of them to render. You can see the *Render* method in Listing 4-1. *Render* takes a single argument of type *HtmlTextWriter*. We'll examine that class later in this chapter. Right now think of it as the conduit through which you send the page's response back to the client.

Other elements of the *Control* class include items such as

- Properties for managing the control's view state

- Properties for managing skins (to accommodate a consistent look and feel across multiple pages within a site)

- Properties for getting the parent control (in the case of composite controls) and the parent page

- Event handlers for the *Init, Load, PreRender*, and *Unload* events

- Methods for raising the *Init, Load, PreRender*, and *Unload* events

- Methods for managing child controls

We'll visit the most important topics in examining both rendered controls and composite controls. The easiest way to start is to jump into building a custom control.

Visual Studio and Custom Controls

In this section, we'll build a simple control (the default control Visual Studio generates for you) and see how it fits on a Web form. Visual Studio will create a simple control that contains a single *Text* property, and it will render that *Text* property to the end browser. It's a good way to discover how server-side controls work.

Create a Custom Control

1.   Begin by opening the ControlORama project from Chapter 3.

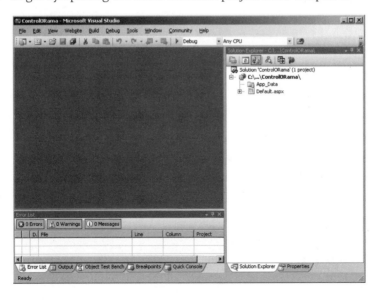

2. Add a new project to ControlORama. Select **File | Add | New Project**. Name the new project CustomControlLib. Choose the project type to be a Windows project, and select **Web Control Library** as the template, like so:

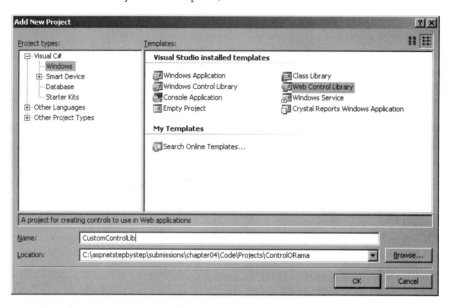

Visual Studio gives you a simple Web control to start with. Listing 4-2 shows the default code generated by Visual Studio for a Web Control Library.

Listing 4-2

```
using System;
using System.Collections.Generic;
using System.ComponentModel;
using System.Text;
using System.Web.UI;
using System.Web.UI.WebControls;

namespace CustomcontrolLib
{
    [DefaultProperty("Text")]
    [ToolboxData("<{0}:WebCustomControl1
        runat=server></{0}:WebCustomControl1>")]
    public class WebCustomControl1 : WebControl
    {
        private string text;

        [Bindable(true)]
        [Category("Appearance")]
        [DefaultValue("")]
        public string text
        {
            get
            {
                return text;
            }
```

```
        set
        {
            text = value;
        }
    }

    protected override void Render(HtmlTextWriter output)
    {
        output.Write(Text);
    }
}
}
```

The code generated by Visual Studio includes a simple class derived from *System.Web.UI.WebControl*. *WebControl* derives from the standard *Control* class, adding some standard properties along the way. Notice the code has a single property named *Text* and overrides *Control's Render* method. This is a real, functioning control (although all it really does is act very much like a label).

3. Build the project by selecting **Build | Build Solution** from the main menu.

4. Add the new control to the toolbox. Switch to the ControlORama project within the Solution Explorer. Highlight the *Default.ASPX* page and switch to the Design view by selecting the Design tab along the bottom of the code window. Reveal the toolbox by hovering the cursor over the Toolbox tab on the left-hand side of Visual Studio. Then right-click anywhere in the toolbox to open the shortcut menu.

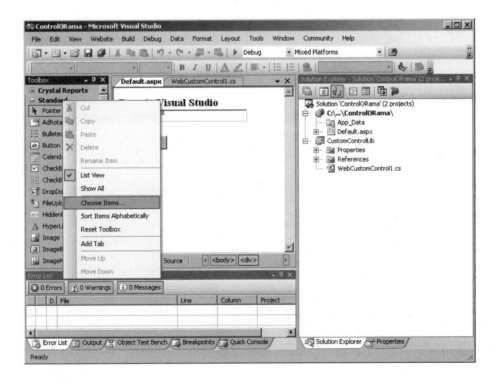

5. Select **Choose Items…** from the local menu. Visual Studio will begin searching your computer for various components that it can add to the toolbox (including both .net components and .com components). Then it will show the Choose Toolbox Items dialog box.

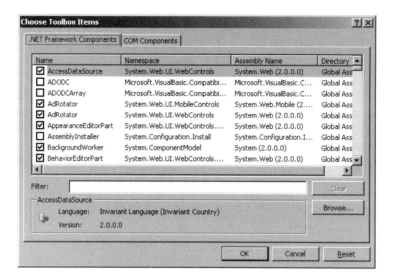

6. Now find the control that Visual Studio just built. Click the Browse button in the Choose Toolbox Items dialog box. Navigate to the ControlORama project directory and then go to the CustomcontrolLib directory. Then open the Bin\Debug directory. (Visual Studio builds debug versions by default.) Select the *CustomControlLib.DLL* assembly and click the **Open** button.

    WebCustomControl1 will appear in the Choose Toolbox Items dialog box. The check box will show it as selected.

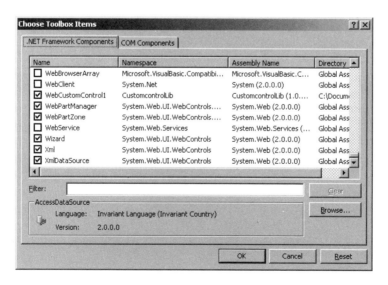

As soon as you click the **OK** button in the Choose Toolbox Items dialog box, the new *WebCustomControl1* will appear in the toolbox. To make it easier to find the control, right-click on the toolbox and select **Sort Items Alphabetically**.

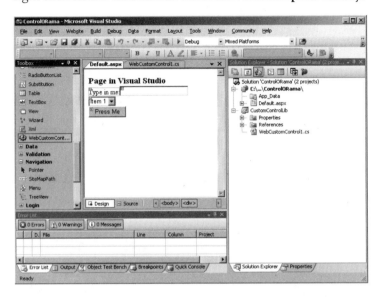

7. Place the control on a page. To see how the control works, you need to give it a home. Add a new page to the Web site. Select the ControlORama project from the Solution Explorer. Select **Web site | Add New Item**, and add a Web form. Name the Web form UseCustomControls.aspx.

   To place the control on the page, switch to Design mode. Pick up the *WebCustomControl1* from the toolbox and drop it onto the Web form.

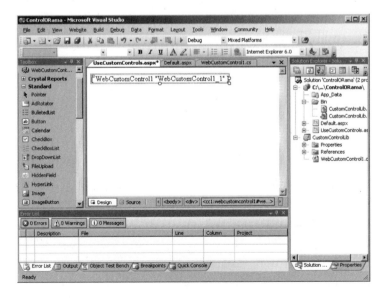

The text showing within the control is the default text shown by a rendered control—basically the control's type. Change the *Text* property in the control and watch it show up in the designer.

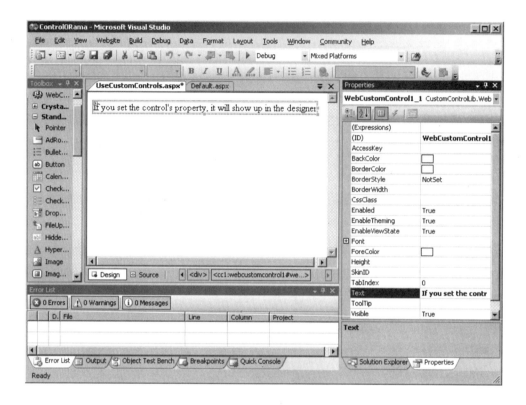

Take a look at the source code for the control again—specifically looking at the *Render* method. Notice the method simply uses the output parameter (an *HtmlTextWriter*) to send the Text property to the browser. That's why the *Text* property is showing after you change it in the designer.

Listing 4-3

```
<%@ Register Assembly="CustomcontrolLib"
Namespace="CustomcontrolLib"
TagPrefix="cc1" %>
```

Listing 4-3 shows the code Visual Studio added to the ASPX file to accommodate the control. You can see it by selecting the **Source** tab from the bottom of the code window in Visual Studio. The *Register* directive tells the ASP.NET runtime where to find the custom control (which assembly) and maps it to a tag prefix. Listing 4-4 shows how the control is declared on the page with the control's *Text* property set to the string *"The control's Text property..."*.

Listing 4-4

```
<form id="form1" runat="server">
<div>
    <cc1:webcustomcontrol1 id="WebCustomControl1_1"
    runat="server"
    text="The control's Text property...">
    </cc1:webcustomcontrol1>
    <br />
</form>
```

Now take a moment to change a few of the control's properties and see what happens in the designer (for example, changing the font is always very noticeable). The properties you see in the Properties page are all standard, and they show up because the control is derived from *System.Web.UI.WebControl*.

8. Now add a text box and a push button to the Web page. After you drop them on the page, Visual Studio adds the code shown in Listing 4-5.

Listing 4-5

```
<form id="form1" runat="server">
<div>
    <cc1:webcustomcontrol1 id="WebCustomControl1_1"
    runat="server"
    text="The control's Text property...">
    </cc1:webcustomcontrol1>
    <br />
    <br />
    <asp:Label ID="Label1"
    runat="server"
    Text="Type something here;">
    </asp:Label>
    <asp:TextBox ID="TextBox1" runat="server"
    Width="282px">
</asp:TextBox>
    <br />
    <asp:Button ID="Button1"
    runat="server" OnClick="Button1_Click"
    Text="Set Control Text" />
    </div>
</form>
```

Notice the standard ASP.NET controls (the button, the text box, and the label) all begin with the *asp:* prefix while the new custom control uses the prefix *cc1:*. Visual Studio made up the tag *cc1:*, although you could change that by adding a tag prefix attribute to the *Control* class.

9. Add an event handler for the push button by double-clicking on the button in the designer. Have the push button pull the text from the *TextBox* and use it to set the control's *Text* property.

```
protected void Button1_Click(object sender, EventArgs e)
    {
        this.WebCustomControl1_1.Text = this.TextBox1.Text;
    }
```

Now surf to the new page with the control. When you type something into the text box and click the button, the browser sends your request to the server. The browser responds by taking the text from the *TextBox* and using it to set the *Text property* of the *WebCustomControl1*.

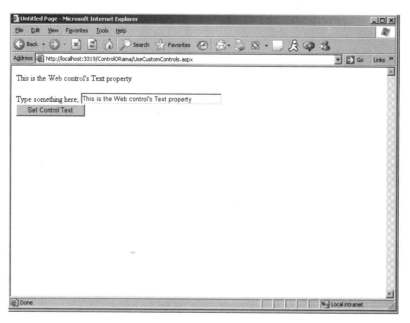

Notice how the new control appears in the control tree with tracing turned on. (You can turn on page tracing by setting the page's *Trace* property to true.)

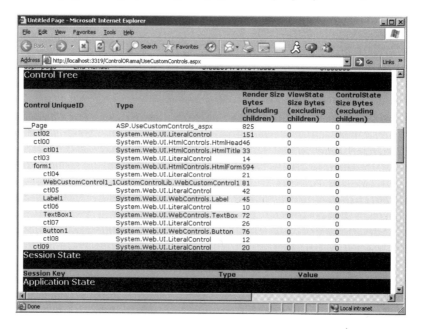

You have now built a simple control. The control framework is pretty flexible, and you can send out anything you want using the *Render* method. Next, we'll develop a more sophisticated control that demonstrates more advanced control rendering.

A Palindrome Checker

The preceding exercise shows the fundamentals of writing a simple server-side control that renders. However, ASP.NET already delivers a perfectly good *Label* control. Why do you need another one? To further illustrate rendered server-side controls, here's a simple control that checks to see if the string typed by the client is a palindrome. We'll observe some more advanced rendering techniques as well as how control events work.

The Palindrome Checker Control

1. Create the *Palindrome checker* control. In the Solution Explorer, highlight the *Custom-ControlLib* node. Right-click on the node and select **Add New Item** from the shortcut menu. Highlight the *Web Custom Control* node. Enter **PalindromeCheckerRendered-Control.cs** in the Name text box and generate the code.

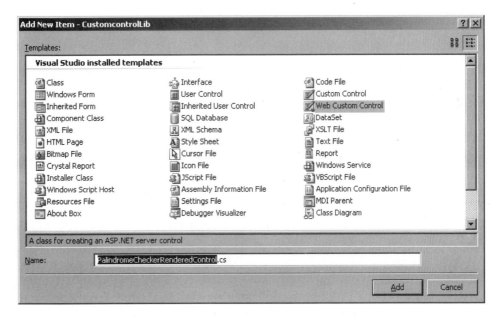

2. Keep the control's *Text* property. This will hold the palindrome text.

3. Add a method to test for a palindrome. A palindrome is a word, sentence, or phrase that reads the same forward as it does backwards. Add a method to the control that checks to see whether the internal text is a palindrome. This is a simple test for a palindrome that converts the text to uppercase, reverses it, and then compares the result

to the original text. You should also strip out nonalphanumeric characters. Here is some code that does the trick.

```
protected string StripNonAlphanumerics(string str)
{
    string strStripped = (String)str.Clone();

    if (str != null)
    {
        char[] rgc = strStripped.ToCharArray();
        int i = 0;
        foreach (char c in rgc)
        {
            if (char.IsLetterOrDigit(c))
            {
                i++;
            }
            else
            {
                strStripped = strStripped.Remove(i, 1);
            }
        }
    }

    return strStripped;
}

protected bool CheckForPalindrome()
{
    if (this.Text != null)
    {
        String strControlText = this.Text;
        String strTextToUpper = null;
        strTextToUpper = Text.ToUpper();

        strControlText =
                    this.StripNonAlphanumerics(strTextToUpper);

        char[] rgcReverse = strControlText.ToCharArray();
        Array.Reverse(rgcReverse);
        String strReverse = new string(rgcReverse);

        if (strControlText == strReverse)
        {
            return true;
        }
        else
        {
            return false;
        }
    }
    else
    {
        return false;
    }
}
```

4. Change the rendering method to print palindromes in blue and nonpalindromes in red. The *Render* method takes a single parameter of type *HtmlTextWriter*. In addition to allowing you to stream text to the browser, *HtmlTextWriter* is full of other very useful features we'll see shortly. For now, you can treat it very much like *Response.Write*. Whatever you send through the *Write* method will end up at the client's browser.

```
protected override void Render(HtmlTextWriter output)
  {
    if (this.CheckForPalindrome())
    {
      output.Write("This is a palindrome: <br>");
      output.Write("<FONT size=5 color=Blue>");
      output.Write("<B>");
      output.Write(Text);
      output.Write("</B>");
      output.Write("</FONT>");
    } else {
      output.Write("This is NOT a palindrome <br>");
      output.Write("<FONT size=5 color=red>");
      output.Write("<B>");
      output.Write(Text);
      output.Write("</B>");
      output.Write("</FONT>");
    }
  }
```

5. Build the project by selecting **Build | Build Solution** from the main menu.

6. Add the *PalindromeCheckerRenderedControl* to the toolbox. Right-click on the toolbox and select **Choose Item**. Use the **Browse** button to find the *CustomcontrolLib.DLL* assembly and select it. Visual Studio will load the new control in the toolbox.

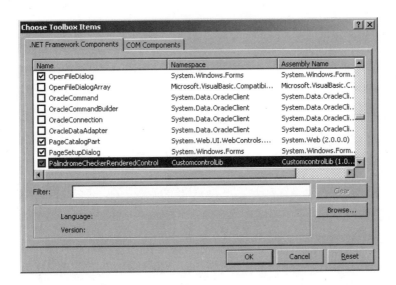

7. Add a page to use the palindrome checker control. Add a new Web form to the Con-
    trolORama project and name it UsePalindromeCheckerControls.aspx. Pick up the
    PalindromCheckerRenderedControl and drop it on the page. Add a *TextBox* and a push but-
    ton so you can add a palindrome to the control and check it.

```
public partial class UsePalindromeCheckerControls : System.Web.UI.Page
{
    protected void Page_Load(object sender, EventArgs e)
    {

    }
    protected void Button1_Click(object sender, EventArgs e)
    {
        this.PalindromeCheckerRenderedControl1.Text = this.TextBox1.Text;
    }
}
```

8. Run the page and test for a palindrome. Palindromes should appear in blue and nonpal-
    indromes in red.

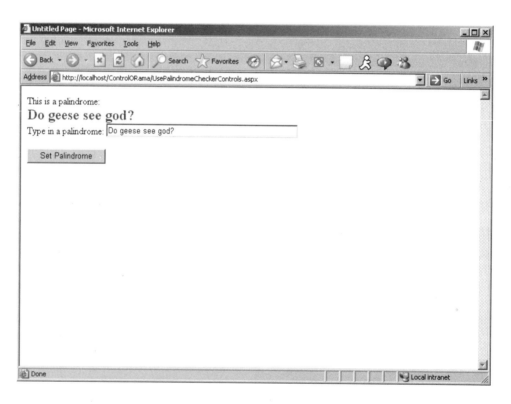

Controls and Events

The *PalindromeCheckerRenderedControl* shows how to render differently depending upon the
state of the *Text* property. While that's a very useful thing in itself, it's often helpful to also alert

the host page to the fact that a palindrome was found. You can do this by exposing an event from the control.

Most of ASP.NET's standard server-side controls already support events. You've already seen how the *Button* control sends an event to the host page when it is clicked. You can actually do this type of thing with any control. Let's add a *PalindromeFound* event to the *PalindromeCheckerRenderedControl*.

Adding a PalindromeFound Event

1. Open the PalindromeCheckerRenderedControl.cs file. To add a *PalindromeFound* event, type in the following line.

```
public class PalindromeCheckerRenderedControl : WebControl
{
        public event EventHandler PalindromeFound; // public event
//...
}
```

2. Once hosts have subscribed to the event, they'll want to know when it happens. To do this, fire an event upon detecting a palindrome. The best place to do this is within the *Text* property's setter.

```
public string Text
{
    get
    {
        return text;
    }

    set
    {
        text = value;
        if(this.CheckForPalindrome()) {
            if (PalindromeFound != null)
            {
                PalindromeFound(this, EventArgs.Empty);
            }
        }
    }
}
```

Rebuild the project.

3. Now wire the event in the host page. Remove the current instance of the *Palindrome-CheckerRenderedControl* from the page and drop a new instance on the page. This will refresh the *CustomControlLib.DLL* assembly so the changes (the new event) will appear in Visual Studio.

4. Select the *PalindromeCheckerRenderedControl* on the page and click the **Events** button (the little lightning bolt) in the property page in Visual Studio.

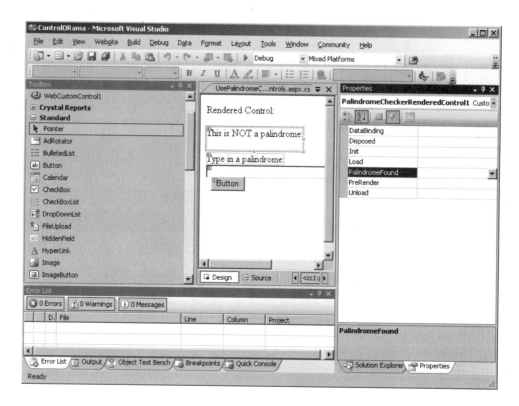

Double-click on the text box next to the *PalindromeFound* event. Visual Studio will create an event handler for you.

5. Respond to the *PalindromeFound* event.

```
public partial class UsePalindromeCheckerControls : System.Web.UI.Page
{
    protected void Page_Load(object sender, EventArgs e)
    {

    }
    protected void Button1_Click(object sender, EventArgs e)
    {
        this.PalindromeCheckerRenderedControl1.Text =
                this.TextBox1.Text;
    }
    protected void PalindromeCheckerRenderedControl1_PalindromeFound(
            object sender, EventArgs e)
    {
        Response.Write("The page detected a PalindromeFound event");
    }
}
```

You should see something like the following when you type a palindrome:

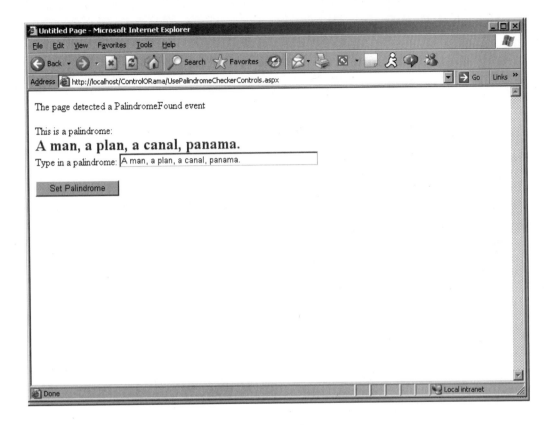

Now that the control renders palindromes correctly and has an event, let's take a closer look at the parameter passed in during the call to *Render: HtmlTextWriter*.

HtmlTextWriter and Controls

Go back and review the control's *Render* method for a minute. Notice the *Render* method places literal font tags to change the color of the palindrome text. While this is certainly effective, this technique has a couple of downsides. For example, HTML is defined by multiple standards. That is, browsers running both HTML version 3.2 and 4.0 occur in nature. Certain HTML elements have changed between version 3.2 and 4.0. If you render all your HTML directly, expecting requests from a certain kind of browser, your users may be taken by surprise if they browse to your page with a new browser that interprets HTML differently.

> **Note**   The .NET framework includes multiple versions of the *HtmlTextWriter* class:
> *Html32TextWriter*, *HtmlTextWriter*, *XhtmlTextWriter*, and *ChtmlTextWriter*. When a request
> comes from a browser, it always includes some header information indicating what kind of
> browser made the request. Most browsers these days are capable of interpreting the current
> version of HTML. In this case, ASP.NET passes in a normal *HtmlTextWriter* into the *Render*
> method. However, if you happen to get a request from a lesser browser that understands only
> HTML 3.2, ASP.NET passes in an *Html32TextWriter*. The classes are similar as far as their use and
> may be interchanged. *Html32TextWriter* emits certain tags (such as table tags) in HTML 3.2 for-
> mat, while *HtmlTextWriter* emits the same tags in HTML4.0 format. Information within
> Machine.Config and the browser capabilities configuration help ASP.NET figure out what kind
> of *HtmlTextWriter* to use. The browser capability information deduced by the ASP.NET runtime
> may be used for more than simply selecting the correct *HtmlTextWriter*. The *Request* property
> (available as part of the *HttpContext* and the *Page*) includes a reference to the   rowser object.
> This object includes a number of flags indicating various pieces of information such as the type
> of browser making the request, whether the browser supports scripting, and the name of the
> platform the browser is running on. This information comes down as part of the headers
> included with each request. The ASP.NET runtime runs the headers against some well-known
> regular expressions within the configuration files to figure out the capabilities. For example,
> here's a short listing illustrating how to figure out if the browser making the request supports
> Frames:

```
public class TestForFramesControl : Control
{
    protected override void Render(HtmlTextWriter output)
    {
        if (Page.Request.Browser.Frames)
        {
          output.Write(
            "This browser supports Frames");
        }
        else
        {
            output.Write("No Frames here");
        }
    }
}
```

To get a feel for using the more advanced capabilities of *HtmlTextWriter*, replace the hard-
coded font tags in the *Render* method of the *PalindromeCheckerRenderedControl* with code that
uses the *HtmlTextWriter* facilities.

Use the *HtmlTextWriter*

1. Open the PalindromeCheckerRenderedControl.cs file.

2. Update the *Render* method to use the *HtmlTextWriter* methods. Use *HtmlTextWriter.Ren-
    derBeginTag* to start a font tag and a bold tag. Use *HtmlTextWriter.AddStyleAttribute* to
    change the color of the font to blue.

```
protected override void Render(HtmlTextWriter output)
{
    if (this.CheckForPalindrome())
    {
        output.Write("This is a palindrome: <br>");
        output.RenderBeginTag(HtmlTextWriterTag.Font);
        output.AddStyleAttribute(HtmlTextWriterStyle.Color, "blue");
        output.RenderBeginTag(HtmlTextWriterTag.B);
        output.Write(Text);
        output.RenderEndTag(); // bold
        output.RenderEndTag(); // font
    } else {
        output.Write("This is a palindrome: <br>");
        output.RenderBeginTag(HtmlTextWriterTag.Font);
        output.AddStyleAttribute(HtmlTextWriterStyle.Color, "blue");
        output.RenderBeginTag(HtmlTextWriterTag.B);
        output.Write(Text);
        output.RenderEndTag(); // bold1
        output.RenderEndTag(); // font
    }
}
```

The *HtmlTextWriter* class and the enumerations include support to hide all the oddities of switching between HTML 3.2 and 4.0. Listing 4-6 shows how the table is rendered using an HTML 4.0–compliant response. Listing 4-7 shows how the table is rendered using an HTML 3.2–compliant response.

Listing 4-6

```
Rendered Control:
<br />
<br />
This is a palindrome: <br>
<b><font>Do geese see god?</font></b><br>
<table width="50%" border="1" style="color:blue;">
    <tr>
    <td align="left" style="font-size:medium;color:blue;">
A man, a plan, a canal, panama.</td>
    </tr>
<tr>
    <td align="left" style="font-size:medium;color:blue;">
Do geese see god?</td>
    </tr>
```

Listing 4-7

```
Rendered Control:<br />
<br />
This is a palindrome: <br>
<b><font>Do geese see god?</font></b><br>
<table width="50%" border="1"">
<tr>
<td align="left">
<font color="blue" size="4">A man, a plan, a canal, panama.</font>
</td>
</tr>
```

```
<tr>
<td align="left"><font color="blue" size="4">Do geese see god?</font>
</td>
</tr>
```

Controls and View State

Before leaving rendered controls, let's take a look at the issue of control state. If you go back to some of the classic ASP examples from earlier chapters, you may notice something disconcerting about the way some of the controls, such as selection boxes, work. After you select something in the combo box and make a round-trip to the server, by the time the response gets back the controls (for example, selection controls) have lost their state. Recall that the Web is all about making snapshots of the server's state and displaying them using a browser. We're essentially trying to perform stateful UI development over a disconnected protocol.

ASP.NET server-side controls include a facility for holding on to a page's visual state—it's a property in the Page named *ViewState*, and you can easily access it any time you need. *ViewState* is a dictionary (a name-value collection) that stores any serializable object.

Most ASP.NET server-side controls manage their visual state by storing and retrieving items in the *ViewState*. For example, a selection control might maintain the index of the selected item between posts so that the control knows which item gets the *<selected>* tag.

The entire state of a page is encoded in a hidden field between posts. For example, if you browse to an ASPX page and view the source code coming from the server, you'll see the ViewState come through as a BASE 64–encoded byte stream.

To get a feel for how *ViewState* works, add some code to keep track of the palindromes that have been viewed through the control.

Using View State

1. Open the PalindromeCheckerRenderedControl.cs file.

2. Add an *ArrayList* to the control to hold the viewed palindromes. Update the *Text* property's setter to store text in the view state if the text is a palindrome.

```
public class PalindromeCheckerRenderedControl : WebControl
{
    public event EventHandler PalindromeFound; // public event

        ArrayList alPalindromes = new ArrayList();

    private string text;

    [Bindable(true)]
    [Category("Appearance")]
    [DefaultValue("")]
    public string Text
```

```
    {
      get
      {
        return text;
      }
      set
      {
        text = value;
        this.alPalindromes =
                  (ArrayList)this.ViewState["palindromes"];
        if (this.alPalindromes == null)
        {
          this.alPalindromes = new ArrayList();
        }

        if(this.CheckForPalindrome()) {
          if (PalindromeFound != null)
          {
            PalindromeFound(this, EventArgs.Empty);
          }
          alPalindromes.Add(text);
        }
        this.ViewState.Add("palindromes", alPalindromes);
      }
    }
}
```

3. Add a method to render the palindrome collection as a table and update the *Render* method to render the viewed palindromes.

```
protected void RenderPalindromesInTable(HtmlTextWriter output)
{
    output.AddAttribute(HtmlTextWriterAttribute.Width, "50%");
    output.AddAttribute(HtmlTextWriterAttribute.Border, "1");
    output.RenderBeginTag(HtmlTextWriterTag.Table); //<table>

    foreach (string s in this.alPalindromes)
    {
        output.RenderBeginTag(HtmlTextWriterTag.Tr); // <tr>
        output.AddAttribute(HtmlTextWriterAttribute.Align, "left");
        output.AddStyleAttribute(HtmlTextWriterStyle.FontSize, "medium");
        output.AddStyleAttribute(HtmlTextWriterStyle.Color, "blue");
        output.RenderBeginTag(HtmlTextWriterTag.Td); // <td>
        output.Write(s);
        output.RenderEndTag(); // </td>
        output.RenderEndTag(); // </tr>
    }

    output.RenderEndTag(); // </table>
}

protected override void Render(HtmlTextWriter output)
{
    if (this.CheckForPalindrome())
    {
        output.Write("This is a palindrome: <br>");
        output.RenderBeginTag(HtmlTextWriterTag.Font);
        output.AddStyleAttribute(HtmlTextWriterStyle.Color, "blue");
```

```
            output.RenderBeginTag(HtmlTextWriterTag.B);
            output.Write(Text);
            output.RenderEndTag(); // bold
            output.RenderEndTag(); // font
        } else {
            output.Write("This is NOT a palindrome: <br>");
            output.RenderBeginTag(HtmlTextWriterTag.Font);
            output.AddStyleAttribute(HtmlTextWriterStyle.Color, "red");
            output.RenderBeginTag(HtmlTextWriterTag.B);
            output.Write(Text);
            output.RenderEndTag(); // bold
            output.RenderEndTag(); // font
        }
        output.Write("<br>");
        RenderPalindromesInTable(output);
    }
```

4. Build and run the application. When you surf to the page holding the palindrome
    checker, you should see the previously found palindromes appearing in the table:

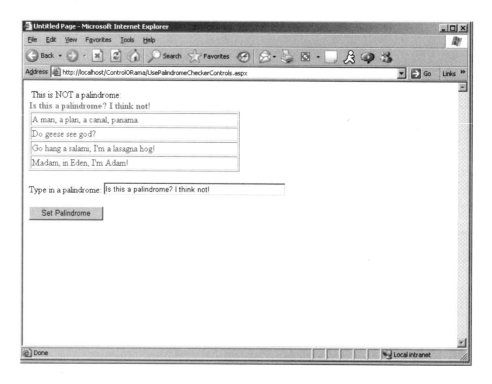

Conclusion

ASP.NET's *Page* infrastructure is set up so that each page is broken down into smaller components (server-side controls) that are responsible for rendering a small amount of HTML into
the page's output stream. After reading this chapter, you probably have a good idea as to how

some of the standard ASP.NET controls work. *Button* controls render an input tag with a type of "submit." *TextBox* controls render an input tag with a type of "text." You can actually see how each of the controls in a page renders by viewing the HTML that comes back to the browser.

Of course, because ASP.NET's *Page* infrastructure is set up this way, it leaves the door open for custom *User* controls. In this chapter we looked at rendered custom controls. Custom controls that render have the ability to squirt anything they want into the output bound for the browser. Custom rendered controls usually manage a set of properties, fire events to their hosts, and render snapshots of themselves to their hosts. In this chapter we built a palindrome checker as an example. Next, we'll see examples of the other kind of custom control—composite-style controls.

Chapter 4 Quick Reference

To	Do This
Create a custom control that takes over the rendering process	Derive a class from *System.Web.UI.Control*
	Override the Render method
	Visual Studio includes a project type, Web Custom Control, that fits the bill
Add a custom control to the toolbox	Show the toolbox if it's not already showing by selecting **View | Toolbox** from the main menu
	Right mouse click anywhere in the toolbox
	Select Choose Items from the local menu
	Choose a control from the list
	OR
	Browse to the assembly containing the control
Change the properties of controls on a page	Make sure the page editor is in Designer mode
	Highlight the control whose property you want to change
	Select the property to edit in the property window
Store view state information that lives beyond the scope of the page	Use the ViewState property of the control
	It's a name/value dictionary that contains serializable types
	Just be sure to use the same index to retrieve the information as you do to store the information
Write browser version-independent rendering code	Use the *HtmlTextWriter* tag-rendering methods for specific tags instead of hard-coding them. The Render method will have the correct HtmlTextWriter based on header information coming down from the browser.

Chapter 5
Composite Controls

After completing this chapter, you will be able to

■ Create a composite custom control

■ Create a composite *User* control

■ Recognize when each kind of control is appropriate

While the last chapter covered the details of controls that did custom rendering, this chapter covers the other kind of control—composite controls. Each type of composite control has advantages and disadvantages, which we'll discuss. First, let's explore the primary differences between rendered controls and composite-style controls.

Composite Controls versus Rendered Controls

Recall that custom rendered controls completely form and tailor the HTML going back to the client via the *System.Web.UI.Control.Render* method. Custom rendered controls take over the entire rendering process. With custom rendered controls, you have extraordinary flexibility and power over the appearance of your Web site.

However, with that power and flexibility also comes the need to keep track of an enormous amount of detail. For example, if were you to add an input button to a custom rendered control, you'd need to insert the correct HTML to describe the button within the response stream heading back to the client. Things get even more difficult when you decide to add more complex controls like selection controls that may need to track collections of items. Even though input buttons and selection controls are easy to describe in HTML, we've seen that ASP.NET already includes server-side control classes that render the correct tags. The standard ASP.NET controls greatly simplify UI programming for Web forms.

Composite controls take advantage of these server-side controls that have already been written. Composite controls are *composed* from other controls. To illustrate the utility of composite controls, imagine you're working on a number of projects whose login screens require a similar look and feel. On one hand, you've already seen that it's fairly easy to build Web forms in Visual Studio. However, if you run into a situation requiring the same group of controls to appear together in several instances, it's pretty tedious to recreate those pages repeatedly. ASP.NET solves this problem with composite controls.

If you need common login functionality to span several Web sites, you might group user name/ password labels and text boxes together in a single control. Then when you want to use the login page on a site, you simply drop the controls *en masse* on the new form. The controls (and the execution logic) instantly combine so you don't need to keep creating the page over and over.

> **Note**   ASP.NET 2.0 now includes a set of login composite controls, so you don't need to write new ones from scratch. However, they are mentioned here because they represent an excellent illustration for the power of composite controls.

Let's begin by looking at custom composite controls.

Custom Composite Controls

In Chapter 4, we saw how binary custom controls render custom HTML to the browser. The factor distinguishing this kind of control most is that these controls override the *Render* method. Remember, the *System.Web.UI.Page* class manages a list of server-side controls. When ASP.NET asks the whole page to render, it goes to each control on the page and asks it to render. In the case of a rendering control, the control simply pushes some text into the stream bound for the browser. Likewise, when the page rendering mechanism hits a composite style control, the composite control walks its list of child controls, asking each one to render—just as the *Page* walks its own list of controls.

Composite controls may contain as many children as memory will accommodate, and the controls may be nested as deeply as necessary. Of course, there's a practical limit to the number and depth of the child controls. Adding too many controls or nesting them too deeply will add complexity to a page, and it may become unsightly.

In Chapter 4, we created a control that checked for palindromes. When the control's *Text* property was set to a palindrome, the control rendered the palindrome in blue text, added it to an *ArrayList*, and then rendered the contents of the palindrome collection as a table. Let's build the same control again—however, this time it will be a composite control.

The Palindrome Checker as a Composite Custom Control

1.   Open the ControlORama project. Highlight the CustomControlLib project in the Solution Explorer. Right-click on the project node and select **Add New Item**. Create a new

class and name the source file PalindromeCheckerCompositeControl.cs. Use the Web
Custom Control template.

2. After Visual Studio creates the code, do the following:

   ❏ Edit the code to change the derivation from *WebControl* to *CompositeControl*. Deriving from the *CompositeControl* also adds the *INamingContainer* interface to the derivation list. (*INamingContainer* is useful to help ASP.NET manage unique IDs for the control's children.)

   ❏ Add an event handler that the host page may use to listen for palindrome detections.

   ❏ Remove the *Render* method.

   ❏ Add four member variables, a *TextBox*, a *Button*, a *Label*, and a *LiteralControl*.

The code should look something like this when you're finished:

```
public class PalindromeCheckerCompositeControl :

        CompositeControl
{
    protected TextBox textboxPalindrome;
    protected Button buttonCheckForPalindrome;
    protected Label labelForTextBox;
    protected Table tablePalindromes;
     protected LiteralControl literalcontrolPalindromeStatus;
    public event EventHandler PalindromeFound;
…
// Render method removed.
}
```

Leave the *Text* property intact. We'll still need it in this control.

The control is very much like the one in Chapter 4. However, this version will include the palindrome *TextBox*, the *Button* to invoke palindrome checking, and will contain a literal control to display whether or not the current property is a palindrome.

3. Borrow the *StripNonAlphanumerics* and *CheckForPalindrome* methods from the *PalindromeCheckerRenderedControl*:

```
protected string StripNonAlphanumerics(string str)
{
    string strStripped = (String)str.Clone();

    if (str != null)
    {
    char[] rgc = strStripped.ToCharArray();

        int i = 0;

        foreach (char c in rgc)
        {
            if (char.IsLetterOrDigit(c))
            {
                i++;
            }
            else
            {
                strStripped = strStripped.Remove(i, 1);
```

```
                }
            }
        }

    return strStripped;
}

protected bool CheckForPalindrome()
{
    if (this.Text != null)
    {
        String strControlText = this.Text;
        String strTextToUpper = null;

        strTextToUpper = Text.ToUpper();

        strControlText = this.StripNonAlphanumerics(strTextToUpper);

        char[] rgcReverse = strControlText.ToCharArray();
        Array.Reverse(rgcReverse);
        String strReverse = new string(rgcReverse);
        if (strControlText == strReverse)
        {
            return true;
        }
        else
        {
            return false;
        }
    }
    else
    {
        return false;
    }
}
```

4. Add an event handler to be applied to the *Button* (which we'll install on the page in just a minute). Because this is a binary control without designer support, you'll need to add the event handler using the text wizard (that is, you'll need to type it by hand).

```
public void OnCheckPalindrome(Object o, System.EventArgs ea)
{
    this.Text = this.textboxPalindrome.Text;
    this.CheckForPalindrome();
}
```

5. This next part is what really distinguishes composite controls from rendered controls. Add an override for the *CreateChildControls* method. In the method, you'll need to create each *UI* element by hand, set the properties you want appearing in the control, and add the individual control to the composite control's list of controls.

```
protected override void CreateChildControls()
{
    labelForTextBox = new Label();
    labelForTextBox.Text = "Enter a palindrome: ";
    this.Controls.Add(labelForTextBox);

    textboxPalindrome = new TextBox();
    this.Controls.Add(textboxPalindrome);
```

```
    Controls.Add(new LiteralControl("<br/>"));

    buttonCheckForPalindrome = new Button();
    buttonCheckForPalindrome.Text = "Check for Palindrome";
    buttonCheckForPalindrome.Click += new EventHandler(OnCheckPalindrome);
    this.Controls.Add(buttonCheckForPalindrome);

    Controls.Add(new LiteralControl("<br/>""));

    literalcontrolPalindromeStatus = new LiteralControl();
    Controls.Add(literalcontrolPalindromeStatus);

    Controls.Add(new LiteralControl("<br/>"));

    this.tablePalindromes = new Table();
    this.Controls.Add(tablePalindromes);
}
```

While the code listed above is pretty straightforward, a couple of lines deserve special note. First is the use of the *LiteralControl* to render the line breaks. Remember—every element on the page (or in this case the control) will be rendered using a server-side control. If you want any literal text rendered as part of your control, you need to package it in a server-side control. The job of a *LiteralControl* is to take the contents (the *Text* property) and simply render it to the outgoing stream.

The second thing to notice is how the event handler is hooked to the *Button* using a delegate. This is usually handled in Visual Studio by clicking on a *UI* element in the designer. However, because there's no designer support here, the event hookup needs to be handled manually.

6. Show the palindrome status whenever the *Text* property is set. Modify the *Text* property's setter so that it checks for a palindrome and renders the result in the *LiteralControl*. It should also raise the *PalindromeFound* event.

```
public string Text
{
    get
    {
        return text;
    }
    set
    {
        text = value;

        if (this.CheckForPalindrome())
        {
            if (PalindromeFound != null)
            {
                PalindromeFound(this, EventArgs.Empty);
            }

            literalcontrolPalindromeStatus.Text =
            "This is a palindrome <br><FONT size=5 color=blue><B>" +
            text +
            "</B> </FONT>";
        } else
```

```
    {
        literalcontrolPalindromeStatus.Text =
        "This is NOT a palindrome <br><FONT size=5 color=red><B>" +
        text +
        "</B> </FONT>";
    }
    }
}
```

7. Show the palindromes in a table, just as the rendered version of this control did. First, add an *ArrayList* and a *Table* control to the *PalindromeCheckerCompositeControl* class.

```
public class PalindromeCheckerCompositeControl :
Control, INamingContainer
{
    protected Table tablePalindromes;

    protected ArrayList alPalindromes;
//...
}
```

8. Add a method to build the palindrome table based on the contents of the *ArrayList*. Check to see if the array list is stored in the *ViewState*. If it's not, then create a new one. Iterate through the palindrome collection and add a *TableRow* and a *TableCell* to the table for each palindrome found.

```
protected void BuildPalindromesTable()
{
    this.alPalindromes = (ArrayList)this.ViewState["palindromes"];
    if (this.alPalindromes != null)
    {
        foreach (string s in this.alPalindromes)
        {
            TableCell tableCell = new TableCell();
            tableCell.BorderStyle = BorderStyle.Double;
            tableCell.BorderWidth = 3;
            tableCell.Text = s;
            TableRow tableRow = new TableRow();
            tableRow.Cells.Add(tableCell);
            this.tablePalindromes.Rows.Add(tableRow);
        }
    }
}
```

9. Update the *Text* property's setter to manage the table. Add palindromes to the *ArrayList* as they're found, and build the palindrome table each time the text is changed.

```
public string Text
{
    get
    {
        return text;
    }
    set
    {
        text = value;
```

```
        this.alPalindromes = (ArrayList)this.ViewState["palindromes"];
        if (this.alPalindromes == null)
        {
            this.alPalindromes = new ArrayList();
        }

    if (this.CheckForPalindrome())
    {
        if (PalindromeFound != null)
        {
            PalindromeFound(this, EventArgs.Empty);
        }
        alPalindromes.Add(text);

        literalcontrolPalindromeStatus.Text =
            "This is a palindrome <br><FONT size=5 color=blue><B>"
                +
            text +
            "</B> </FONT>""";
    } else
    {
        literalcontrolPalindromeStatus.Text =
        "This is NOT a palindrome <br><FONT size=5 color=red><B>" +
        text +
        "</B> </FONT>";
    }
    this.ViewState.Add("palindromes", alPalindromes);
    this.BuildPalindromesTable();
    }
}
```

10. Build the project and add the *User* control to the ControlORama UsePalindromeCheckerControls.aspx page. You can pick up the *User* control directly from the toolbox and drop it on to the page. When you run the page, it will check for palindromes and keep a record of the palindromes that have been found, like so (tracing is turned on in this example so we can see the control tree a bit later on):

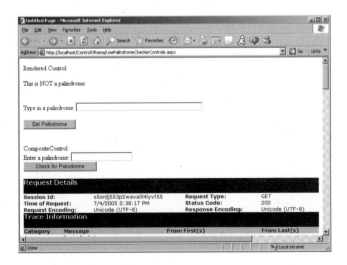

With tracing turned on, you can look further down and see the control tree. Notice how the *PalindromeCheckerCompositeControl* acts as a main node on the tree, and that the composite control's child controls are shown under the *PalindromeCheckerCompositeControl* node.

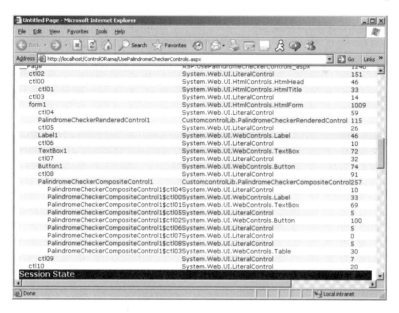

When you type palindromes and click the button, the control will detect them. The control displays the current *Text* property in red if it's *not* a palindrome, and in blue if it *is* a palindrome. You can also see the table rendering, showing the currently found palindromes.

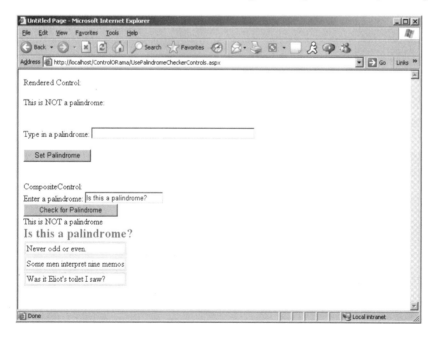

The palindrome checker is a good example of a binary composite control. The composite control lives entirely within the *CustomcontrolLib* assembly and does not have any designer support. Here's an alternative to coding a composite control entirely by hand—the second way to create composite controls is via a *User* control.

User Controls

User controls are very like binary composite controls. However, instead of deriving from *System.Web.UI.CompositeControl*, they derive from *System.Web.UI.UserControl*. Perhaps a better description is that they're very much like miniature Web forms. The have a UI component (an .ascx file) that works with the Visual Studio designer, and they employ a matching class to manage the execution. However, unlike a Web form, they may be dragged onto the toolbox and then dropped into a Web form.

To get a good idea as to how Web *User* controls work, here's how to build the palindrome checker as a *User* control.

The Palindrome Checker as a *User* Control

1. Open the ControlORama project (if it's not already open). Highlight the ControlORama Web site within the Solution Explorer. Right-click on the site and select **Add New Item**. Select the Web *User Control* template and name the control *PalindromeCheckerUserControl.ascx*.

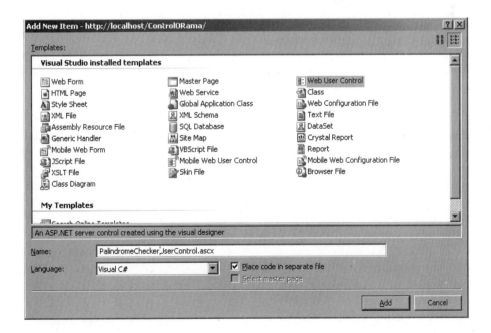

2. Notice that Visual Studio immediately drops you into the designer. *User* controls are designer friendly. Drag a *Label*, a *TextBox*, a *Button*, and another *Label* from the toolbox. Drop them into the *User* control like so:

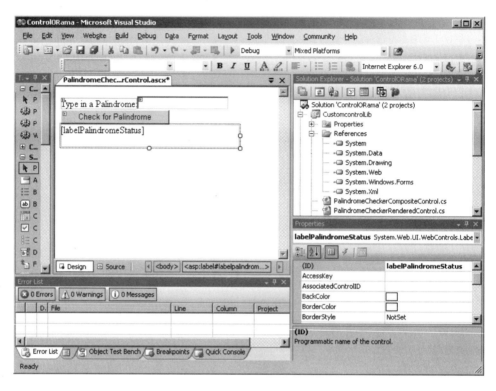

Name the second label *labelPalindromeStatus* to distinguish it from the label applying to the text box.

3. Borrow the *StripNonAlphanumerics* and *CheckForPalindrome* from the *PalindromeCheckerCompositeControl* class.

```
protected string StripNonAlphanumerics(string str)
{
    string strStripped = (String)str.Clone();
    if (str != null)
    {
        char[] rgc = strStripped.ToCharArray();
        int i = 0;
        foreach (char c in rgc)
        {
            if (char.IsLetterOrDigit(c))
            {
                i++;
            }
            else
            {
                strStripped = strStripped.Remove(i, 1);
```

```
                }
            }
        }
    return strStripped;
}
protected bool CheckForPalindrome()
{
    if (this.Text != null)
    {
        String strControlText = this.Text;
        String strTextToUpper = null;

        strTextToUpper = Text.ToUpper();

        strControlText = this.StripNonAlphanumerics(strTextToUpper);

        char[] rgcReverse = strControlText.ToCharArray();
        Array.Reverse(rgcReverse);
        String strReverse = new string(rgcReverse);
        if (strControlText == strReverse)
        {
            return true;
        }
        else
        {
            return false;
        }
    }
    else
    {
        return false;
    }
}
```

4. Add the *PalindromeFound* event to the control class.

```
public event EventHandler PalindromeFound; // public event
```

5. Unlike binary composite controls, *User* controls aren't generated with any default properties. Open the code file and add a text member variable and a *Text* property, very much like the other composite control implemented.

```
private String text;

public string Text
{
    get
    {
        return text;
    }
    set
    {
        text = value;
```

```
        if (this.CheckForPalindrome())
        {
          if (PalindromeFound != null)
          {
            PalindromeFound(this, EventArgs.Empty);
          }

          this.labelPalindromeStatus.Text =
                "This is a palindrome <br><FONT size=5 color=blue><B>" +
          text +
          "</B> </FONT>";
        }
        else
        {
          labelPalindromeStatus.Text =
                "This is NOT a palindrome <br><FONT size=5 color=red><B>" +
          text +
          "</B> </FONT>";
        }
      }
    }
```

6. Now add support for keeping track of palindromes. Add an ArrayList to the control class:

```
        ArrayList alPalindromes;
```

7. Add a *Table* to the control. Switch to the PalindromeCheckerUserControl Design view and drag a *Table* onto the form.

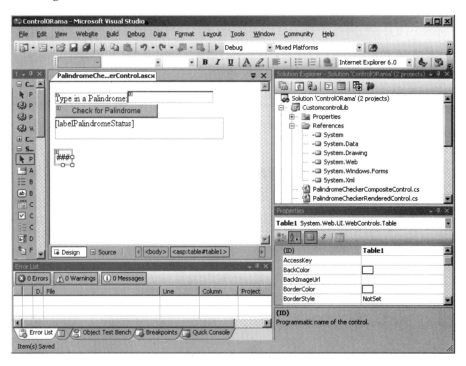

8. Add a method to build the table of palindromes. It's very much like the one in the *Pal-indromeCheckerCompositeControl*, except the name of the table has changed. *Table1* is the name given the table by Visual Studio.

```
protected void BuildPalindromesTable()
{
    this.alPalindromes = (ArrayList)this.ViewState["palindromes"];
    if (this.alPalindromes != null)
    {
        foreach (string s in this.alPalindromes)
        {
            TableCell tableCell = new TableCell();
            tableCell.BorderStyle = BorderStyle.Double;
            tableCell.BorderWidth = 3;
            tableCell.Text = s;
            TableRow tableRow = new TableRow();
            tableRow.Cells.Add(tableCell);
            this.Table1.Rows.Add(tableRow);
        }
    }
}
```

9. Add support for keeping track of the palindromes in the *Text* property's setter.

```
public string Text
{
    get
    {
        return text;
    }

    set
    {
        text = value;
        this.alPalindromes =
                (ArrayList)this.ViewState["palindromes"];
        if (this.alPalindromes == null)
        {
            this.alPalindromes = new ArrayList();
        }

        if (this.CheckForPalindrome())
        {
            if (PalindromeFound != null)
            {
                PalindromeFound(this, EventArgs.Empty);
            }
            alPalindromes.Add(text);

            this.labelPalindromeStatus.Text =
                    "This is a palindrome <br><FONT size=5 color=blue><B>" +
                text +
                "</B> </FONT>";
        }
```

```
        else
        {
            labelPalindromeStatus.Text =
                        "This is NOT a palindrome <br><FONT size=5 color=red><B>" +
            text +
            "</B> </FONT>";
        }
        this.ViewState.Add("palindromes", alPalindromes);
        this.BuildPalindromesTable();
    }
}
```

10. Build and run the project. When you type palindromes into the *PalindromeCheckerUser-Control*, it should look something like this:

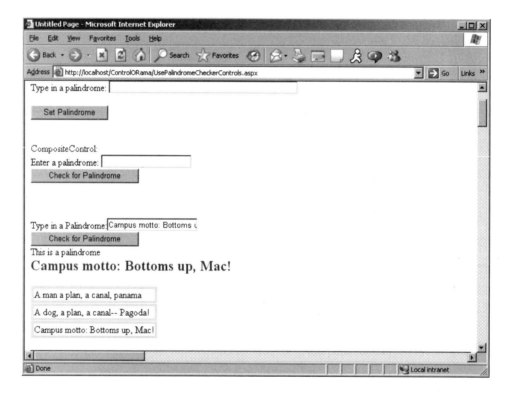

Before leaving, take a look at the page with tracing turned on. Here you can see how the page/control hierarchy is laid out in memory.

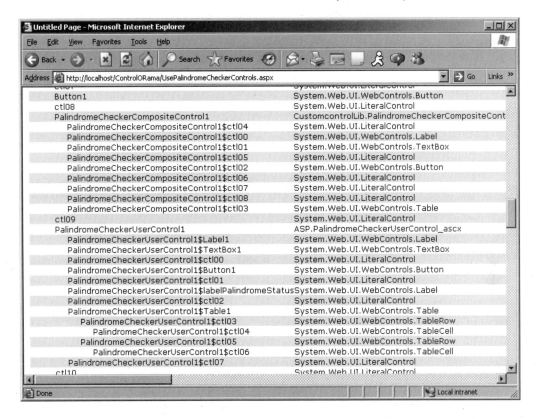

Notice how similar the *User* control is to the composite control. Both composite-style controls nest multiple single controls. They're very convenient ways of grouping rich Web-based user interface functionality into single units.

When to Use Each Type of Control

With composite controls and *User* control having so many similarities, there seems to be some redundancy in the framework. Since *User* controls have such an affinity with the designer, perhaps it seems you don't need custom composite controls at all. However, each style of composite controls has distinct advantages and disadvantages.

The biggest advantage of custom composite controls is that they are deployed as individual assemblies. Because custom composite controls are packaged in distinct assemblies, you may sign them and deploy them across the enterprise. You also may install them in the Global Assembly Cache. The primary downside to using custom composite controls is that they require more attention to detail in the coding process (there's no designer support).

The primary advantage to *User* controls is that they *do* include designer support. That makes them very easy to design visually. However, *User* controls have a downside in their deployment—they go with the project in which they were created, and they are deployed that way. You can include them as part of other projects, but that requires copying the ASCX and the CS files to the new project. They are not deployed as signed, secure assemblies.

Conclusion

This look at composite style controls wraps up ASP.NET's custom control story. Composite controls are a great way to package UI functionality into manageable chunks. Custom composite controls and *User* controls both maintain internal lists of controls and render them on demand. However, custom composite controls live entirely within an assembly, whereas *User* controls are split between ASCX files and a backing source code file and/or assembly.

In the next chapter, we'll take a look at some of the other more extensive controls available within ASP.NET.

Chapter 5 Quick Reference

To	Do This
Create a custom control composed of other server-side controls that lives in its own assembly	Derive a class from *System.Web.UI.Control*
	Override the *CreateChildControls* method
	Visual Studio includes a project type, Web Custom Control, that fits the bill
Add controls to a custom composite control	Instantiate the child control
	Add the child control to the composite control's Control collection
Add a custom control to the toolbox	Show the toolbox if it's not already showing by selecting **View | Toolbox** from the main menu
	Right mouse click anywhere in the toolbox
	Select Choose Items from the local menu
	Choose a control from the list
	OR
	Browse to the assembly containing the control
Tell ASP.NET to make up unique IDs for the child controls within the composite control	Add *INamingContainer* to the control's inheritance list
Raise events within a custom composite control	Expose the events using the *event* keyword
Create composite controls with designer support	Within a Visual Studio Web Site project, select **Web site | Add New Item...** from the main menu
	Select the Web User Control template

Chapter 6
Control Potpourri

After completing this chapter, you will be able to

- Use ASP.NET validation controls

- Use *TreeView*

- Use *MultiView*

ASP.NET has always evolved with the goal of reducing the effort developers must expend to get their Web sites up and running. One of the things you'll find as you tour ASP.NET is that Microsoft has done a great job of anticipating what the developer needs and putting it in the framework. In Chapters 3, 4, and 5 we saw the architecture behind ASP.NET Web forms and controls. With this architecture in place, you can easily extend the framework to do almost anything you want it to do.

ASP.NET versions 1.0 and 1.1 took over much of the functionality developers were building into their sites with classic ASP. For example, server-side controls handled much of the arduous coding that went into developing Web sites displaying consistent user interfaces (such as combo boxes that always showed the last selection that was chosen).

ASP.NET 2.0 continues that theme by introducing new server-side controls that insert commonly desired functionality into the framework. In this chapter, we look at support provided by ASP.NET for validating the data represented by controls as well as a couple of the various navigation controls (the *MultiView* control and the *TreeView* control).

Let's start with the validation controls.

Validation

One of ASP.NET's primary goals has been to provide functionality to cover the most often used scenarios. For example, we'll see later on that authorization and authentication requirements are common among Web sites. Most sites won't let you get to the real goodies until you authenticate as a user. ASP.NET 2.0 includes some new login controls to make authorization and authentication easier.

Another scenario you often find when surfing Web sites is that most sites include a page onto which you are to enter various types of information. For example, when applying for credentials to enter a Web site, you often need to enter things such as user names and passwords. If you want to have something mailed to you, you may be asked to enter your e-mail address.

When the company sponsoring a Web site wants some information from you, they want to make sure they have accurate information. While they can't guarantee that whatever you enter is 100 percent accurate, they can at least have a fighting chance of getting accurate information by validating the fields you've entered. For example, some fields may be absolutely required, and the Web site will ensure that data is entered into them. If you're asked to enter a phone number, the site may ask for it in a certain format and then apply a regular expression to validate whatever you enter as a user. If you're asked to enter a password, the site may ask you to enter it twice to be sure you really meant what you typed.

ASP.NET includes a host of validation controls that accompany standard controls (like a *Text-Box*) on a Web form. They work in concert with the standard controls and emit error messages (and sometimes alerts) if the user has typed in something that looks amiss.

ASP includes six validator controls:

- **RequiredFieldValidator**   Ensures that a field is filled in
- **RangeValidator**   Ensures the value represented by a control lies within a certain range
- **RegularExpressionValidator**   Validates that data within a control matches a specific regular expression
- **CompareValidator**   Ensures that the data represented by a control compares to a specific value or another control
- **CustomValidator**   Provides an opportunity to specify your own server-side and client-side validation functions
- **ValidationSummary**   Shows a summary of all the validation errors on a page

The validation controls all work the same way. First define a regular control on the page. Then place the accompanying validators wherever you want the error messages to appear on the page. The validator controls have a property named *ControlToValidate*. Point the validator control to the control needing validation and the rest works automatically. Of course, the validator controls have a number of properties you may use to customize the appearance of the error messages coming from the controls.

The ASP.NET validator controls work with the following server-side controls:

- *TextBox*
- *ListBox*
- *DropDownList*
- *RadioButtonList*
- *HtmlInputText*
- *HtmlInputFile*
- *HtmlSelect*
- *HtmlTextArea*

To see how they work, follow the next example, which applies validation controls to a Web form.

Creating a page that employs validation controls

1. Begin by creating a new Web site named ControlPotpourri.

2. Add a new Web form named ValidateMe.aspx. This form will hold the regular server-side controls and their accompanying validation controls. The form will resemble a sign-in form that you often see on Web sites. It's the canonical example for employing user input validation.

3. Add a *TextBox* to hold the user's first name text box. Name the control *TextBoxFirstName*.

4. Add a last name *TextBox*. Name the control *TextBoxLastName*.

5. Add an address *TextBox*. Name the control *TextBoxAddress*.

6. Add a ZIP Code *TextBox*. Name the control *TextBoxZip*.

7. Add a phone *TextBox*. Name the control *TextBoxPhone*.

8. Add *TextBoxes* to hold a password and a password confirmation. Name them *TextBoxPassword* and *TextPasswordAgain*, respectively. Set the *TextMode* property for both of them to Password so that they don't display the text being typed by the end user. This is a common scheme to ensure the user types a password he or she really means to enter because the *Password* property on the *TextBox* prevents the user from seeing the characters as they are keyed.

9. Add a *TextBox* to hold the user's age. Name the control *TextBoxAge*.

10. Add a *Button* to submit the form.

The form should look something like this when you're done.

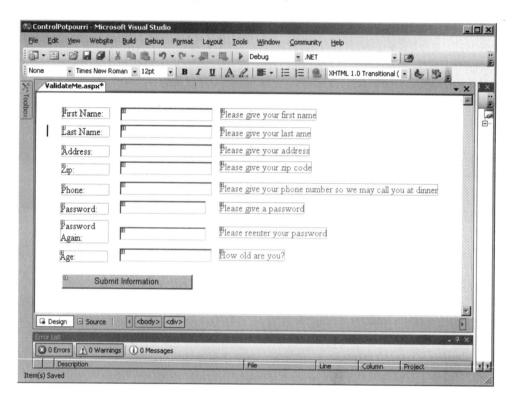

11. Now start adding validators. Add a *RequiredFieldValidator* control for the first name. In the properties for the first name validator control, pull down the combo box in the *ControlToValidate* property. Select the *TextBoxFirstName* control. Set the *ErrorMessage* property to a useful error message such as "Please give your first name."

12. As with the first name text box, add a RequiredFieldValidator control for the last name. In the properties for the last name validator control, pull down the combo box in the *ControlToValidate* property. Select the *TextBoxLastName* control. Set the *ErrorMessage* property to a useful error message such as "Please give your last name."

13. Add *RequiredFieldValidator* controls for the ZIP Code, the phone number, and the password text boxes. In the properties for the ZIP Code validator control, pull down the combo box in the *ControlToValidate* property. Select the *TextBoxZip* control. Set the *ErrorMessage* property to a useful error message such as "Please give your zip code." In the properties for the phone validator control, pull down the combo box in the *ControlToValidate* property. Select the *TextBoxPhone* control. Set the *ErrorMessage* property to a useful error message such as "Please give your phone number so we may call you at dinner." In the properties for the first password validator control, pull down the

combo box in the *ControlToValidate* property. Select the *TextBoxPassword* control. Set the *ErrorMessage* property to a useful error message such as "Please make up a password." In the properties for the second password validator control, pull down the combo box in the *ControlToValidate* property. Select the *TextBoxPasswordAgain* control. Set the *ErrorMessage* property to a useful error message such as "Please confirm your password."

14. Add a *RequiredFieldValidator* control for the age field. In the properties for the age required field validator control, pull down the combo box in the *ControlToValidate* property. Select the *TextBoxAge* control. Set the *ErrorMessage* property to a useful error message such as "Please give your age."

15. Compile and run the program. At first, all you'll see is a collection of input boxes. Before entering any fields, click the **Submit** button. Watch the error messages appear, as shown in the following graphic.

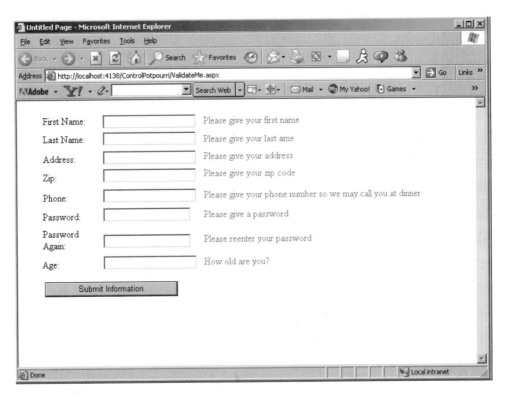

16. Type a first name and then press the **Tab** key to move the focus to another control. Watch what happens. The ASP.NET validator controls insert some JavaScript into the HTML sent to the browser (if the browser understands JavaScript). With the client-side script in place, required field validators can manage their error messages without a round-trip to the server, as shown in the following graphic.

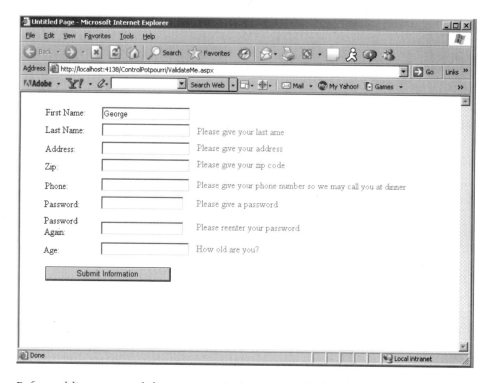

Before adding more validation controls, let's take a look at how ASP.NET user input validation works.

How Page Validation Works

ASP.NET's page validation is set up very cleverly—and it's all based on the *page* server-side control architecture. As with many other features in ASP.NET, the validation mechanism solves the most common use cases you encounter during Web site development. Most sites include both client-side and server-side validation. By supporting client-side validation, users are spared a round-trip when validating data input to the page. In addition to client-side validation, most sites also support server-side validation for two reasons: to make sure no data was garbled or modified during transmission, and to support clients unable to support client-side scripting (perhaps the client browser doesn't support JavaScript). Let's start with a look at client-side validation.

Client-Side Validation

If you looked at the ASPX source code generated by Visual Studio as you placed controls on the page, you probably noticed the page became littered with even more tags, such as server-side control tags to support text boxes and selection controls. In addition, each validator control placed on the page corresponds to a separate tag. Validators are server-side controls, too. They render standard browser-interpretable code—similar to the regular server-side controls.

ASP.NET validator controls support client-side validation by linking a JavaScript file named WebUIValidation.js into the HTML sent to the browser. The file contains the client-side validation functions necessary to support client-side validation.

When the validation controls render to the browser, they add span elements with custom attributes to the rendered HTML. The validation handlers are hooked up when the HTML document is loaded in the browser.

Because client-side validation requires JavaScript support in the client, clients without JavaScript support will need to rely on server-side validation. If you want, you may disable the client-side script for each control by setting the *EnableClientScript* property on the validator to false.

Server-Side Validation

Once the client has passed the client-side validation tests, the request is posted back to the server and the server-side validation kicks in. Server-side validation is managed by infrastructure within the *Page* class. As you add validator controls to the page, they're added to a collection of validators managed by the page. Each validation control implements an interface named *IValidator*. The *IValidator* interface specifies a *Validate* method, an *ErrorMessage* property, and an *IsValid* property. Of course, each validator has its own custom logic to determine the validity of the data held within the control it's validating. For example, the *RequiredFieldValidator* checks to see that there's data within the control it's associated with. The *RegularExpressionValidator* compares the data within a control to a specific regular expression.

During the post-back sequence for a page, validation occurs just after the *Page_Load* event fires. The page checks each validator against its associated control. If validation fails, the server-side validation controls that failed render themselves as visible span elements.

The page itself has a property named *IsValid* that you can check to ensure your confidence in the data passed in from the client before you actually start using the data in the controls. In addition, the Page class implements a method named *Validate()*. *Validate* walks the list of validation controls, running each control's *Validate* method.

Add Finer-grained Validation

Once you've ensured users fill the required fields, it's important to make sure that the data coming from users is likely to be correct. For example, you may not be able to ensure the veracity of the user's phone number, but at least you can make sure it is in the right format and doesn't contain garbage.

1. Dismiss the browser and go back to the designer window. Now that you have controls that show error messages when the user forgets to type something, let's take a look at some fine-grained validation. When you look at the fields being entered, you can see a couple more opportunities for the user to enter bad data.

2. There's not much you can do for the first name, last name, and address fields except hope that the users type what they really mean to type. However, you might want to ensure the user types only numbers into the Zip Code field. The way to ensure that is to use a *RegularExpressionValidator* for the *TextBoxZip* control.

3. Set the *ValidationExpression* button to **U.S. Zip code**. Highlight the *ValidationExpression* property, and then click the little button with an ellipsis to bring up the Regular Expression Editor:

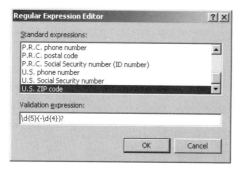

4. Add a regular expression validator for the *TextBoxPhone* control. Set the *ControlToValidate* property to *TextBoxPhone*. Bring up the Regular Expression Validator and choose **U.S. phone number** as the regular expression to validate, as shown in the following graphic.

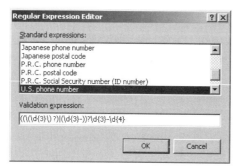

5. Add a *CompareValidator* for the *TextBoxPasswordAgain* control. In the properties for the password again validator control, pull down the combo box in the *ControlToValidate* property. Select the *TextBoxPasswordAgain* control. Set the *ControlToCompare* property to *TextBoxPassword*. Set the *ErrorMessage* property to a useful error message such as "Please reenter your password."

6. Add another *CompareValidator* for the *TextBoxAge* control. Enter **18** for *ValueToCompare* and **Integer** as the data type to compare. The operator property should be *GreaterThanEqual*.

7. Add a *ValidationSummary* to the form. This will show any errors occurring at once. If you want an alert to pop up in the browser, set the *ValidationSummary.ShowMessageBox* property to True.

8. Build and run the program. Enter some erroneous data. See what happens. You should see the error messages emitted by the validator controls. For example, if you type **17** as the age, the *CompareValidator* for the control should emit an error message. The *CompareValidator* should throw up an error in this case because the validator is looking for values greater than or equal to 18.

Other Validators

In addition to the validators mentioned above, ASP.NET includes two other validators: the *RangeValidator* and the *CustomValidator*. Let's take a quick look at each of those.

The *RangeValidator* is similar to the *CompareValidator* in that you may use it to check the data in a control against a value. However, the RangeValidator's purpose is to report an error if the data held in a control is out of a range. The validator specifies a minimum and a maximum value and reports the error if the value in the control falls beyond these thresholds.

You can try to fit any other kind of validation you might encounter into the *CustomValidator*. The *CustomValidator* fits on the page in the same way as the other validators. However, rather than predefining validation methods (on the server and within the client script), these pieces are left open. When you put a *CustomValidator* onto a page, you assign it an associated control. Then you refer to a validation function (that you write into the page). You may also specify a script block to be shipped to the client and run (along with the other client-side script).

Validator Properties

In looking through the validator controls, you can see that they contain the standard properties available to the other standard ASP.NET controls. For example, there's a *Text* property, a *Font* property, and various coloring properties. In addition, you'll find a couple of other properties useful for managing the error output sent to the browser.

The first property is the *Display* property. Its value may be either static or dynamic. This property manages the client-side rendering of the error message. *Static* (the default value) causes the span element emitted by the control to take up layout space in the HTML bound for the client, even when hidden. When the *Display* property is *Dynamic*, the span element emitted by the control changes the layout and dynamically expands when displayed.

A new feature for ASP.NET 2.0 is the ability to group validation controls. That is, each validation control may belong to a named group. The *ValidationGroup* property controls the name of the group. When a control belongs to a group, controls in that group only validate when one of the other validators in that group fires. This gives you a "multiple forms" effect within a single page.

Let's take a look at two other interesting controls: the *TreeView* and the *MultiView*.

TreeView

One of the most common user interface idioms in modern software is a hierarchy represented by expandable nodes. For example, whenever you browse for a file using Windows Explorer, you need to expand and contract various folders (subdirectories) to see what's inside. This type of control is known generically as a tree control.

Tree controls let users navigate hierarchies by representing expandable and collapsible nodes. For example, when you explore your C drive using Windows Explorer, the directories appear as closed folders with small plus signs to the left. When you click on a plus sign, Windows Explorer displays an open folder and then shows the subdirectories directly underneath. If there are further subdirectories, you may open them the same way.

ASP.NET provides this functionality via the *TreeView*. It's useful any time you want to represent a nested data structure and have a way of drilling down into it. To see how the *TreeView* works, let's look at an example.

Using the *TreeView* control

This exercise illustrates the *TreeView* control by showing a hierarchical, expandable list of 1970s bands that are still around today. The example will illustrate the hierarchical nature of the bands mentioned by showing the name of the band followed by a list of roles performed by each particular member.

1.   Begin by adding a new Web form to the ControlPotpourri Web site. Name it *UseTreeView*.

2.   Pick up a *TreeView* from the toolbox and add it to the default page. You'll find it under the Navigation controls.

3.   Visual Studio presents a number of options you can apply to the *TreeView*. Select the Auto Format option. Visual Studio presents a dialog box showing a number of styles for the *TreeView*. Browse through a few of them, highlighting them to see what the styles look like. The following graphic shows the local menu which you may use to bring up the AutoFormat dialog box.

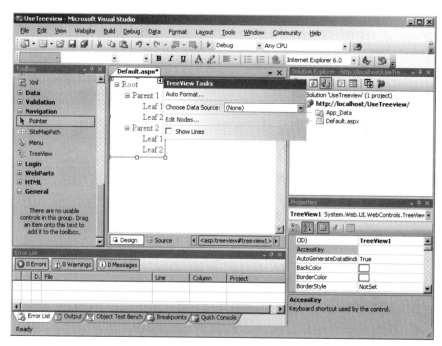

4. After selecting a style for the *TreeView*, select the **Edit Nodes** task. You may edit the nodes by right-clicking on the *TreeView* control and selecting **Edit Nodes** from the local menu. From this dialog box you may edit each of the nodes. The leftmost button adds new root nodes. In this example, the bands are represented as root nodes. The next button over is for adding child nodes. You may nest these nodes as deeply as necessary. In this example, the second layer of nodes represents the members of the bands, and the third layer represents their roles. The following graphic show the *TreeView* node editor.

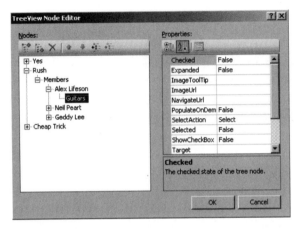

5. Add a border around the *TreeView* using the *Border* property.

6. Build the project and browse to the page. You should be able to expand and contract the nodes. After running the page, take a quick look at the ASPX source code to see how the *TreeView* manages its nodes. The following graphic shows how the *TreeView* appears in the browser.

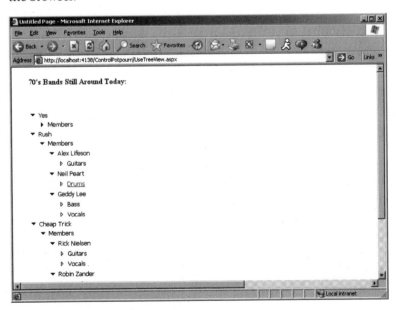

7. To make it a bit more interesting, add some functionality to handle some of the tree node events. First add a label to show the selected node. Name the label *LabelSelected-Node* so that you have programmatic access to it. Add a *TextBox* to show information about the selected node. Make the *TextBox* multiline. Then add an event handler for the *SelectedNodeChanged* event. Add code to interrogate the selected node to list information about the child nodes.

```
protected void TreeView1_SelectedNodeChanged(object sender, EventArgs e)
{

    this.LabelSelectedNode.Text = "Selected Node changed to: " +
    this.TreeView1.SelectedNode.Text;
    TreeNodeCollection childNodes = this.TreeView1.SelectedNode.ChildNodes;
    if (childNodes != null)
    {
    this.TextBox1.Text = "";
        foreach(TreeNode childNode in childNodes)
        {
            this.TextBox1.Text += childNode.Value + "\n";
        }
    }

}
```

The following graphic shows how the selected details appear in the *ListBox*.

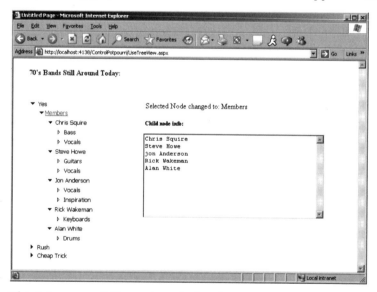

This is just a small illustration of what the *TreeView* is capable of doing. In addition to building nodes using the designer, you may build them programmatically. You may expand and contract nodes as well. Finally, the *TreeView* supports databinding, allowing you to throw a hierarchical data structure at the control so it will render properly for you.

Finally, let's take a look at ASP.NET 2.0's *MultiView* and *View controls*.

MultiView

From time to time, it's useful to gather controls together in several panes and give the user the opportunity to page through the panes. During the lifetime of ASP.NET 1.0, Microsoft released several rich dynamic (though officially unsupported) controls that emitted DHTML instead of regular HTML. A trio of these controls, the *TabStrip*, the *MultiView* (an older version), and the *PageView*, worked together to form essentially a set of tabbed panes.

These controls aren't available in ASP.NET 2.0; however, two controls—the *MultiView* and the *View*—go a long way toward providing similar functionality. The *MultiView* acts as a container for *Panel*-like controls (*View* controls). The *MultiView* includes support for paging through the various *Views* held within it. The *MultiView* shows a single *View* at a time.

The following exercise provides an example that shows how the *MultiView* and the *View* controls work together.

Using the *MultiView* and *View* controls

1. Add a new Web form to the ControlPotpourri site. Name it *UseMultiview*. You'll add a *MultiView* to this form and then add some *Views* to it.

2. Add a *MultiView* to this Web form.

3. The main purpose of the *MultiView* is to manage a set of *Views*. To add a *View* to a *MultiView*, pick it up and drop it *inside* the *MultiView*. Add three *Views* to the Web form like so:

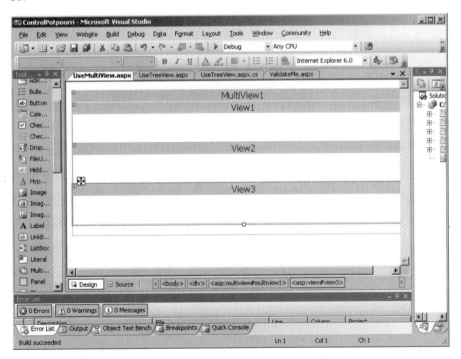

4. Add some content to each of the *Views*. You can think of the *Views* very much like panes. In this example, the first view includes a *TextBox* and a button. The second view includes a *DropDownList*, and a *PalindromeCheckerCompositeControl* from Chapter 5. The following graphic illustrates how the *Views* look in the designer.

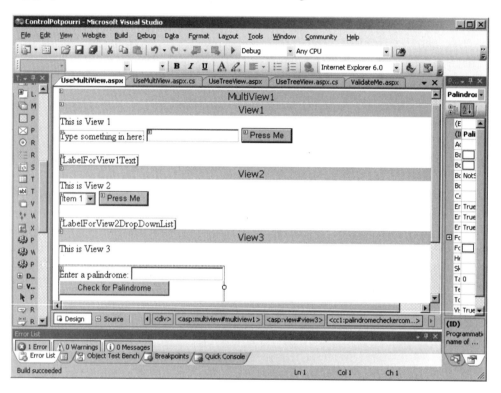

5. To cause the *MultiView* and the first *View* to show up, set the *ActiveViewIndex* property to 0 to show the first pane.

6. Add some controls to navigate between the *Views* in the *MultiView*. Add two buttons to the bottom of the form. Call them Previous and Next—they'll be used to page through the *Views*.

7. Add event handlers for the buttons by double-clicking on each of them.

8. Add code to the page through the *Views*. This code responds to the button clicks by changing the index of the current *View*.

```
protected void ButtonPrev_Click(object sender, EventArgs e)
{
    if (MultiView1.ActiveViewIndex == 0)
    {
        MultiView1.ActiveViewIndex = 2;
    }
    else
```

```
        {
            MultiView1.ActiveViewIndex -= 1;
        }
    }
    protected void ButtonNext_Click(object sender, EventArgs e)
    {
        if (MultiView1.ActiveViewIndex == 2)
        {
            MultiView1.ActiveViewIndex = 0;
        }
        else
        {
            MultiView1.ActiveViewIndex += 1;
        }
    }
}
```

9. Compile the project and browse to the Web page. Pressing the navigator buttons will cause post-backs to the server, which will render the individual views. The following graphic shows how the *MultiView* and *View* number 3 appear in a browser.

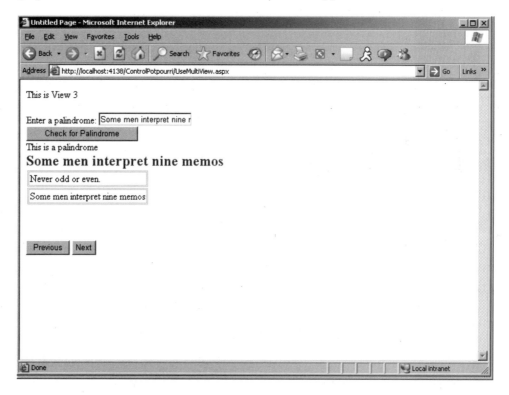

As you can see, the *MultiView* and the *View* classes act as panes that you can swap in and out. They represent a great way to manage the surface area involved in collecting large amounts of data. We'll see another version of this kind of control when we look at the *Wizard* control in conjunction with the session state.

Conclusion

In this chapter, we looked at both the ASP.NET validations and several of the new controls available in ASP.NET 2.0. ASP.NET has always strived to lessen the drudgery of Web development by solving the most common use cases encountered during the development of Web sites.

Whenever you sign onto a commercial Web site, you almost invariably hit a form that asks you for information. When creating such forms, you will want to ensure that the data coming from the user is as accurate as possible. It's a good idea to check certain things, such as making sure all the required fields are filled, the fields have data in the correct format, and that certain data matches specific values or falls within a stated range. ASP.NET validators perform this function.

The ASP.NET *TreeView* helps users browse hierarchical data structures (such as directories). The *TreeView* renders expandable and collapsible nodes that let users drill down into the data structures. The *MultiView* and the *View* work very much like panels that can be swapped in and out.

Next up: *Web Parts* (server-side controls on steroids).

Chapter 6 Quick Reference

To	Do This
Validate Form input	ASP.NET includes a number of validator controls that check data entered via server-side controls. These controls include
	CompareValidator
	RangeValidator
	RequiredFieldValidator
	RegularExpressionValidator
	ValidationSummary
	CustomValidator
	To validate the input of a server-side control, drag the appropriate validator control onto the page and set the *ControlToValidate* property to the target control
	Set the other validator properties appropriately
	Instantiate the child control
	Add the child control to the composite control's Control collection
Display hierarchical data sets in an intuitive way	Use the *TreeView* control
	Either add items by hand, or bind the *TreeView* control to a hierarchical data source

To	Do This
Swap between several pages of information on the same Web page	Use the *MultiView* and *View* controls
	You can think of the *View* control as a miniature page managing controls
	The *MultiView* manages a collection of *Views*
	The *MultiView* supports swapping between *Views*

Chapter 7
Web Parts

After completing this chapter, you will be able to

- Understand ASP.NET Web Parts

- Use standard Web Parts in a Web page

- Create a custom Web Part

- Use the custom Web Part in a Web page

In Chapters 4 and 5, we took a look at both rendered and composite controls. Chapter 6 covered a few of the controls already available within ASP.NET 2.0. Because rendering an ASP.NET Web form is broken down into small, manageable chunks, arbitrarily extending the framework by adding new controls is a straightforward affair. Server-side controls offer very fine-grained control over the HTML rendered by your application.

In this chapter we get a taste of Web Parts. The topic of Web Parts could take up an entire book—they represent a whole new level of interaction with Web sites. Web Parts are in many ways like custom controls. They give you a way to customize the HTML coming out of your Web site without having to hard-code the output of your page.

While custom controls derive either from *System.Web.UI.Control* or *System.Web.UI.WebControl*, Web Parts derive from *Microsoft.SharePoint.WebPartPages.WebPart*. While *WebPart* does inherit from *System.Web.UI.Control*, it goes beyond the regular control functionality by handling interactions with *WebPartPage* and *WebPartZone* classes to support adding, deleting, customizing, connecting, and personalizing Web Parts on a page.

One big advantage of using Web Parts is that they combine the flexibility of rendered custom controls with the drag-and-drop manageability of *User* controls. As a developer you can drag completed Web Parts from Web Parts galleries and drop them onto Web Parts zones. You can modify the shared properties of a group of Web Parts and make them persistent. In addition to being a useful way of packaging UI components, Web Parts can connect with each other via standard interfaces.

A Brief History of Web Parts

In the early 2000s, SharePoint emerged as a highly leveraged way for organizations to build portals and collaboration environments. For example, coordinating large teams toward a common goal is an excellent reason for a portal. Team endeavors such as software development require systems such as version control and bug tracking. If the team is distributed geographically or in some other way not part of the office network, the next logical thing is to be able to share information over the Web.

Without a framework such as SharePoint, developers would likely duplicate much effort between them. SharePoint introduced some prefabricated components to ease building collaboration sites (rather than building them from scratch). SharePoint Web pages are based upon a type of component named Web Parts. Web Parts are a way to package information and functionality for users.

While SharePoint is a stand-alone framework dedicated to building collaboration portals, ASP.NET 2.0 represents a broad-spectrum Web development framework that happens to have a built-in portal framework. That is, SharePoint represents a dedicated means to build portals, and ASP.NET 2.0 includes some classes useful for building portal-like applications. However, even though they're different development environments, they do share a principal concept between them—Web Parts. While ASP.NET Web Parts and SharePoint Web Parts aren't exactly the same animal, they operate similarly.

What Good Are Web Parts?

WebPart controls are useful for developing portal-type Web sites. Work flow and collaboration management is quickly becoming one of the most important application areas for Web site development. Because portals often have much of the same functionality from one to the other, it makes more sense to build portals from a framework than to build them completely from scratch. Much of this functionality includes such items as file transfers, implementing user profiles, and user administration.

ASP.NET offers three distinct Web Parts development scenarios. These scenarios include (1) building regular pages to consume Web Parts controls, (2) developing Web Parts controls, and (3) implementing Web Parts pages and Web Parts within a portal-type application.

Developing Web Parts Controls

Web Parts controls represent a superset of the existing ASP.NET server-side controls (including rendered controls, *User* controls, and composite controls) regardless of who wrote them. For maximum programmatic control of your environment, you can also create custom Web Parts controls that derive from the *System.Web.UI.WebControls.WebParts.WebPart* class.

Web Parts Page Development

Regular Web pages may use Web Parts. Visual Studio includes support for creating pages to host *WebPart* controls. Developing a *WebPart* page involves introducing a *WebPartManager* to the page, specifying a number of zones on the page, and then populating them with *WebPart* controls.

Web Parts Application Development

Finally, you may develop entire applications out of *WebPart* controls. For example, you may decide to build a portal. *WebPart* controls enable you to write personalized pages that are customizable. Web Parts are also ideal for building a commonly used application (such as sharing records or documentation) and shipping it as a unit so it can be deployed on another company's Web site wholesale.

The Web Parts Architecture

The Web Parts architecture serves multiple purposes. Given that the job of Web Parts is to behave as a bigger UI lever, the functional components have been broken into overall page management and zone management. *WebPart* controls need to be coordinated together. In addition, the different functional areas of a page often need to be handled as a group of controls (for managing layout, for example).

In terms of framework classes, Web Parts are nested within zones, which are managed by a singular *WebPartManager* that talks to the application data store. Figure 7-1 illustrates how the parts are related.

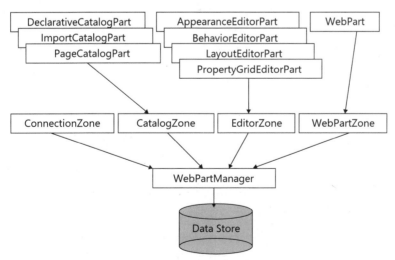

Figure 7-1 How Web Parts are managed within zones, which in turn are managed by an instance of *WebPartManager*.

WebPartManager and *WebZones*

As Figure 7-1 illustrates, *WebPartManager* manages each *WebZone*, which in turn manages each individual *WebPart*. Any page using at least one *WebPart* needs an instance of *WebPartManager*. The *WebPartManager* is responsible for managing and coordinating the zone(s) and the controls lying within them. The *WebZone* also manages any extra *UI* elements that go with the group of controls.

Within the zone, the *ZoneTemplate* contains all Web Parts. If a regular ASP.NET control is in a *ZoneTemplate*, ASP.NET will wrap it as a Web Part.

Built-in Zones

Web Parts zones manage the layout for a group of controls. Out of the box, ASP.NET includes four built-in zones. These are:

- **WebPartZone**   This class represents basic functionality for managing server-side controls within zones on a page. *WebPartZone* controls are responsible for hosting both normal server-side controls as well as *WebPart* controls. Normal controls become wrapped by the *GenericWebPart* control at run time to add *WebPart* qualities to them.

- **CatalogZone**   This zone hosts *CatalogPart* controls. Catalogs generally manage the visibility of parts on a page. The *CatalogZone* control shows and hides its contents based upon the catalog display mode. Web Part Catalogs are named such because they act as catalogs of controls from which the end user may select.

- **EditorZone**   The *EditorZone* control represents the means through which end users may modify and personalize Web pages according to their preferences. Personalizing a Web site includes such things as setting up personal information (such as birthdays, gender-specific addressing, number of visits to the site, etc.). Other kinds of personalization involve setting up color schemes and layouts. The *EditorZone* helps manage this functionality as well as saves and loads those settings so they're available the next time the user logs on.

- **ConnectionZone**   Web Parts are often more useful when they're connected together and communicate dynamically. The *ConnectionZone* manages this functionality.

Built-in Web Parts

In addition to including several zones straight out of the box, ASP.NET provides some ready-to-use *WebPart* controls as well. The *WebPart* controls fit into various functional categories. Some are for managing catalogs, while others are for managing editing. Each specific kind of *WebPart* fits within a particular zone. Here's a rundown of the currently available *WebPart* toolbox.

- **DeclarativeCatalogPart**   When building a *WebPart* page, you may add parts dynamically or declaratively. Adding parts to a page dynamically means executing code that adds parts to the page at runtime. For example, imagine you had a Web Part represented as a class named "MyWebPart" (ultimately derived from *System.Web.UI.Controls.WebParts*). You may add the part to the page by creating an instance of the part and adding it to the *WebPartManager* using *WebPartManager.AddWebPart*. Adding parts to a page declaratively means including tag declarations within the ASPX file representing the *WebPart* page. The *DeclarativeCatalogPart* control manages server-side controls added declaratively to a catalog on a Web page.

- **PageCatalogPart**   One way end users will probably want to customize a site is by opening and closing controls. The *PageCatalogPart* represents a page catalog for holding controls that were previously added to a page that is now closed. By managing the controls in a *PageCatalogPart*, the end user may add the controls back to the page.

- **ImportCatalogPart**   The *ImportCatalogPart* enables users to import a Web Part description from XML data.

- **AppearanceEditorPart**   The *AppearanceEditorPart* is used to edit the appearance properties of an associated *WebPart* or *GenericWebPart*.

- **BehaviorEditorPart**   To support editing the behavior of a *WebPart* or *GenericWebPart*, ASP.NET provides the *BehaviorEditorPart*.

- **LayoutEditorPart**   The *LayoutEditorPart* is for editing the layout properties and associated *WebPart* (or *GenericWebPart* control).

- **PropertyGridEditorPart**   To support users in editing custom properties of *WebPart* controls, ASP.NET provides the *PropertyGridEditorPart* (the other *EditorPart* controls only support editing existing properties from the *WebPart* class).

To get a feel as to how to use *WebPart* controls let's run an example. The following exercise shows how to build a Web page from *WebPart* controls.

Using Web Parts

1. Create a new site. Name it UseWebParts.

2. In the default page, add a *WebPartManager*.

3. Drag a *WebPartZone* onto the page. Set the ID to **WebPartZoneLinks**. Set the *HeaderText* to **Links**. Set the *HeaderStyle* font Fore color to a blue (so you can see it better later during editing mode). Set the *AutoFormat* to a nice style such as Professional.

4. Add some *HyperLinks* to the *WebPartZone*, as shown here:

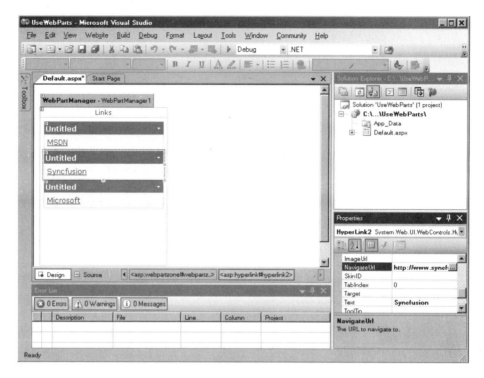

5. Run the page. You should see the links appear on the left side of the page.

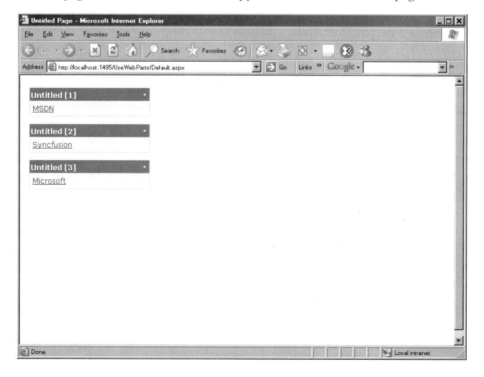

6. Add a *DropDownList* to the page. Name it *DropDownListDisplayModes*. This will be used to switch the display mode back and forth.

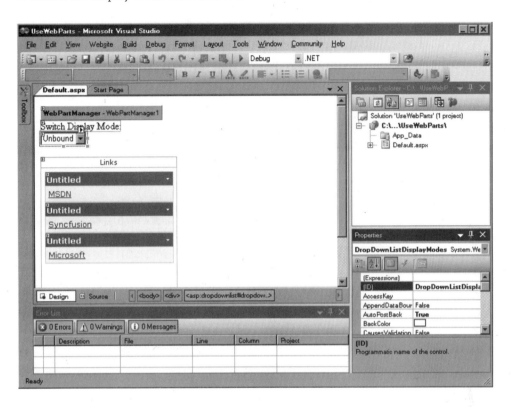

ASP.NET 2.0 Web Parts support five separate display modes. They are:

- **BrowseDisplayMode**   This is normal mode. No personalization or editing is available here.

- **DesignDisplayMode**   This mode turns on drag-and-drop layout personalization.

- **EditDisplayMode**   This option turns on personalization or customization of *Web-Part* properties and permits a user to delete Web Parts that have been added to the page dynamically.

- **ConnectDisplayMode**   This mode allows a user to connect Web Parts at runtime.

- **CatalogDisplayMode**   This mode allows a user to add Web Parts into a *WebPart-Zone* at runtime.

7. Update the *_Default* class to support switching modes. Add a *WebPartManager* member named *_wpManager* to the class to hold an instance of the current *WebPartManager*. Update the *Page_Init* method to attach an event handler to the page's *InitComplete* event. In the *InitializationComplete* handler, get the current *WebPartManager* and stash the reference in the *_wpManager* member, as shown in this listing:

```
public partial class _Default : System.Web.UI.Page
{
    WebPartManager _wpManager;
    protected void Page_Load(object sender, EventArgs e)
    {
    }

    void Page_Init(object sender, EventArgs e)
    {
        Page.InitComplete += new EventHandler(InitializationComplete);
    }

    public void InitializationComplete(object sender, System.EventArgs e)
    {
        _wpManager = WebPartManager.GetCurrentWebPartManager(Page);
        String browseModeName = WebPartManager.BrowseDisplayMode.Name;
        foreach (WebPartDisplayMode mode in
          _wpManager.SupportedDisplayModes)
        {
            String modeName = mode.Name;
            // Make sure a mode is enabled before adding it.
            if (mode.IsEnabled(_wpManager))
            {
                ListItem item = new ListItem(modeName, modeName);
                DisplayModeDropdown.Items.Add(item);
            }
        }
    }
}
```

The code listed in the above handler interrogates the current *WebPartManager* for the supported display modes and puts them in the *DropDownList*.

8. Add a handler for the *DropDownListDisplayModes* drop-down list box when the *Selected-IndexChanged* event occurs. Have the handler switch the *WebPart* page into the selected mode. The following code shows how.

```
protected void
    DropDownListDisplayModes_SelectedIndexChanged(
            object sender, EventArgs e)
{
    String selectedMode = DropDownListDisplayModes.SelectedValue;
    WebPartDisplayMode mode =
     _wpManager.SupportedDisplayModes[selectedMode];
    if (mode != null)
        _wpManager.DisplayMode = mode;
}
```

9. Finally, override the *Page_PreRender* method to display the selected display mode in the drop-down list box.

```
void Page_PreRender(object sender, EventArgs e)
{
    ListItemCollection items = this.DropDownListDisplayModes.Items;
    int selectedIndex =
      items.IndexOf(items.FindByText(_wpManager.DisplayMode.Name));
    DropDownListDisplayModes.SelectedIndex = selectedIndex;
}
```

10. Run the site. Immediately (without doing anything else), you may enter Design mode, as shown in the following graphic:

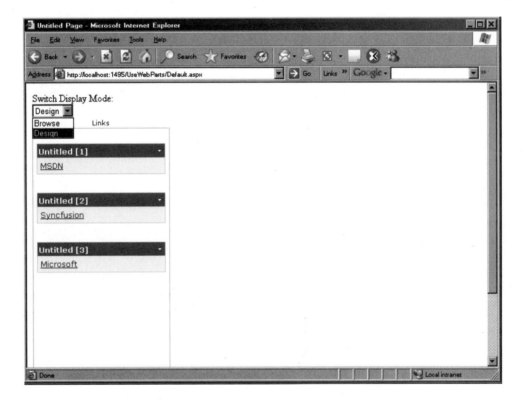

You'll see more modes later as you add more zones. Notice how the title now shows up. You may pick up items on the page and move them around now. For example, you may pick up one of the links and move it into the Links *WebPartZone*.

11. Now add some more functionality. Add an *EditorZone* to the page. Then in the *Editor-Zone*, add an *AppearanceEditorPart*, as shown in the following graphic:

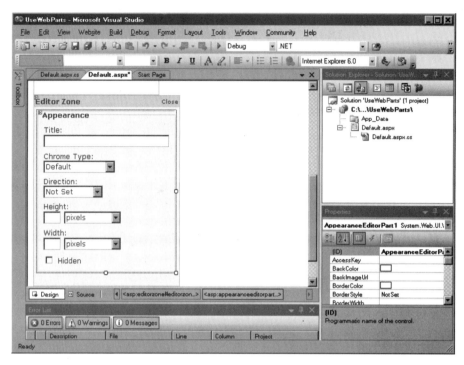

12. Now run the site. You'll see a new option in the Display Mode drop-down list box: the Edit mode.

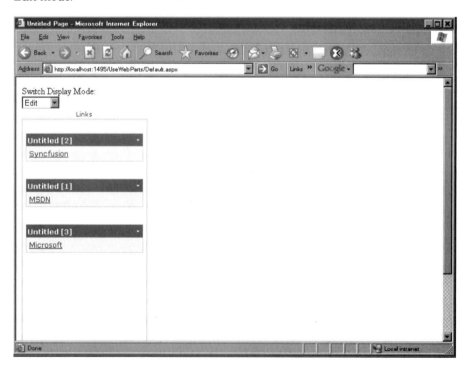

13. Now go back and add a *CatalogZone*. Drop a *DeclarativeCatalogPart* into the new *Web-PartZone* and select **Edit Template**.

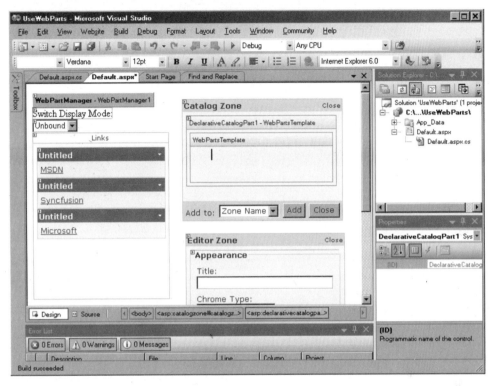

14. While in Template Editing mode, pick up a *TextBox* control from the toolbox and drop it into the *DeclarativeCatalogPart*. Then update the actual source code to add a *Title* attribute, as shown:

```
<ZoneTemplate>
  <asp:DeclarativeCatalogPart
    ID="DeclarativeCatalogPart1" runat="server">
    <WebPartsTemplate>
      <asp:TextBox ID="TextBox1"
        Title="A TextBox"
        runat="server">
      </asp:TextBox>
    </WebPartsTemplate>
  </asp:DeclarativeCatalogPart>
</ZoneTemplate>
```

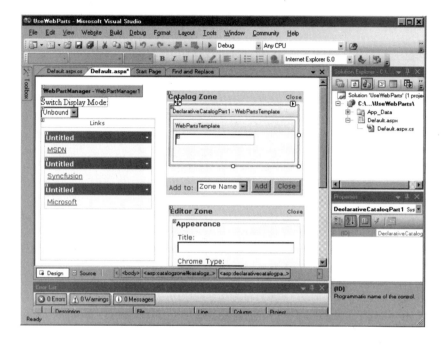

15. Now run the page again. Switch to Catalog Mode. Mark the **A TextBox** check box and add a *TextBox* to the Links zone. (This may not seem too interesting yet. However, in the next exercise, you'll write a hyperlink Web Part that you may add to the links page from the catalog—and then update it with your own links and display names).

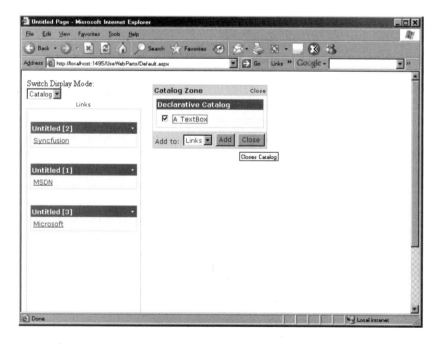

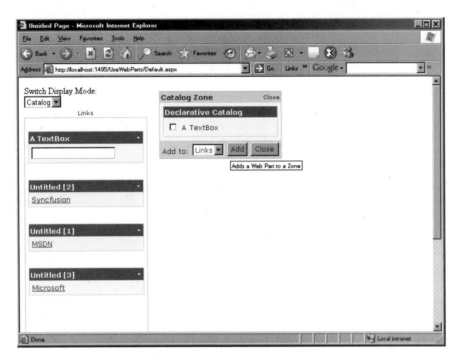

16. Run the page and get into Edit mode. Select a local menu from one of the Web Parts. Select **Edit**. You should see a collection of controls for editing the Web Part appearing in the Editor Zone, like so:

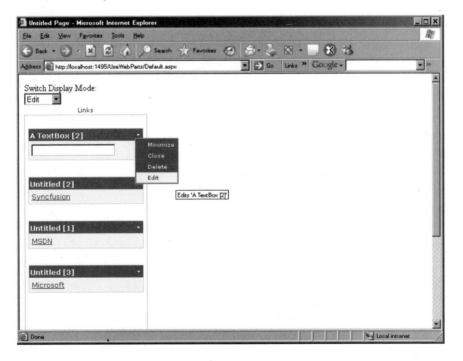

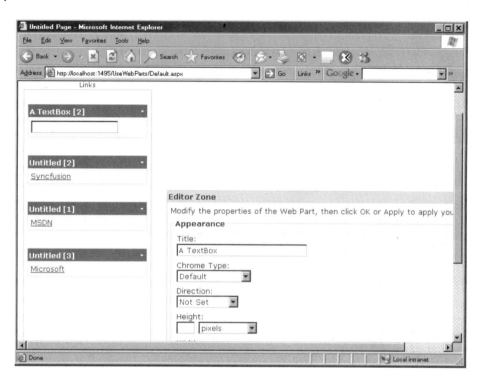

Developing a Web Part

The previous example showed how to use Web Parts within a page and how to switch the page between various modes at runtime. The catalog built into the page includes a *TextBox* control that you may add to a *WebPartZone* on the page. The example delivers a small glimpse into the flexibility and power of Web Parts. However, simply dropping a *TextBox* onto a *WebPartZone* isn't very interesting. In this example, we'll build a hyperlink Web Part that you may use to augment the Links *WebPartZone*.

Developing a Web Part is actually fairly straightforward and quite similar to developing a custom control (like the ones from Chapters 4 and 5). Instead of deriving a class from *System.Web.UI.Controls.WebControl* or *System.Web.UI.Controls.CompositeControl*, you derive a class from *System.Web.UI.WebControls.WebParts.WebPart*. From that point, you have the choice of either rendering HTML or composing a Web Part from other controls. The *WebPart* includes considerable functionality for integrating with the Web Part architecture. For example, in the next sample, the navigation URL and display name properties of the hyper link Web Part will be exposed as properties that the end user may modify through the *PropertyGridEditorPart*.

The following example illustrates how to create a hyperlink Web Part that you may add to the Links *WebPartZone* in the UseWebParts project. While, you could add a regular *HyperLink* control to the catalog, normal controls don't have the same support for the user to modify the links. For that, the link need to be represented as a Web Part.

Developing the HyperLinkWebPart

1. Add a new subproject to the UseWebParts solution. Make it a class library and name the library WebPartLib. When Visual Studio asks you to name the first class being placed in the library, name the file "HyperLinkWebPart.cs." (Visual Studio will name the class *HyperLinkWebPart*.)

2. Make a reference to the System.Web assembly within the new subproject. Right mouse click on the WebPartLib node in Solution Explorer and use the Add Reference option from the local menu to add the System.Web assembly.

3. Derive the new class from *System.Web.UI.WebControls.WebParts.WebPart* by adding it to the inheritance list, as shown here:

```
using System;
using System.Collections.Generic;
using System.Text;
using System.Web;
using System.Web.UI;
using System.Web.UI.WebControls;
using System.Web.UI.WebControls.WebParts;

namespace WebPartLib
{

    public class HyperLinkWebPart :
      System.Web.UI.WebControls.WebParts.WebPart
    {

    }
}
```

4. Add two string member variables to the HyperLinkWebPart class—one to represent the display name of the Web Part and the other to represent the actual URL. Initialize them with reasonable values:

```
using System;
using System.Collections.Generic;
using System.Text;
using System.Web;
using System.Web.UI;
using System.Web.UI.WebControls;
using System.Web.UI.WebControls.WebParts;

namespace WebPartLib
{

    public class HyperLinkWebPart :
    System.Web.UI.WebControls.WebParts.WebPart
    {

        string _strURL = "http://www.microsoft.com";
        string _strDisplayName = "This is a link";
    }
}
```

5.   Add a member variable of type *HyperLink* to the class. The Web Part will leverage the already-existing functionality of the *HyperLink* control. Override *CreateChildControls* to create an instance of *HyperLink* and add it to the *HyperLinkWebPart* controls collection. Initialize the *HyperLink.Text* property to the member variable representing the display name. Initialize the *HyperLink.NavigateUrl* property to the member variable representing the URL:

```
using System;
using System.Collections.Generic;
using System.Text;
using System.Web;
using System.Web.UI;
using System.Web.UI.WebControls;
using System.Web.UI.WebControls.WebParts;

namespace WebPartLib
{

    public class HyperLinkWebPart :
    System.Web.UI.WebControls.WebParts.WebPart
    {

        HyperLink _hyperLink;

        string _strURL = "http://www.microsoft.com";
        string _strDisplayName = "This is a link";
        protected override void  CreateChildControls()
        {
            _hyperLink = new HyperLink();
            _hyperLink.NavigateUrl = this._strURL;
            _hyperLink.Text = this._strDisplayName;
            this.Controls.Add(_hyperLink);
            base.CreateChildControls();
        }
    }
}
```

6.   Finally, expose the URL and the display name as properties so that the Web Parts architecture can understand and work with them. To allow the exposed properties to work with the Web Parts architecture through the *PropertyGridEditorPart*, be sure to adorn the properties with the following attributes: *Personalizable*, *WebBrowsable*, and *Web-DisplayName*, as shown here:

```
using System;
using System.Collections.Generic;
using System.Text;
using System.Web;
using System.Web.UI;
using System.Web.UI.WebControls;
using System.Web.UI.WebControls.WebParts;

namespace WebPartLib
{
```

```csharp
public class HyperLinkWebPart :
System.Web.UI.WebControls.WebParts.WebPart
{

    HyperLink _hyperLink;

    string _strURL = "http://www.microsoft.com";
    string _strDisplayName = "This is a link";
    [Personalizable(), WebBrowsable, WebDisplayName("Display Name")]
    public string DisplayName
    {
        get
        {
            return this._strDisplayName;
        }
        set
        {
            this._strDisplayName = value;
            if (_hyperLink != null)
            {
                _hyperLink.Text = this.DisplayName;
            }
        }
    }
    [Personalizable(), WebBrowsable, WebDisplayName("URL")]
    public string URL
    {
        get
        {
            return this._strURL;
        }
        set
        {
            this._strURL = value;
            if (_hyperLink != null)
            {
                _hyperLink.NavigateUrl = this.URL;
            }

        }
    }
    protected override void CreateChildControls()
    {
        _hyperLink = new HyperLink();
        _hyperLink.NavigateUrl = this._strURL;
        _hyperLink.Text = this._strDisplayName;
        this.Controls.Add(_hyperLink);
     base.CreateChildControls();
    }
  }
}
```

7. Make sure the project's compiler output is going to a sensible directory (for example, the bin\debug directory for the project).

8. Now add the *HyperLinkWebPart* to the catalog. First, right mouse click in the toolbox and select "Choose Item" (just as you did when adding custom controls to a page). Find the WebPartLib.dll assembly and load it into Visual Studio. You should see the Hyper-LinkWebPart appear in the toolbox, as shown here:

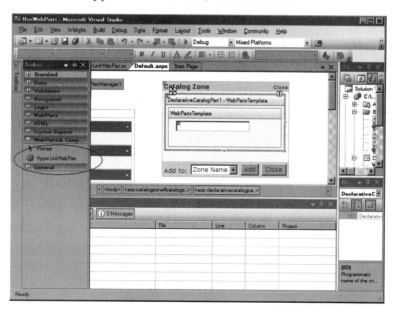

9. Put the *CatalogZone* into "Edit Template" mode by clicking on the small arrow in the Web Template. Then drag the *HyperLinkWebPart* into the *CatalogZone*, just as you did earlier with the *TextBox*, as shown here:

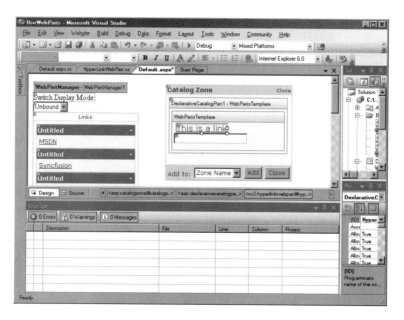

10. Add a title to the new catalog item. Switch to the source code window in Visual Studio. Within the source code, add a title to the new control:

```
<ZoneTemplate>
    <asp:DeclarativeCatalogPart
     ID="DeclarativeCatalogPart1" runat="server">
        <WebPartsTemplate>
            <cc2:HyperLinkWebPart
            Title="A Hyper Link"
            ID="HyperLinkWebPart1"
            runat="server" />
            <asp:TextBox ID="TextBox1"
            Title="A TextBox"
            runat="server">
            </asp:TextBox>
        </WebPartsTemplate>
    </asp:DeclarativeCatalogPart>
</ZoneTemplate>
```

The HyperLinkWebPart should now appear in the catalog with a title, as shown here:

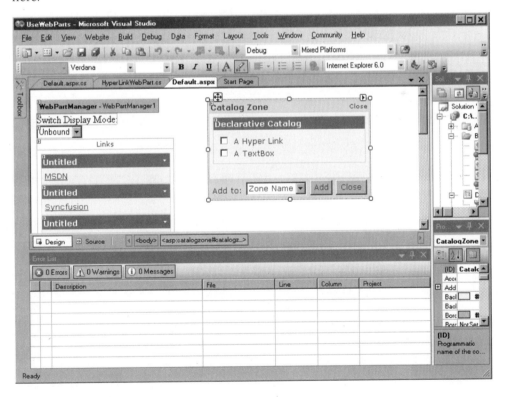

11. Add a *PropertyGridEditorPart* to the *EditorZone* on the page. Just pick one up out of the toolbox and drop it onto the *EditorZone*, as shown in the following graphic:

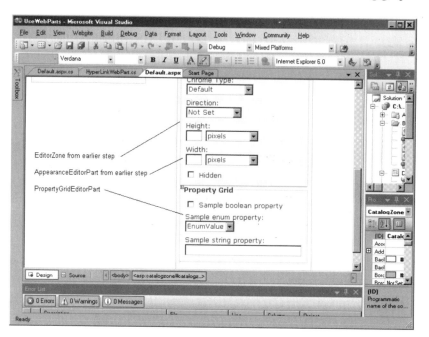

12. Surf to the Web site. Put the page in Catalog mode by selecting Catalog from the drop-down list box.

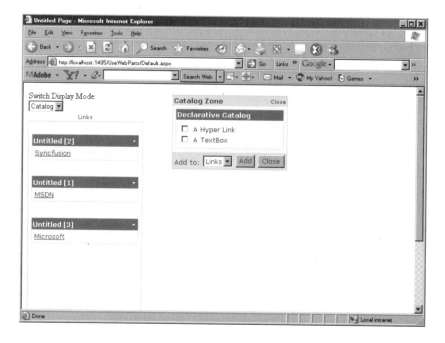

13. Select "A Hyper Link" from the catalog and add it to the Links Web Part Zone.

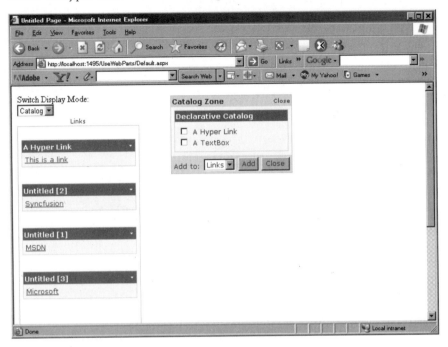

14. Put the Web Parts Page into Edit mode by selecting Edit from the drop-down list box. Click on the local menu area on the upper-right corner of the newly added link.

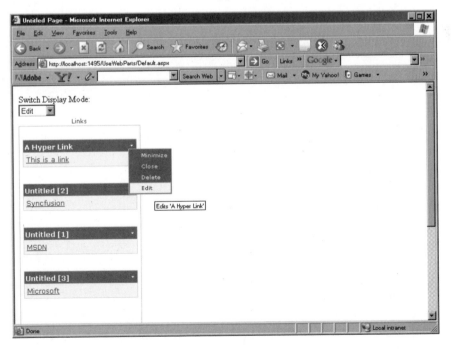

15. Select Edit to edit this link. You should see the Editor Zone appear, along with the new property grid showing text boxes for editing the *DisplayName* and the *URL*:

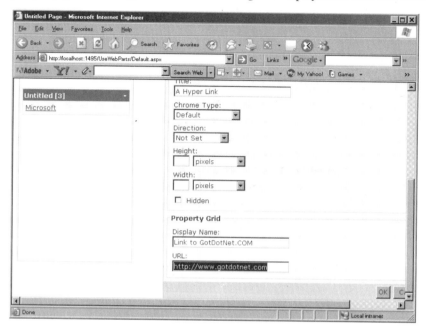

16. Type in a new *DisplayName* and a new *URL*. (The example points to *www.gotdotnet.com*) Select OK. The browser should now show the new properties for the *HyperLinkWebPart*, and you should be able to surf to the site represented by the link.

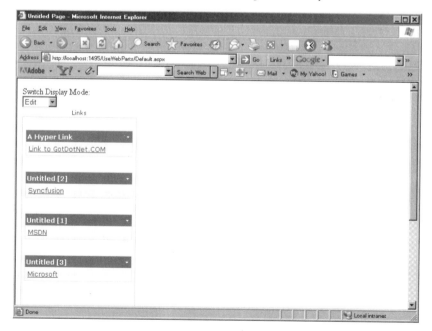

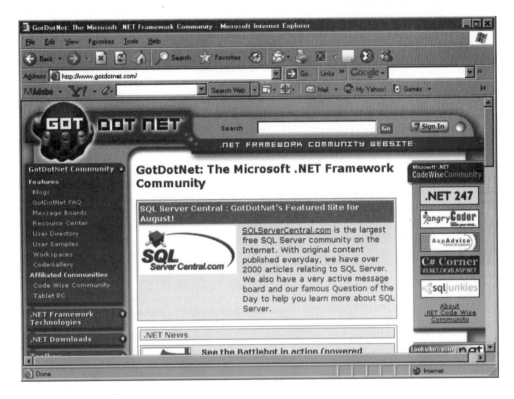

Conclusion

In this chapter, we took a brief look at Web Parts from an ASP.NET point of view. Web Parts are like server-side controls on steroids. They provide layout and control management above and beyond normal server-side controls. The Web Part architecture is built around three fundamental concepts: *WebPart* zones, Web Parts themselves, and the server-side controls that may populate them. Web Parts are especially useful for portal-type applications because of their ability to leverage the personalization and customization facilities of ASP.NET 2.0.

Chapter 7 Quick Reference

To	Do This
Enable a Web page to use *WebPart* controls	Add a *WebPartManager* to the page on which you wish to use *WebPart* controls
Add various editing capabilities to a Web Parts page	Add an *EditorZone* to the page
Add a place in which to position server-side controls to be managed by the Web Part architecture	Add a *WebZone* to the page

To	Do This
Allow users to dynamically add controls from a collection of controls	Add *CatalogZone* to the page
	Add controls to the catalog while in Edit Template mode
Create a Web Part	Derive a class from *System.Web.UI.WebControls.Web-Parts.WebPart*
	Render some HTML OR Create child controls

Chapter 8
A Common Look and Feel

After completing this chapter, you will be able to

- Use Master Pages to develop a common look and feel for your entire site

- Use Themes to apply a style to a page *en masse*

- Use Skins to stylize custom controls

This chapter covers one of ASP.NET 2.0's most useful features as far as developing an identity for your site: Master Pages. A distinguishing characteristic of most well-designed modern Web sites is the consistent look and feel of each page within the site.

For example, many sites incorporate a specific color scheme and fonts. In addition, the way a well-designed site frames information and provides navigation tools is consistent from one page to another. Can you imagine visiting a site where each page appeared radically different from the previous page? At the very least you'd probably be confused. At the very worst, you might even be repulsed.

ASP.NET 2.0 introduces a new feature named Master Pages to help you make your site appear consistent as visitors move around it. In addition, ASP.NET 2.0 features a way to stylize controls. Let's take a look at how they work.

A Common Look and Feel

Getting to the point where Web development tools support creating a common look and feel between all the pages in a site has been a long process. Classic ASP provided a very crude way of spreading a common look and feel throughout a site by incorporating a file inclusion mechanism that pulled one .asp file into another wholesale. It was brute force to say the least. While it worked to a certain degree, you had very little control over the nuances of your site while clumping files together.

ASP.NET 1.0 went quite a bit further by composing the whole page-rendering mechanism out of smaller server-side controls and user controls. We saw this in Chapters 2 and 3. However, even though you could package portions of a Web application's UI into separate modules, you still had some heavy lifting to do to implement a common look and feel among the pages in your application. User controls also support developing a common look and feel. For example, you can create a user control with specific navigation controls and links and use it in the same place on every page in your site. That in itself creates a common look and feel.

While using the custom control/user control approach to break apart a site's user interface is useful for developing a consistent UI, it falls short of being an ideal solution in a couple of ways. First, all the pages in an application need to include the surrounding code. That means that you have to apply the controls in the same way to *each page*. If you decide to change the placement of the controls (or some other aspect not governed by the controls), you have to change each page. Second, every page using a custom control needs a *Register* directive—and more code that needs to be copied. As a reuse model it went much further than earlier approaches (i.e., classic ASP). What you really want is a single place in the site where you can lay out the look and feel of the page *once* and have it propagate across the site.

One way to accomplish this goal and avoid building pages one at a time is to build a primary class from which all the pages in your application will derive. Because ASP.NET is built on an object model based on the *Page* class, why not simply add a new layer to your application? Figure 8-1 shows a diagram illustrating how you might build a set of pages from a single base page.

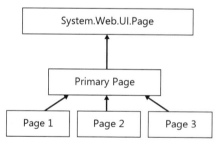

Figure 8-1   A base class to implement functionality common among several pages.

All the ASPX pages inherit from the same code-behind class deriving from the primary class (which in turn derives from *System.Web.UI.Page*). The primary class takes responsibility for loading the controls necessary for the site's look and feel. Then each separate page is responsible for managing the rest.

This approach works, as long as you don't mind doing a lot of coding . In addition, there was no design support in ASP.NET 1.*x* for this sort of thing, and messing with the *Page* class hierarchy in Visual Studio sometimes would break the project.

ASP.NET 2.0 introduced Master Pages to support developing a common look and feel across your entire site.

ASP.NET 2.0 Master Pages

Master Pages represent a sort of metapage. They have much the same structure as normal pages. However, they live in files named with the "master" extension. A Master Page serves as a template that renders a common appearance to all pages based on it. Master Pages use XHTML document tags (such as *<html>*, *<head>*, and *<body>*) that apply only to the Master Page. When you surf to a page that has a Master Page applied to it, the request and response are filtered through the Master Page. The Master Page may not be served by itself, ensuring that each page has a common look and feel. ASP.NET merges the Master Page and the ASPX page (the content page) into a single class. At that point, the class processes requests and renders output like any other *System.Web.UI.Page*–derived class.

Because Master Pages are similar to normal ASPX pages, they may contain the same sort of content and functionality as normal pages. That is, they may contain server-side controls, user controls, and markup. In addition to markup and controls, a Master Page may contain instances of the *System.Web.UI.WebControls.ContentPlaceHolder* control. As its name implies, the content placeholder stands in place of the real content that will eventually appear in pages based upon the Master Page. A Master Page renders all the elements it contains. That is, those elements not contained within a *System.Web.UI.WebControls.ContentPlaceHolder* control.

Because Master Pages play a part in how the final page handler is synthesized, they work a bit differently than the straight inheritance technique described above (that is, writing a base class to implement common functionality via inheritance). As the page executes, the Master Page injects its own content into the ASPX page using the Master Page. Specifically, the Master Content ends up being represented by a control that is added to the ASPX page's *Controls* collection, where it's rendered in the same way all other controls are.

In addition to most normal page attributes and functionality, Master Pages may contain the following directives (which are also available to ASC files).

- *AutoEventWireup*
- *ClassName*
- *CompilerOptions*
- *Debug Description*
- *EnableViewState Explicit*
- *Inherits*
- *Language*
- *Strict*
- *Src*
- *WarningLevel*
- *Master*

The following exercise illustrates developing a site around a Master Page.

Using a Master Page

1. Create a new site named MasterPageSite.

2. Add a new item to the page. Select **MasterPage** from the available templates. Name it MasterPage.master. The following graphic shows adding a Master Page template.

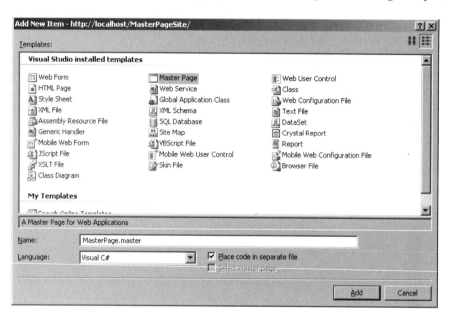

Visual Studio will pump out code like this in a file named MasterPage.master:

```
<%@ Master Language="VB"
CodeFile="ASPNetStepByStepMasterPage.master.vb"
Inherits="ASPNetStepByStepMasterPage" %>

<!DOCTYPE html PUBLIC "-//W3C//DTD XHTML 1.1//EN"
"http://www.w3.org/TR/xhtml11/DTD/xhtml11.dtd">

<html xmlns="http://www.w3.org/1999/xhtml" >
<head runat="server">
    <title>Untitled Page</title>
</head>
<body>
    <form id="form1" runat="server">
    <div>
        <asp:contentplaceholder
        id="ContentPlaceHolder1" runat="server">
        </asp:contentplaceholder>
    </div>
    </form>
</body>
</html>
```

This is what the Master Page looks like in design mode:

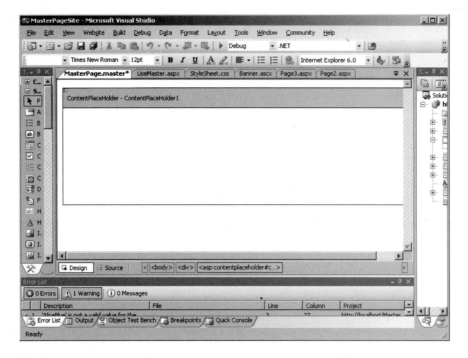

3. Update the background color of the Master Page. In the Properties dialog box, select the **Document** element from the combo box and update the document's background color. The example here uses light gray. This will let you see that the Master Page is really being used in subsequent ASPX files.

4. Create a new form and name it UseMaster.aspx. Make sure the Select master page check box is checked, like so:

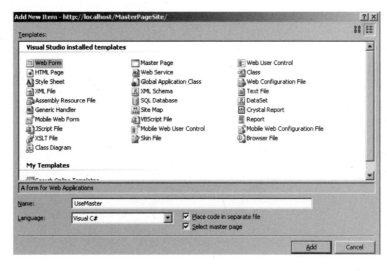

Visual Studio will ask you to select a Master Page, as shown in the following graphic.

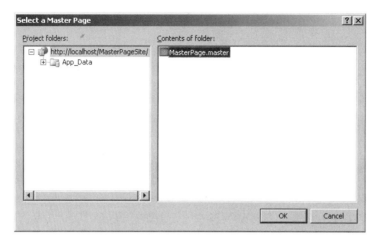

When you view UseMaster.aspx in the designer, it looks like the MasterPage.master file. Notice the grayish hue applied to the page. This lets you know the Master Page is really being applied here.

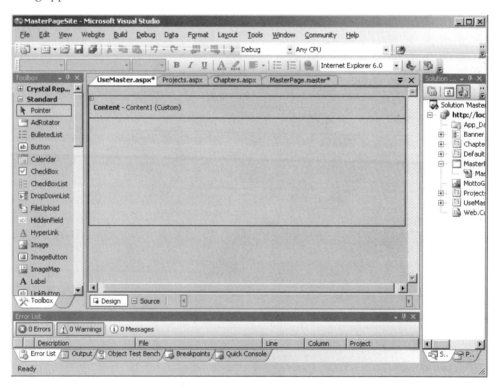

This is the code generated by Visual Studio to support using the Master Page:

```
<%@ Page Language="C#"
    MasterPageFile="~/MasterPage.master" AutoEventWireup="true"
    CodeFile="UseMaster.aspx.cs" Inherits="UseMaster"
    Title="Untitled Page" trace="false" %>

<%@ Register Src="Banner.ascx"
TagName="Banner"
TagPrefix="uc1" %>
<asp:Content ID="Content1"
    ContentPlaceHolderID="ContentPlaceHolder1" Runat="Server"">
</asp:Content>
```

5. Now add some content to UseMaster.aspx. Add a label to the content placeholder. Have it say something so you can distinguish this as a separate page.

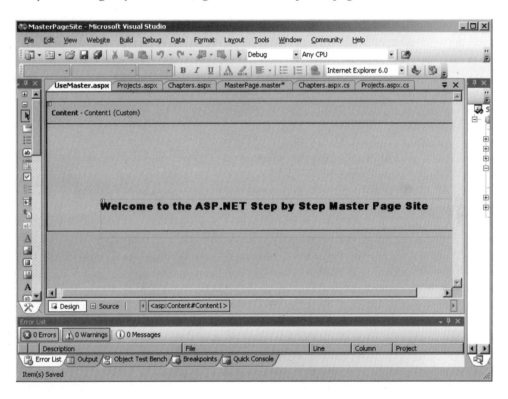

6. Add two more pages to the site. The example here includes a page describing the chapter content of this book and a second page describing the projects. You may use this, or add your own content. The important thing is to add two more pages and apply the Master Page to them (that is, create the Web forms with the Select master page box checked).

    Add some content to the two pages in the content placeholders. That way you can distinguish the pages (we'll add navigation support later).

The following two graphics show the example site's pages containing a *ListBox* to select the topic and a *TextBox* to hold information about the topic.

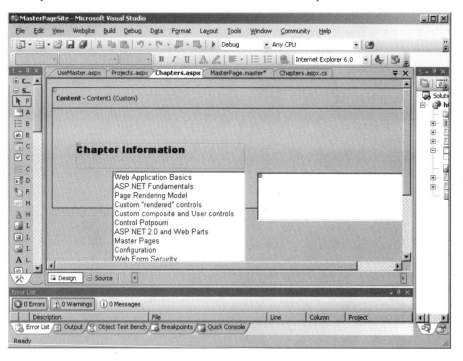

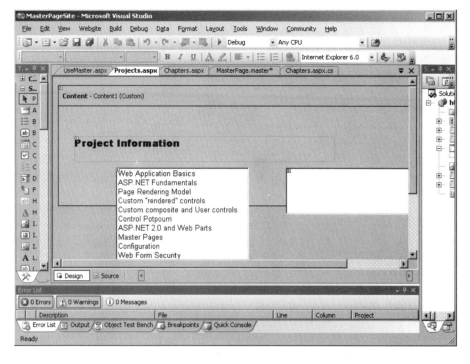

7. Go back to the MasterPage.master page and update it so it has a bit more content. Use the **Layout | Insert Table** menu option to insert a table immediately above the content pane on the Master Page. Give the table one row and two columns. Size it so that the left cell is narrow and the right cell is wide. It should look something like this:

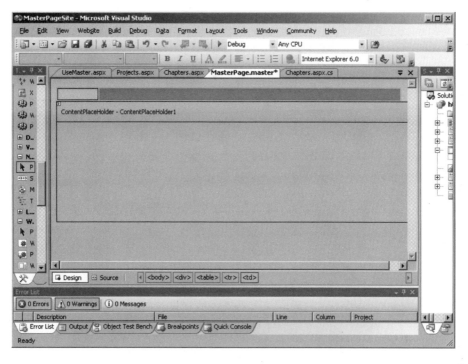

8. Add a menu to the leftmost cell in the table. In customizing the menu, add an AutoFormat style to it. The example here uses the Classic style. Add three items to the menu for navigating to the three pages in this site—the Home page, the Chapters page, and the Projects page.

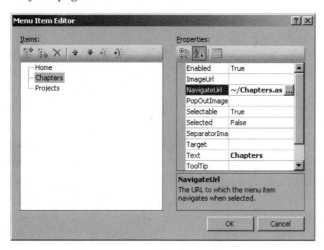

Set up the appropriate navigation for each menu option. That is, have the Home menu item navigate to the UseMaster.aspx page. Have the Chapters menu item navigate to the Chapters.aspx file. Finally, have the Projects menu item navigate to the Projects.aspx file. You may do this by clicking the navigation button in the *Navigation* field of the *Property* page:

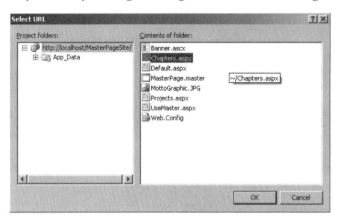

You should end up with something like this:

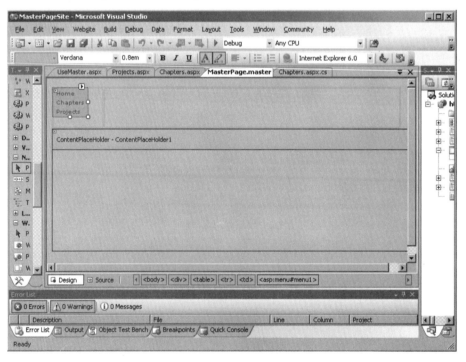

9. Finally, no Master Page is complete without a banner. Use the bitmap editor (or Paint-brush–Pbrush.exe) to draw a banner. The one in this example is about 1000 pixels wide by 90 pixels high. Drop the banner into the table cell on the right. Your Master Page should something look like this now:

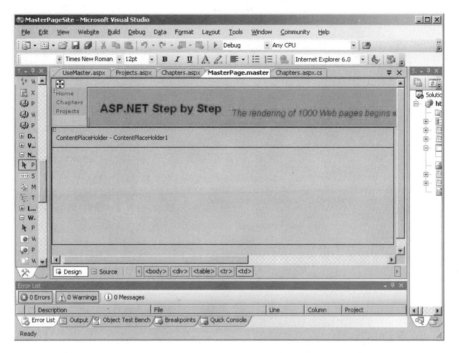

Because the UseMaster.aspx, Chapters.aspx, and Projects.aspx files were created using the Master Page, they have the menu and banner built in automatically. Surf to the Use-Master.aspx file and browse through the menu items. You should see that each page has a common look and feel, but with the correct content.

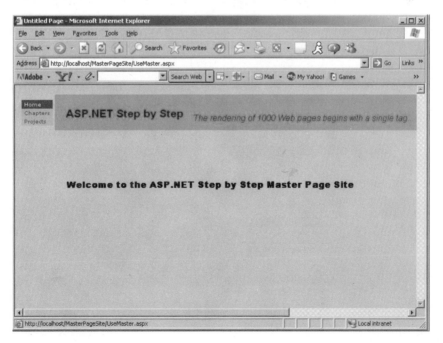

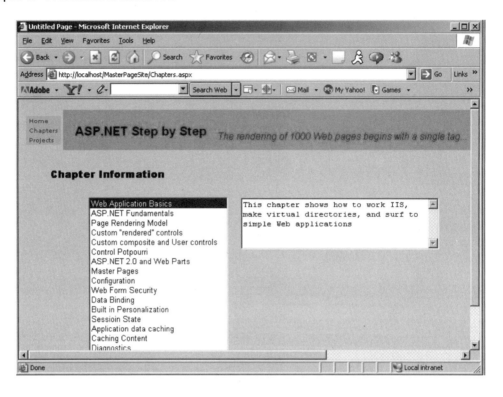

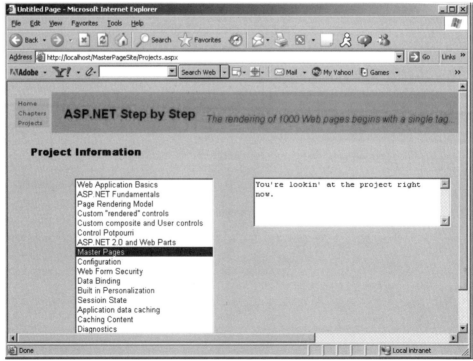

Master Pages offer significant improvements over earlier versions of classic ASP and ASP.NET for developing a common look and feel among all the pages in your application. Of course, you may use multiple Master Pages in a project, and you may also nest them.

A second way to help manage the look and feel of your application is ASP.NET Themes.

Themes

Master Pages control the general layout of a series of pages within an application. However, there are other elements (those that are subject to change between pages) that you might like to have remain constant. Themes provide a means of applying common styles to the elements on each page in your site.

If you're familiar with Cascading Style Sheets (CSS), you will feel very at home with Themes. The two techniques are similar because through both techniques you may define the visual styles for your Web pages. Themes go a step beyond Cascading Style Sheets. You may use Themes to specify styles, graphics, and even CSS files within the pages of your applications. When available, you may apply ASP.NET Themes at the application, page, or server control level.

Themes are represented as text-based style definitions in ASP.NET 2.0. ASP.NET 2.0 already includes a number of Themes straight out of the box. You'll find these Themes located at `C:\WINDOWS\Microsoft.NET\Framework\v2.0.xxxxx\ASP.NETClientFiles\Themes`. ASP.NET 2.0 includes some predefined Themes. In addition, you may define and use your own Themes.

The following exercise shows how to create and use a Theme.

Creating and Using a Theme

1. Add a new form to the MasterPagesSite project. Name the page UseThemes.aspx. Turn off the Select master page check box if it happens to be turned on before you commit to creating the page.

2. Add a Theme folder to your project. Highlight the Web site node in the Solution Explorer. Right-click and select **Add Folder**. Select **Theme Folder**. This will create an App_Themes directory for you.

3. Create a Default Themes folder under the App_Themes folder. Right-click on the App_Theme folder. Select **Add Folder**, and then select **Theme Folder** from the menu. Name the folder Default.

4. Add a new Style sheet to the Default Themes folder. Right-click on the Default Themes folder and select **Add New Item**. Select the Style Sheet template. Name the Style sheet Default.css.

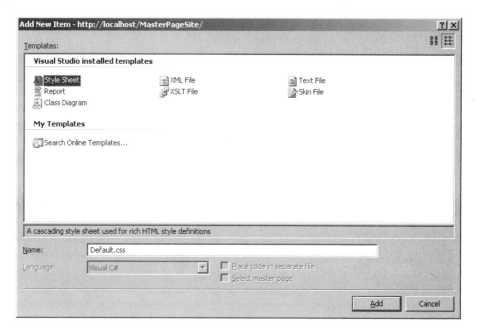

5. Build the style sheet. When the style sheet is open in Visual Studio, you may right-click on the Elements node to modify the style for the node. For example, if you want to change the style of the *<H1>* tag, you would right-click on the Elements node and select **Add Style Rule**. To change the style of the *<H1>* tag, select it from the list of elements and move it into the Style rule hierarchy by clicking the **>** button, as shown here:

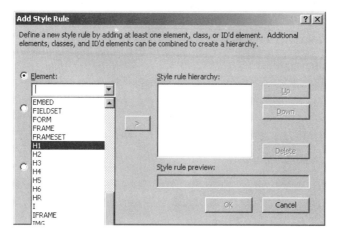

To modify the style, right-click on the H1 node in the CSS outline page and select **Build Style**. Here's the Style Builder dialog box:

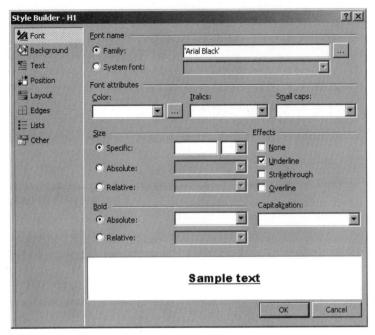

The sample application included with the CD sets the font to Arial Black with an underscore.

6. Now test the Theme by declaring it in the page and by typing a heading with H1 tags, like so:

```
<%@ Page Language="C#" AutoEventWireup="true"
CodeFile="UseThemes.aspx.cs

"Theme=<Default"
trace="false" Inherits="UseThemes" %>
<%@ Register Src="Banner.ascx" TagName="Banner" TagPrefix="uc1" %>

<!DOCTYPE html PUBLIC "-//W3C//DTD XHTML 1.1//EN"
"http://www.w3.org/TR/xhtml11/DTD/xhtml11.dtd">

<html xmlns="http://www.w3.org/1999/xhtml" >
<head runat="server">
    <title>Untitled Page</title>
</head>
<body>
    <form id="form1" runat="server">
    <div>
    <H1> How does this look? </H1>
    </div>
    </form>
</body>
</html>
```

Here's how the Themed page appears in the browser with the new theme (the H1 Tag set to the new font and set to use the underscore in this example):

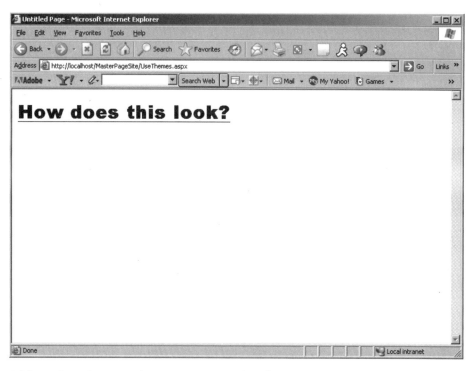

7. Add another Theme to the project. Name the Theme SeeingRed. That is, create a new Theme folder and add a new style sheet of the same name. Make the *<H1>* tag use a red color font this time. Then change the Theme used by the page to SeeingRed:

```
Theme="SeeingRed"
```

Surf to the page to see the *<H1>* tag printed in red.

This is just a taste of the kinds of things you can do by providing Themes for a page. Once a Theme is defined, you may apply it by declaring it as part of the *Page* declaration, or by intercepting the *PreInit* event and changing the Theme property in the page to a valid Theme.

Going hand in hand with Themes are Skins. Let's look at those.

Skins

Skins complement Master Pages and Themes as a way to manage the style of your Web site. Using Skins is almost like combining *WebControl*-based controls with Cascading Style Sheets. Another way to think of Skins is as a way to set certain properties of a control as a group. For example, you may want to define different coloring schemes for a control such as the *Table* control. The *Calendar* control is also a good one because it's so rich. By providing Skins for controls, you can have a number of different appearance options for various controls at your disposal without having to go into detail and manage the control properties one by one.

You have actually used Skins already. Many server-side controls already support style templates. For example, when working with the *TreeView* earlier, you saw that you could apply one of several styles to it. Earlier in this chapter we looked at applying a set of color attributes to the *Menu* control. In this section we'll see how Skins work and how to apply them.

Skin files define specific controls and the attributes that apply to them. That is, a .skin file contains server-side control declarations. The Skin file's job is to preset the style properties for the control. Skin files reside in named Theme folders for an application, accompanied by any necessary CSS files.

The following exercise illustrates how to create Skins for some controls on your Web site.

Create a Skin

1. Create a Skin file by right-clicking on the **SeeingRed** folder in the App_Theme node on the Solution Explorer and selecting **Add New Item**. Choose **Text File** from the templates. Name the file SeeingRed.skin.

2. In the "SeeingRed".skin file, pre-declare some controls for which you'd like to have default property values set. For example, the following SeeingRed.skin file declares default properties for some controls. These controls have their various colors defaulting to assorted shades of red.

    ```
    <asp:Label runat="server" ForeColor="red"
    Font-Size="14pt" Font-Names="Verdana" />
    <asp:button runat="server" borderstyle="Solid"
    borderwidth="2px" bordercolor="#ff0000" backcolor="#cc0000"/>
    <asp:CheckBoxList runat=server ForeColor="#ff0000" />
    <asp:RadioButtonList runat=server ForeColor="#ff9999" />
    <asp:Table runat="server" Bordercolor="#ff9999" Borderwidth="2"
    ForeColor="#ff3366"/>
    ```

3. Now add those controls for which you've pre-declared attributes in the Skin file onto the UseThemes.aspx page to see how the SeeingRed.skin file applies. While you probably won't be able to see the effect in the following graphic, you will no doubt see the effect when running the sample application.

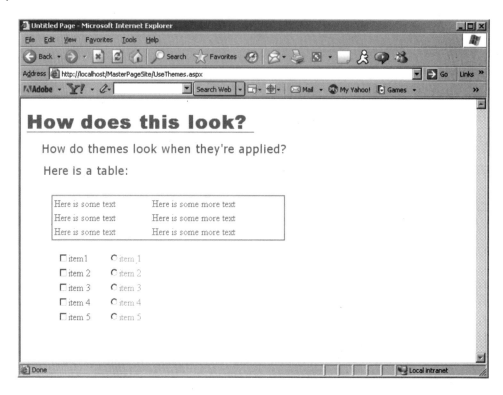

The SeeingRed.skin file will automatically be applied by declaring the SeeingRed Theme within the page. You may also prescribe different Skins at runtime, and you can apply separate Skins to each control.

Conclusion

One of the most often requested features for ASP.NET has been to support a common look and feel for a site. The Master Pages feature within ASP.NET 2.0 pushes this capability to the forefront and makes developing a set of pages with similar aspects a very doable proposition. In addition to Master Pages, ASP.NET 2.0 Themes represent a way to apply global style attributes to all the pages in your application.

ASP.NET also supports specifying default values for specific server-side controls through a Skin file. Skins offer a finer-grained approach to applying styles in a control-centric manner.

Chapter 8 Quick Reference

To	Do This
Define a page that will represent the common look and feel of a series of pages in a Web site	Add a Master Page to the site

To	Do This
Create a page based on the Master Page	Check the Select master page check box when creating forms for a site
Add elements to the Master Page that will show up in pages based on the Master Page	Place elements outside the area represented by the content pane. A Layout table is useful for this
Add individual elements to content pages	Add elements within the content page shown on the page
Create a Theme for a page	Add a new Theme folder to the App_Theme folder within your application. Use a Cascading Style Sheet (CSS) to define styles and classes for the Theme
Apply a Theme to a page	Set the Theme property within the *Page* Directive OR Set the Theme property within the page during the page's *PreInit* event
Create a Skin	Create a text file within a Theme folder. Name the file <whateverthethemefolderis>.skin. Add control declarations with their properties set to default values

Chapter 9

Configuration

After completing this chapter, you will be able to

■ Understand the way .NET handles configuration

■ Apply configuration settings to ASP.NET Applications

■ Manage ASP.NET configuration using the ASP.NET Administration tool

■ Manage ASP.NET configuration using the MMC Snap-in

This chapter introduces the method in which ASP.NET manages configuration information. It gives a taste of how ASP.NET configuration works. We'll see details about ASP.NET configuration in later chapters. ASP.NET is a feature-rich system for developing and deploying Web sites. The features we'll see in more detail as we examine ASP.NET further include some the following:

■ session state

■ caching content to help optimize your Web site's responses

■ tracing requests

■ mapping specific file extensions to custom handlers

■ authenticating users

Each of these features are controlled by a number of separate parameters. For example, when you enable session state for your application, you may choose where to locate your application's session state (in process, on a separate machine using a daemon process, or using SQL Server). You may also configure the lifetime of your session state and how your application tracks the session state (via a cookie or some other method).

A second feature controlled through the configuration file is caching output. When you cache the content of your site, you may vary the lifetime of your cached content and where it's cached (on the server, on the client, or on the proxy).

For both these features (and others) the configuration options are governed by various configuration files. Here we first examine the nature of Windows configuration, and then look specifically at how ASP.NET handles configuration. In ASP.NET 1.x, modifying the configuration of your application meant editing the XML-based configuration file by hand. Fortunately, ASP.NET 2.0 offers two tools that make configuration a much easier proposition. One tool is the ASP.NET configuration tab available through the normal IIS configuration panel. The second tool is the Web site Administration tool, available through the Web site | Web Administration menu in Visual Studio. We'll cover these tools as well.

Windows Configuration

Every computing platform needs a configuration mechanism. That is, a number of various parameters can govern the behavior of the operating system and programs. For example, Windows provides an environment variable named *PATH* that controls the search path for executable programs. Other environment variables include one named *TEMP* (controls the location of temporary files) and *USERPROFILE* (identifies the location of the current user's profile information).

In addition, individual applications may require different settings specific to that program. For example, many applications require some version checking or that specific DLLs be available. These actions may vary from one installation to the next, and it's not a good idea to hard-code the settings into your application. Instead, you store values in a secondary file that accompanies the application.

During the early days of Windows, .INI files worked quite well; there is even a set of Windows API functions for managing configuration parameters. Now that we are a few years into the new millennium, XML is the way to go. .NET depends upon XML files (Machine.Config and Web.Config) for its configuration.

A name/value pair in Win.INI that turns on OLE messaging looks like:

```
OLEMessaging=1
```

> **Note** The second way in which applications have configured themselves in the past is through the Registry. The Registry is a centralized database applications may use to store name/value pairs. The reason ASP.NET doesn't use the registry to configure information is because global nature Registry is in direct conflict with ASP.NET's need for flexibility during deployment. Settings stored in the Registry would need to be copied through the Registry API, whereas Configuration files may simply be copied.

.NET Configuration

.NET configuration files are well-formed XML files whose vocabulary is understood by the .NET runtime. You can see a listing of all the files by looking in the configuration directory. The .NET runtime reads these configuration files into memory on various occasions to set the various .NET runtime parameters. The first configuration file we'll take a look at is Machine.Config.

Machine.Config

The default .NET configuration for your machine is declared within a file named Machine.Config. You can find Machine.Config within the directory c:\Windows\ Microsoft.NET\Framework\ver<*whatevertheversionis*>\config. Machine.Config sets the default .NET application behaviors for the entire machine.

.NET version 2.0 has made a number of improvements to the Machine.Config arrangement. ASP.NET 1.x lumped all of Machine.Config into a single file—even comments and configuration information for all separate browsers. The current version of Machine.Config is trimmed down substantially from version 1.x. The comments have been moved to a separate file named Machine.Config.Comments, and separate browser definition capability files have been moved to separate configuration files. This is important to know because the Machine.Config comments are often more useful as documentation for configuring .NET than the regular online documentation. As you configure your various ASP.NET applications, the Machine.Config comments should be the first place you look for information.

Configuration Section Handlers

At the top of Machine.Config you'll see a number of Configuration Section Handlers. Each of these handlers understands a specific vocabulary for configuring .NET (and ultimately ASP.NET). While Machine.Config controls the settings for the entire machine, ASP.NET applications rely on files named "Web.Config" to manage configuration. We'll see much more about Web.Config shortly. However, for now here is a small snippet that you might find in a Web.Config file for a specific application.

```
<?xml version="1.0" encoding="utf-8"?>
<configuration
xmlns="http://schemas.microsoft.com/.NetConfiguration/v2.0">
    <system.web>
        <authentication mode="Forms" />
        <sessionState mode="SQLServer" cookieless="UseUri" timeout="25" />
    </system.web>
</configuration>
```

This small segment tells the ASP.NET runtime to use Forms Authentication (one of ASP.NET's authentication options) to authenticate users of this site. The configuration information also tells ASP.NET to use SQL Server to manage session state, to allow session state information to expire after 25 minutes, and to track session information using a session ID embedded within the request URI.

You can see from this example that configuring ASP.NET relies on the ability of the runtime to understand some keywords. In this case, the keywords *authentication*, *mode*, and *Forms* tell ASP.NET how to manage authentication. ASP.NET must correctly interpret *sessionState*, *mode*, *SQLServer*, *cookieless*, *UseURI*, and *timeout* to know how to manage an application's session state.

The .NET components that understand these vocabularies are listed near the top of Machine.Config.

```
<configuration>
  <configSections>
    <section name="appSettings"
     type="entire strong assembly name here… "
        restartOnExternalChanges="false" />
    <section name="connectionStrings"
      type="entire strong assembly name here… " />
    …
    <sectionGroup name="system.web"
      type="entire strong assembly name here.. ">
      <section name="authentication"
        type=" entire strong assembly name here.. "
          allowDefinition="MachineToApplication" />
      <section name="sessionState"
        type=" entire strong assembly name here.. "
          allowDefinition="MachineToApplication" />
    …
    </sectionGroup>
  </configSections>
</configuration>
```

The listing above is necessarily abbreviated. Go ahead and take a look at Machine.Config and you'll see the section handlers in their full glory. The *sessionState* configuration settings are interpreted by an assembly with the strong name *System.Web.Configuration.SessionStateSection, System.Web, Version=2.0.0.0, Culture=neutral, PublicKeyToken=b03f5f7f11d50a3a*. A *strong name* fully specifies the name of an assembly including a version (to ensure version compatibility) and a public token (to ensure the assembly has not been tampered with).

Web.Config

While Machine.Config lays out the default setting for your applications, the default settings are generally targeted toward the most common use cases (rather than some special configuration you may need to apply to your application). For example, *sessionState* is configured to be handled in process by default. That's fine when you're developing, but almost certainly is not appropriate for a commercial-grade application that is servicing many diverse clients.

Because all your .NET applications depend upon Machine.Config to configure them, making changes to Machine.Config could potentially affect your other applications. It's a bad idea to update Machine.Config directly.

Stand-alone .NET applications depend upon configuration files modeled after the application name to configure themselves. For example, an application named MyApp.EXE would have a configuration file named Myapp.EXE.Config. Of course, ASP.NET applications aren't named in that way. Instead, the ASP.NET runtime expects configuration information to be declared in a file named Web.Config.

To override the default settings within Machine.Config, you simply need to include a file named Web.Config in your application's virtual directory. For example, the following code sets up the Web application to which it applies. The Config file turns on Forms Authentication and tracing.

```xml
<?xml version="1.0" encoding="utf-8"?>
<configuration
xmlns="http://schemas.microsoft.com/.NetConfiguration/v2.0">
    <system.web>
        <authentication mode="Forms" />
        <trace enable=true/>
    </system.web>
</configuration>
```

The configuration settings your application actually sees have been inherited from a (potentially) long line of other Web.Config files. Figure 9-1 illustrates how the configuration settings accumulate through the Web.Config file standing in the directory path taken by the request. After Machine.Config sets up the default configuration settings, different configuration files in the same path have the opportunity to tweak the settings for a single application. Figure 9-1 shows how configuration settings are modified via individual configuration files.

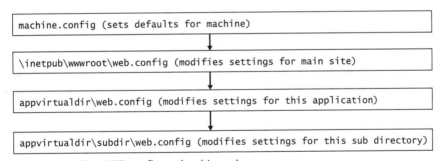

Figure 9-1 The .NET configuration hierarchy.

In Figure 9-1, you can see that Machine.Config sets the default configuration. The subsequent Web.Config files are merged into a new set of configuration parameters along the way. After Machine.Config sets up the configuration parameters, the Web.Config in Inetpub takes over, modifying the settings in Machine.Config. As soon as the Web.Config from the Inetpub directory touches the configuration, the Web.Config contained in the application's virtual directory gets a crack at changing the settings. Finally, the Web.Config within a subdirectory of the main virtual directory modifies the settings. Note that ASP.NET configuration happens *after* IIS configures itself through the Metabase.

This way of managing configuration information works well. Many of the normal defaults work well and you need to tweak only a few items, so you just drop a Web.Config in your virtual directory and/or subdirectory.

However, managing settings that way (by littering your hard disk with Web.Config files) can get a bit unwieldy if lots of different parts of your application need separate configurations. The ASP.NET configuration schema includes a *Location* element for specifying different settings for different directories—but they can all go in a master configuration file for your application.

For example, the following configuration section will remove the ability for the AppSubDir directory to process standard ASP.NET Web Services. The *remove* instruction causes ASP.NET to have amnesia about all files with the extension .asmx.

```
<configuration>
  <location path="appSubDir">
    <system.web>
      <httpHandlers>
        <remove verb="*" path="*.asmx" />
      </httpHandlers>
    </system.web>
  </location>
</configuration>
```

You could also apply other specific settings to the subdirectory. We'll look at security in depth in the next chapter. Of course, ASP.NET configuration files include terms to manage authorization and authentication. This is a perfect use for the *local* element. The following configuration snippet allows all users into the main (virtual) directory while requiring users wanting access to the PagesRequiringAuth subdirectory to be authenticated.

```
<configuration>
  <system.web>
    <authorization>
      <allow users="*" />
    </authorization>
  </system.web>
  <location path="pagesRequiringAuth">
    <system.web>
      <authorization>
        <deny users="?" />
      </authorization>
    </system.web>
  </location>
</configuration>
```

Configuration in ASP.NET 1.*x*

Configuration within ASP.NET 1.*x* was done entirely by typing changes into a target Web.Config file manually. For example, if you wanted your application to use *SQLServer* as a session state database, you'd need to insert the correct verbiage into the application's

Web.Config file keystroke by keystroke. Unfortunately, there was no configuration compiler to help ensure the syntax was correct. If you typed something wrong, you usually wouldn't know about it until you ran the application, at which point ASP.NET would cough up a cryptic error message.

Configuration in ASP.NET 2.0

ASP.NET 2.0 introduces some major improvements to the process of managing ASP.NET applications. While you may still type configuration information into the Web.Config file manually, ASP.NET 2.0 provides some new configuration utilities. These tools include the Web site Administration tool available in Visual Studio, and the ASP.NET configuration tab available through IIS.

Configuring Your Application

In this exercise, you'll change some application settings within an application's configuration and see how they're reflected within Web.Config.

1. Begin by creating a new Web site named ConfigORama. Make it a regular ASP.NET site (not an empty one). It can be a File Web site.

2. After Visual Studio generates the application, select the **Web site | ASP.NET** Configuration menu item. This will bring up the ASP.NET Administration tool:

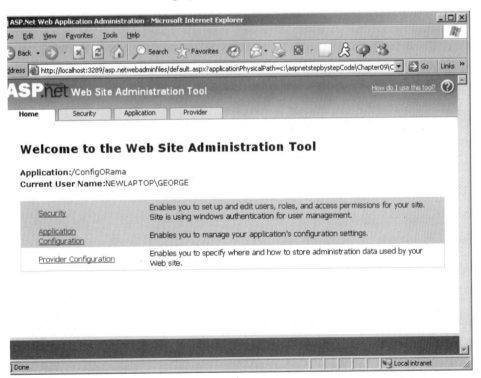

The ASP.NET Administration Tool

> **Note** Notice the Administration tool includes three tabs: Security, Application, and Provider. The Security tab manages authentication and authorization settings. That is, you may use the Security tab to add users and assign roles to them. We'll explore that process in detail in the next chapter.
>
> The Application tab is for maintaining various settings related to your application. Some basic configuration settings are controlled here, including maintaining key-value pairs specific to your application, SMTP settings for defining how the site manages e-mail, and turning debugging and tracing on and off. You can also use the Application tab to take your application offline in case you need to perform maintenance.
>
> Finally, the Provider tab is used to manage database providers. While earlier versions of .NET (ADO.NET) supported a managed layer between your application and various data sources, managing the providers still took a bit of programming skill. ADO.NET includes multiple implementations of the same interfaces. If you're diligent and disciplined enough, you can minimize the amount of code that needs to be changed if your enterprise decides to go with another database vendor. ASP.NET 2.0 introduces the Data Provider architecture to further abstract the details of connecting and using a data source.
>
> ASP.NET hooks you up with a database stored in the Web site's App_Data folder. The Provider tab is where you go when you decide to use another database in your application.

The Web Site Administration tool lets you manage parts of Web.Config without having to type things by hand. It's accessible from Visual Studio. Visual Studio doesn't provide a Web.Config by default. The Web Site Administration tool will create a Web.Config file for you. The tool will also create a database suitable for consumption by SQL Server Express in the Data folder of your Web site for storing application data.

The ASP.NET configuration facilities include a number of inherited settings. Those types of settings are likely to be found in many Web sites and are represented as inherited settings. For example, many sites use a database connection string. To avoid hard-coding the string into the site's code, connection strings are usually included as part of Web.Config. The *Connection-String* application setting is an inherited setting.

3. Continue working with configuration. Go to the Application tab and add a couple of application settings. Add a setting named *ConnectionString* and one named *AnotherString*. In this exercise, it doesn't matter what you type as the corresponding value (it will later). The example on the CD uses a realistic connection string for the *ConnectionString* value and *AnotherValue* for the value associated with the other string.

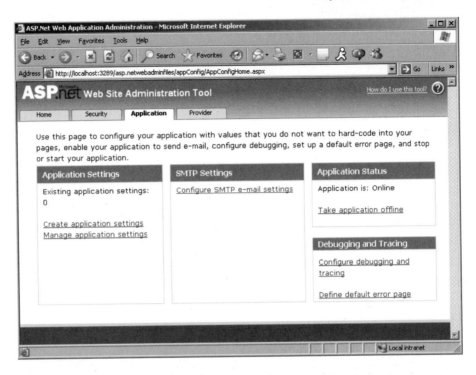

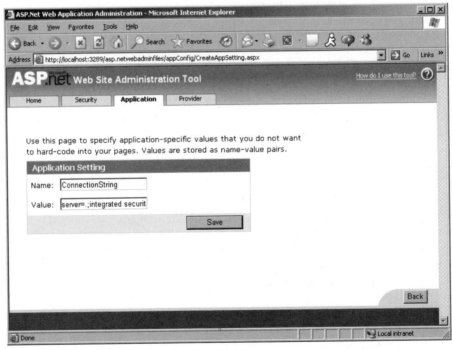

4. Open the application's Web.Config file. You should see an entry for *AnotherString*. Then look for *ConnectionString*—it's not there. That's because *ConnectionString* is an inherited application setting.

   Web.Config should look like this now:

   ```
   <?xml version="1.0" encoding="utf-8"?>
   <configuration
   xmlns="http://schemas.microsoft.com/.NetConfiguration/v2.0">
       <appSettings>
           <add key="AnotherString" value="AnotherValue" />
       </appSettings>
   </configuration>
   ```

5. Now write some code to access the application settings you just added. They're available via a class named *ConfigurationManager*. Add a combo box to the Default.aspx form to hold the *Application Settings* keys and another label to display the values. Also add a button that will look up the value associated with the *Application Settings* key. In the *Page_Load* handler, interrogate the *ConfigurationManager* for all the application settings.

   ```
   public partial class _Default : System.Web.UI.Page
   {
       protected void Page_Load(object sender, EventArgs e)
       {


           if (!this.IsPostBack)
           {
               foreach (String strKey
                   in ConfigurationManager.AppSettings.AllKeys)
               {
                   this.
                       DropDownListApplicationSettings.
                       Items.Add(strKey);
               }
           }

       }
       protected void ButtonLookupSetting_Click(object sender, EventArgs e)
       {

           String strSetting;
           strSetting =
               ConfigurationManager.AppSettings[this.
                   DropDownListApplicationSettings.
                   SelectedItem.Text];
           this.LabelSetting.Text = strSetting;

       }
   }
   ```

6. Compile the program and run the site. When you start the page, it will load the combo box with all the keys from the *ConfigurationManager.AppSettings* collection. When you

select the Application Settings using the key from the combo box, the code looks up the value of the application setting and displays it in the label.

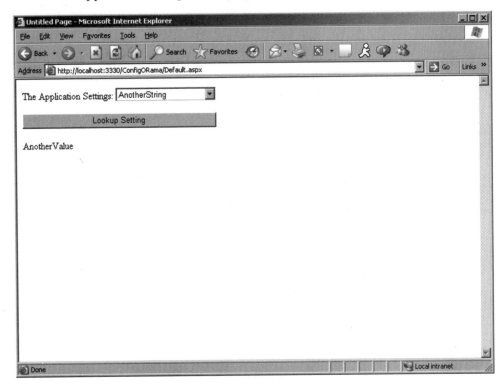

ASP.NET also supports another way to manage Application Settings. It's the MMC Snap-in for ASP.NET.

ASP.NET MMC Snap-in

If your site is running from within a virtual directory (through IIS), you may use the ASP.NET Snap-in (available through the Microsoft Management Console, or MMC) to edit configuration information. To use this, you need to have your site managed by IIS.

While the Snap-in is only available on the computer hosting the site, it is much more extensive in its ability to manage your ASP.NET application.

Here's an exercise to familiarize yourself with the ASP.NET MMC Snap-in.

Use the MMC Snap-in

1. Begin by creating a new Web site. Call it ConfigORamaIIS. Make it an HTTP site managed by IIS (that is, select HTTP in the Location combo box on the page). Run it from

your own computer (*localhost*). Visual Studio will create a virtual directory for you and point itself to the virtual directory.

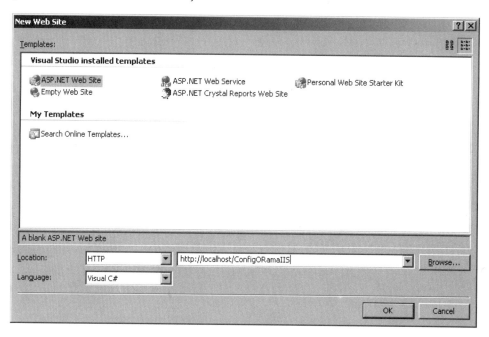

2. Open up IIS. Look for the ConfigORamaIIS site:

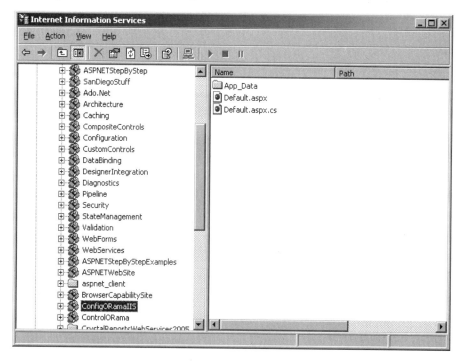

3. Right-click on the virtual directory node to get to the Properties. Select the **ASP.NET** tab.

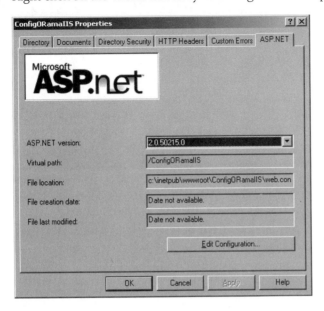

4. Click the **Edit Configuration** button to get to the configuration editor.

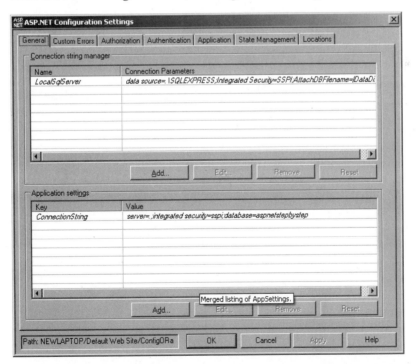

The first tab in the Configuration Settings dialog box is the General tab. Notice there is a Connection string manager section (with a default connection string) and an

Application settings section. Click the **Add** button underneath the Application settings window. Here's where you may add application settings—just as you did with the ASP.NET Configuration tool. Clicking the Add button brings up the Edit/Add Application Settings editor. Add a key-value pair.

5. Open Web.Config within your application. It should now include an entry for *AnotherString*.

```xml
<?xml version="1.0" encoding="utf-8"?>
<configuration
xmlns="http://schemas.microsoft.com/.NetConfiguration/v2.0">
    <appSettings>
        <add key="AnotherString" value="AnotherValue" />
    </appSettings>
</configuration>
```

6. Add a setting named *BackgroundColor*. Give it a value of **#00FF**. This will expose a setting that administrators can use to change the background color of Default.aspx (after support is built into the code).

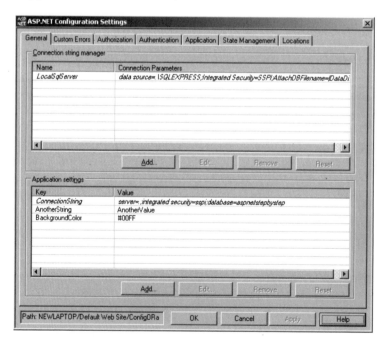

7. Now add a method to the Default page (Default.aspx.cs) to retrieve the background color. It should be available from the *ConfigurationManager.AppSettings* collection.

```
public partial class _Default : System.Web.UI.Page
{
    protected String BackgroundColor()
    {
        return
          ConfigurationManager.AppSettings["BackgroundColor"];
    }

    protected void Page_Load(object sender, EventArgs e)
        {
        }
}
```

8. Open the Default.aspx page to the Source view and update the body tag to retrieve the background color from the Application Settings. Use the <% and %> braces to mark executable code. Also add a line to the ASPX file to display background color value.

```
<%@ Page Language="C#" AutoEventWireup="true"
CodeFile="Default.aspx.cs" Inherits="_Default" %>
<!DOCTYPE html PUBLIC
"-//W3C//DTD XHTML 1.1//EN"
"http://www.w3.org/TR/xhtml11/DTD/xhtml11.dtd">
<html xmlns="http://www.w3.org/1999/xhtml" >
<head runat="server">
    <title>Untitled Page</title>
</head>
<body bgcolor="<%=BackgroundColor()%>">
    Body background color: <%=BackgroundColor()%>
    <form id="form1" runat="server">
    <div>
    </div>
    </form>
</body>
</html>
```

9. Compile the program and run the page. The value #00FF translates to a bright green, so the background for your page should now appear bright green.

10. Browse through some of the other tabs in the ASP.NET Configuration Settings dialog box available through IIS. We'll encounter many of these settings as we go through ASP.NET.

   ❑ The Custom Errors page allows you to specify specific pages to which ASP.NET will redirect clients when the application throws an exception.

   ❑ The Authentication tab is for setting up users and assigning them roles within your application.

   ❑ The Authentication tab is also for specifying what type of authentication ASP.NET should apply to your site.

   ❑ The Application tab manages such issues as localization and themes/master pages.

❑ The State management tab is for managing session state. You can tell ASP.NET to store session state in any of a number of places, including in process on the host machine, out of process using a dedicated state server, or on a dedicated *SQL Server* database.

❑ The Location tab manages specific settings for specific resources.

The configuration story doesn't end here. ASP.NET relies on Web.Config for almost all of its settings. While we touched on only a couple of settings in this chapter, we'll see most of them throughout the next chapters. We'll revisit configuration when covering features such as security, session state, error messages, and HttpHandlers/HttpModules.

Conclusion

In this section, we saw how to manage configuration for a specific ASP.NET application. The configuration defaults are found within Machine.Config and Machine.Config.Default. When it comes time for the ASP.NET runtime to apply configuration settings to a specific application, ASP.NET looks for overridden configuration settings within an XML file named Web.Config.

The Web.Config file configuring a specific application lives in that application's virtual directory. If you're happy with the way Microsoft set up Web application settings using Machine.Config, you don't need to change anything in Web.Config. However, the default settings (using defaults such as *inproc* session state Windows authentication) aren't useful for a production Web site.

To change these settings, you may edit the Web.Config file directly (as you had to do in the days of ASP.NET 1.*x*). However, ASP.NET 2.0 includes new configuration tools that make configuring your site a very straightforward proposition.

We'll encounter ASP.NET configuration many more times in forthcoming chapters. In fact, we'll visit configuration heavily in the next chapter on ASP.NET security.

Chapter 9 Quick Reference

To	Do This
View raw configuration files	Look in the Windows directory under Microsoft.NET\Framework\ ver<whatevertheversionis>\config
Change configuration settings in a specific ASP.NET application	Place a Web.Config file in the application's virtual directory and modify the settings
Change configuration settings for a specific subdirectory underneath a virtual directory	Place a separate Web.Config file in the subdirectory OR Use the *Local* element in the virtual directory's Web.Config file

To	Do This
Modify a Web application's settings using the Web site Administration tool	Select **Web site | Administer Web site** from the main menu in Visual Studio
Modify a Web application's settings using the IIS ASP.NET Configuration table	Open the IIS control panel
	Highlight the virtual directory setting
	Right mouse click to bring up the Properties page
	Push the Configuration button
	Select the ASP.NET tab
Retrieve settings from the configuration file	Use the ASP.NET *ConfigurationManager* class

Chapter 10

Logging In

After completing this chapter, you will be able to

- Manage Web-based security

- Implement Forms Authentication

- Work with Forms Authentication in the raw

- Work with ASP.NET login controls to make writing login pages painless

- Work with ASP.NET role-based authorization

This chapter covers managing access to your ASP.NET application. Web site security is a major concern for most enterprises. Without any means of securing a site, the Web site can expose areas of your enterprise you may not want exposed. We'll take a quick look at what security means when it comes to Web applications. Then we'll look at various services available within ASP.NET for authenticating and authorizing users.

> **Note** "Authenticating users" means determining a user really is who he or she says (verifying the identity of a user). This is often done using a shared secret such as a password. "Authorizing users" means granting or restricting access to a specific user who has identified himself or herself. For example, clients in an administrative role are often granted more access than clients in a role as simple users.

Finally, we'll look at the new login controls, which greatly reduce the amount of development effort you might otherwise put into securing your site.

Web-Based Security

Software security is a prevalent topic these days, especially with ever increasing public awareness of security issues such as privacy. When a Web application runs on the Microsoft platform, several security issues arise immediately. They include (1) IIS's security context, (2) being sure your clients are who they say they are, and (3) specifying what those clients may and may not do with your application.

Managing Web-based security is similar to managing normal network security in that you still need to manage the authentication and authorization of users. However, Web-based security involves managing clients running different platforms in an open system. That is, you may not have any idea who your site clients are.

While not quite a trivial problem, Windows security is at least a solved problem. Anyone's who's configured a Windows network knows there are myriad issues involved in getting all the users of a network set up appropriately. *But* a Windows network is a closed system, and everyone on the network is connected and has a baseline level of trust between them (that is, they're all on the network). When you log on to a Windows network, you prove who you are (you *authenticate*) by providing your user name and password. If the security subsystem believes you are who you say you are, it issues a security token to your Windows session, and every application you start runs with that security token.

The resources (files, folders, drives, applications, etc.) on your computer and on your network are associated with Discretionary Access Control Lists (DACLs). If the security context under which your application runs belongs to a resource's DACL, then you may use it. Otherwise, the system will prevent you from using the resource. This is known as *authorization*.

In a closed system such as a Windows network, an administrator can effectively survey the whole system and assign users access to various resources. Because it's a closed system, the system can determine very easily whether or not a user belongs in the system and what that user may do.

Contrast this with a Web application. When considering a Web application, you realize first that the range of users of your application is quite wide. They are not necessarily part of your network. That means you need another way (outside of the Windows infrastructure) of authenticating and authorizing the users of your Web application.

Securing IIS

The first security issue you encounter in programming Web applications on the Windows platform is understanding the security context for IIS. Virtually all access to your Web site will be directed through IIS. As with all Windows applications, IIS runs under a specific context. When you install IIS on your machine, the install process creates a separate security identity specifically for IIS.

You can see the identity under which your version of IIS runs by starting the IIS control panel, selecting a virtual directory, right-clicking to get the properties, and then selecting the directory security tab. On my computer, the name of the user is IUSR_D6XXH351, as you can see in Figure 10-1.

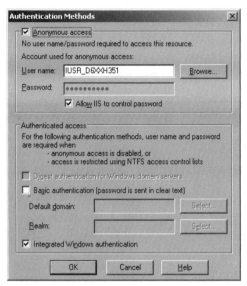

Figure 10-1   Managing IIS's authentication settings.

Notice the top left corner of the dialog box includes a check box labeled Anonymous access. When this box is checked, IIS uses the principle identified in the *User name* field as its security principle. That is, IIS runs with access to the resources as being available for IUSR_D6XXH351.

If you turn off the Anonymous access check box, you may apply Windows authentication to your Web application. In this case, you'd need to give all the potential clients a Windows user name and password. This only works when the clients are running on Windows-based platforms. Users logging on to your site are *challenged* (meaning they'll be asked to authenticate themselves). They'll see a Windows login dialog box when they log on to your Web site (perhaps you've run into this type of site before). This method of authentication does work well if you're writing an enterprise-wide site and you can count on your audience running Windows-based browsers. However, for a Web site with a wider audience, you'll want to use other means of authentication.

Fortunately, ASP.NET includes *Forms Authentication*, a straightforward means of authenticating clients. The Forms Authentication subsystem in ASP.NET 1.0 and 1.1 was a huge improvement from having to write your own authentication subsystem. ASP.NET 2.0 includes and improves upon the Forms Authentication model by adding an Authorization subsystem as well.

Let's start by taking a look at Forms Authentication in the raw.

Basic Forms Authentication

ASP.NET 1.0 and 1.1 introduced a straightforward means of authenticating users. Forms Authentication is driven by an application's Web.Config file. In addition to controlling such aspects as session state, tracing and debugging, and application key-value pairs, Web.Config includes authentication and authorization nodes.

To require users of your site to authenticate, you simply need to place some instructions into your Web.Config file. (You may edit the file directly, or you may use a tool such as the Web Site Administration tool available through Visual Studio.)

Web.Config has a section for specifying how your site should deal with authentication and authorization. In the absence of the authentication and authorization elements, ASP.NET allows unrestricted access to your site. However, once you add these elements to your Web.Config file ASP.NET will force a redirect to a file you specify. Most of the time, the file will be some sort of login page where users must do something such as type in a user name and password.

Before looking at the code, take a look at Figure 10-2, which illustrates how control flows on your Web site when you turn on Forms Authentication using Web.Config.

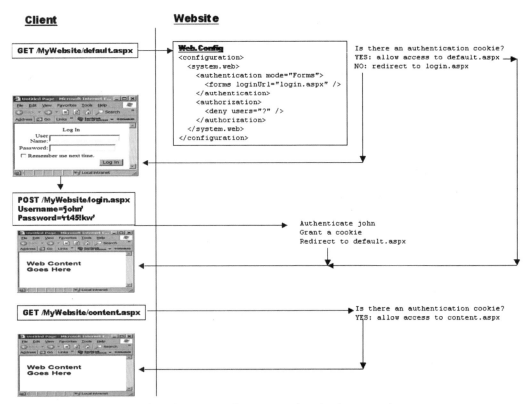

Figure 10-2   The control flow for a site with Forms Authentication turned on.

The CD that comes with this book includes this login page. To see an example of the most basic authentication you can use in your application, take a look at the files Login.aspx and Web.ConfigFormsAuthentication. The Web.Config includes the *Authentication* and *Authorization* elements to support Forms Authentication for the site. Listing 10-1 shows the Web.Config to force authentication.

Listing 10-1

```
<configuration>
  <system.web>
    <authentication mode="Forms">
      <forms loginUrl="login.aspx" />
    </authentication>

    <authorization>
      <deny users="?" />
    </authorization>
  </system.web>
</configuration>
```

The login page that goes with it is shown in Listing 10-2.

Listing 10-2

```
<%@ Page language=C# %>
<html>
  <script runat=server>

  protected bool AuthenticateUser(String strUserName,
                                  String strPassword) {
    if (strUserName == "Gary") {
      if(strPassword== "K4T-YYY") {
        return true;
      }
    }
    if(strUserName == "Jay") {
      if(strPassword== "RTY!333") {
        return true;
      }
    }
    if(strUserName == "Susan") {
      if(strPassword== "erw3#54d") {
        return true;
      }
    }
    return false;
  }

  public void OnLogin(Object src, EventArgs e) {
    if (AuthenticateUser(m_textboxUserName.Text,
                         m_textboxPassword.Text)) {
      FormsAuthentication.RedirectFromLoginPage(
         m_textboxUserName.Text, m_bPersistCookie.Checked);
    } else {
      Response.Write("Invalid login: You don't belong here...");
    }
  }
  </script>
```

```
<body>
  <form runat=server>
    <h2>A most basic login page</h2>
    User name:
    <asp:TextBox id="m_textboxUserName" runat=server/><br>
    Password:
    <asp:TextBox id="m_textboxPassword"
        TextMode="password" runat=server/>
    <br/>
    Remember password and weaken security?:
    <asp:CheckBox id=m_bPersistCookie runat="server"/>
    <br/>
    <asp:Button text="Login" OnClick="OnLogin"
                runat=server/>
    <br/>
  </form>
</body>
</html>
```

This is a simple login page that keeps track of three users—Gary, Jay, and Susan. Of course, in a real application this data would come from a database rather than being hard-coded into the page.

In this scenario, even if users try to surf to any page in the virtual directory, ASP.NET will stop them dead in their tracks and force them to pass the login page shown in Figure 10-3.

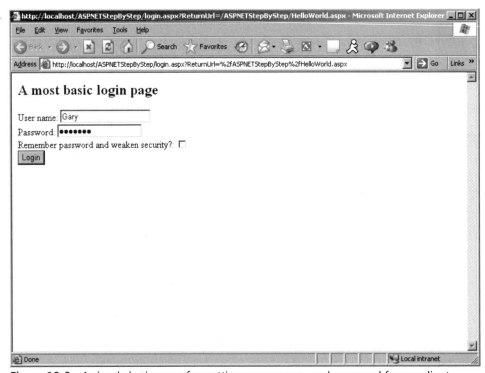

Figure 10-3   A simple login page for getting a user name and password from a client.

This simple login page authenticates the user (out of a group of three possible users). In a real Web site, the authentication algorithm would probably use a database lookup to see if the user identifying himself or herself is in the database and whether the password matches. Later in this chapter, we'll see the ASP.NET 2.0 authentication services. The login page then issues an authentication cookie using the *FormsAuthentication* utility class.

Here's what the Web page looks like in the browser with tracing turned on. Here you can see the value of the Authentication cookie in the cookie collection.

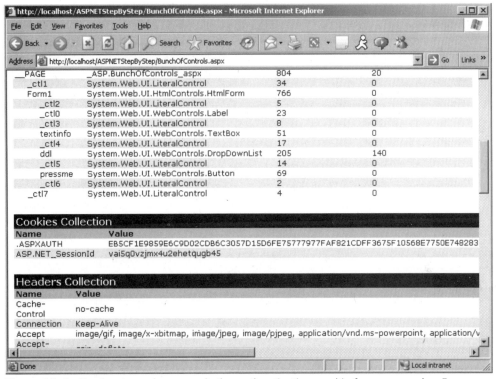

Figure 10-4 Tracing turned on reveals the authentication cookie for a page using Forms Authentication.

Run the Forms Authentication Example

This example shows how to employ Forms Authentication on your site.

1. To run the Forms Authentication example, create a virtual directory to hold the site. Alternatively, you can use an already existing site and employ Forms Authentication there.

2. Copy the Login.aspx page from the Chapter 10 examples into the virtual directory for which you want to apply Forms Authentication.

3. Copy the Web.ConfigForceAuthentication file from the Chapter 10 examples into the virtual directory for which you want to apply Forms Authentication. Make sure the configuration file is named Web.Config after you copy it.

4. Try to surf to a page in that virtual directory. ASP.NET should force you to complete the Login.aspx page before moving on.

5. Type in a valid user name and password. Subsequent access to that virtual directory should work just fine because now there's an Authentication ticket associated with the request and response.

While you may build your own authentication algorithms, ASP.NET 2.0 includes a number of new features that make authenticating users a straightforward and standard proposition. We'll look at those in a moment.

Briefly, ASP.NET allows two other types of authentication: Passport authentication and Windows authentication. Passport authentication relies upon Passport—a centralized authentication service provided by Microsoft. If you've ever used hotmail.com, you've used Passport. The advantage of Passport authentication is that it centralizes login and personalization information at one source.

The other type of authentication supported by ASP.NET is Windows authentication. If you specify Windows authentication, ASP.NET relies upon IIS and Windows authentication to manage users. Any user making his or her way through IIS authentication (using basic, digest, or Integrated Windows Authentication as configured in IIS) will be authenticated for the Web site. These other forms of authentication are available when configuring IIS. However, for most ASP.NET Web sites, you'll be bypassing IIS authentication in favor of ASP.NET authentication. ASP.NET will use the authenticated identity to manage authorization.

ASP.NET Authentication Services

ASP.NET includes a great deal of support for authenticating users (outside of IIS's support). Most of it comes from the *FormsAuthentication* class.

The *FormsAuthentication* Class

Many of ASP.NET's authentication services center around the *FormsAuthentication* class. Listing 10-3 shows the *FormsAuthentication* class. In the example above, the Login.aspx page uses the *FormsAuthentication.RedirectFromLoginPage* method to issue an authentication cookie and render the originally requested page. *FormsAuthentication* includes a number of other services, including issuing an authentication token without redirecting and encrypting passwords.

Listing 10-3

```
public class FormsAuthentication
{
...
  public static bool CookiesSupported {get;}
  public static string FormsCookieName {get;}
  public static string FormsCookiePath {get;}
  public static string LoginUrl {get;}
```

```
  public static bool RequireSSL {get;}
  public static bool SlidingExpiration {get;}
  public static bool Authenticate(string strName,
      string strPassword);
  public static string Encrypt(FormsAuthenticationTicket ticket);
  public static FormsAuthenticationTicket Decrypt(string str);
  public static HttpCookie GetAuthCookie(string strUserName,
      bool bPersist);
  public static string GetRedirectUrl(string strUserName,
      bool bPersist);
  public static string HashPasswordForStoringInConfigFile(
      string strPassword, string strFormat);
  public static void RedirectFromLoginPage(string struserName,
      bool bPersist);
  public static void Initialize();
   public static FormsAuthenticationTicket RenewTicketIfOld(
   FormsAuthenticationTicket tOld
);
  public static void SignOut();
}
```

The example shown in Listings 10-1 and 10-2 show how the rudimentary authentication works by installing an authentication cookie in the response and redirecting the processing back to the originally requested page. There are some other interesting methods in the *Forms-Authentication* class that allow for finer-grained control over the authentication process. For example, you can authenticate users manually (without forcing a redirect). That's useful for creating optional login pages that vary their content based upon the authentication level of the client.

An Optional Login Page

The code accompanying this book also includes an example showing how to authenticate separately. The page in Listing 10-4 uses the same authentication algorithm (three users—Gary, Jay, and Susan—with hard-coded passwords). However, the page authenticates users and then redirects them back to the same page (OptionalLogin.aspx).

Listing 10-4

```
<%@ Page language=C# trace="false"%>
<html>
  <script runat=server>

  protected bool AuthenticateUser(String strUserName,
                                  String strPassword)
  {
    if (strUserName == "Gary")
    {
       if(strPassword== "K4T-YYY")
       {
          return true;
       }
    }
    if(strUserName == "Jay")
```

```
            {
               if(strPassword== "RTY!333")
               {
                  return true;
               }
            }
            if(strUserName == "Susan")
            {
               if(strPassword== "erw3#54d")
               {
                  return true;
               }
            }
            return false;
         }

         public void OnLogin(Object src, EventArgs e)  {
            if (AuthenticateUser(m_textboxUserName.Text,
                             m_textboxPassword.Text))
            {
             FormsAuthentication.SetAuthCookie(
                      m_textboxUserName.Text,
              m_bPersistCookie.Checked);
                  Response.Redirect("optionallogin.aspx");
            } else {
               Response.Write("Invalid login: You don't belong here...");
            }
         }

         protected void ShowContent()
         {
            if(Request.IsAuthenticated)
            {
               Response.Write("Hi, you are authenticated. <br>" );
               Response.Write("You get special content...<br>" );
            } else
            {
               Response.Write("You're anonymous. Nothing special for you... ");
            }
         }
</script>
<body><form runat=server>

     <h2>Optional Login Page</h2>

     User name:
     <asp:TextBox id="m_textboxUserName" runat=server/><br>
     Password:
     <asp:TextBox id="m_textboxPassword"
         TextMode="password" runat=server/>
     <br/>
     Remember password and weaken security?:
     <asp:CheckBox id=m_bPersistCookie runat="server"/>
     <br/>
     <asp:Button text="Login" OnClick="OnLogin"
                 runat=server/>
```

```
    <br/>

    <%ShowContent(); %>
  </form></body>
</html>
```

Notice the page sets the authentication cookie manually by calling *FormsAuthentication.Set-AuthCookie* and then redirects the processing back to the page. Each time the page shows, it calls the *ShowContent* method, which checks the authentication property in the page to decide whether or not to display content specialized for an authenticated user. Because the page redirects manually after authenticating, the Web.Config file needs to look a bit different. To make it work, the authentication node should remain, but the authorization node that denies anonymous users needs to be removed. That way, any user can log in to the OptionLogin.aspx page (they won't be denied) but they may proceed after they're authenticated. Here's the new Web.Config file, shown in Listing 10-5. The file on the CD is named Web.ConfigForOptional-Login. To make it apply to the application, copy the file and name it as Web.Config.

Listing 10-5

```
<configuration>
  <system.web>
    <authentication mode="Forms">
    </authentication>
  </system.web>
</configuration>
```

Here's how the optional login page appears before the user has been authenticated, shown in Figure 10-5.

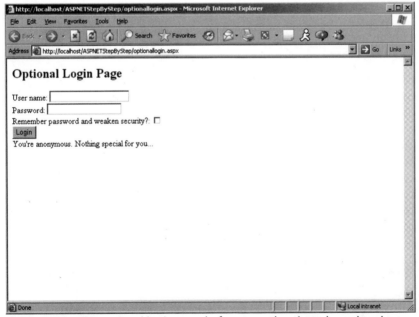

Figure 10-5   The optional login page before an authenticated user logs in.

Run the Optional Login Page

This example shows how to run the optional login page.

1. To run the optional login page, create a virtual directory to hold the site. Alternatively, you can use an already existing site and try the optional login page from there.

2. Copy the OptionalLogin.aspx page from the Chapter 10 examples into the virtual directory.

3. Copy the Web.ConfigOptionalLogin from the Chapter 10 examples into the virtual directory. Make sure the configuration file is named Web.Config so ASP.NET picks up on it.

4. Try to surf to a page in that virtual directory. ASP.NET should allow you to see the page, but as an unauthenticated user.

5. Type in a valid user name and password. You should see the content tailored for authenticated users. Subsequent requests/responses to and from the site will include an authentication token.

    After the user has been authenticated, the optional login page shows the content tailored to the specific authenticated user. Figure 10-6 shows the page after an authenticated user logs in.

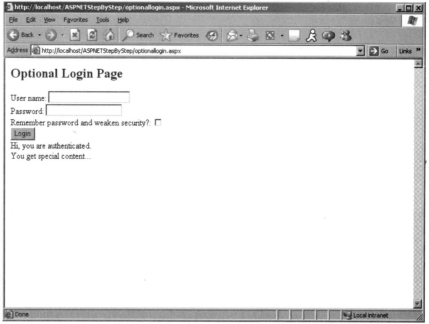

Figure 10-6   An Authenticated user has logged in.

Managing Users

So far, you can see that the fundamentals behind employing Forms Authentication are easy to manage. In the examples above, the sites are inaccessible until you prove your identity. The example above shows raw authentication with the users and passwords being hard-coded into the *Page* file. This is useful for illustration. However, in a real application you'll undoubtedly want to assign user identities to various clients visiting your site.

ASP.NET and Visual Studio include facilities for both managing user identities and for managing roles. The following exercise shows how to set up a secure site in which users are allowed access only after they identify themselves correctly.

Managing User Access

1. Create a new Web site named SecureSite. The example included with the CD is a File system Web site so that the site focuses strictly on Forms Authentication. Of course, HTTP Web sites using IIS will also have to go through the IIS authentication process.

2. Open the ASP.NET Administration Tool by selecting **Web site | ASP.NET Configuration** from the main menu. Go to the **Provider** tab. Select the **Select a single provider for all site management data** link. Then select **AspNetSqlProvider** as the provider, as shown here:

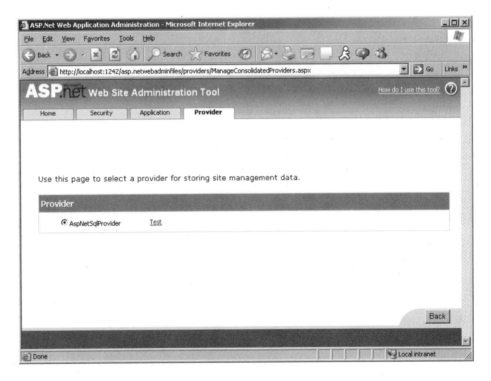

> **Tip** IIS includes an ASP.NET configuration utility as well. If your site has a virtual directory, you can get to it by opening IIS, selecting the virtual directory of interest, right-clicking to get Properties, and selecting the ASP.NET tab from the configuration dialog.

3.   Go to the **Security** tab. You'll see the page shown in the following graphic. Click the **Select authentication type** link:

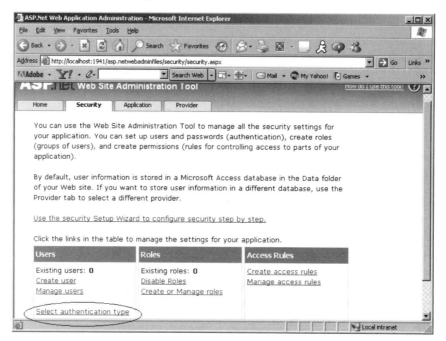

4.   Select **From the internet** as the access method. This will cause the site to use Forms Authentication.

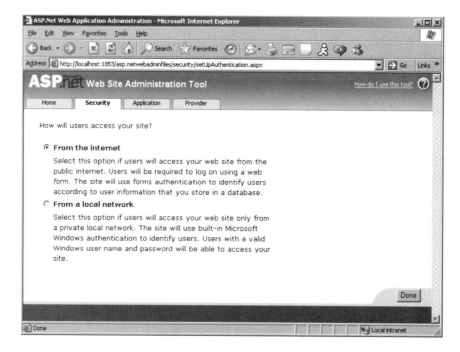

5. Select **Enable Roles** and then select **Create or manage roles**. Add some roles to the site. The example here includes three roles: Administrator, Joe User, and Power user. Add these roles now. We'll assign real users to them shortly.

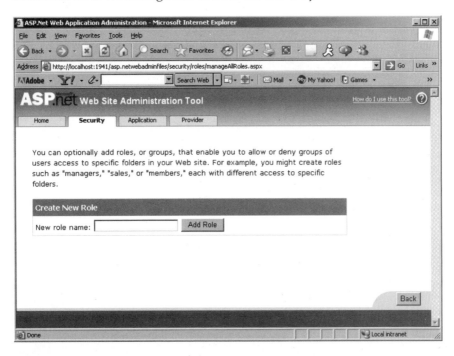

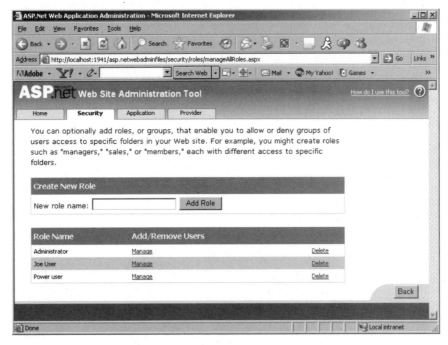

6.   Now add some users and assign some roles. From the main security page, select the **Create User** link. Add some users. You may assign them to roles now if you wish.

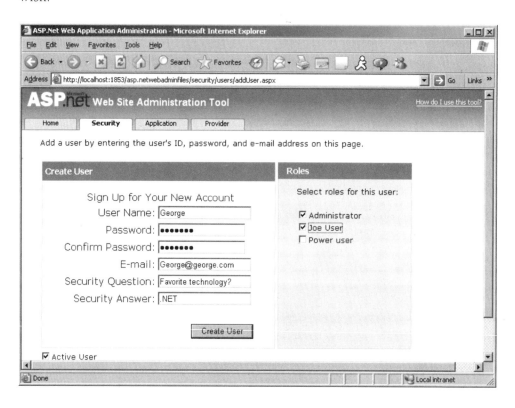

After you've added some users and assigned roles to them, Web.Config should look something like this:

```
<?xml version="1.0"?>
<configuration xmlns="http://schemas.microsoft.com/.NetConfiguration/v2.0">
   <system.web>
      <authorization>
   <deny users="?" />
   <allow roles="Administrator" />
  </authorization>
    <authentication mode="Forms" />
      <roleManager enabled="true"/>
      <compilation debug="true"/></system.web>
</configuration>
```

7. At this point, you may authenticate users to your site. However, you would probably like to control what parts of your site they may access. To do that, create some access rules. Select the **Create Access Rules (on security tab)** link to manage authorization. Deny anonymous users, as shown in the following graphic:

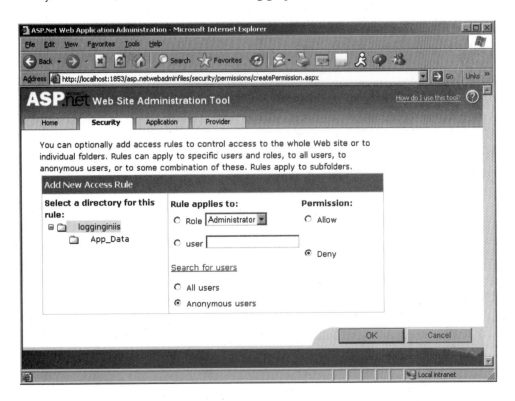

Denying access to anonymous users causes the following changes in Web.Config. Notice the *authorization* and the *roleManager* elements.

```
<?xml version="1.0" encoding="utf-8"?>
<configuration
  xmlns="http://schemas.microsoft.com/.NetConfiguration/v2.0">
  <system.web>
    <authorization>
      <deny users="?" />
    </authorization>
    <roleManager enabled="true"
      defaultProvider="AspNetSqlRoleProvider" />
    <authentication mode="Forms" />
  </system.web>
</configuration>
```

8. Now try running the site. ASP.NET should deny you access to the site, as shown
    here:

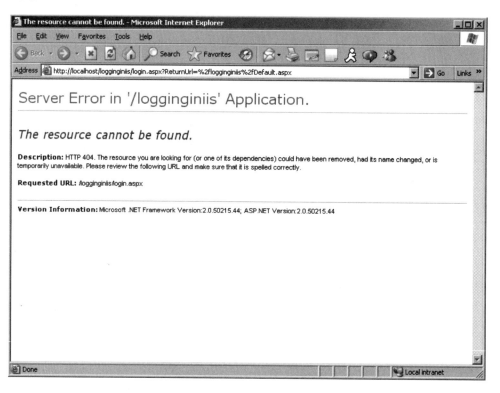

ASP.NET is looking for a way to authenticate the user. However, the site doesn't have one yet.
The Forms Authentication setting is set to true, anonymous users are denied access, but
there's no instruction to ASP.NET about what to do. There's no login redirect and no login
page yet, so ASP.NET simply stops you in your tracks. Let's provide a login page using the
ASP.NET login controls.

ASP.NET Login Controls

Earlier in this chapter, we handcrafted a couple of different login pages. During the heyday of
ASP.NET 1.1, that's what you had to do to get Forms Authentication working. ASP.NET 2.0
improves things by adding a number of login controls that perform the most common login
scenarios you might need for your site.

These controls include the *Login, LoginView, PasswordRecovery, LoginStatus, LoginName,
ChangePassword, and CreateUserWizard* controls. Here's a summary of what each control
does.

Login—The *Login* control is the simplest login control and supports the most common login scenario—signing in using a user name and password. The control includes user name and password text boxes and a check box for users who want to compromise password security by saving their passwords on the machine. The control exposes properties through which you can change the text and appearance of the control. You may also add links to manage registration or password recovery. The *Login* control interacts with the ASP.NET membership component for authentication by default. If you want to manage authentication yourself, you may do so by handling the control's *Authenticate* event.

LoginView—The *LoginView* control is very like the optional login page mentioned earlier. It's useful for managing the content you display for authenticated versus nonauthenticated users. The *LoginView* displays the login status via the display templates *AnonymousTemplate* and *LoggedInTemplate*. The control renders a different template depending on the status of the user. The *LoginView* also lets you manage text and links within each template.

PasswordRecovery—The *PasswordRecovery* control supports Web sites that send user passwords to clients when they forget their passwords. The control collects the user's account name, and then follows up with a security question (provided that functionality is set up correctly). The control either e-mails the current password to the user or creates a new one.

LoginStatus—The *LoginStatus* control displays whether or not the current user is logged on. Nonlogged-in users are prompted to log in, while logged-in users are prompted to log out.

LoginName—The *LoginName* control displays the user's login name.

ChangePassword—The *ChangePassword* control gives users a chance to change their passwords. An authenticated user may change his or her password by supplying the original password and a new password (along with a confirmation of the new password).

CreateUserWizard—The *CreateUserWizard* control collects information from users so it can set up an ASP.NET membership account for each user. Out of the box, the control gathers a user name, a password, an e-mail address, a security question, and a security answer. The *CreateUserWizard* will collect different information from users, depending on the membership provider used by your application.

The following exercise illustrates how to write a login page using the login controls.

Write a Login Page

1. ASP.NET wants to see a login page for the SecureSite application called Create a login page. Add a regular Web form to your application. Name the form Login.aspx. Grab a *Login* control from the toolbox and drag it onto the form, like so:

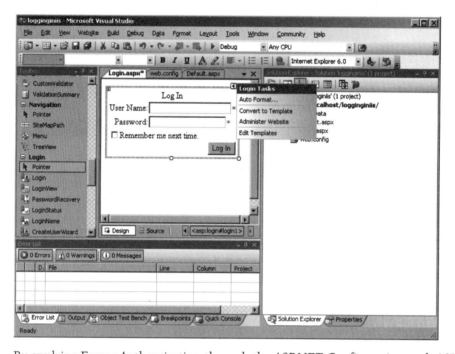

2. By applying Forms Authentication through the ASP.NET Configuration tool, ASP.NET understands to use Forms Authentication. The default Login URL is Login.aspx.

   Now try to surf to the default page. ASP.NET will now confront you with the login page, like so:

You'll see the default page (provided you logged in successfully):

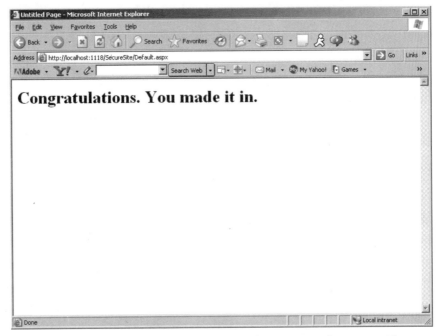

Authentication is an important step in managing the security of your site. The second half is managing access to your site once users have authenticated themselves. This is known as *authorization*.

Authorizing Users

Once you have authenticated a user, you have established his or her identity. While that information is sometimes useful by itself, a system becomes secure when authentication is combined with authorization. Authentication establishes identity, while authorization establishes what users can do when they're signed onto your site.

In the previous example, we added a couple of roles to the site. The following example illustrates how to limit access to certain areas of your site based on the user's identity.

Managing Authorization

1. Add a folder for Administrators to access. Name the folder Administrators. Add a Web form to the folder that says something like "Administrators Only." Make a JoeUsers folder (and a Web form for Joe Users). Also make a PowerUsers folder and resource.

2. Now set up associations between the roles you've defined and these new resources. Go to the Web Site Administration tool again. Add some more users, each with various roles assigned. For example, this site includes a user named George associated to the Administrator role, a user named Joe assigned to the Joe User role, and a user named Frodo assigned to the Power User role.

3. After adding the new users, set up some new access roles. You may do this by selecting the **Manage Access Rules** link and then selecting the **Add New Access Rule** link. You may selectively allow or deny various users or classes of users, as shown here:

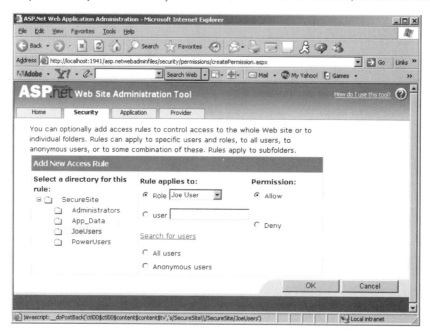

4. Add some hyperlinks to the default page so that clients can try to navigate to the various restricted pages.

Now surf to the site. Depending upon which identity you logged in as, you should be allowed or restricted to the various resources.

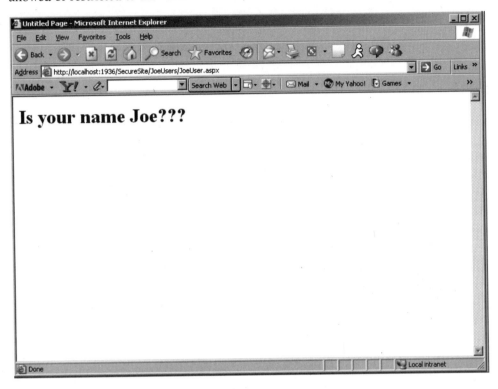

Table 10-1 shows the users' names and their passwords for the example included with this chapter.

Table 10-1   User names and passwords for the example code available for this book.

User Name	Password
George	abc!123
Joe	abc!123
Frodo	abc!123

This touches upon the utility provided by the login controls. For even more robust login scenarios (including password recovery and optional logins), try some of the other login controls.

Conclusion

In this chapter we saw the ASP.NET security model. While IIS does have its own security model, leveraging it for Web site security often amounts to giving users to your site a Windows user identity. Perhaps that's okay for a small confined Web site. However, for a site that will be available to potentially the entire globe, that's not such a good thing.

If you decide to let ASP.NET handle authentication, then you have more control over how the authentication happens while at the same time leaving your set of Windows user identities unadulterated. To let a request get past IIS, allow anonymous access to your virtual directory.

Once a request gets past IIS, it's up to ASP.NET to figure out who the user is and how to dole out access. ASP.NET includes an authentication model named Forms Authentication. You turn on Forms Authentication through the Web.Config file. Either use the typing Wizard (that is, type the *<authentication>* element by hand, *or* use the Web Site Administration tool (or the IIS ASP.NET tab) to turn on Forms Authentication.

The Web Site Administration tool is useful for adding users, adding roles, and assigning users to roles. It's the most convenient way to manage users and roles. (If you want to, you may set up your own authentication scheme and database, bypassing the ASP.NET support.)

By using ASP.NET Authentication and Authorization support, the Login controls work automatically. The Login controls supply login functionality for the majority of use cases. (As always, you may bypass the support for an authentication and authorization scheme of your own choosing.)

Chapter 10 Quick Reference

To	Do This
Use Forms Authentication in your application	1. Use the ASP.NET Web Site Administration tool (select **Web site | ASP.NET Configuration**)
	2. Use the ASP.NET tab in IIS
Configure the security aspects of your Web site	1. Use the ASP.NET Web Site Administration tool (select **Web site | ASP.NET Configuration**)
	2. Use the ASP.NET tab in IIS
Authenticate a request by hand	Use the *FormsAuthentication* class's Set Auth cookie
Invalidate an authentication cookie	Call the *FormsAuthentication* class's *SignOff* method
View the authentication cookie	Turn on tracing

Chapter 11

Databinding

After completing this chapter, you will be able to

- Represent collections using databound controls

- Talk to database providers in ASP.NET

- Customize databound controls

This chapter covers one of ASP.NET's most useful features: databinding. A number of controls within ASP.NET have the capability to understand the form and content of a collection and to render the correct tags to represent such user elements as list boxes, radio button lists, and combo boxes. Here we'll examine how these controls work and how to use them on a Web page.

Representing Collections without Databinding

One of the most common problems encountered in building any software (and Web sites in particular) is representing collections as user interface elements. Think about some of the sites you have recently visited. If you ordered something from a commercial site, you no doubt hit a page that asked you to enter your address. What happened when you reached the *State* field? Most Web sites display a drop-down list box from which you may choose a state abbreviation.

How was that drop-down list filled? In HTML, the *<selection>* tag nests several *<option>* tags that represent the elements to be listed. The state abbreviations probably came from a database or some other well-established source. Somewhere (most likely at the server), some piece of code had to go through the collection of states and render *<selection>* and *<output>* tags for it.

ASP.NET server-side controls, such as the *ListBox* and the *DropDownList*, include *Items* collections. For example, one way to render a collection as a combo box is to declare a combo box on your ASP.NET page and add the items individually via the *Items.Add* method like so:

```
protected void BuildComboBox(IList techList)
{
    for(int i = 0; i < techList.Count; i++)
    {
        this.DropDownList2.Items.Add(techList[i]);
    }
}
```

Because representing collections as UI elements is such a prevalent programming task, it makes a lot of sense to push that down into the framework if at all possible. ASP.NET includes a number of databound controls that are capable of taking collections and rendering the correct tags for you. Let's see how this works.

Representing Collections with Databinding

Each of the databound controls within ASP.NET includes properties to attach it to a data source. For simple databinding, these controls include a *DataSource* property to which you may attach any collection that implements the *IEnumerable* interface (as well as the *DataSet* and *DataTable* classes that we'll see shortly). After attaching the collection to the control, you call *DataBind* on the page (or the control) to instruct the control to iterate through the collection.

For more complex databinding, some controls include a property named *DataSourceID*. This new style of databinding is named *declarative databinding*. Instead of simply iterating through a collection, the declarative databinding classes use a separate *Data* control to manage data for the databound control. These data managers support the databound controls in implementing standard functionality such as sorting, paging, and editing. Declarative binding greatly simplifies the process of rendering collections. They work by referencing the ID of a *DataSource* control on the page. .NET includes several of these *DataSource* controls—including one for XML data, one for Access databases, and one for SQL Server, among others. With declarative databinding, calling *DataBind* is optional. The control will call *DataBind* during the *PreRendering* event.

ASP.NET includes a number of controls that support at least simple databinding, while others support declarative databinding as well. These controls include those based upon the *ListControl*, the *CheckBoxList*, the *RadioButtonList*, the *DropDownList*, and the *ListBox*. In addition, the more advanced controls include the *TreeView*, the *Menu*, the *GridView*, the *DataGrid*, the *Repeater*, the *FormView*, and the *DetailsView*.

Here's a rundown of how each control works.

ListControl-Based Controls

The most common databound controls are those based upon the *ListControl* base class. These controls include the *ListBox*, the *BulletedList*, the *RadioButtonList*, the *CheckBoxList*, and the *DropDownList*. We'll see these controls in detail in a moment. The names are self-explanatory for the most part. They all have direct analogs in Windows desktop programming as well as standard HTML control tags. The *ListBox* displays a list of strings. The *DropDownList* is similar to a *ComboBox*. The *RadioButtonList* displays a group of mutually exclusive radio buttons. The *CheckBoxList* displays a column of check box controls.

TreeView

We saw an example of the *TreeView* in Chapter 6. The *TreeView* control represents hierarchical data. It's perfect for matching up with XML data sources. The *TreeView* features collapsible nodes that allow users to drill down from abstract data elements into more detailed ones. The *TreeView* supports declarative databinding.

Menu

The *Menu* control also handles hierarchical databinding. The *Menu* control gives users the ability to navigate the site in much the same way that menus for desktop applications do. The *Menu* supports declarative databinding.

FormView

The *FormView* control supports free-form layout for individual controls (such as a *TextBox* or a *ListBox*) that render data from a data source. The *FormView* also supports editing of data in the data source through the controls. The *FormView* supports declarative databinding.

GridView

While ASP.NET 1.*x* supported only the *DataGrid* control, ASP.NET 2.0 supports a *DataGrid* on steroids—the *GridView*. The *GridView* control is what it says it is—it renders collections via a grid with individual columns and rows. Each row in the grid represents an individual record in a collection. Each column within that row represents an individual field within the record. While the original *DataGrid* required *you* as a developer to manage paging and sorting of data, the *GridView* control supports automatic paging and sorting. The *GridView* also supports editing (something that requires hand-coding in the *DataGrid*). The *GridView* supports declarative databinding.

DetailsView

Whereas the *GridView* gives you the whole gestalt of a data source, the *DetailsView* control is for drilling down to display one record at a time. The *DetailsView* is often paired with controls such as the *ListBox*, the *DropDownList*, or the *GridView*. Users select the row using one of these controls and the *DetailsView* shows the associated data. The *DetailsView* supports declarative databinding.

DataList

Whereas the *DataGrid* and the *GridView* display the data in a data source using regular rows and columns, the *DataList* control displays the records in a data source in a format you determine using template controls.

Repeater

The *Repeater* control also displays data from a data source in a format you determine (rather than forcing it into rows and columns). The *Repeater* control uses both raw HTML and server-side controls to display the rows. The *Repeater* control repeats the format you define for each row.

Simple Databinding

The simplest databinding entails attaching a simple collection to one of the *ListControl*-based control's *DataSource* property. If you have a collection, you can simply set the *DataSource* property of one of these controls and it will render the correct tags automatically.

The following example shows how to use some of the databound controls by hooking up an *ArrayList* to several of the *ListControl*-based controls.

Databinding with an ArrayList

1. Start a new Web site named DataBindORama.

2. From the Web site menu, select **Add New Item...** and add a class named *TechnologyDescriptor*. Add two member variables to the class: *String* types named *_strTechnologyName* and *_strDescription*. This class will represent a technology name and an accompanying description. Expose these two member variables as public properties.

Important   Exposing the member variables as properties is important so the controls will work correctly with databinding. When a control binds to a collection composed of classes, it will look for the fields to expose via their property names. Using the databinding controls, you may specify a "display name" (that is, the value that will appear in the control), and you may specify a second "hidden" value to be associated with the item that was selected. In the case of rendering collections of managed objects, the binding architecture depends upon these fields being exposed as properties.

Listing 11-1 shows the *TechnologyDescriptor* that exposes a technology name and description as properties.

Listing 11-1

```
public class TechnologyDescriptor
{
    protected String _strTechnologyName;
    protected String _strDescription;

    public String TechnologyName
    {
        get
        {
            return this._strTechnologyName;
        }
        set
        {
            this._strTechnologyName = value;
        }
    }
    public String Description
    {
        get
        {
            return this._strDescription;
        }
        set
        {
            this._strDescription = value;
        }
    }

    public TechnologyDescriptor(String strTechnologyName,
                String strDescription)
    {
        this._strTechnologyName = strTechnologyName;
        this._strDescription = strDescription;
    }
}
```

3. After developing the *TechnologyDescriptor* class, add four databound controls to the default page: a *ListBox*, a *DropDownList*, a *RadioButtonList*, and a *CheckBoxList*.

4. Underneath each of these controls, place a *Label*. The label will be used to show the value associated with each selected item.

5. Set the *AutoPostBack* property for the *ListBox*, the *DropDownList*, the *RadioButtonList*, and the *CheckBoxList* to true. That way, selecting an item in each of the controls will cause a post back during which the selected item may be interrogated.

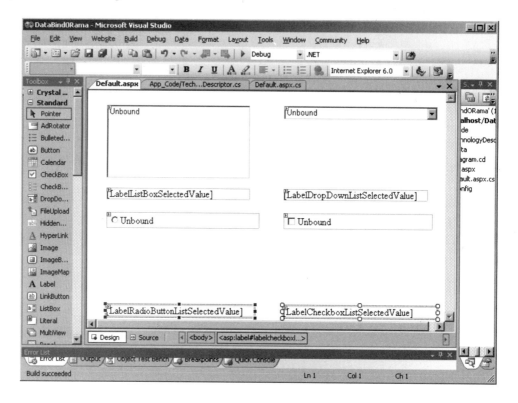

6. Now update the page to build a list of *TechnologyDescriptors* and to attach the collection of *TechnologyDescriptors* for each control. For each control, set the *DataTextField* property to "*TechnologyName*" (to map it to the *TechnologyDescriptor's TechnologyName* property). This will ensure that the technology name will appear in the control. Then set the *Data-ValueField* for each control to "Description" to map the *Description* property to be the associated value. Listing 11-2 shows creating a collection of *TechnologyDescriptors* and attaching the collection to each of the controls.

7. Add selection handlers for each of the controls (by double-clicking them). Upon receiving the selection events, interrogate the control for the selected item's value. Listing 11-2 also shows the handlers.

Listing 11-2

```
protected void Page_Load(object sender, EventArgs e)
{
    Ilist techList = CreateTechnologyList();
    if (!this.IsPostBack)
    {
        this.ListBox1.DataSource = techList;
        this.ListBox1.DataTextField = "TechnologyName";

        this.DropDownList1.DataSource = techList;
        this.DropDownList1.DataTextField = "TechnologyName";
```

```
        this.RadioButtonList1.DataSource = techList;
        this.RadioButtonList1.DataTextField = "TechnologyName";

        this.CheckBoxList1.DataSource = techList;
        this.CheckBoxList1.DataTextField = "TechnologyName";

        this.DataBind();
    }
}

protected Ilist CreateTechnologyList()
{
    ArrayList alTechnologies = new ArrayList();

    TechnologyDescriptor technologyDescriptor;

    technologyDescriptor =
    new TechnologyDescriptor("ASP.NET", "Handle HTTP Requests");
    alTechnologies.Add(technologyDescriptor);

    technologyDescriptor =
    new TechnologyDescriptor("Windows Forms",
    "Local Client UI technology");
    alTechnologies.Add(technologyDescriptor);

    technologyDescriptor =
    new TechnologyDescriptor("ADO.NET",
    "Talk to the database");
    alTechnologies.Add(technologyDescriptor);

    technologyDescriptor =
    new TechnologyDescriptor(".NET CLR",
    "Modern runtime environment for managed code");
    alTechnologies.Add(technologyDescriptor);

    technologyDescriptor =
    new TechnologyDescriptor(".NET IL",
    "Intermediary representation for .NET applications");
    alTechnologies.Add(technologyDescriptor);

    technologyDescriptor =
    new TechnologyDescriptor(".NET Compact Framework",
    "Modern runtime environment for small devices");
    alTechnologies.Add(technologyDescriptor);

    return alTechnologies;
}

protected void ListBox1_SelectedIndexChanged(object sender, EventArgs e)
{
    this.LabelListBoxSelectedValue.Text = this.ListBox1.SelectedValue;
    }
protected void DropDownList1_SelectedIndexChanged(object sender,
    EventArgs e)
{
    this.LabelDropDownListSelectedValue.Text =
    this.DropDownList1.SelectedValue;
}
protected void RadioButtonList1_SelectedIndexChanged(object sender,
    EventArgs e)
```

```
{
    this.LabelRadioButtonListSelectedValue.Text =
    this.RadioButtonList1.SelectedValue;
}
protected void CheckBoxList1_SelectedIndexChanged(object sender,
    EventArgs e)
{
    this.LabelCheckboxListSelectedValue.Text =
    this.CheckBoxList1.SelectedValue;
}
```

8. Compile the site and browse to the page.

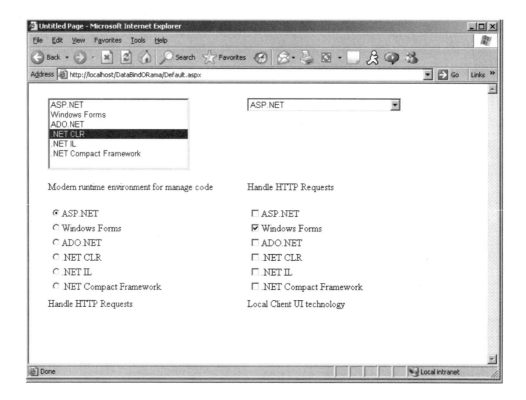

In the above example, selecting one of the items within the databound controls will reveal the related value in the label beneath the control.

In certain programming situations, you may find yourself doing this kind of databinding. For example, simple collections such as states within the United States or short lists (perhaps of employee or contact names) work great with these *ListControl*-based controls. However, very often you'll find yourself dealing with data in a more complex format—beyond simply an *ArrayList*. A number of controls can deal with more complex *DataSets*. However, we first need to look at ADO.NET because it provides the easiest way to reach these more complex data compositions.

Accessing Databases

The previous example shows how to attach in-memory collections (such as *ArrayLists*) to a server-side control and have it render the correct tags to the client. While this is useful, the server-side controls are capable of working with other collections—including ones that come from databases. Before seeing how to render database queries using UI elements, let's take a quick look at the .NET database story.

The .NET Database Story

Just as .NET includes a library of classes for managing rich client UI (Windows Forms) and for handling HTTP requests (ASP.NET), .NET includes a library for connecting to a wide range of databases. That library is named ADO.NET.

ADO.NET is similar to Microsoft's previous database technology (named simply ADO). ADO stands for Active Data Objects. While Microsoft has dropped "Active" from its marketing lexicon, it kept the name ADO and appended ".NET" to name the managed database technology (surely for brand name recognition). ADO represents a set of managed providers that is very similar in function and form to classic ADO. ADO.NET centers around three main units of functionality: connecting to a database, commanding the database, and using the results.

Connections

When you want to talk to a specific database, you usually need to *connect* to it. At the very least, most of the time this involves specifying the location of the database. For many scenarios, connecting also requires managing security (via user names and passwords). More advanced scenarios may also require dealing with such issues as connection pooling and transactions. These are all handled as part of the process of *connecting* to the database. The connection information is usually passed in via a string, which sets various connection parameters.

ADO.NET has classes for making connections to a database. ADO.NET 1.x included only two: a connection for Microsoft SQL Server and another for connecting to OLEDB databases. ADO.NET 2.0 adds classes specialized for more database types and includes a new set of database services using the *provider pattern*.

Working with ADO.NET 1.x involved writing most of the data access code using the ADO interfaces (rather than directly instantiating the database classes). This allowed you to isolate the vendor-specific details in a single place in the code—in the spot where the connection is managed. After that, getting the other parts required for making queries (for example, getting the correct command object) was a matter of asking the connection for it. While you may still write code to connect to the database using ADO.NET 1.x–style code, there's now a better way—using the ADO.NET 2.0 database provider factories.

As mentioned previously, ADO.NET 2.0 offers the provider pattern, an improvement in connecting to and using databases. By using the provider pattern, you limit exposing the kind of database you're using to a single call to a *provider factory*. You choose the kind of database in one place and the provider takes care of making sure the correct connection and command objects are used. This was less important in ADO 1.*x* when ADO divided the database world into two kinds of databases: SQL Server and OLEDB databases. However, with its support of new database types, the provider pattern is a welcome addition.

If you look in Machine.Config, you'll see providers for the following database types:

- *Odbc Data Provider*
- *OleDb Data Provider*
- *OracleClient Data Provider*
- *SqlClient Data Provider*
- *SQL Server CE Data Provider*

Listing 11-3 shows a snippet from Machine.Config illustrating how the provider keys are mapped to provider factories.

Listing 11-3

```
<system.d<configuration>
 <system.data>
    <DbProviderFactories>
       <add name="Odbc Data Provider"
            invariant="System.Data.Odbc"
            type="System.Data.Odbc.OdbcFactory…" />
       <add name="OleDb Data Provider"
            invariant="System.Data.OleDb"
            type="System.Data.OleDb.OleDbFactory…"/>
       <add name="OracleClient Data Provider"
            invariant="System.Data.OracleClient"
            type="System.Data.OracleClient.OracleClientFactory…"/>
       <add name="SqlClient Data Provider"
            invariant="System.Data.SqlClient"
            "System.Data.SqlClient.SqlClientFactory" />
       <add name="SQL Server CE Data Provider"
            invariant="Microsoft.SqlServerCe.Client"
            type="Microsoft.SqlServerCe.Client.SqlCeClientFactory…" />
    </DbProviderFactories>
  </system.data>
</configuration>>
```

To get a connection to a database, you ask the runtime for a reference to the right factory and then get a connection from the factory, as shown in Listing 11-4. You use the name of the database type (*System.Data.SqlClient* or *Microsoft.SqlServerCe.Client*, for example). After getting the right kind of factory, you ask it to create a connection for you.

Listing 11-4

```
DbConnection GetConnectionUsingFactory()
{
  DbProviderFactory dbProviderFactory =
      DbProviderFactories.GetFactory("System.Data.SqlClient")
  return dbProviderFactory.CreateConnection();
}
```

Once you have a connection, you may use it to connect to the database. Given a SQL Server database named *AspDotNetStepByStep* available on your machine, you'd insert a connection string as shown in Listing 11-5 in your Web.Config. You could type it in manually—or, as we saw in Chapter 9, you may use the ASP.NET configuration utilities to add the connection string to the application's configuration. Listing 11-5 shows how this might appear in a Web.Config file.

Listing 11-5

```
<configuration>
 <connectionStrings>
<add name="AspDotNetStepByStep"
    connectionString=
        "server=.;integrated security=sspi;database= AspDotNetStepByStepDB "/>
</connectionStrings>
</configuration>
```

Once you have a reference to the database connection, you may open the connection and start commanding the database.

Commands

Once connected, the database is waiting for you to send database commands. These commands usually include querying the database, updating existing data, inserting new data, and deleting data. Most databases support Structured Query Language (SQL) to manage these commands. (Some databases may support specialized variations of SQL, so the actual command text may differ from one implementation to the other.) Commanding the database usually entails writing SQL statements such as

```
Select * from DotNetReferences where AuthorLastName = Petzold
```

For example, to connect to an SQL database named *AspDotNetStepByStepDB* and query the *DotNetReferences* table for all the references by someone with the last name "Petzold," you'd use code as shown in Listing 11-6.

Listing 11-6

```
class UseDBApp {
 static void Main(string[] args) {
  DbProviderFactory dbProviderFactory =
      DbProviderFactories.GetFactory("System.Data.SqlClient")
  DbConnection conn = dbProviderFactory.CreateConnection()
```

```
using(conn) {
 ConfigurationSettings s =
  ConfigurationSettings.ConnectionStrings["AspDotNetStepByStep"];
 conn.ConnectionString = s.ConnectionString;
 conn.Open();

 DbCommand cmd = conn.CreateCommand();
 cmd.CommandText =
   "SELECT * FROM DotNetReferences WHERE AuthorLastName=Petzold";
 DbDataReader reader = cmd.ExecuteReader();
 // do something with the reader
 }
}
```

Executing the command using *ExecuteReader* sends a query to the database. The results come back via an instance of the *IDataReader* interface. The code listed above stops short of using the results. Let's take a look at how that works.

Managing Results

Once you've connected to the database and issued a query, you probably need to sift through the data to use it. ADO.NET supports two broad approaches to managing result sets: the *IDataReader* interface and the *DataSet* class.

DataReader

The example above retrieves an *IDataReader* from the query operation. The IDataReader interface is useful for iterating through the results of the query. Listing 11-7 shows part of the *IDataReader* interface.

Listing 11-7
```
public interface IDataReader
{
    bool IsClosed {get;}
    int    RecordsAffected {get;}
    void Close();
    bool NextResult();
    bool Read();
//..…
}
```

When iterating through the results of a query, *Read* fetches the next row. *NextResult* will fetch the next result set.

Accessing data through *IDataReader* is often termed "fire hose mode" because you have to eat your way through the data one row at a time *going forward only*. There's no way to revert back to a previous row except by resetting the reader and starting again. An alternative to accessing data through the *IDataReader* interface is to use a *DataSet*.

DataSet

In addition to the *IDataReader*, ADO.NET supports the notion of a disconnected record set—the *DataSet* class in ADO.NET. The ADO.NET is primarily designed to help you write large, highly scalable applications. One of the biggest hindrances to scalability is the limits of database connectivity. Databases usually have a limit on the number of active connections available at one time, and if all the connections are in use at any particular time, any piece of code wanting a database connection will need to wait. If the number of users of a system is about the same as the number of connections available, then perhaps that's not a problem. However, if the number of users of a system is greater than the number of database connections, the system performance will likely be impacted greatly.

To encourage scalability, ADO.NET includes a class named *DataSet* that's designed to give you an easily navigable snapshot of your application's database. The idea behind a database is to get in and get out quickly with a copy of the data.

Objects in the *DataSet* class are usually built using a *DataAdapter*. A *DataSet* includes a *DataTable* array—one for each selection statement in the query. Once the *DataAdapter* comes back from fetching the *DataSet*, you have the latest snapshot of the database in memory. The *DataSet* contains a *DataTable* collection and creates a *DataTable* element for each *SELECT* statement in the query. You may access the *Tables* collection using either ordinal or *String*-type indices. Once you get to a table, iterating through the rows and columns is a matter of indexing into the table using ordinal indices for the rows and ordinal or *String*-type indices for the columns. Listing 11-8 shows an example of using the *SqlDataAdapter* to get a *DataSet*.

Listing 11-8

```
public static void UseDataSet()
{
   DataSet ds = new DataSet();
   try
   {
      SqlDataAdapter da = new SqlDataAdapter(
         "select * from customer; select * from country",
         "server=.;uid=sa;pwd=;database=ASPNetStepByStepDB");
      da.Fill(ds, "DotNetReferences");
   }
   catch(SqlException e)
   {
      System.Console.WriteLine(e);
   }

   foreach (DataTable t in ds.Tables)
   {
      Console.WriteLine("Table " + t.TableName + " is in dataset"");
      Console.WriteLine("Row 0, column 1: " + t.Rows[0][1]);
      Console.WriteLine("Row 1, column 1: " + t.Rows[1][1]);
      Console.WriteLine("Row 2, column 1: " + t.Rows[2][1]);
   }
   ds.WriteXml("c:\\dataset.xml");
   ds.WriteXmlSchema("c:\\dataset.xsd");
```

```
// also- may bind to the tables here:
this.ListBox1.DataSource = ds.Tables[0];
this.ListBox1.TextDataField = "AuthorLastName"
this.ListBox1.DataBind();
}
```

The code in Listing 11-8 illustrates using a *DataAdapter* and a *DataSet*. The code prints out the first two columns of the first three rows of each table in the *DataSet*. The example in Listing 11-8 shows that a *DataTable* is valid as a *DataSource* for databound controls. The example also shows that the *DataSet* objects also serialize as XML. Both the table schema and the contents may be serialized this way–making it especially useful for transferring data between systems.

Here's one final note about items in the *DataSet* class. They're disconnected and are not restricted to the "fire hose mode" of data access. You have complete random access to any table, any column, and/or any row in the *DataSet*. In fact, objects in the *DataSet* class are also smart enough to keep track of any data you change inside of them. You may flush the data back to the physical database by using the *CommandBuilder* to prepare the *DataSet* for an *Update* through the *DataAdapter*.

Given either an *IDataReader* or a *DataSet*, the databound controls will automatically render themselves appropriately to show the control on the browser. While you may always connect to the database and fetch the data manually through the standard connection/command architecture, ASP.NET 2.0 and Visual Studio 2005 support an even easier-to-use way to render data–via declarative databinding.

ASP.NET Data Sources

After seeing how to access data in the raw using ADO.NET, let's look at an easier way. ASP.NET 2.0 includes some new classes that hide the complexity of managing connections and of gathering data. They're the *DataSource* controls.

These *DataSource* controls abstract the entire connection and command mechanism so that all you need to do is decide on a data source, point the control there, and invent a query. Visual Studio provides a wizard that guides you through this. Once you have a *DataSource*, you may attach it to a databound control that uses it.

Let's take a look at making a query and populating some controls with the results of the query.

Use a *DataSource* to Populate Controls in *DataReader* Mode

1. Add a new form to DataBindingORama named *DataBindingWithDB*.

2. The example for this chapter (named DataBindORama), available on the CD that comes with this book, includes an Access database named ASPNETStepByStep.MDB. Set up an accessor for the database. Go to the *Data* controls in the toolbox. Drag an

AccessDataSource onto the form. Select **Configure Data Source...** from the local menu displayed by Visual Studio. Click **Browse** in the Configure Data Source dialog box. You'll see a directory named App_Data in the list box on the left side. Highlight it. Then select ASPStepByStep.mdb from the list box on the right side. This will insert an Access database accessor into your project. Configure the data accessor to use the AspDotNetStepByStep database that comes with this book.

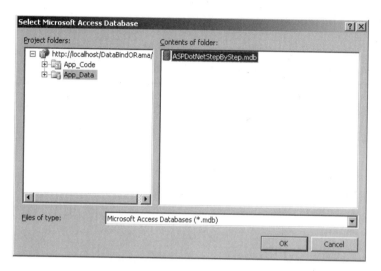

3. Select all the columns and all the rows from the *DotNetReferences* table when configuring the query (that is, choose "*" to query for all the columns).

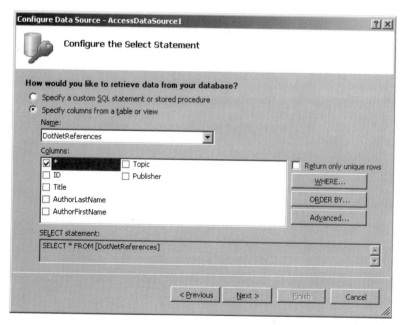

4. Test the query if you want to by clicking the **Test Query** button.

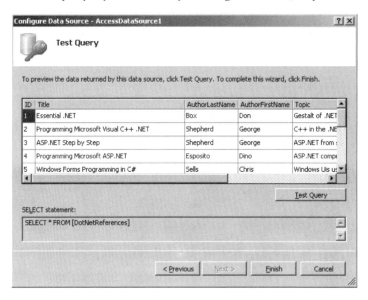

5. Set the *DataSourceMode* property to *DataReader*.

6. Now drag a *ListBox* onto the page. Set the *AutoPostback* property to true. Handle the *Page_Load* method by attaching the *ListBox DataSource* to the *AccessDataSource1* like so:

```
protected void Page_Load(object sender, EventArgs e)
{
  if (!this.IsPostBack)
  {
    this.ListBox1.DataSource = this.AccessDataSource1;
    this.ListBox1.DataTextField = "AuthorLastName";
    this.ListBox1.DataValueField = "Title";
    this.ListBox1.DataBind();
  }
}
```

7. Put a label near the bottom of the page. This label will hold the selected value from the combo box.

8. Double-click on *ListBox1* to handle the item changed event. In the event handler, set the *Label1* text property to the value field of the selected item.

```
protected void RadioButtonList1_SelectedIndexChanged(object sender,
    EventArgs e)
{
  this.Label1.Text = this.RadioButtonList1.SelectedItem.Value;
}
```

9. Now drag a *RadioButtonList* onto the form. When you finish dropping it on the form, Visual Studio will ask you if you want to choose a data source. Click **Choose Data Source**....

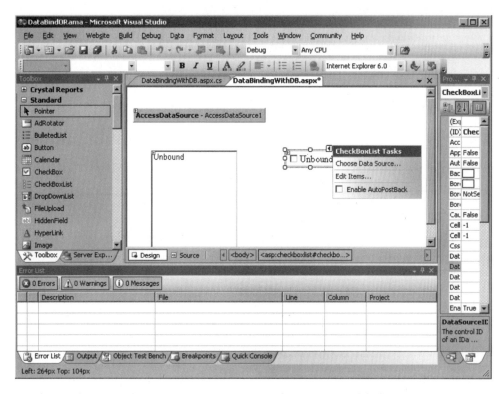

10. Configure the control to use *AccessDataSource1* that you just added.

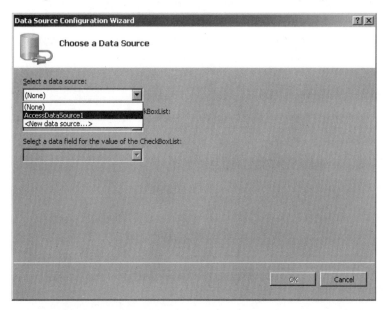

11. Configure the control to use the *AuthorLastName* column for the text field and the *Title* column for the value field.

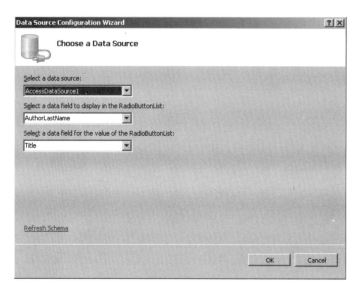

12. Double-click on the *RadioButtonList1* object on the form to create a handler for the radio button selection. Handle the selection by updating the *Label1* object with the value associated with the current radio button selection.

```
protected void RadioButtonList1_SelectedIndexChanged(object sender,
    EventArgs e)
{
    this.Label1.Text = this.RadioButtonList1.SelectedItem.Value;
}
```

13. Now run the program. The *ListBox* and the *RadioButton* list should show the *AuthorLastName* field. Selecting one name out of either list will cause a post back and show the title (the associated value) in the label near the bottom of the page.

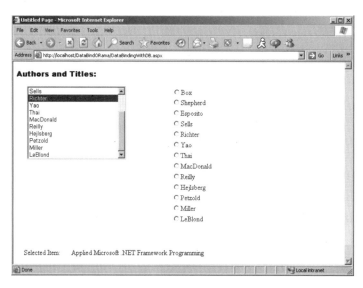

Now we've had a taste of how binding to the simple controls works. While using these controls is common in many scenarios, the databound controls don't end there. ASP.NET includes other more complex controls that render data such as complex UI elements as grids and control constellations.

Other Databound Controls

In addition to the simple bound controls, ASP.NET includes several more complex controls. They work very much like the simple bound controls in that you attach a data source to them and they render automatically. However, these controls differ by displaying the data in more elaborate ways. These controls include the *GridView*, the *FormView*, the *DetailsView*, and the *DataList*.

The best way to understand the nature of these controls is to work through a couple of examples. Let's start with the *GridView*.

The *GridView*

1. Add a new Web form to the DataBindORama site. Name it *UseGridView*.

2. Pick up a *GridView* from the toolbox (it's under the *Data* controls). Drop it on the form. Visual Studio will ask you to configure the *GridView*. Under the Choose Data Source... option, select **<New data source...>**. Point Visual Studio to the ASPNetStepByStep.mdb under the App_Data directory. When specifying the query, select "*" to query for all the columns. Finally, enable Paging, Sorting, and Selection from the *GridView* Configuration menu. After configuring the *GridView*, Visual Studio will show you a representation of the format the query will use when it is rendered to the browser:

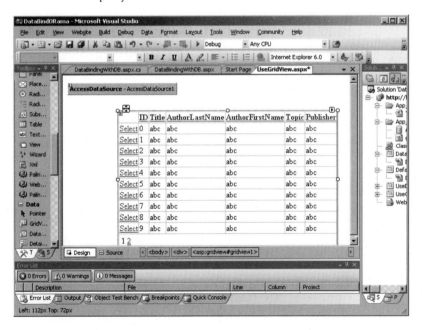

3. Run the program. Try the various options such as paging through the data and sorting to get a feel as to how the *GridView* works.

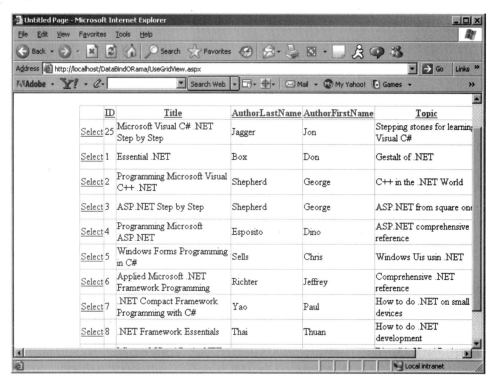

4. Go back to Visual Studio and try formatting the *GridView* to change its appearance. As with all the other ASP.NET controls, the *GridView* includes a number of configurable properties such as the foreground and background colors. Some of the other specialized properties within the *GridView* include the *AlternateRowStyle*, the *PagerSettings*, and the *PagerStyle*.

The *GridView* is useful for displaying tables in a format where you can see all the rows and columns at once. While the classic *DataGrid* is still available, the *GridView* handles tasks such as selecting rows and sorting by column.

Here's a look at another complex control: the *FormView*.

The *FormView*

1. Add a new Web form to the DataBindORama site named *UseFormView*.

2. Pick up a *FormView* from the toolbox (it's under the *Data* controls). Drop it on the form. Visual Studio will ask you to configure the *FormView*. Under the Choose Data Source… option, select **<New data source…>**. Point Visual Studio to the ASPNetStepByStep.mdb under the App_Data directory. When specifying the query, select "*" to query for all the columns.

3. Select the AutoFormat option from the Configuration menu. Here you have the opportunity to apply a couple of canned styles to the *FormView*. The example accompanying this text uses the *classic* style.

4. Finally, enable paging from the *FormView* Configuration menu by selecting the **Enable Paging** check box. Set the *HeadingText* property to give the *FormView* a title (perhaps something like ".NET Reference Authors and Titles").

5. After configuring the *FormView*, Visual Studio will show you a representation of the format the query will use when it is rendered to the browser:

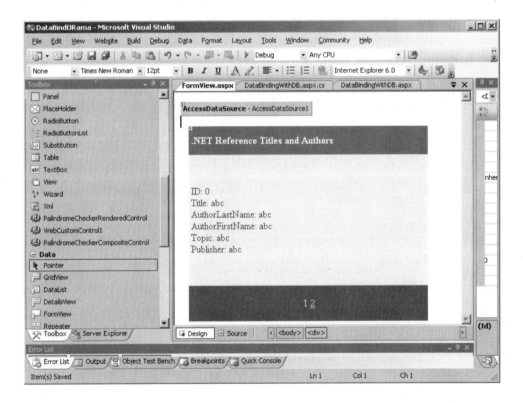

6. Run the program. Try the various options such as paging through the data to get a feel for how the *FormView* works.

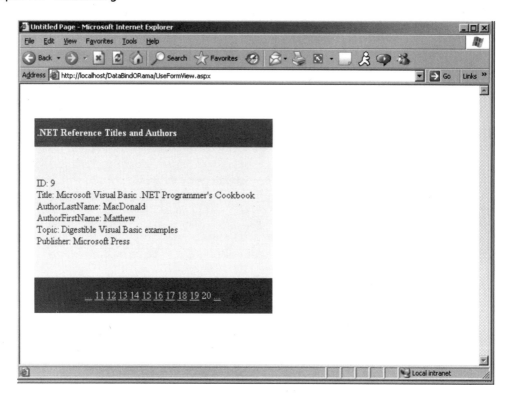

The *FormView* is useful for gathering the information for singular rows in one place. The user navigates between each row, but the focus is always on the current row.

The *DetailsView*

1. Add a new Web form to the DataBindORama site named *UseDetailsView*.

2. Pick up a *DetailView* from the toolbox (it's under the *Data* controls). Drop it on the form. Visual Studio will ask you to configure the *DetailsView*. Under the Choose Data Source... option, select **<New data source...>**. Point Visual Studio to the ASPNetStep-ByStep.mdb under the App_Data directory. When specifying the query, select "*" to select all the columns.

3. Select the AutoFormat option from the Configuration menu. Here you have the opportunity to apply a couple of canned styles to the *DetailsView*. The example accompanying this text uses the *classic* style.

4. Select the **Edit Fields...** option from the Configuration menu. Check the **Auto-Generate fields** check box on the dialog box.

5. Finally, enable paging from the *DetailsView* Configuration menu. Set the *HeadingText* property to give the *FormView* a title (perhaps something like ".NET Reference Authors and Titles").

6. After configuring the *DetailsView*, Visual Studio will show you a representation of the format the query will use when it is rendered to the browser:

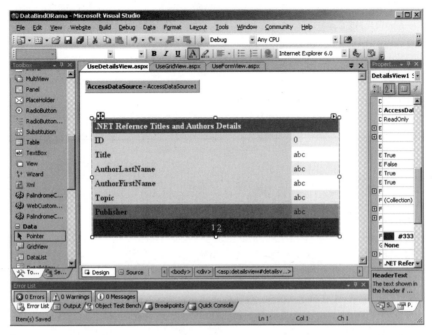

7. Run the program. Try the various options such as paging through the data to get a feel as to how the *DetailsView* works.

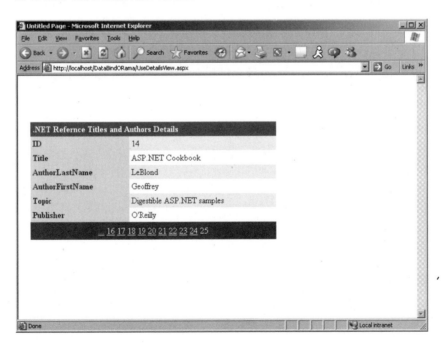

The *DataList* control was available in ASP.NET 1.*x*. It's been updated to support declarative databinding. Here's a look at the *DataList*.

The *DataList*

1. Add a new Web form to the DataBindORama site named *UseDataList*.

2. Pick up a *DataList* from the toolbox (it's under the *Data* controls). Drop it on the form. Visual Studio will ask you to configure the *DataList*. Under the Choose Data Source... option, select **<New data source...>**. Point Visual Studio to the ASPNetStepByStep.mdb under the App_Data directory. When specifying the query, select "*" to query for all the columns.

3. Select the AutoFormat option from the Configuration menu. Here you have the opportunity to apply a couple of canned styles to the *DataList*. The example accompanying this text uses the *slate* style.

4. Select the *DataList* Properties dialog box from the *DataList* Configuration menu by selecting **Property Builder**. Make sure the Show header and the Show footer check boxes are selected.

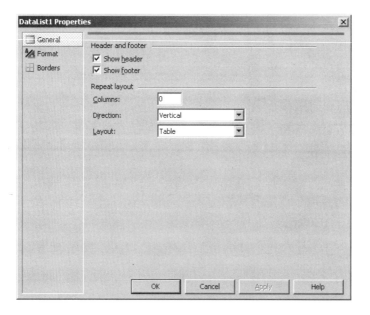

5. Set the *Caption* property to give the *DataList* a title (perhaps something like: ".NET Reference Authors and Titles").

6. After configuring the *DataList*, Visual Studio will show you a representation of the format the query will use when it is rendered to the browser:

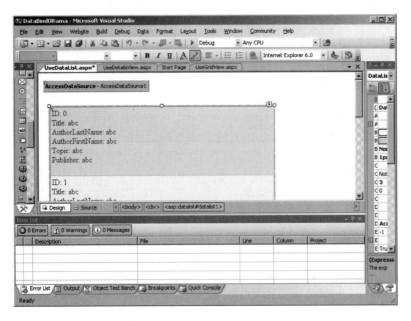

7. Run the program to see how the *DataList* renders itself.

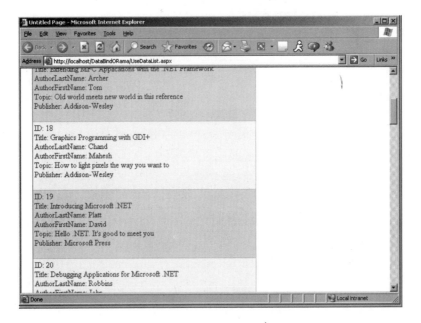

Conclusion

In this chapter, we looked at ASP.NET's support for databound controls. While it's not rocket science to iterate through a collection and add the data to ASP.NET's server-side controls, it's a fairly common operation. That Microsoft pushed it down into the Framework classes is a good thing.

One of the advantages of these controls is that they don't care at all where their data comes from. The data might be as simple as an *ArrayList* composed of .NET types (with each element in the array representing a row and each property representing a column). On the other hand, the data bound to a control might be as complex as *IDataReader* or a *DataSet* acquired from a physical database.

Looking at databound controls invariably involves mentioning the ASP.NET database story: ADO.NET. The ADO.NET managed classes are for connecting to the database, commanding the database, and harvesting the results afterward. While connecting to the database manually (via .NET 1.*x*-style code) is still supported, .NET version 2.0 and Visual Studio 2005 offer an easier way to associated controls with data via the *DataSource* controls.

ASP.NET includes a number of databound controls that may be matched up with a collection or (in the case of certain *DataSource* controls) a data source. The controls then assume the burden of iterating through the data and rendering the correct tags to the client.

Chapter 11 Quick Reference

To	Do This
Bind a collection to a control	Set the control's *DataSource* property to the collection
Choose a column to display in the control	Set the control's *TextTextField* property to the column name
Choose a column to use programmatically (that's NOT displayed in the control)	Set the control's *TextValueField* property to the column name
Display a *DataTable* as a grid	Use the *DataGrid* or the *GridView* controls
Display a *DataTable* as a formatted, repeating list	Use either the *DataList* or the *Repeater*
Make a class' member variables available as DataTextFields and DataValueFields within a control	Expose the members as properties

Chapter 12

Personalization

After completing this chapter, you will be able to

■ Use ASP.NET personalization

■ Apply personalization to a Web site

This chapter covers ASP.NET's built-in personalization features. A major Theme throughout ASP.NET 2.0 is to provide frameworks and support for implementing features most Web sites need. For example, we saw the support ASP.NET 2.0 provides for making a common look and feel throughout a site in Chapter 8. We saw the new login controls in Chapter 10. The new login controls are there so you don't have to hash out yet one more login control.

Personalizing Web sites is another feature that often makes for a great Web site. Up until ASP.NET 2.0, it was up to you to provide any personalization support for your site. Now these features are rolled into ASP.NET 2.0.

Let's take a look at Web personalization.

Personalizing Web Visits

When the Internet and the Web first began coming into prominence, most of the sites you could surf to contained only static content. That is, they offered only text, graphics, and perhaps links to other pages. The early Web surfing community consisted of a host of anonymous voyeurs peering into the contents of those early Web servers.

Until the Web began exploding with interactive sites, there was really no need for the Web site to care who was looking at it. However, any businessperson worth his or her salt will tell you that tailoring and targeting content toward specific individuals is good for business.

The next time you go online to shop or visit a subscription-type site, take note of how much the site knows about you. Very often (if you've provided login information) the site will greet you with your name. It may point you to information or products that might interest you. This demonstrates the notion of personalizing a Web site.

In the past, any personalization of your site resulted from code you wrote, such as code to manage user preferences in cookies or code to store personal information in back-end databases. In addition to simply storing and managing the personal information, you had to integrate the personal information management with whatever authentication and authorization scheme you decided to use.

ASP.NET 2.0 now includes services for personalizing a Web site to suit a particular client's taste. There's no reason you couldn't write your own database and services to provide this functionality. However, as with all these services provided by ASP.NET, they bring with them some consistency and prevent your having to write all the code yourself.

Personalization in ASP.NET

ASP.NET 2.0 provides specific support for personalizing Web sites. The support ASP.NET provides for personalization service greatly simplifies the whole management and storage of personal information. Defining a Web site's personalization facilities begins with defining User Profiles.

User Profiles

The heart of the new ASP.NET personalization service is the User Profile. A User Profile defines what kind of personal information your Web site needs. For example, you may want to know personal data about users of your Web site, such as name, gender, number of visits to the site, and so forth. User Profiles are also handy for storing user preferences for your site. For example, you might include a Theme as part of a personal profile so that users can tailor the pages to their particular tastes.

Once the personalization properties are defined in Web.Config, a component within .NET has to be able to read it and use it. That job is handled by ASP.NET personalization providers.

Personalization Providers

In Chapter 11 on databinding, we saw that .NET includes a new provider pattern. Providers hide the coding differences involved in creating the necessary objects for connecting to various databases. Just pick a provider (for example, SQL Server or Access), and the provider does the dirty work of manufacturing connections and such. ASP.NET includes two personalization providers out of the box: a profile provider for custom user data and a personalization provider for Web Parts as we saw in Chapter 7.

ASP.NET defines the fundamental provider capabilities in an abstract class named *PersonalizationProvider*. Those capabilities include such things as loading and saving personalization properties and managing their relationship to any Web Parts used within a site.

ASP.NET provides a default implementation of these capabilities in a concrete class named *SqlPersonalizationProvider*, which is derived from *PersonalizationProvider*.

Using Personalization

Using personalization is pretty straightforward. You basically define personalization properties in Web.Config. ASP.NET will synthesize a class you may use to manage personalization settings. At that point, profile information is available in much the same way as session state is available.

Defining Profiles in Web.Config

Profile schema is defined within Web.Config as name/type pairs. Imagine that in the course of designing your site, you decided you'd like to track the following information about a particular user:

- User name
- Gender
- Visit count
- Birthday

Defining these properties is a matter of populating them in Web.Config. A definition for the properties listed above might look like this Web.Config:

```
<system.web>
   <profile automaticSaveEnabled="true" >
      <properties>
         <add name="NumVisits" type="System.Int32"/>
         <add name="UserName" type="System.String"/>
         <add name="Gender" type="bool">
         <add name="Birthday" type="System.DateTime">
      </properties>
   </profile>
</system.web>
```

The personalization properties consist of name/type pairs and will basically become the schema under which the personalization data will be stored. Once defined in the Web.Config file, the profile may be used in the site through the *Profile* property found in the current *Http-Context* (and is also available via the *Page*).

Use Profile Information

To use the profile in the Web site, you access it in much the same way you might access session state. However, instead of being represented by name/value pairs accessed through an indexer, the ASP.NET compiler will synthesize a profile object based upon the scheme defined in the Web.Config file.

For example, given the schema listed above, ASP.NET will synthesize a class named *Profile-Common*, based upon the *ProfileBase* class. The synthesized class will reflect the instructions written into the Web.Config by inserting properties, shown here in bold:

```
public class ProfileCommon : ProfileBase
{
    public  virtual  HttpProfile GetProfile(string username);
    public  object GetPropertyValue(string propertyName);
    public  void SetPropertyValue(string propertyName,
            object propertyValue);
    public  HttpProfileGroupBase GetProfileGroup(String groupName);
    public  void Initialize(String username,Boolean isAuthenticated);
    public  virtual void Save();
    public  void Initialize(SettingsContext context,
            SettingsPropertyCollection properties,
            SettingsProviderCollection providers);
    public string UserName{get; set;};
    public int NumVisits{get; set;};
    public bool Gender(get; set; );
    public DateTime Birthdate{get; set; };
}
```

To access the profile properties, simply use the *Profile* property within the page. The *Profile* property is an instance of the *ProfileCommon* class synthesized by ASP.NET. Just access the members of the *Profile*, like so:

```
protected void Page_Load(object sender, EventArgs e)
{
    if (Profile.Name != null)
    {
        Response.Write("Hello " + Profile.Name);
        Response.Write("Your birthday is " +
            Profile.Birthdate);
    }
}
```

Saving Profile Changes

The preceding code snippet assumes there's already personalization information associated with the user. To insert profile data for a particular user, simply set the properties of the *Profile* object. For example, imagine a page that includes a handler for saving the profile. It might look something like this:

```
protected void ProfileSaveClicked(object sender, EventArgs e)
{
    Profile.Name = this.TextBoxName.Text;
    Profile.Birthdate = this.Calendar1.SelectedDate;
}
```

The easiest way to ensure that the personalization properties persist is to set the *automaticSaveEnabled* to true. Personal profile data will be saved automatically by the provider.

Alternatively, you may call *Profile.Save* as necessary to save the personalization properties. In addition to saving and loading profiles, you may also delete the profile for a specific user by calling *Profile.DeleteProfile*.

Profiles and Users

Profile information is associated with the current user based upon the identity of the user. By default, ASP.NET uses the *User.Identity.Name* within the current *HttpContext* as the key to store data. By default, profiles are available only for authenticated users.

ASP.NET supports anonymous profiles as well. Turn this on within Web.Config. The default tracking mechanism for anonymous profiles is to use cookies. However, as with tracking session state, you may tell ASP.NET to use a mangled URL.

The following exercise illustrates using personalization profiles based on the user's login ID.

Using Profiles

1. Create a new project. Name the project MakeItPersonal.

2. Add a Web.Config file to the project. Update Web.Config to include some profile properties. The example here includes a user name, a Theme, and a birthdate. Be sure to turn *anonymousIdentification* to true. The following example shows that you may group and nest profile structures using the *<group>* element.

```
<system.web>

    <profile>
      <properties >
        <add name="Theme" type="System.String"/>
        <add name="Name" type="String"/>
        <add name="Birthdate"" type="System.DateTime"/>
        <group name="Address">
            <add name="StreetAddress"/>
            <add name="City"/>
            <add name="State"/>
            <add name="ZipCode"/>
        </group>
      </properties>
    </profile>

</system.web>
```

Note Supporting Anonymous Personalization This example uses the authenticated user name as the key for locating personalization information. However, ASP.NET supports "anonymous" personalization. That is, ASP.NET supports personalization information for anonymous users—but tracks the users via a cookie. You may add support for anonymous personalization tracking by turning the anonymousIdentification element to "true" and specifying cookie parameters like this:

```
<anonymousIdentification enabled="true"
cookieName=".ASPXANONYMOUSUSER"
cookieTimeout="120000"
cookiePath="/"
cookieRequireSSL="false"
cookieSlidingExpiration="true"
cookieProtection="Encryption"
cookieless="UseDeviceProfile" />
```

By configuring the site this way, ASP.NET will store the personalization settings based on a cookie it generates when a user first hits the site.

3. Borrow the Default and SeeingRed Themes from the MasterPagesSite project (Chapter 8). This will let the user pick the Theme.

4. Borrow the UseThemes.aspx and .cs files from the MasterPagesSite project.

5. Borrow the Banner.ascx file from the MasterPagesSite.

6. Now update the Default.aspx page. This will be where users type profile information.

   Add text boxes for the name, address, city, state, and zip code.

   Add a drop-down list box populated with Default and SeeingRed items. This will be used for selecting the Theme.

   Also add a calendar control to pick the birthdate.

7. Add a button the user may click to submit profile information. Add a handler to input these values into the profile. Double-click on the button to add the handler.

   The input screen should look something like this:

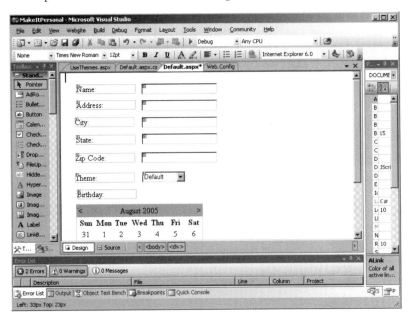

> **Note   Adding Users to Authenticate** This example uses the authenticated user name as the key for storing personalization values. Use the ASP.NET Configuration Utility to apply Forms Authentication to this application (as described in chapter 10). Also add at least one user so that you have one to personalize. Add a Login.ASPX screen to the site and modify the site's access rules to enforce authentication. Then you will be able to see the personalization information being stored and retrieved.

8. Update *Page_Load* to display profile information (if it's there). Grab the profile object and set each of the text boxes and the calendar control.

```
using System.Web;
using System.Web.Security;
using System.Web.UI;
using System.Web.UI.WebControls;
using System.Web.UI.WebControls.WebParts;
using System.Web.UI.HtmlControls;

public partial class _Default : System.Web.UI.Page
{
    protected void Page_Load(object sender, EventArgs e)
    {
        if (!this.IsPostBack)

        {
            ProfileCommon pc = this.Profile.GetProfile(Profile.UserName);
            if (pc != null)
            {
                this.TextBoxName.Text = pc.Name;
                this.TextBoxAddress.Text = pc.Address.StreetAddress;
                this.TextBoxCity.Text = pc.Address.City;
                this.TextBoxState.Text = pc.Address.State;
                this.TextBoxZipCode.Text = pc.Address.ZipCode;
                this.DropDownList1.SelectedValue = pc.Theme;
                this.Calendar1.SelectedDate = pc.Birthdate;
            }
        }
    }
// ...
}
```

9. Update the profile submission handler to store the profile information.

```
protected void ButtonSubmitProfile_Click(object sender, EventArgs e)
{

ProfileCommon pc = this.Profile.GetProfile(Profile.UserName);

    if (pc != null)
    {
        pc.Name = this.TextBoxName.Text;
        pc.Address.StreetAddress = this.TextBoxAddress.Text;
        pc.Address.City = this.TextBoxCity.Text;
        pc.Address.State = this.TextBoxState.Text;
```

```
        pc.Address.ZipCode = this.TextBoxZipCode.Text;
        pc.Theme = this.DropDownList1.SelectedValue;
        pc.Birthdate = this.Calendar1.SelectedDate;

        pc.Save();
    }
}
```

10. Finally, update the UseThemes.aspx page to use the Theme. Override the page's *OnPreInit* method. Have the code apply the Theme as specified by the profile.

```
protected override void OnPreInit(EventArgs e)
{
    ProfileCommon pc = this.Profile.GetProfile(Profile.UserName);
        if (pc != null)
        {
            String strTheme = pc.Theme.ToString();
            if (strTheme != null &&
                strTheme.Length > 0)
            {
                this.Theme = strTheme;
            }
        }
    base.OnPreInit(e)
}
```

11. When you surf to the page, you should be able to enter the profile information and submit it. Following your initial visit, the profile will be available whenever you hit the site.

Conclusion

Profiles represent an effective way to add personalization to your site. The profile scheme in the Web.Config defines the profiles available to the application. ASP.NET will synthesize a *ProfileCommon* class that includes support for the properties defined in Web.Config. To access the properties, grab the Profile object from the Page for the current *HttpContext*. ASP.NET will take care of the details of serializing the property data and tracking it either anonymously or by using the identity of the logged in user.

Chapter 12 Quick Reference

To	Do This
Define personalization profile settings	Use the *<profile>* element in Web.Config. Define name/type pairs to create the profiles schema
Access the profile properties	Profile properties are available through the page and through the current *HttpContext*
Track the profiles with cookies	Enable *anonymousIdentification* in Web.Config

Chapter 13

Session State

After completing this chapter, you will be able to

- Explain the importance of managing session state in a Web application

- Use the session state manager (the *Session* object)

- Configure session state

- Store session state on a state server

- Store session state in a database

This chapter covers managing session state within your ASP.NET application. Programming Web applications requires you to be very mindful of how the state of your application is distributed at any moment. One of the most important types of state in a Web application is session state—the state associated with a single particular session. Because Web applications are distributed by nature, keeping track of any single client has to be done deliberately.

ASP.NET session state support is extensive, reliable, and flexible—offering many advantages over the session state support available in classic ASP. For starters, ASP.NET session state is handled by the *Session* object—an object dictionary that's automatically created with each new session (if you have session state enabled). The *Session* object is easily accessible through the

HttpContext object, which you can reference at any point during the request. The process of associating user state with a particular user's session is handled automatically by ASP.NET. Whenever you want to access session state, you just grab it from the context (it's also mapped into a member variable living on the page). You may choose how ASP.NET tracks session state, and you may even tell ASP.NET where to store session state.

Let's begin with a look at how various pieces of state are managed by ASP.NET, and the gap filled by the session state manager.

Why Session State?

After working with ASP.NET during the previous chapters, one theme should be emerging. Web-based programming distinguishes itself as a programming idiom in which you're trying to manage an application serving multiple users distributed over a wide area. What's more, you're doing it over a disconnected protocol.

For example, imagine you're writing some sort of shopping portal. Certain types of the application data can be kept in a central database—things like inventory and supplier lists. We've seen that *System.Web.UI.Page* and server-side controls themselves manage view state. However, when you think about the nature of data in a user's shopping cart, you see the data clearly belongs elsewhere.

You don't really want to store that data in the page's *ViewState*. While it's possible for simple applications, storing large chunks of data in view state will bog down your users' experience of the site (it'll be much slower) and it poses a security risk by having items travel back and forth with each request. In addition, only serializable types may be stored in view state.

Unfortunately, a single user's data doesn't really belong in the central database, either. Perhaps if you expected only one user over the lifetime of your application, that might work. However, remember the nature of a Web application is to make your application available to as many clients as possible. Suddenly, it becomes clear that you want to be able to carve out a small data holding area that persists for the lifetime of a single user's session. This type of data is known as *session state*.

ASP.NET and Session State

Since its inception, ASP.NET has supported session state. When session state is turned on, ASP.NET creates a new *Session* object for each new request. The *Session* object becomes part of the context (and is available through the page). ASP.NET stamps the *Session* object with an identifier (more on that later), and the *Session* object is reconstituted when a request comes through containing a valid session identifier. The *Session* object follows the page around and becomes a convenient repository for storing information that has to survive throughout the session (and not simply for the duration of the page).

The *Session* object is a dictionary of name-value pairs. You can associate any CLR-based object with a key of your choosing and place it in the *Session* object so it will be there when the next request belonging to that session comes through. Then you may access that piece of data using the key under which it was stored. For example, if you wanted to store some information provided by the user in the *Session* object, you'd write code like this:

```
void StoreInfoInSession()
{
   String strFromUser = TextBox1.Text;
   Session["strFromUser"] = strFromUser;
}
```

To retrieve the string during the next request, you'd use code like this:

```
void GetInfoFromSession()
{
   String strFromUser = Session["strFromUser"] ;
   TextBox1.Text = strFromUser;
}
```

The square braces on the *Session* object indicate an *indexer*. The indexer is a convenient syntax for express keys—both when inserting data into and retrieving data from the *Session* object.

Managing session state in ASP.NET is extraordinarily convenient. In ASP.NET, session state may live in a number of places including (1) in proc—in the ASP.NET worker process, (2) on a separate state server running a daemon process, and (3) in a SQL Server database.

Let's start by getting a taste of using session state right now.

Getting a Taste of Session State

To see how session state works, here's an exercise that involves creating a Web site whose page stores a value as a member variable in the page and as an element of session state. It will illustrate the difference between page state during a request and session data that persists beyond a request.

Trying Session State

1. Create a new Web site. Name it SessionState. Make sure it's an HTTP site so you may use IIS to configure the session state.

2. In the default page (Default.aspx), drag a text box (and a label to identify the *TextBox* if you want) onto the form. Then drag two buttons and another label onto the form like so:

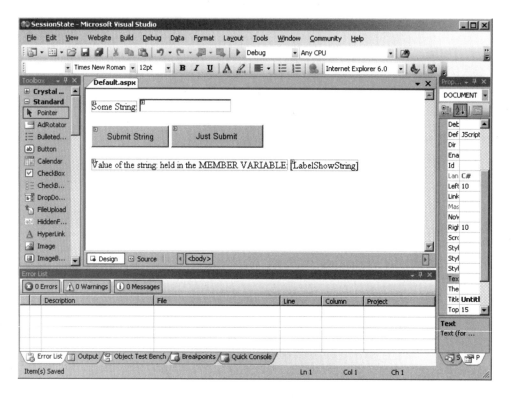

3. Name the first button Submit String. That is, set the ID to *SubmitString*. It doesn't matter what you name the second button. The first button will submit the string to the form, and the other button will just perform a post back. That way, you'll be able to see the ephemeral nature of page member variables. Name the label *LabelShowString*. We'll use it to display the value of the string.

4. Add a *String* variable member to the page. In the *Page_Load* handler, set the text box on the page to the value of the string. Then add a handler for the Submit String button. Have the handler take the *Text* property from the *TextBox1* and store it in the page member variable. Then set the *LabelShowString* label text to the value of the string like so:

```
public partial class _Default : System.Web.UI.Page
{

    String _str;

    protected void Page_Load(object sender, EventArgs e)
    {
```

```
      this.LabelShowString.Text = this._str;

  }
  protected void SubmitString_Click(object sender, EventArgs e)
  {

    this._str = this.TextBox1.Text;
    this.LabelShowString.Text = this._str;

  }
}
```

5. Now run the program. Type a string into the text box and click **Submit String**. When the post goes to the page, the page will show the string in the label.

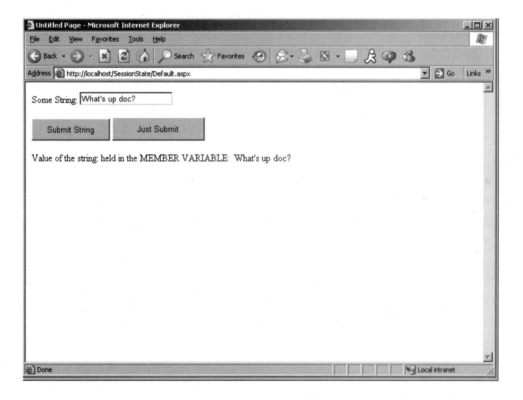

6. Now click the **Submit String** button. What happens? Remember, *Page_Load* simply looks at the value of the *_str* member variable and stuffs it into the label. Pages (and HTTP handlers in general) are very short-lived objects. They live for the duration of the request and then are destroyed—along with all the data they hold. The *_str* member variable evaporated as soon as the last request finished. A new *_str* member variable (which was empty) was instantiated as soon as the page was recreated.

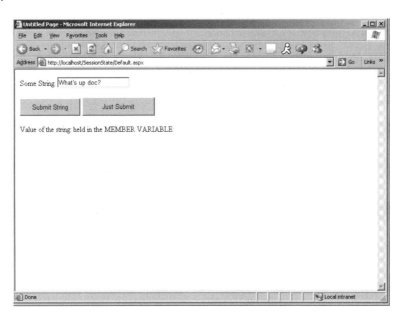

To sum up, we saw in Chapter 4 that controls manage their own state. But in this case, we're taking the data from the text box and storing it in a member variable in the *Page* class. The lifetime of the page is very short. The page lives long enough to generate a response, then it disappears. Any state you've stored as data members in the page disappears, too.

7. Session state is a way to solve this issue. To show this, add a new label to the page. This one will show the data as retrieved from the *Session* object.

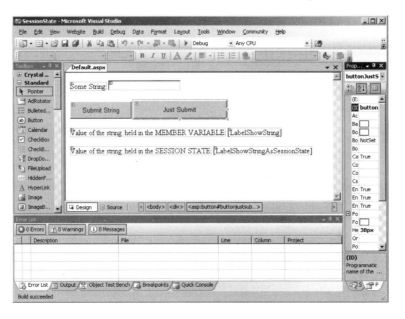

8. Write code to store the string in session state. Have the *SubmitString* take the text from the *TextBox1* and store it into the *Session* object. Then update the *Page_Load* method to display the value as it came from session state as shown below:

```
public partial class _Default : System.Web.UI.Page
{
    String _str;

    protected void Page_Load(object sender, EventArgs e)
    {
        this.LabelShowString.Text = this._str;

        this.LabelShowStringAsSessionState.Text =
            (String)this.Session["str"];

    }
    protected void SubmitString_Click(object sender, EventArgs e)
    {
        this._str = this.TextBox1.Text;
        this.Session["str"] = this.TextBox1.Text;
        this.LabelShowString.Text = this._str;

        this.LabelShowStringAsSessionState.Text =
            (String)this.Session["str"];
    }
}
```

9. Run the program. Type in a string and click the **Submit String** button. Both labels should contain data. The *LabelShowString* label will hold data because the *SubmitString* handler made the assignment. The *LabelShowStringAsSessionState* label also shows data because the handler set that text.

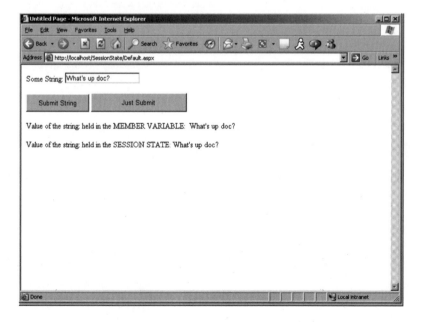

10. Now click the **Just Submit** button and see what happens:

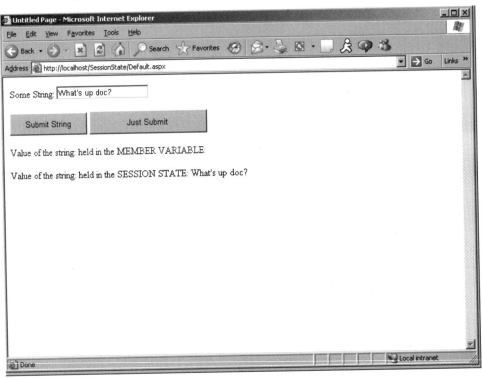

In this case, the page was simply submitted, causing only the *Page_Load* to be executed. *Page_Load* displays both the *_str* member variable (which is blank because it lives and dies with the page) and the data from the *Session* object (which lives independently of the page).

As you can see, session state is pretty convenient. However, we wouldn't get very far if all we could do was store simple strings and scalars. Fortunately, the session dictionary stores all manner of CLR objects.

Session State and More Complex Data

ASP.NET's *Session* object will store any object running within the CLR. That goes for larger data—not just small strings or other scalar types. One of the most common uses for the *Session* object is for implementing features like shopping carts (or any other data that has to go with a particular client). For example, if you're developing a commerce-oriented site for customers to purchase products, you'd probably implement a central database representing your inventory. Then as each user signs on, they will have the opportunity to select items from your inventory and place them in a temporary holding area associated with the session they're running. In ASP.NET that holding area is the *Session* object.

A number of different collections are useful for managing shopping cart-like scenarios. Probably the easiest to use is the good ol' *ArrayList*—an automatically sizing array that supports both random access and the *IList* interface. However, for other scenarios you might use a *DataTable*, a *DataSet*, or some other more complex type.

We took a quick look at ADO and data access in Chapter 11—all about databinding. The next example revisits databound controls (the *DataList* and the *GridView*. We'll also see the *DataTable* in depth.

Session State, ADO.NET Objects, and Databound Controls

This example illustrates using ADO.NET objects, databound controls, and session state to transfer items from an inventory (represented as a *DataList*) to a collection of selected items (represented using a *GridView*).

1. Create a new page on the SessionState site named UseDataList.aspx.

2. Drag a *DataList* onto the page and place it on the right side of the page.

3. When setting up the *DataList*, select *AutoFormat* to give the *DataList* a sleeker appearance. The style used in the application accompanying this chapter is the *slate* style.

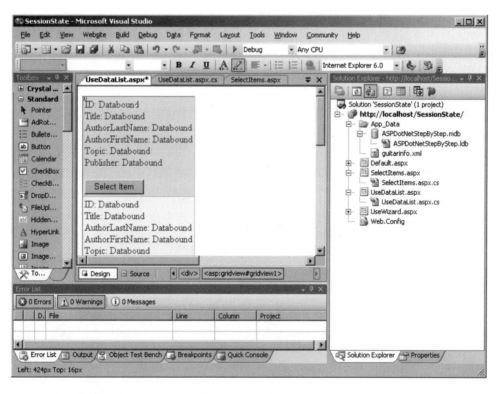

4. Give this *DataList* a caption of **Items in Inventory**.

5. Switch to the Source view in the designer. In the declaration template, add a button as shown in the code highlighted below. The button *Text* property should be **Select Item**. The button ID should be **ButtonSelectItem**.

```
<asp:DataList ID="DataList1"
    runat="server" BackColor="White" BorderColor="#E7E7FF"
    BorderStyle="None" BorderWidth="1px" CellPadding="3"
    GridLines="Horizontal"
    Style="z-index: 100; left: 8px; position: absolute; top: 16px"
    OnItemCommand="DataList1_ItemCommand" Caption="Items in Inventory" >
<FooterStyle BackColor="#B5C7DE" ForeColor="#4A3C8C" />
<SelectedItemStyle BackColor="#738A9C"
        Font-Bold="True" ForeColor="#F7F7F7" />
<AlternatingItemStyle BackColor="#F7F7F7" />
<ItemStyle BackColor="#E7E7FF" ForeColor="#4A3C8C" />
        <ItemTemplate>
        ID:
        <asp:Label ID="IDLabel"
        runat="server" Text='<%# Eval("ID") %>'></asp:Label><br />
        Title:
        <asp:Label ID="TitleLabel"
        runat="server" Text='<%# Eval("Title") %>'></asp:Label><br />
        AuthorLastName:
        <asp:Label ID="AuthorLastNameLabel"
        runat="server" Text='<%#
Eval("AuthorLastName")
        %>'></asp:Label><br />
        AuthorFirstName:
        <asp:Label ID="AuthorFirstNameLabel"
        runat="server" Text='<%#
Eval("AuthorFirstName")
        %>'></asp:Label><br />
        Topic:
        <asp:Label ID="TopicLabel" runat="server"
        Text='<%# Eval("Topic") %>'></asp:Label><br />
        Publisher:
        <asp:Label ID="PublisherLabel"
        runat="server"
        Text='<%# Eval("Publisher") %>'></asp:Label><br />
        <br />

        <asp:Button ID="SelectItem"
            CommandName="DataList1_ItemCommand"
            runat=server Text="Select Item" />

         
        </ItemTemplate>
            <HeaderStyle BackColor="#4A3C8C" Font-
    Bold="True"
                ForeColor="#F7F7F7" />
    </asp:DataList>
```

6. Stub out a shell for the *SelectItem* button on handler. The button handler should be named *DataList1_ItemCommand* to match the identifier in the *DataList1*. We'll use it shortly to move items from the inventory to the selected items table.

```
public partial class UseDataList : System.Web.UI.Page
{

    protected void DataList1_ItemCommand(object source,
            DataListCommandEventArgs e)
    {
    }

}
```

7. Go back to the code for the page and add some code to open a database and populate the *DataList*. Name the function *GetInventory*. The examples that come with this book include a database named ASPDotNetStepByStep.mdb that will work. You can use the connection string listed below to connect to the database. Make sure the database path points to the file correctly using your directory structure.

```
public partial class UseDataList : System.Web.UI.Page
{

    protected DataTable GetInventory()
    {
        String strConnection =
        @"Provider=Microsoft.Jet.OLEDB.4.0;
        DataSource=
        c:\\inetpub\\wwwroot\\SessionState\\App_Data\\ASPDotNetStepByStep.mdb";

        DbProviderFactory f =
            DbProviderFactories.GetFactory("System.Data.OleDb");

        DbConnection connection = f.CreateConnection();
        connection.ConnectionString = strConnection;

        connection.Open();

        DbCommand command = f.CreateCommand();
        command.CommandText = "Select * from DotNetReferences";
        command.Connection = connection;

        IDataReader reader = command.ExecuteReader();

        DataTable dt = new DataTable();
        dt.Load(reader);
        reader.Close();
        connection.Close();
        connection.Dispose();

        return dt;
    }

    protected DataTable BindToinventory()
    {
        DataTable dt;
        dt = this.GetInventory();
        this.DataList1.DataSource = dt;
        this.DataBind();
```

```
        return dt;
    }

// more goes here…
}
```

8. Now add a method named *CreateSelectedItemsData*. This will be a table into which selected items will be placed. The method will take a *DataTable* object that will describe the schema of the data in the live database (we'll see how to get that in a minute). You can create an empty *DataTable* by constructing it and then adding *Columns* to the column collection. The schema coming from the database will have the column name and the data type.

```
public partial class UseDataList : System.Web.UI.Page
{

  protected DataTable CreateSelectedItemsTable(DataTable tableSchema)
  {

      DataTable tableSelectedItemsData = new DataTable();

      foreach(DataColumn dc in tableSchema.Columns)
      {
          tableSelectedItemsData.Columns.Add(dc.ColumnName,
              dc.DataType);
      }
      return tableSelectedItemsData;

  }
}
```

9. Update the page code to handle *Page_Load*. When the initial request to a page is made (that is, if the request is *not* a post back), *Page_Load* should call *BindToInventory* (which returns the *DataTable* snapshot of the *DotNetReferences* table). Use the *DataTable* as the schema upon which to base the selected items table. That is, declare an instance of a *DataTable* and assign it the result of *CreateSelectedItemsTable*. Then store the (now empty) table in the *Session* object using the key *tableSelectedItems*.

```
public partial class UseDataList : System.Web.UI.Page
{
    protected void Page_Load(object sender, EventArgs e)
    {

        if (!IsPostBack)
        {
            DataTable dt = BindToInventory();
            DataTable tableSelectedItems =
                this.CreateSelectedItemsTable(dt);
            Session["tableSelectedItems"] = tableSelectedItems;
        }

    }
}
```

Browse to the Web site to make sure that the database connects. It should look something like this:

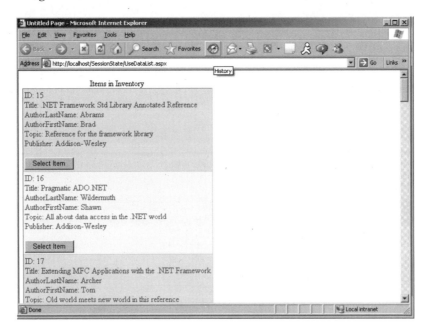

10. Now add a *GridView* to the page. Don't bother to give it a data source. It represents the table of selected items held in session state. We'll add that shortly. Make sure the *Auto-GenerateColumns* property is set to true.

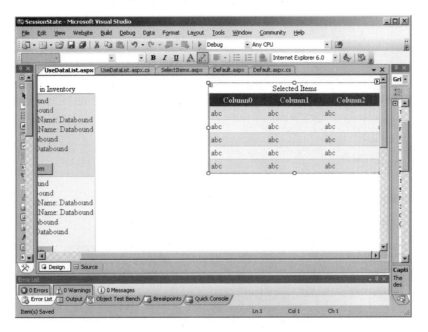

11.   Finally, add a handler for the *SelectItem* button. This method should move items from the inventory to the selected items table. You can get the selected item index from the *DataListCommandEventArgs* coming into the handler. Calling *BindToInventory* will set up the *DataList* data source so you can fetch the selected item. You may access the columns within the selected row using ordinal indices. From the values in each column, construct a new *DataRow* and add it to the selected items table. Store the modified table back in session state. Finally, apply the new selected items table to the *DataSource* in the *GridView1* and bind the *GridView1*.

```
public partial class UseDataList : System.Web.UI.Page
{
    protected void DataList1_ItemCommand(object source,
        DataListCommandEventArgs e)
    {

        int nItemIndex = e.Item.ItemIndex;
        this.DataList1.SelectedIndex = nItemIndex;

        BindToinventory();

        // Order of the columns is:
        // ID, Title, FirstName, LastName, Topic, Publisher

        DataTable dt = (DataTable)DataList1.DataSource;
        String strID = (dt.Rows[nItemIndex][0]).ToString();
        String strTitle = (dt.Rows[nItemIndex][1]).ToString();
        String strAuthorLastName = (dt.Rows[nItemIndex][2]).ToString();
        String strAuthorFirstName = (dt.Rows[nItemIndex][3]).ToString();
        String strTopic = (dt.Rows[nItemIndex][4]).ToString();
        String strPublisher = (dt.Rows[nItemIndex][5]).ToString();

        DataTable tableSelectedItems;
        tableSelectedItems = (DataTable)Session["tableSelectedItems"];

        DataRow dr = tableSelectedItems.NewRow();
        dr[0] = strID;
        dr[1] = strTitle;
        dr[2] = strAuthorLastName;
        dr[3] = strAuthorFirstName;
        dr[4] = strTopic;
        dr[3] = strPublisher;

        tableSelectedItems.Rows.Add(dr);

        Session["tableSelectedItems"] = tableSelectedItems;

        this.GridView1.DataSource = tableSelectedItems;
        this.GridView1.DataBind();

    }
}
```

12. Run the site. When the page first comes up, you should see only the inventory list on the left side of the page. Click the **Select Item** button on some of the items. You should see your browser post back to the server and render the *DataList and* the *GridView* with the newly added selected item.

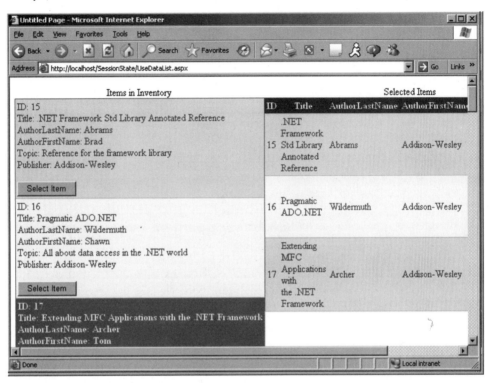

Now that you have a working application that uses session state, let's take a look at the different ways in which you may configure ASP.NET session state.

Configuring Session State

ASP.NET gives you several choices for managing session state. You can turn it off completely, you may run session state in the ASP.NET worker process, you may run it on a separate state server, or you may run it from a SQL Server database. Here's a rundown of the options available:

- **Don't use it at all.** By disabling session state, your application performance will increase because the page doesn't need to load the session when starting, nor does it need to store session state when it's going away. On the other hand, you won't be able to associate any data with a particular user.

- **Store session state in proc.** This is how session state is handled by default. In this case, the session dictionaries (the *Session* objects) are managed in the same process as the page and handler code. The advantage of using session state in process is that it's very fast and convenient. However, it's not durable. For example, if you restart IIS or somehow knock the server down, all session state is lost. In some cases, this may not be a big deal. However, if your shopping cart represents a shopping cart containing sizeable orders, losing that might be a big deal. In addition, the in process Session manager is confined to a single machine, meaning you can't use it in a Web form.

■ **Store session state in a state server.**   This option tells the ASP.NET runtime to direct all session management activities to a separate daemon process running on a particular machine. This option gives you the advantage of running your server in a Web farm. A Web farm is a group of servers tied together to serve Web pages. The ASP.NET Session State facilities support Web farms explicitly. To run in a Web form, you would direct all your applications to go to the same place to retrieve session information. The downside to this approach is that it does impede performance somewhat–applications need to make a network round-trip to the state server when loading or saving session information.

■ **Store session state in a database.**   Configuring your application to use a SQL Server database for state management causes ASP.NET to store session information within a SQL Server database somewhere on your network. Use this option when you want to run your server from within a Web form when you want session state to be durable and safe.

There are two ways to configure ASP.NET: the hard way and the easy way. As with most other configuration settings, the ASP.NET session state configuration ultimately happens within the Web.Config file. As always, you may configure Web.Config the hard way by using the typing Wizard (that is, typing the settings in by hand). Alternatively, you may use the ASP.NET Configuration Settings dialog box from IIS.

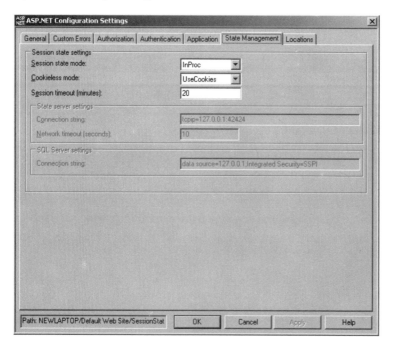

Turning Off Session State

The ASP.NET session state configuration tool available through IIS will touch your Web site's Web.Config file and insert the right configuration strings to enforce the settings you choose. To turn off session state completely, select Off from the session state mode control.

Storing Session State *InProc*

To store session state in the ASP.NET worker process, select *InProc* from the session state mode control. Your application will retrieve and store session information very quickly, but it will be available only to your application (and not on a Web form).

Storing Session State in a State Server

To have ASP.NET store session state on another server on your network, select *StateServer* from the *SessionState* mode control. When you select this item, the dialog box will enable the Connection String text box and the network timeout text box. Insert the protocol, IP address, and port for the state server in the Connection String text box. For example, the string:

```
tcpip=127.0.0.1:42424
```

will store the session state on the local machine over port 42424. If you want to store the session state on a machine other than your local server, change the IP address. Before session state is stored on a machine, you need to make sure the ASP.NET state server is running on that machine. You may get to it via the Services panel under the control panel.

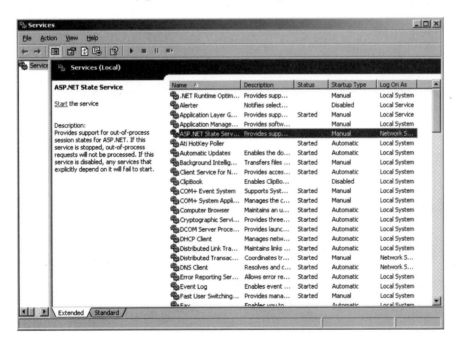

Storing Session State in a Database

The final option for storing session state is to use a SQL Server database. Select *SQLServer* from the ASP.NET session state mode combo box. You'll be asked to enter the connection string to the SQL Server state database. Here's the string they provide by default:

```
data source=127.0.0.1;Integrated Security=SSPI
```

You may point ASP.NET so it references a database on another machine. Of course, you need to have SQL Server installed on the target machine to make this work. In addition, you'll find some SQL scripts to create the state databases in your .NET system directory (C:\WINDOWS\Microsoft.NET\Framework\v2.0.50215 on this machine at the time of this writing). The Aspnet_regsql.exe tool will set up the databases for you.

Tracking Session State

Because Web-based applications rely on HTTP to connect browsers to servers and HTML to represent the state of the application, ASP.NET is essentially a disconnected architecture. When an application needs to use session state, the runtime needs a way of tracking the origin of the requests it receives so that it may associate data with a particular client. ASP.NET 2.0 offers three options for tracking the Session ID, via cookies, the URL, or client profiles.

Tracking Session State with Cookies

This is the default option for an ASP.NET Web site. In this scenario, ASP.NET generates a hard-to-guess identifier and uses it to store a new *Session* object. You can see the session identifier come through the cookie collection if you have tracing turned on.

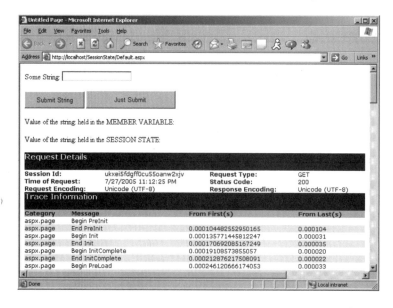

Tracking Session State with the URL

The other main option is to track session state by embedding the session ID as part of the request string. This is useful if you think your clients will turn off cookies (thereby disabling cookie-based session state tracking).

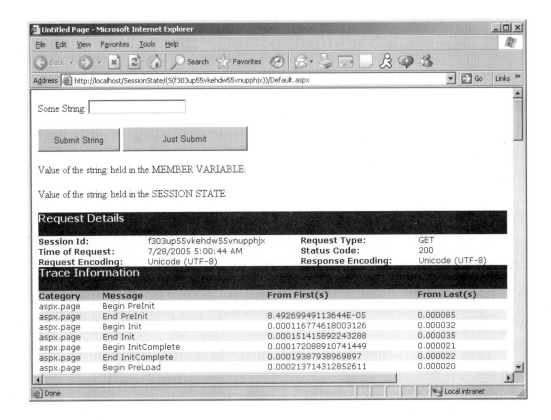

Using AutoDetect

By selecting AutoDetect, the ASP.NET runtime will determine if the client browser has cookies turned on. If cookies are turned on, then the session identifier is passed around as a cookie. If not, the session identifier will be stored in the URL.

Applying Device Profiles

The *UseDeviceProfile* option tells ASP.NET to determine if the browser supports cookies based on the *SupportsRedirectWithCookie* property of the *HttpBrowserCapabilities* object set up for the request. Requests that flip this bit to true cause session identifier values to be passed as cookies. Requests that flip this bit to false cause session identifiers to be passed in the URL.

Session State Timeouts

The *timeout* configuration setting manages the lifetime of the session. The lifetime of the session is the length of time in minutes a session may remain idle before ASP.NET abandons it and makes the session ID invalid. The maximum value is 525,601 minutes (one year), and the default is 20.

Other Session Configuration Settings

ASP.NET supports some other configuration settings not available through the IIS configuration utility. These are values you need to type into the Web.Config file directly.

If you don't like the rather obvious name of the session ID cookie made up by ASP.NET (the default is SessionID), you may change it. The *cookieName* setting lets you change that name. You might want to rename the cookie as a security measure to hamper hackers in their attempts to hijack a session key.

If you want to replace an expired session ID with a new one, setting the *regenerateExpiredSessionId* setting to true will perform that task. This is only for cookieless sessions.

If you don't like the SQL Server database already provided to support ASP.NET's session state, you may apply your own database. The *allowCustomSqlDatabase* setting turns this feature on.

When using SQL Server to store session data, ASP.NET has to act as a client of SQL Server. Normally, the ASP.NET process identity is impersonated. You may instruct ASP.NET to use the user credentials supplied to the *identity* configuration element within Web.Config by setting the *mode* attribute to Custom. By setting the *mode* attribute to *SQLServer*, you tell ASP.NET to use a trusted connection.

Used when the mode attribute is set to *StateServer*, the *stateNetworkTimeout* is for setting the number of seconds for the idle time limits of the TCP/IP network connection between the Web server and the state server. The default is 10.

Finally, you may instruct ASP.NET to use a custom provider by setting the name of the provider in the *custom* element. For this to work the provider must be specified elsewhere in Web.Config (specifically in the *providers* element).

The Wizard Control: Alternative to Session State

One of the most common uses for session state is to keep track of information coming from a user even though the information is posted back via several pages. For example, scenarios such as collecting mailing addresses, applying for security credentials, or purchasing something on a Web site introduce this issue.

Sometimes gathering information is minimal and may be done through only one page. However, when collecting data from users requires several pages of forms, you need to keep track of that information between posts. For example, most commercial Web sites employ a multi-stage checkout process. After placing a bunch of items into your shopping cart, you click "Check Out" and the site redirects you to a checkout page. From there, you are usually required to perform several distinct steps—setting up a payment method, confirming your order, and getting an order confirmation.

While you could code something like this in ASP.NET 1.x, ASP.NET 2.0 now includes a *Wizard* control to deal with this sort of multistage data collection.

If you were to develop a multistage input sequence, you'd need to build in the navigation logic and keep track of the state of the transaction. The *Wizard* control provides a template that performs the basic tasks of navigating though multiple input pages while you provide the specifics. The *Wizard* control logic is built around specific steps, and includes facilities for managing these steps. The *Wizard* control supports both linear and nonlinear navigation.

Using the Wizard Control

This example shows using the *Wizard* control to gather several different pieces of information from the client: a name and address, what kinds of software he or she uses, and the kind of hardware he or she uses. For example, this might be used to qualify users for entry into a certain part of the Web site or perhaps to qualify them for a subscription.

1. Create new page in the SessionState project named UseWizard.

2. Drop a *WizardControl* onto the page.

3. When the local menu appears in the designer, select **Add Wizard Steps...** to show this dialog box:

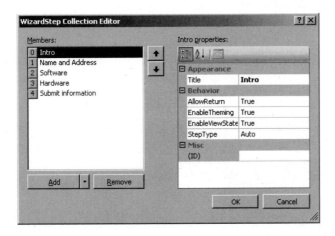

4. Add an Intro step, a Name and Address step, a Software step, a Hardware step, and a Submit information step. Make sure Intro is a *StartNavigationTemplate*.

5. Make sure the Submit information step is a *FinishNavigationTemplate*.

6.   Add controls to the steps. The Intro step gets a label that describes what the user is entering:

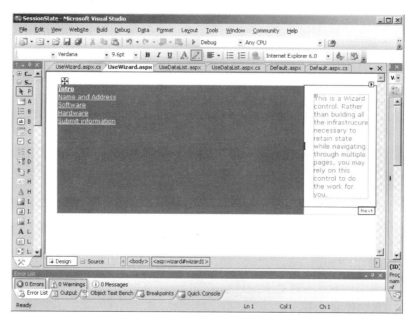

7.   The Name and Address step should include labels and text boxes to get personal information. Be sure to give useable IDs to the text boxes. You'll need them during the submission step:

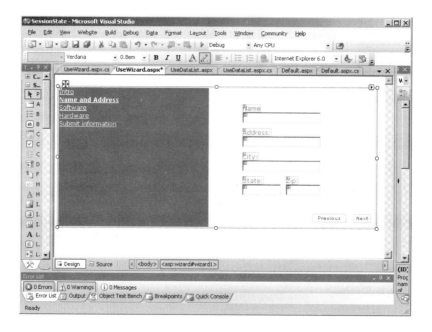

8. The Software step should include a list of check boxes listing common software types:

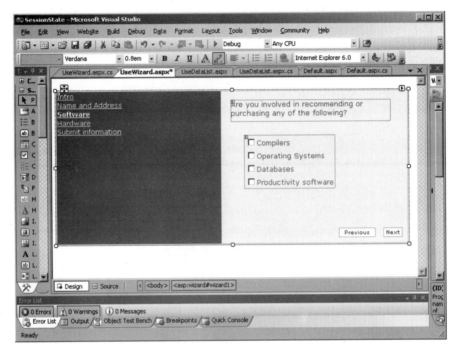

9. The Hardware step should include a list of check boxes listing common hardware types:

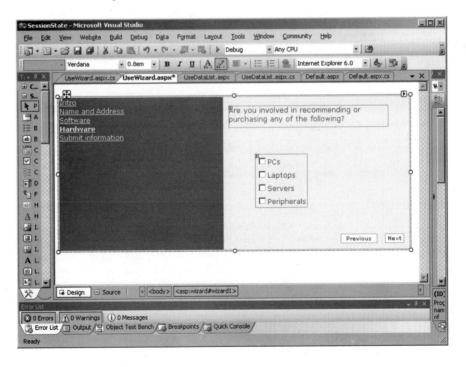

10. The summary information step (which you may use to show information before submitting) should include a label that will summarize the information collected. Name the label *LabelSummary* so you can use it to display the summary.

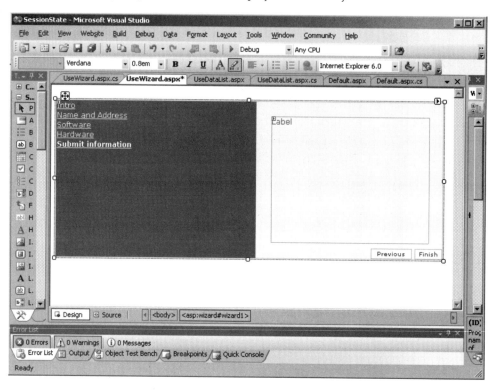

11. Finally, edit the *Form_Load* method to collect the information from each of the controls in the *Wizard*. The controls are actually available as member variables on the page. This information will be loaded every time the page is loaded. However, it will be hidden from view until the user selects the step. Double-clicking on the *Wizard* control will add a handler for the Finish button that you may use to harvest the information gathered via the wizard.

```
protected void Page_Load(object sender, EventArgs e)
{

    String strSummary =
        "About to submit. \n ";
    strSummary += " You are: \n";
    strSummary += this.TextBoxName.Text + " ";
    strSummary += this.TextBoxAddress.Text + " ";
    strSummary += this.TextBoxCity.Text + " ";
    strSummary += this.TextBoxState.Text + " ";
    strSummary += this.TextBoxZip.Text + " \n";

    strSummary += "Software: ";
    foreach (ListItem listItem in CheckBoxListSoftware.Items)
```

```
    {
        if (listItem.Selected)
        {
            strSummary += listItem.Text + " ";
        }
    }

    strSummary += "\nHardware: ";
    foreach (ListItem listItem in CheckBoxListHardware.Items)
    {
        if (listItem.Selected)
        {
            strSummary += listItem.Text + " ";
        }
    }

    this.TextBoxSummary.Text = strSummary;

}
protected void Wizard1_FinishButtonClick(object sender,
    WizardNavigationEventArgs e)
{
    // Do something with the data here
}
```

12. Now run the page and go through the steps. You'll see each step along the way and then finally a summary of the information collected.

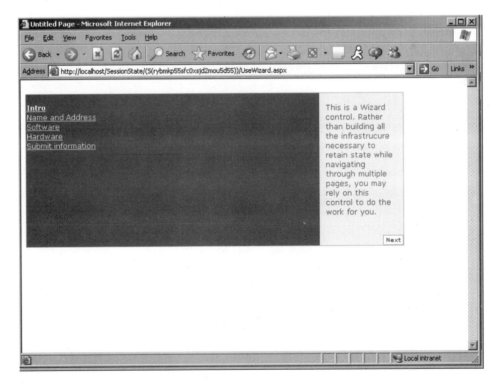

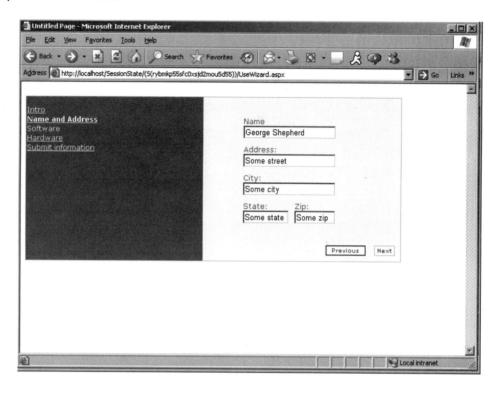

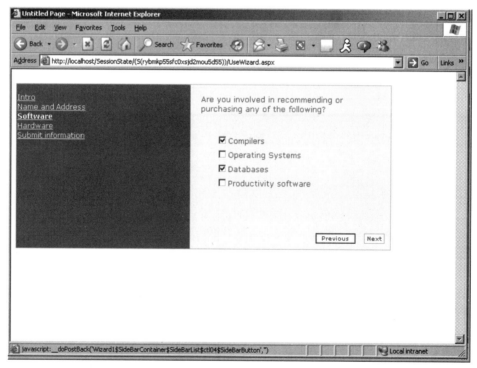

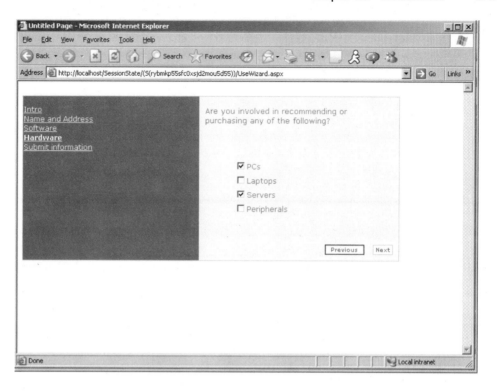

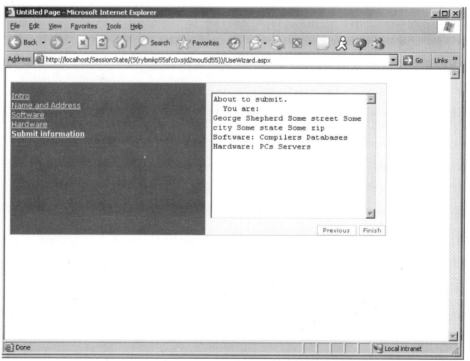

Conclusion

If anything distinguishes Web-based programming from other types of programming, it's probably the issue of tracking the state of any particular user. Because Web development inherently involves distributing state and managing that state, it needs to be done deliberately.

Session state is one of the most important pieces of state in any application because it is associated with the particular client making the request. This is most important for applications where you want to have the state associated with a single user available (as in the case of a shopping cart).

Session state is always available through the *Page* (and through the *HttpContext*) via the *Session* object. It's a name value dictionary that holds any kind of CLR object. Adding and retrieving information is accomplished most easily via indexers. In addition, session state may be configured in its location, in how it's tracked, and in how long it lasts. ASP.NET supports a number of other more advanced settings, too.

In this chapter, we also looked at the *Wizard* control as a way to retain information between several posts without resorting to session state. This is most useful when several kinds of related data need to be collected at once.

Chapter 13 Quick Reference

To	Do This
Access the current client's session state	Use the *Page.Session* property
	Use the current context's *HttpContext.Session* property
Access a specific value in the current client's session state	Session state is a set of key-value pairs. Access the data with the string key originally used to insert the data in the cache
Store session state in-proc	Set the <SessionState> attributes in Web.Config. Set mode to InProc
Store session state in a state server	Set the <SessionState> attributes in Web.Config. Set mode to StateServer. Be sure to include a stateConnection string
Store session state in SQL Server	Set the <SessionState> attributes in Web.Config. Set mode to SQLServer. Be sure to include a sqlConnection string
Disable session state	Set the <SessionState> attributes in Web.Config. Set mode to Off
Use cookies to track session state	Set the <SessionState> attributes in Web.Config. Set cookieless to false
Use URL to track session state	Set the <SessionState> attributes in Web.Config. Set cookieless to true
Set session state timeout	Set the <SessionState> attributes in Web.Config. Set timeout to a value (representing minutes)

Chapter 14
Application Data Caching

After completing this chapter, you will be able to

- Improve the performance of your application by using the application cache
- Avoid unnecessary round-trips to the database
- Manage items in the cache

This chapter covers ASP.NET's built-in data caching features. Caching is a long-standing means of improving the performance of any software system. The idea is to place frequently used data in quickly accessed media. Even though access times for mass storage continue to improve, accessing data from a standard hard disk is *much* slower than accessing it in memory. By taking often-used data and making it available quickly, you can improve the performance of your application dramatically.

The ASP.NET runtime includes a dictionary (key-value map) of CLR objects. The map (named *Cache*) lives with the application and is available via the *HttpContext* and *System.Web.UI.Page*. Using the cache is very much like using the *Session* object. You may access items in the cache using an indexer. In addition, you may control the lifetime of objects in the cache and even set up links between the cached objects and their physical data sources. Let's start by examining a case in which using the cache is justified.

Making an Application that Benefits from Caching

1. Create a new site. Call it **UseDataCaching**.

2. Borrow the *UseDataList* code from the example in Chapter 13. To bring it into your new project, right-click on the project in solution explorer. Choose **Add Existing Item**. Navigate the to the UseDataList.aspx and UseDataList.aspx.cs code from Chapter 13.

    The code you imported refers to the database in the *SessionState* example. That's okay. If you want to, you can change it to the database in this application's App_Data directory, but it's not strictly necessary as long as the path points to an available database somewhere on your system.

3. Examine the *GetInventory, the BindToInventory*, and the *Page_Load* methods. Listing 14-1 shows the code.

   Listing 14-1

   ```
   protected DataTable GetInventory()
   {
   String strConnection =
       @"Provider=Microsoft.Jet.OLEDB.4.0;
       DataSource=
       c:\\inetpub\\wwwroot\\SessionState\\App_Data\\ASPDotNetStepByStep.mdb";

       DbProviderFactory f =
           DbProviderFactories.GetFactory("System.Data.OleDb");

       DbConnection connection = f.CreateConnection();
       connection.ConnectionString = strConnection;

       connection.Open();
       DbCommand command = f.CreateCommand();
       command.CommandText = "Select * from DotNetReferences";
       command.Connection = connection;

       IDataReader reader = command.ExecuteReader();

       DataTable dt = new DataTable();
       dt.Load(reader);
       reader.Close();
       connection.Close();
       connection.Dispose();

       return dt;
   }
   protected DataTable BindToInventory()
   {
       DataTable dt;
       dt = this.GetInventory();
       this.DataList1.DataSource = dt;
       this.DataBind();
       return dt;
   }

   protected void Page_Load(object sender, EventArgs e)
   {

       if (!IsPostBack)
       {
         DataTable dt = BindToInventory();
         DataTable tableSelectedItems =
           this.CreateSelectedItemsTable(dt);
           Session["tableSelectedItems"] = tableSelectedItems;
       }
   }
   ```

4. Run the application to make sure it works. That is, it should connect to the DotNetReferences table and bind the *DataList* to the table from the database.

The *GetInventory* and *BindToInventory* methods are called by the *Page_Load* method. How often is *Page_Load* called? Every time a new page is created—which happens for every single HTTP request destined for the UseDataList page. In the case of running this application on a single computer with one client (in a testing situation), perhaps connecting to the database for every request isn't a big deal. However, for applications expecting to serve thousands of users making frequent requests, repeated database access actually becomes a very big deal. Accessing a database is actually a very expensive operation. As we'll see shortly, it may take up to a half second to simply connect to this access database and read the mere 25 rows contained in the DotNetReferences table. Data access can only get more expensive as the size of the tables in the database grows. A half-second in the computer processing time scale is eons to the program.

Now think about the nature of the inventory table. Does it change often? Of course, not in the case of this simple application. However, think about how this might work in a real application. The items carried within an inventory will probably not change often (and such changes will probably occur at regular, predictable intervals). If that's the case, why does the application need to hit the database each time a page is loaded? Doing so is certainly overkill. If you could take that data and store it in a medium offering quicker access than the database (for example, the computer's internal memory), your site could potentially serve many more requests than if it had to make a round-trip to the database every time it loads a page. This is a perfect opportunity to cache the data.

Using the Data Cache

Using the data cache in the simplest and most naïve way supported by ASP.NET is very like accessing the *Session* object. Remember, accessing the *Session* object involves using an indexer (the square brace syntax) and a consistent index to store and retrieve data. The data cache works in exactly the same way (although it has some other features for managing items in the cache).

The strategy for caching a piece of data usually involves these steps:

1.   Look in the cache for the data element.

2.   If it's there, use it (bypassing the expensive database round-trip).

3.   If the data is unavailable in the cache, make a round-trip to the database to fetch it.

4.   Cache the data so it's available next time around.

The next example modifies the UseDataList page so that it stores the data in the cache after acquiring it for the first time. While the first time *Page_Load* is called, subsequent calls are infinitely faster.

Using the Cache

1.   Open the UseDataList.aspx.cs file and go to the *GetInventory* method.

2. Modifying the method to use the cache is fairly straightforward. The following listing highlights the changes. First, check to see if the item is in the cache. If searching the cache for the *DataSet* turns up a valid pointer, then you may bypass the database lookup code and return the *DataSet*. If searching the cache turns up a null pointer, go ahead and make the round-trip to the database. When the database lookup finishes, you'll have a good *DataSet*. Cache it before returning the reference to the caller. If you include the *Trace* statements, you'll be able to see exactly how big an impact caching can make.

```
protected DataTable GetInventory()
{
  DataTable dt;

  Trace.Warn("Page_Load", "looking in cache");
  C:dt = (DataTable)Cache["InventoryDataTable"];
  Trace.Warn("Page_Load", "done looking in cache");

  if (dt == null)
  {

      Trace.Warn("Page_Load", "Performing DB lookup");

      dt = new DataTable();

      String strConnection =
      @"Provider=Microsoft.Jet.OLEDB.4.0;
       DataSource=c:
\\inetpub\\wwwroot\\SessionState\\App_Data\\ASPDotNetStepByStep.mdb";

      DbProviderFactory f =
      DbProviderFactories.GetFactory("System.Data.OleDb");

      DbConnection connection = f.CreateConnection();
      connection.ConnectionString = strConnection;

      connection.Open();
      DbCommand command = f.CreateCommand();
      command.CommandText = "Select * from DotNetReferences";
      command.Connection = connection;

      IDataReader reader = command.ExecuteReader();

      dt.Load(reader);

      reader.Close();
      connection.Close();
      connection.Dispose();

      Cache["InventoryDataTable"] = dt;
      Trace.Warn("Page_Load", "Done performing DB lookup");

  }
  return dt;
}
```

This code reduces the cost of loading the page significantly (after the data is loaded in the cache, of course). Next time the page is loaded, it'll use the cached version—available through *Cache* at a tremendously reduced cost. How much is the cost savings? It's huge—as you can see looking at the trace pages for the application. Let's take a peek.

Impact of Caching

If you included the *Trace* statements in the *GetInventory* method, then you can surf to the trace page to see the effect of caching. The UseDataCaching application included here has the *Trace* attribute turned off in the page, but has *application tracing* turned on. That is, the Web.Config includes the following section:

```
<configuration>
   <system.web>
   <trace enabled="true" />
   <system.web>
</configuration>
```

You can see the trace information by surfing to the virtual directory with a file name of Trace.axd. Here's the URI for following the trace information:

```
http://localhost/UseDataCaching/trace.axd
```

Figure 14-1 shows the trace statements produced by accessing the page for the first time. The column furthest to the right indicates the time elapsed since the previous trace statement. The trace statement shows that 0.558656 seconds passed while the page was loading the *DataSet*. That's over a half-second.

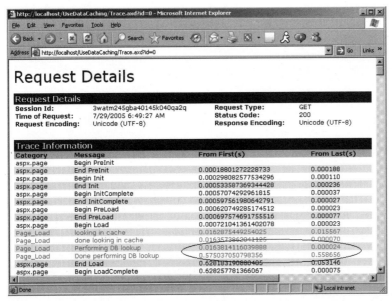

Figure 14-1   Hitting the database takes over a half second in this scenario.

Make a few more posts to the page (for example, add some items from the inventory to the selected items grid). Then go back and look at the tracing information for the subsequent post-backs. Figure 14-2 shows some example trace statements. Fetching from the *Cache* is dramatically faster than hitting the database—by several orders of magnitude! Again, you may not notice the difference with just one client surfing the page every once in a while. However, when multiple clients are surfing to the same page simultaneously, they'll get their responses much more quickly than if the page had to make a round-trip to the database.

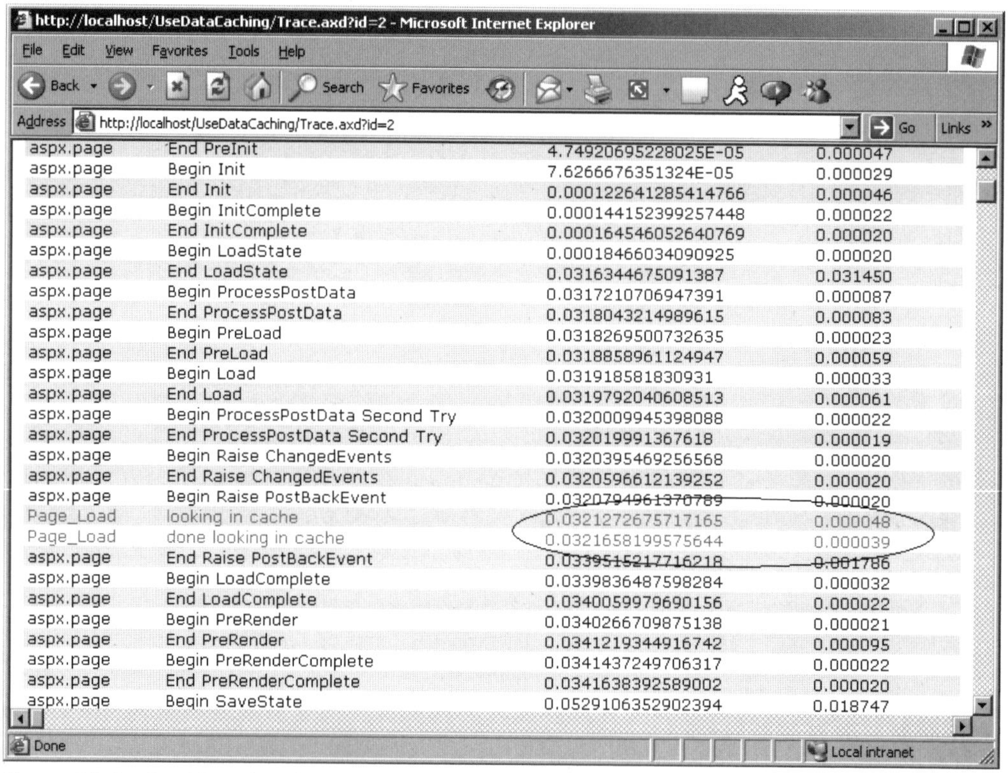

Figure 14-2   Fetching data from the cache takes 0.000039 seconds.

Managing the Cache

The last example cached items in the most naïve way possible. They were simply placed in the cache and given an index. However, at times you may need a bit more control over the items in the cache. For example, what if the physical source backing one of the items you cache changes? If getting accurate information out to your users is important, you may want to know about the change so you can handle it (perhaps by reloading the new information into the cache). As another example, what if you knew that the data in your cache would become invalid after a certain period of time, or on a certain date? You'd want to make sure the data in the cache is invalidated and appropriately refreshed with new data.

In addition to placing items in the cache using the indexer, the *Cache* object implements a parameterized method named *Insert* that allows you control over many aspects of the cached item. The ways in which you may control cache entries include the following:

- Setting up an absolute expiration time

- Setting up a sliding expiration time

- Setting up dependencies between cached items and their backing sources (for example database, file, directory dependencies, or dependencies upon other cache entries)

- Managing a relative priority of cached items

- Setting up callback functions to be called when items are removed

The *Cache's* insert method includes four overloads. Table 14-1 enumerates them.

Table 14-1   Overloads for the *Cache.Insert* method

Insert Overload	Description
Insert (String, Object)	Directly corresponds to the indexer version. Blindly places the object in the *Cache* using the string key in the first parameter.
Insert (String, Object, CacheDependency)	Inserts an object into the *Cache* and associates it with a dependency.
Insert (String, Object, CacheDependency, DateTime, TimeSpan)	Inserts an object into the *Cache*, associating it with a dependency and an expiration policy.
Insert (String, Object, CacheDependency, DateTime, TimeSpan, CacheItemPriority, CacheItemRemovedCallback)	Inserts an object into the *Cache*. Associates a dependency and expiration and priority policies. Also associates the *Cache* entry with a delegate for a callback to notify the application when the item is removed from the cache.

The following example illustrates some of these settings and how they work. In addition, the forthcoming examples illustrate another way to get *DataTables* and *DataSets*. You may actually create them programmatically. The next few examples use a *DataTable* that is created in memory rather than being fetched from a database. While the impact of caching isn't quite as dramatic when using the in-memory *DataTable*, it is still appreciable—and you can see this other approach to managing data. We'll also see how the *DataTable* serializes as XML as well (which will be useful for examining cached items with file dependencies).

DataSets in Memory

In Chapter 11, we looked at making a round-trip to the database to gather data suitable to bind to a control. Then we looked at maintaining data between requests by using the *Session* object. The *Session* object holds any .NET CLR object—even a *DataReader*. However, it's not a good idea to hold on to a *DataReader* for long periods of time as that means holding a connection open. Having too many open connections will ultimately slow your site to a crawl.

A better approach is to make single round-trips to the database and hold on to a *DataTable* or a *DataSet*.

In addition to fetching them from databases, a *DataTable* may be synthesized programmatically. Doing so involves constructing a *DataTable* and adding *DataRows* to describe the schema. After constructing a *DataTable*, you may use it to create columns with the correct "shape," populate them, and then add them to the table's columns collection. Listing 14-2 shows an example of creating a *DataTable* in memory. The table is a collection of famous quotes and their originators that will be useful in the next examples.

Listing 14-2
```
public class QuotesCollection : DataTable
{
    public QuotesCollection()
    {
        //
        // TODO: Add constructor logic here
        //
    }

    public void Synthesize()
    {
        // Be sure to give a name so that it will serialize as XML
        this.TableName = "Quotations";
        DataRow dr;

        Columns.Add(new DataColumn("Quote", typeof(string)));
        Columns.Add(new DataColumn("OriginatorLastName", typeof(strin)));
        Columns.Add(new DataColumn("OriginatorFirstName",
        typeof(string)));

        dr = this.NewRow();
        dr[0] = "Imagination is more important than knowledge.";
        dr[1] = "Einsten";
        dr[2] = "Albert";
        Rows.Add(dr);

        dr = this.NewRow();
        dr[0] = "Assume a virtue, if you have it not";
        dr[1] = "Shakespeare";
        dr[2] = "William";
        this.Rows.Add(dr);

        dr = this.NewRow();
        dr[0] = @"A banker is a fellow who lends you his umbrella
            when the sun is shining, but wants it back the
            minute it begins to rain.";
        dr[1] = "Twain";
        dr[2] = "Mark";
        this.Rows.Add(dr);

        dr = this.NewRow();
        dr[0] = "A man cannot be comfortable without his own approval.";
        dr[1] = "Twain";
```

```
        dr[2] = "Mark";
        this.Rows.Add(dr);

        dr = this.NewRow();
        dr[0] = "Beware the young doctor and the old barber";
        dr[1] = "Franklin";
        dr[2] = "Benjamin";
        this.Rows.Add(dr);

        dr = this.NewRow();
        dr[0] = @"Reality is merely an illusion, albeit a
                  very persistent one.";
        dr[1] = "Einstein";
        dr[2] = "Albert";
        this.Rows.Add(dr);

        dr = this.NewRow();
        dr[0] = "Beer has food value, but food has no beer value";
        dr[1] = "Sticker";
        dr[2] = "Bumper";
        this.Rows.Add(dr);

        dr = this.NewRow();
        dr[0] = @"Research is what I'm doing when I don't know
                  what I'm doing";
        dr[1] = "Von Braun";
        dr[2] = "Wernher";
        this.Rows.Add(dr);

        dr = this.NewRow();
        dr[0] = "Whatever is begun in anger ends in shame";
        dr[1] = "Franklin";
        dr[2] = "Benjamin";
        this.Rows.Add(dr);

        dr = this.NewRow();
        dr[0] = "We think in generalities, but we live in details";
        dr[1] = "Whitehead";
        dr[2] = "Alfred North";
        this.Rows.Add(dr);

        dr = this.NewRow();
        dr[0] = "Every really new idea looks crazy at first.";
        dr[1] = "Whitehead";
        dr[2] = "Alfred North";
        this.Rows.Add(dr);

        dr = this.NewRow();
        dr[0] = @"The illiterate of the 21st century will not be
                  those who cannot read and write, but those who cannot learn,
                  unlearn, and relearn.";
        dr[1] = "Whitehead"";
        dr[2] = "Alfred North";
        this.Rows.Add(dr);
    }
}
```

Building a *DataTable* in memory is straightforward—it's mostly a matter of defining the column schema and adding rows to the table. This class is available on the CD accompanying this book, so you don't need to type the whole thing. You may just import it into the next examples.

Now let's take a look at managing items within the cache.

Cache Expirations

The first way of managing cached items is to give them expiration thresholds. In some cases, you may be aware of certain aspects of your cached data that allow you to place expiration times on it. The *Cache* supports both absolute expirations and sliding expirations.

Absolute Expiration

1. To try out absolute expirations, add a new page to the UseDataCaching site named **CacheExpirations**.

2. Use the **Website | Add Existing Item** to bring the QuoteCollection.cs file from the CD accompanying this book and make it part of this project.

3. Drag a *GridView* onto the CacheExpirations page. Don't bind it to a data source yet. We'll handle that in the *Page_Load* method.

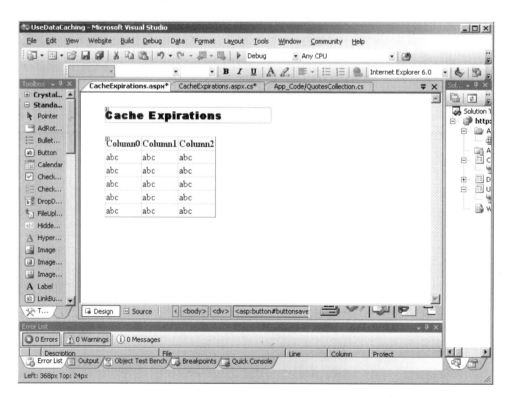

4. In the *Page_Load* method of the CacheExpirations page, check the cache to see if there's already an instance of the *QuoteCollections* object (just as in the previous example). If the data's not available from the cache, create an instance of the *QuoteCollections* class and call the *Synthesize* method to populate the table. Finally, add it to the cache using the overloaded *Insert* method. You can use the *DataTime* class to generate an absolute expiration. Bind the *QuotesCollection* object to the *GridView*. The caching policy should be *Cache.NoSlidingExpiration*. Set up some trace statements so you may see how the expiration times affect the lifetime of the cached object.

```
protected void Page_Load(object sender, EventArgs e)
{

        QuotesCollection quotesCollection;

        DateTime dtCurrent = DateTime.Now;
        Trace.Warn("Page_Load",
"Testing cache at: " +
dtCurrent.ToString());
        quotesCollection = (QuotesCollection)Cache["QuotesCollection"];

        if (quotesCollection == null)
        {

                quotesCollection = new QuotesCollection();
                quotesCollection.Synthesize();

                DateTime dtExpires = new DateTime(2005, 12, 31, 23, 59, 59);
                dtCurrent = DateTime.Now;

                Trace.Warn("Page_Load",
"Caching at: " +
dtCurrent.ToString());
                Trace.Warn("Page_Load",
"This entry will expire at: " +
dtExpires);
                Cache.Insert("QuotesCollection",
                        quotesCollection,
                        null,
                        dtExpires,
                        Cache.NoSlidingExpiration,
                        CacheItemPriority.Default,
                            null);
        }

        this.GridView1.DataSource = quotesCollection;
        this.DataBind();

}
```

5. Experiment with changing the dates and times to see how setting the expiration time forces a reload of the cache.

An absolute expiration time applied to the cached item tells ASP.NET to flush the item from the cache at a certain time. Now let's try using a different kind of expiration technique–the sliding expiration. Using a sliding expiration tells ASP.NET to keep the data in the cache as long as it has been accessed within a certain period of time. Items that have not been accessed within that time frame are subject to expiration.

Sliding Expirations

1. Now try setting a sliding expiration for the cached data. Modify the *Page_Load* method in the CacheExpirations page. Getting a sliding expiration to work is simply a matter of changing the parameters of the *Insert* method. Make up a time span after which you want the cached items to expire. Pass *DateTime.MaxValue* as the absolute expiration date and the *timespan* as the final parameter like so:

```
protected void Page_Load(object sender, EventArgs e)
{
    QuotesCollection quotesCollection;

    DateTime dtCurrent = DateTime.Now;
    Trace.Warn("Page_Load",
        "Testing cache: " + dtCurrent.ToString());
    quotesCollection =
        (QuotesCollection)Cache["QuotesCollection"];

    if (quotesCollection == null)
    {
        quotesCollection = new QuotesCollection();
        quotesCollection.Synthesize();

        TimeSpan tsExpires = new TimeSpan(0, 0, 15);
        dtCurrent = DateTime.Now;

        Trace.Warn("Page_Load",
            "Caching at: " + dtCurrent.ToString());
        Trace.Warn("Page_Load",
            "This entry will expire in: " +
            tsExpires.ToString());
        Cache.Insert("QuotesCollection",
            quotesCollection,
                null,
                DateTime.MaxValue,
                tsExpires);
    }

    this.GridView1.DataSource = quotesCollection;
    this.DataBind();
}
```

2. Surf to the page. You should see the cache reloading if you haven't accessed the cached item within the designated time frame.

   Cache dependencies represent another way to manage cached items. Let's take a look at how they work.

Cache Dependencies

In addition to allowing objects in the cache to expire by duration, you may set up dependencies for the cached items. For example, imagine our program loads some data from a file and places it into the cache. The backing file (that is, the source of the cached information) may change, making the data in the cache invalid. ASP.NET supports setting up a dependency between the cached item and the file so that changing the file invalidates the cached item. The conditions under which the cached items may be flushed include when a file changes, a directory changes, another cache entry is removed, or data in a table in an SQL Server changes (this is an often requested feature finally available in ASP.NET 2.0!).

Here's an example that illustrates setting up cache dependencies.

Setting Cache Dependencies

1. Add a new page to the UseDataCache site. Name it **CacheDependencies.aspx**.

2. Place a button on the page that you may use to post a request to the page to generate an XML file from the *QuotationsCollection*. Also, drag a *GridView* onto the page like so:

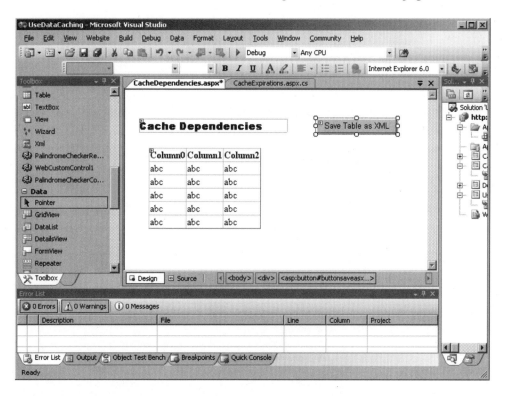

3. Double-click the button to generate a handler for the button that will save the XML Schema and the XML from the *DataTable* to .XML and .XSD files in the App_Data directory.

4. Within the handler, instantiate a *QuotesCollection* object and call *Synthesize* to generate the data. Within the page, you have a reference to the *Server* object. Call the *MapPath* method in the *Server* object to get the physical path for saving the file. Then use that path to create an XML file and a schema file. The *DataTable* will do this for you automatically by calling the *WriteXmlSchema* and *WriteXml* methods, respectively.

```
protected void ButtonSaveAsXML_Click(object sender, EventArgs e)
{

    QuotesCollection quotesCollection = new QuotesCollection();
    quotesCollection.Synthesize();
    String strFilePathXml =
    Server.MapPath(Request.ApplicationPath +
    "\\app_data\\QuotesCollection.xml");
    String strFilePathSchema =
    Server.MapPath(Request.ApplicationPath +
    "\\app_data\\QuotesCollection.xsd");
    quotesCollection.WriteXmlSchema(strFilePathSchema);
    quotesCollection.WriteXml(strFilePathXml);

}
```

5. Now write a method to load the XML into the *QuotationsCollection* object and cache the data. You can use the file path to the XML file to create a dependency on the file. When it changes, ASP.NET will empty the cache. Turn off the absolute expiration and the sliding expiration by passing in *Cache.NoAbsoluteExpiration* and *Cache.NoSlidingExpiration*. If you put trace statements in, you can see the effect of updating the file after it's been loaded in the cache. Finally, make sure to bind the *GridView* to the *QuotationCollection*.

```
protected void CacheWithFileDependency()
{
    QuotesCollection quotesCollection;

    Trace.Warn("Page_Load", "Testing cache ");
    quotesCollection = (QuotesCollection)Cache["QuotesCollection"];

    if (quotesCollection == null)
    {
        Trace.Warn("Page_Load", "Not found in cache");
        quotesCollection = new QuotesCollection();

        String strFilePathXml =
            Server.MapPath(Request.ApplicationPath +
            "\\app_data\\QuotesCollection.xml");
        String strFilePathSchema =
            Server.MapPath(Request.ApplicationPath +
            "\\app_data\\QuotesCollection.xsd");

        quotesCollection.ReadXmlSchema(strFilePathSchema);
        quotesCollection.ReadXml(strFilePathXml);
```

```
        CacheDependency cacheDependency =
                new CacheDependency(strFilePathXml);

        Cache.Insert("QuotesCollection",
                        quotesCollection,
                        cacheDependency,
                        Cache.NoAbsoluteExpiration,
                        Cache.NoSlidingExpiration,
                        CacheItemPriority.Default,
                            null);
    }

    this.GridView1.DataSource = quotesCollection;
    this.DataBind();
}
```

6. Call the *CacheWithFileDependency()* within the *Page_Load* method.

```
protected void Page_Load(object sender, EventArgs e)
{
    CacheWithFileDependency();
}
```

7. Now run the page. It should load the XML and schema into the *QuotesCollection*, save the *QuotesCollection* in the cache, and then show the data in the grid. Clicking the **Save As XML** button will refresh the XML file (upon which a cache dependency was made). Because the file on the disk changes, ASP.NET will flush the cache. Next time you load the page, the cache will need to be reloaded.

Now let's look at the final cache dependency: the SQL Server dependency.

The SQL Server Dependency

ASP.NET 1.0 had a huge gap in its cache dependency functionality. The most useful type of dependency was completely missing—that is, a dependency between a cached item coming from SQL Server and the physical database. Because so many sites use data provided by SQL Server to back their *DataGrids* and other controls, establishing this dependency is definitely a most useful way to manage cached data.

For the SQL Server dependency to work, you first configure SQL Server using the program aspnet_regsql.exe. The dependency is described in the configuration file, whose name is passed into the *SqlCacheDependency* constructor. The *SqlCacheDependency* class monitors the table. When something causes the table to change, ASP.NET will remove the item from the *Cache*.

Listing 14-3 shows a configuration file with a dependency upon SQL Server. Listing 14-4 shows an ASP.NET page that loads the data from the SQL Server database and establishes a dependency between the database and the cached item.

Listing 14-3

```
<caching>
 <sqlCacheDependency enabled="true" >
   <databases >
     <add name="DBName" pollTime="500"
         connectionStringName="connectionString"/>
   </databases>
 </sqlCacheDependency>
</caching>
```

Listing 14-4

```csharp
<%@ Page Language="C#" %>
<script runat="server">
    protected void Page_Load(Object sender, EventArgs e)
    {
        DataSet ds = null;
        ds = (DataSet)Cache["SomeData"];
        if (ds == null)
        {
            string cconnectionString =
                ConfigurationSettings.ConnectionStrings["connectionString"].
                ConnectionString;
                SqlDataAdapter da =
                    new SqlDataAdapter("select * from DBName.table",
                    connectionString);
                ds = new DataSet();
                da.Fill(ds);
                SqlCacheDependency sqlCacheDependency =
                    new SqlCacheDependency("DBName", "table");
                Cache.Insert("SomeData",
                            ds,
                            sqlCacheDependency);
        }
        GridView1.DataSource = ds;
        DataBind();
    }
</script>
<html><body>
    <form id="form1" runat="server">
        <asp:GridView ID="GridView1" Runat="server">
        </asp:GridView>
    </form>
</body></html>
```

Once items are in the cache and their lifetimes are established through expirations and cached item dependencies, one other way to manage the cache remains—reacting when items are removed.

Clearing the Cache

As you can see from the previous examples, ASP.NET clears the cache on several occasions by

■ removing items explicitly by calling *Cache.Remove*

- removing low-priority items due to memory consumption
- removing items that have expired

One of the parameters to one of the *Insert* overloaded methods is a callback delegate so that ASP.NET can tell you that something's been removed from the cache. To receive callbacks, you simply need to implement a method that matches the signature, wrap it in a delegate, and then pass it when calling the *Insert* method. When the object is removed, ASP.NET will call the method you supply.

The next example illustrates setting up a removal callback function.

Removal Callback

1. One of the main tricks to getting the removal callback to work is finding an appropriate place to put the callback. What happens if you make the callback a member of your *Page* class? It won't work. The callback will become disconnected after the first page has come and gone. The callback has to live in a place that sticks around. The perfect class for establishing the callback is in the global application area. We'll see the application services in more detail in Chapter 17. For now, add a global application object to your application. Select **Website | Add New Item**. Find the Global Application template and insert it into the project. Visual Studio will add a new file named Global.asax to your application.

2. Global.asax will include a server-side script block. Write a method to handle the callback within the Global.asax file. In this case, the response will be to set a flag indicating the cache is dirty. Then the code will simply place the data back into the cache during the *Applicationi_BeginRequest* handler. The code for doing so will look very much like the code in the *CacheWithFileDependency* method shown earlier. You can get a reference to the cache through the current *HttpContext*.

```
<%@ Application Language="C#" %>

<script runat="server">

    bool _bReloadQuotations = false;

    public void OnRemoveQuotesCollection(string key, object val,
        CacheItemRemovedReason r)
    {
        // Do something about the dependency Change
        if (r == CacheItemRemovedReason.DependencyChanged)
        {
            _bReloadQuotations = true;
        }
    }

    protected void Application_BeginRequest(object sender, EventArgs e)
    {
        if (_bReloadQuotations == true)
        {
```

```
            ReloadQuotations();
            _bReloadQuotations = false;
        }
    }

    protected void ReloadQuuotations()
    {
        QuotesCollection quotesCollection = new QuotesCollection();

        String strFilePathXml =
            Server.MapPath(HttpContext.Current.Request.ApplicationPath +
            "\\app_data\\QuotesCollection.xml");
        String strFilePathSchema =
            Server.MapPath(HttpContext.Current.Request.ApplicationPath +
            "\\app_data\\QuotesCollection.xsd");

        quotesCollection.ReadXmlSchema(strFilePathSchema);
        quotesCollection.ReadXml(strFilePathXml);

        System.Web.Caching.CacheDependency
            cacheDependency =
            new System.Web.Caching.CacheDependency(strFilePathXml);

        HttpContext.Current.Cache.Insert("QuotesCollection",
            quotesCollection,
            cacheDependency,
            Cache.NoAbsoluteExpiration,
            Cache.NoSlidingExpiration,
            CacheItemPriority.Default,

            this.OnRemoveQuotesCollection);
    }

</script>
```

3. Update the *CacheWithFileDepenedency* method to use the callback method when establishing the *QuotesServer* in the cache. You may access the callback method through the page's *Application* member.

```
protected void CacheWithFileDependency()
{
    QuotesCollection quotesCollection;

    Trace.Warn("Page_Load", "Testing cache ");
    quotesCollection = (QuotesCollection)Cache["QuotesCollection"];

    if (quotesCollection == null)
    {
        Trace.Warn("Page_Load", "Not found in cache");
        quotesCollection = new QuotesCollection();

        String strFilePathXml =
            Server.MapPath(Request.ApplicationPath +
            "\\app_data\\QuotesCollection.xml");
        String strFilePathSchema =
            Server.MapPath(Request.ApplicationPath +
            "\\app_data\\QuotesCollection.xsd");
```

```
        quotesCollection.ReadXmlSchema(strFilePathSchema);
        quotesCollection.ReadXml(strFilePathXml);
        CacheDependency cacheDependency =
            new CacheDependency(strFilePathXml);

        Cache.Insert("QuotesCollection",
            quotesCollection,
            cacheDependency,
            Cache.NoAbsoluteExpiration,
            Cache.NoSlidingExpiration,
            CacheItemPriority.Default,
            this.ApplicationInstance.OnRemoveQuuotesCollection);
    }

    this.GridView1.DataSource = quotesCollection;
    this.DataBind();
}
```

When you surf to the page, you should never see the *Page_Load* method refreshing the cache. That's because when the XML file is overwritten, ASP.NET immediately calls the *ReloadQuotations* method—which loads the cache again.

Conclusion

Caching is one of the easiest and most well-understood ways of wringing better performance out of an application. ASP.NET implements an easy-to-use application cache. The application cache stores any CLR object and is available at any time while processing a request. You can dig it out of the current context (the *HttpContext*), and it's also available as a member variable of *System.Web.UI.Page*.

Probably the most common way to use the cache is to store database query results to avoid round-trips to a database. Accessing memory is often orders of magnitude faster than hitting the database. In addition, you sidestep issues such as limited connection resources and database contention.

While you can effectively improve the performance of your application by simply putting items in the cache, ASP.NET's caching mechanism provides facilities for putting limits on the amount of time items remain cached. You may also set up dependencies between cached items and their physical data sources so that you may be alerted when items need to be reloaded into the cache.

Chapter 14 Quick Reference

To	Do This
Access the data cache	The data cache is available as
	1. the *Cache* property in the page
	2. the *Cache* property in the current *HttpContext*

To	Do This
Insert an item in the cache	Use the indexer notation to add an object and a value to the cache
Insert an item in the cache with a dependency	Create a *CacheDependency* object and add the object to the cache using the overloaded insert method
Insert an item in the cache with an expiration time	Create a *DateTime* object and add the object to the cache using the overloaded insert method
Delete an item from the cache	Call the cache's Remove method
Be notified that an item is being removed from the cache	Include a callback delegate when inserting an item in the cache

Chapter 15
Caching Output

After completing this chapter, you will be able to

- Cache content

- Improve the performance of Web applications by using output caching

- Manage the cached content through the *OutputCache* directive

- Manage the cached content through the *HttpCachePolicy* class

This chapter covers ASP.NET's support for caching output. In Chapter 14, we saw what an impact data caching could make on your application. By avoiding round-trips to the database, you can make parts of your Web site run much faster than they otherwise would. In addition to data caching, ASP.NET supports *output caching*.

After spending a bit of time watching the whole page-rendering process, you now know it can be pretty involved. A lot happens between the time a page loads and the final closing tag is sent to the browser. For example, the page may require database access. It may have a number of controls declared on it. Furthermore, perhaps some of those controls are the more complex controls like the *DataList* or the *GridView* whose rendering process is expensive. All these things usually take time to process.

Just as you can bypass whole round-trips to a database by caching data in memory, you may configure ASP.NET to bypass the whole page-rendering process and send back content that's already been rendered once. This is called output caching.

Caching Content

As you surf the Web, you see all manner of pages. Some sites churn their content very quickly, while others change much more slowly. Some pages have portions that change while other portions of the page remain static. If you have a page whose content changes infrequently, you may cache the output instead of regenerating it every time a request comes in.

At the outset, turning on output caching is easy. To set up caching, place the *OutputCache* directive on the page. It's a separate directive, like the *Page* directive. The *OutputCache* directive enables caching and provides certain control over its behavior. The following exercise introduces caching output.

Create a Cacheable Page

1. Create a new Web site named OutputCaching.

2. Open the Default.aspx file and insert the *OutputCache* directive near the top, immediately after the *Page* directive. For now, set the *Trace* attribute to false (we'll turn it on a bit later when we look at caching User Controls). At the very least, the *OutputCache* directive needs two things: (1) the *Duration* attribute to be set, and (2) the *VaryByParam* attribute to "none." We'll see more about these attributes shortly. The *Duration* attribute specifies how long the content should be cached. The *VaryByParam* attribute is for managing caching multiple versions of the page. The following listing shows the syntax of the *OutputCache* directive. This example caches the page's content for 15 seconds. The code following the output directive was generated by Visual Studio.

```
<%@ Page Language="C#" AutoEventWireup="true"
CodeFile="Default.aspx.cs" Inherits="_Default" trace="false"%>
<%@ OutputCache Duration="15" VaryByParam="none" %>

<!DOCTYPE html PUBLIC
"-//W3C//DTD XHTML 1.1//EN"
"http://www.w3.org/TR/xhtml11/DTD/xhtml11.dtd">

<html xmlns="http://www.w3.org/1999/xhtml" >
<head runat="server">
    <title>Untitled Page</title>
</head>
<body>
    <form id="form1" runat="server">
    <div>
    </div>
    </form>
</body>
</html>
```

3. Update the *Page_Load* method to print the date and time that this page was generated, like so:

```
using System;
using System.Data;
```

```
using System.Configuration;
using System.Web;
using System.Web.Security;
using System.Web.UI;
using System.Web.UI.WebControls;
using System.Web.UI.WebControls.WebParts;
using System.Web.UI.HtmlControls;

public partial class _Default : System.Web.UI.Page
{
    protected void Page_Load(object sender, EventArgs e)
    {
        Response.Write("This page was generated and cached at: " +
            DateTime.Now.ToString());
    }
}
```

The first time the content is produced, the *Page_Load* method runs and produces the following output:

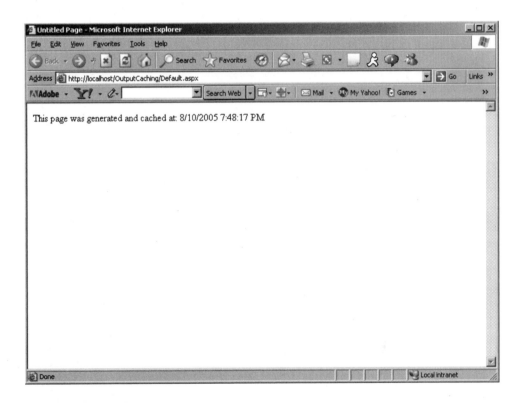

No matter now many times you refresh the browser (you may do this by pressing **F5** while running Internet Explorer within 15 seconds of first accessing the page), ASP.NET will grab the cached content and display that. As soon as 15 seconds has expired,

ASP.NET runs the page in the normal way, calling *Page_Load*, regenerating the content, and caching it again. The following graphic illustrates the new page accessed just moments later than 15 seconds following the first hit:

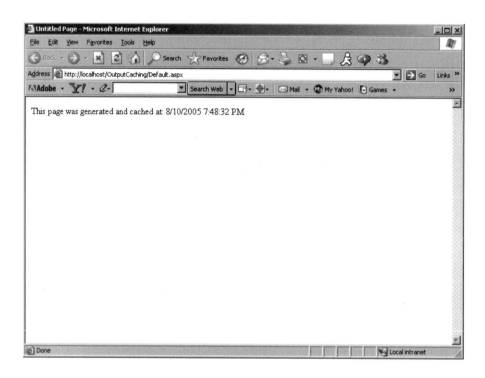

4. To get an idea as to how caching content might improve performance, add a small amount of code to the *Page_Load* method to put the executing thread to sleep for perhaps 10 seconds (this is to simulate an expensive content-generating routine). You'll need to use the *System.Threading* namespace to access the threading functions.

```
using System;
using System.Data;
using System.Configuration;
using System.Web;
using System.Web.Security;
using System.Web.UI;
using System.Web.UI.WebControls;
using System.Web.UI.WebControls.WebParts;
using System.Web.UI.HtmlControls;
using System.Threading;

public partial class _Default : System.Web.UI.Page
{
    protected void Page_Load(object sender, EventArgs e)
    {
```

```
    Thread.Sleep(10000);
    Response.Write("This page was generated and cached at: " +
       DateTime.Now.ToString());
  }
}
```

5. Now surf to the page. Notice how long the page took to load (about 10 seconds). Immediately refresh the page. Notice the browser displays the content right away—without the long wait time. For pages that are expensive to generate and that don't change very often, caching the content represents an enormous performance boost for your Web site—especially as the number of clients increases.

Managing Cached Content

In some cases, it's enough to blindly cache the content of certain pages by simply putting the *OutputCache* directive in the page. However, sometimes you need a bit more control over what's happening in the output cache. ASP.NET supports a number of parameters you may use to manage the way the cache functions. You may control the output caching behavior by either changing the parameters in the *OutputCache* directive or by tweaking the *HttpCachePolicy* property available through the *Response* object.

Modifying the *OutputCache* Directive

It's often very useful to be able to govern output caching. For example, some pages present the exact same content to all the users who access the page. In that case, caching a single version of the content is just fine. However, there are other circumstances in which sending the same content to everyone is inappropriate. The easiest way to control the behavior of output caching is to modify the *OutputCache* directive.

One obvious case in which controlling the cache is important is while caching different versions of content for different browsers making requests. Different browsers often have different capabilities. If you send content requiring a feature not supported by all browsers, some browsers making requests will get a spurious response. The *VaryByCustom* parameter within the *OutputCache* directive allows you to cache different content based on different browsers.

Controlling the output caching is also important when your page renders content based upon the parameters that are sent within the query string. For example, imagine you have a page through which a user has identified himself or herself by typing a name in a text box. The browser will insert that name inside a parameter inside the query list. You may instruct the output cache to cache different versions based on parameters in the query string. For example, users identifying themselves as "John Doe" can get a different version of cached content than users identifying themselves as "Jane Smith." The *VaryByParam* attribute controls this behavior.

Table 15-1 shows a summary of these parameters.

Table 15-1   Summary of output cache parameters.

Attribute	Option	Description
DiskCacheable	true false	Specifies that the output may be written to a disk-based cache (or not)
NoStore	true false	Specifies that the "no store" cache control header is sent (or not)
CacheProfile	A String	Name of a profile (found in Web.Config) to control output cache settings
VaryByParam	none * param name	A semicolon delimited list of strings specifies query string values in a GET request or variables in a POST request
VaryByHeader	* header names	A semicolon delimited list of strings specifying headers that might be submitted by a client
VaryByCustom	browser custom string	Tells ASP.NET to vary the output cache by browser name and version, or by a custom string; must be handled by an override of *GetVaryByCustomString*
Location	Any Client Downstream Server None	Manages which header and metatags are sent to clients to support caching; here are their meanings: Any== page may be cached anywhere Client== cached content remains at browser Downstream== cached content stored both downstream *and* on the client Server== content cached on the server only None== disables caching
Duration	number	Number of seconds the page or control is cached

The following exercise illustrates creating separate versions of cached content based upon how the user identifies himself or herself.

Varying Cached Content by Query String Parameters

1. Add a *TextBox* and a *Button* to the default.aspx page. Give the *TextBox* an ID of **TextBox-Name**. This will hold the client's name and will server as the parameter controlling the number of cached versions of the page.

2. Double-click on the button to add a handler for it. In the handler, respond to the user's request by displaying a greeting using the contents of the text box. Also, modify the

processing time of the page loading by reducing the amount of time the current thread sleeps (or by removing that line completely):

```
using System;
using System.Data;
using System.Configuration;
using System.Web;
using System.Web.Security;
using System.Web.UI;
using System.Web.UI.WebControls;
using System.Web.UI.WebControls.WebParts;
using System.Web.UI.HtmlControls;
using System.Threading;

public partial class _Default : System.Web.UI.Page
{
    protected void Page_Load(object sender, EventArgs e)
    {
        Thread.Sleep(0);
        Response.Write("This page was generated and cached at: " +
            DateTime.Now.ToString());
    }
    protected void ButtonSubmitName_Click(object sender, EventArgs e)
    {
        Response.Write("<br><br>");
        Response.Write("<h2> Hello there, " +
        this.TextBoxName.Text + "</h2>");
    }
}
```

3. Increase the time that the content will be cached (this example uses a minute). That will give you time to change the contents of the *TextBox* to view the effects of caching. Also, include *TextBoxName* as the parameter by which to vary the content within the *Output-Cache* directive.

```
<%@ Page Language="C#" AutoEventWireup="true"
CodeFile="Default.aspx.cs" Inherits="_Default"
trace="false"%>

<%@ OutputCache Duration="60" VaryByParam="TextBoxName" %>
```

4. Surf to the page and type in a name. Click the button to submit the form and note the time stamp of the page. Type a second name into the *TextBox* and click the button to submit the form. Note the time stamp. Then type the same name you typed the first time. Click the button to submit the form. If you do all this within the 60-second window, you should see the cached versions of the page, which you can discern using the time stamp displayed as part of each page. The following three graphics illustrate the caching varying by the value of the *TextBoxName* parameter. The first graphic shows the original request:

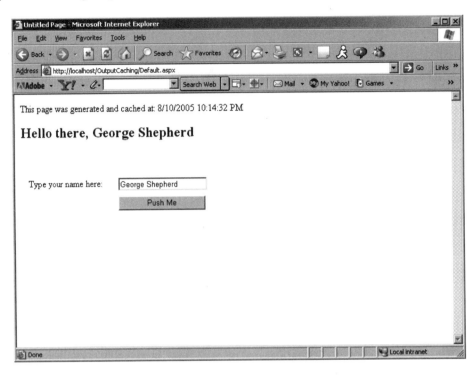

The second graphic shows a request with a new value for the *TextBoxName* parameter:

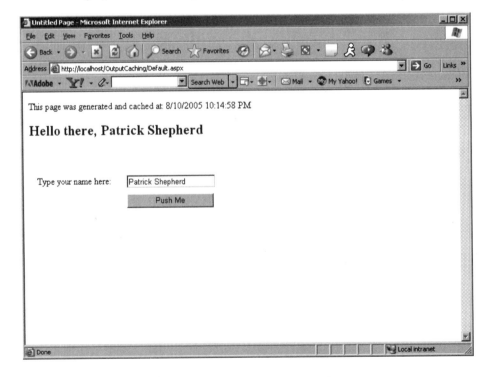

The third graphic shows making a request to the page using the same name as the original request. Note the cached page shows.

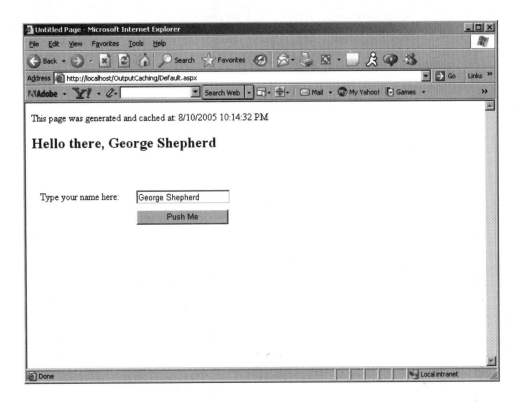

There are other ways to modify the *VaryByParam* attribute. One way is to use the word "none," which means ASP.NET will cache only one version of the page for each type of request (for example, GET, POST, and HEAD). Using an asterisk for *VaryByParam* ("*") tells ASP.NET to cache as many different versions of the page as there are query string or POST body requests. The example above caches as many different versions of the page as there are unique names typed by users.

Using *VaryByHeader* in the *OutputCache* directive tells ASP.NET to generate a separate cache entry for each new header string that comes down (for example, UserAgent and UserLanguage represent HTTP headers that may be sent by the client).

We'll cache a User Control shortly. The *VaryByControl* attribute lets you cache separate content versions for each page that has a User Control with unique properties.

Finally, *VaryByCustom* tells ASP.NET to manage separate cache entries dependent upon a couple of factors. The first factor is the browser types and versions. Alternatively, you may provide a custom *GetVaryByCustomString* method that tells ASP.NET to create separate cached versions of a page based on a custom defined string.

The *HttpCachePolicy*

The second way to manage the output cache is through the *HttpCachePolicy*, which is available from the *Response* class. Listing 15-1 shows a C# representation of a portion of the *Http-CachePolicy* class.

Listing 15-1
```
public class HttpCachePolicy
{
  public HttpCacheVaryByHeaders VaryByHeaders {get;}
  public HttpCacheVaryByParams VaryByParams {get;}
  public void AppendCacheExtension(string extension);
  public void SetRevalidation(HttpCacheRevalidation
        revalidation);
  public void SetETag(String str);
  public SetValidUntilExpires(bool b);
  public void SetExpires(DateTime date);
  public void SetLastModified(DateTime date);
  public void SetMaxAge(TimeSpan delta);
  public void SetNoServerCaching();
  public void SetNoStore();
  // more methods and properties…
}
```

When you set up an *OutputCache* directive, you tell ASP.NET to populate this class during the *Page* class's *InitOutputCache* method. The *Response* object makes the *HttpCachePolicy* available through its *Cache* property. The name "*Cache*" is unfortunate because you might easily confuse it with the application data cache. Perhaps *CachePolicy* would have been a better name for the property to avoid such confusion. You can use the *HttpCachePolicy* class to control the behavior of the server-side caching as well as the headers used for content caching. The *OutputCache* directive may also be used to control some of the same aspects as the *HttpCachePolicy* class. However, some features such as sliding the expiration date or changing the "last modified" stamp for a page are available only through the *HttpCachePolicy* class.

For example, Listing 15-2 shows a page fragment ensuring that all origin-server caching for the current response is stopped. It also sets the last modified date to the current date and time.

Listing 15-2
```
public partial class _Default : System.Web.UI.Page
{
    protected void Page_Load(object sender, EventArgs e)
    {
      Thread.Sleep(0);
      Response.Write("This page was generated and cached at: " +
          DateTime.Now.ToString());

      Response.Cache.SetNoServerCaching();
      Response.Cache.SetLastModified(DateTime.Now);
    }
}
```

Caching Locations

In addition to varying the number of cached versions of a page, you may tell ASP.NET where to cache the content. This is controlled through either the *Location* attribute in the *Output-Cache* directive or by using the *HttpCachePolicy* class's *SetCacheability* method.

ASP.NET supports several output caching locations for which you can specify using the *OutputCache* directive:

- **Any**   Page can be cached by the browser, a downstream server, or on the server
- **Client**   Page should be cached on the client browser only
- **Downstream**   Page should be cached on a downstream server and the client
- **Server**   Page will be cached on the server only
- **None**   Disable caching

The *HttpCachePolicy* also allows you to determine the location of the cached content programmatically. This is done through the *HttpCachePolicy.SetCacheability* method, which takes a parameter of the *HttpCacheability* enumeration. The enumeration is a bit easier to read than the attributes used in the *OutputCache* directive. They include:

- **NoCache**   Disable caching
- **Private**   Only cache on the client
- **Public**   Cache on the client *and* the shared proxy
- **Server**   Cache on the server
- **ServerAndNoCache**   Specify that the content is cached at the server but all others are explicitly denied the ability to cache the response
- **ServerAndPrivate**   Specify that the response is cached at the server and at the client but nowhere else; proxy servers are not allowed to cache the response

Output Cache Dependencies

We saw how ASP.NET supports data caching in Chapter 14. The contents of the data cache in ASP.NET may be flushed due to various dependencies. The same is true of ASP.NET output caching. The response object has a number of methods for setting up dependencies based on cached content. For example, you may want to set up a page that renders data from a text file. You can set up a *CacheDependency* on that text file so that when the text file is changed, the cached output is invalidated and reloaded.

Caching Profiles

One of the problems associated with using the *OutputCache* directive directly is that the values become hard-coded. Changing the caching behavior means going in and changing the source code of the page. A new feature for ASP.NET 2.0 is the ability to add caching profiles. That way, setting the caching behavior variables is offloaded to the configuration file, and output caching becomes an administration issue and not a programming issue (as it should be).

The Web.Config file may include an *outputCacheSettings* section that may contain a list of *outputCacheProfiles*. The *outputCacheProfiles* are simply key-value pairs whose keys are the output caching variables (such as *Duration*). When you mention the profile name in the *OutputCache* directive, ASP.NET will simply read the values out of the configuration file and apply them to the *OutputCache* directive.

The following exercise illustrates setting up a cache profile instead of hard-coding the values into the page.

Set Up a Cache Profile

1. Add a cache profile to the Site's Web.Config file. If Web.Config isn't already there, go ahead and add one to the project. Then add a cache profile to Web.Config nested between the system.web elements. Name the cache profile "profile."

```
<configuration>
  <system.web>
    <caching>
      <outputCacheSettings>
        <outputCacheProfiles>
          <add name="profile"
            duration="60"
            varyByParam="TextBoxName" />
        </outputCacheProfiles>
      </outputCacheSettings>
    </caching>
  </system.web>
</configuration>
```

2. Change the *OutputCache* directive in the Default.aspx page to use the new profile:

```
<%@ Page Language="C#" AutoEventWireup="true"
CodeFile="Default.aspx.cs" Inherits="_Default"
trace="false"%>

<%@ OutputCache CacheProfile=<;$QD>profile" %>
```

3. Surf to the page. It should work exactly as it did before when the caching values were hard-coded. That is, run the page, type a name, and note the date and time stamp. Type a new name and note the date and time stamp. Type the original name, submit it, and you should see the original cached page appear (as long as you complete the post within the specified time window).

Caching User Controls

Just as whole pages may be cached, ASP.NET supports caching User Controls as well. Imagine your job is to create a sizeable Web site that allows users to navigate through information via various navigation controls (menus, hyperlinks, and so forth). For example, imagine a part of your page shows links or other navigation controls that lead users to the most recent news, summary information, and other places. The actual content may change, but the links probably don't. If the links don't change very often and the cost of generating that section of the page is expensive, it makes sense to move the functionality into a User Control and apply the *OutputCache* directive to the User Control. Doing so will cause ASP.NET to cache the portion of the page represented by the control.

The *OutputDirective* may be applied to the ASCX file that comprises a User Control. The *OutputDirective* for a User Control may also use the *Shared* property to tell ASP.NET to cache one version of the control for all pages that use it, resulting in potentially even higher performance over the span of many hits (the default is false).

The following exercise illustrates caching the output of a User Control.

User Controls and Output Caching

1. Create a simple User control for the OutputCaching project. Navigation controls are perfect for caching, so create a control that has a menu. Name the control *SiteMenu.ascx*. Drag a *Menu* control onto the User Control, as shown here:

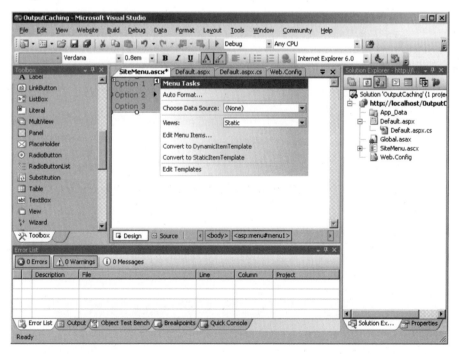

Add some menu items, as shown in this graphic:

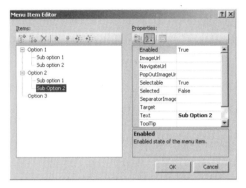

2. Add the *OutputCache* directive with the following parameters in the control source, like so:

```
<%@ Control Language="C#" AutoEventWireup="true"
CodeFile="SiteMenu.ascx.cs" Inherits="SiteMenu" %>
<%@ OutputCache Duration="60" VaryByParam="none" %>
```

3. Create a new page in the project. Name it UseSiteMenuControl.aspx.

4. Drag the *SiteMenu* User Control onto the UseSiteMenuControl page. When ASP.NET loads and runs your Web page, ASP.NET will cache the User Control because the User Control mentions the *OutputDirective*.

5. Make sure tracing is turned on in the UseSiteMenuControl.aspx file. (That is, set the *Trace="true"* attribute in the *Page* directive.) Surf to the page. The first time you surf to the page, you'll see the following information in the control tree section of the *Trace* output:

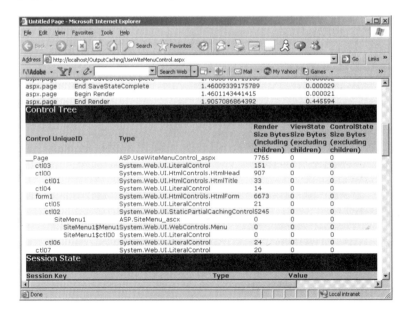

Notice the entire control tree was rendered. Push the refresh key (**F5** in Internet Explorer) while looking at UseSiteMenuControl.aspx. Examine the control tree portion of the *Trace* output again. Notice that ASP.NET uses the cached control instead of re-rendering the entire *SiteMenu* control.

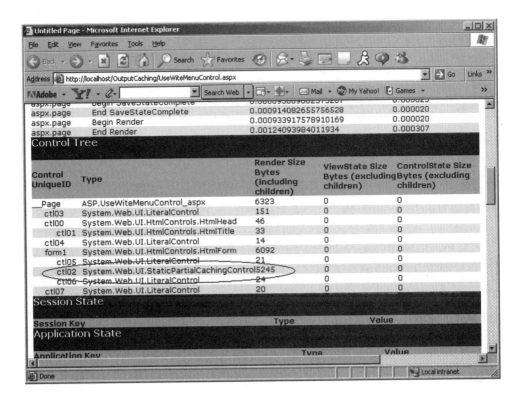

When Output Caching Makes Sense

As with other caching techniques, one of the most important strategies is to turn on output caching for those pages that are accessed frequently and expensive to generate. Also, be sure to cache only those pages that don't change frequently (otherwise, you may be better off simply *not* using output caching).

For example, pages full of controls that render a great deal of HTML are probably expensive. Imagine a page including a *DataGrid* displaying an employee directory. This is a perfect candidate for caching due to several reasons. First, a database hit (or even an in-memory cache hit) Is required. Second, a *DataGrid* is pretty expensive to render—especially if it needs to figure out the schema of the employee directory table on the fly. Finally, an employee directory probably doesn't change very often. By caching it once, you can avoid spending a great deal of unnecessary cycles.

A related issue here is to be careful when typing asterisks into the output caching parameters such as *VaryByParam*. Using *VaryByParam*=* tells ASP.NET to generate a new page for every single request in which *any* query string parameter has changed. That's almost the same as *not* caching altogether—with the added cost of the memory consumed by the output cache. However, this may make sense for Web sites with limited audiences where the parameter variance between requests remains limited.

In addition, be wary of how caching might affect the appearance of your page on different browsers. Much of the time, content will appear the same regardless of the browser. However, if you cache some content that depends upon a specific browser feature (such as Dynamic HTML), clients whose browsers don't understand the feature may see some very weird behavior in the browser.

Tuning the behavior of the output cache is also important. Effective caching is always a matter of balance. While you can potentially speed up your site by employing output caching, the cost is memory consumption. Using instrumentation tools can help you balance performance against cost.

Finally, User Controls often represent a prime output caching opportunity—especially if they don't change frequently. Wrapping the portion of a page that *doesn't* change in an output cached User Control will usually enhance the perceived performance of your application at a minimal cost because only the User Control content is cached.

Conclusion

Caching is a tried and true way to improve the performance of almost any system. By making frequently used content available quickly through the output cache, you can speed up the perceived performance of your application by a wide margin.

Turning on output caching in ASP.NET is a matter of including the correct directive at the top of your page. Naive use of the cache involves simply placing it on the page code and setting the *Duration* to some number and the *VaryByParam* attribute to none. However, you may also control various behaviors of the output cache by setting variables within the *OutputCache* directive. You may also control output caching behaviors through the *HttpCachePolicy* class, available through the *Cache* property of the *Response* object. ASP.NET supports cache profiles so you don't have to hard-code the caching parameters into the *OutputDirective*.

User Controls often represent a prime output caching opportunity—especially if they're navigation controls or some other control that doesn't change very often. By applying the *OutputCache* directive to the User Control, ASP.NET caches that part of the page on which it was placed.

Chapter 15 Quick Reference

To	Do This
Cache a page's output	Add the *OutputCache* directive to the page
Store multiple versions of a page based on varying query string parameters	Use the *VaryByParam* attribute of the *OutputCache* directive
Store multiple versions of a page based on varying headers	Use the *VaryByHeader* attribute of the *OutputCache* directive
Store multiple versions of a page based on varying browsers	Use the *VaryByCustom* attribute of the *OutputCache* directive, selecting "browser" as the value
Specify the location of the cached content	Specify the *Location* attribute in the *OutputCache* directive
Access caching attributes programmatically	Use the *Cache* property of the *Response* object, which is an instance of the *HttpCachePolicy* class
Offload output caching configuration to the Web.Config file	Add *outputCacheProfile* elements to your Web.Config file. Use them as necessary
Cache a User Control	Apply the *OutputCache* directive to the control's ASCX file

Chapter 16
Diagnostics and Debugging

After completing this chapter, you will be able to

- Turn on page tracing

- Insert custom trace messages into the page trace

- Turn tracing on for the entire application

- Manage custom error pages

- Manage exceptions within your application

Even with all the software architecture methodologies and development practices available these days, software is still very much a craft. Software libraries such as ASP.NET and Windows Forms go a long way towards making development more standardized and predictable (good things in software practice). However, there are still almost inevitable periods when you need to figure out what's wrong with an application that decides to behave differently than you expected it to.

This chapter covers the support provided by ASP.NET for figuring out what's wrong with your ASP.NET application. As you can imagine, debugging Web applications introduces a whole new set of challenges. Remember, HTTP is basically connectionless, and the only thing the client really gets to see is a snapshot of the application. This chapter shows you how to watch your application as it runs and trace the state of any particular request. We'll also cover managing error pages and trapping application exceptions within ASP.NET.

Page Tracing

The first place to start with debugging is to examine ASP.NET page tracing. The *Page* class has a property named *Trace*. When *Trace* is turned on, it tells the ASP.NET runtime to insert a rendering of the entire context of the request and response at the end of the HTML sent to the client.

We've already seen page tracing to some extent. When we looked at the ASP.NET server-side control architecture, the page trace was invaluable in understanding the structure of the page. Remember, a rendered page is composed of a number of server-side controls collected together as a hierarchical tree. A *Page* nests several controls, and the controls themselves may nest other controls (they may be nested several levels deep, as a matter of fact). The page trace includes a section displaying the composition of the page in terms of server-side controls.

Turning on Tracing

Turning tracing on is easy. Simply set the *Trace* property of the page to True. You may turn tracing on either by modifying the ASPX code directly, or by setting the *Trace* property using the designer. Here's the *Trace* property being turned on directly within the ASPX code as part of the page directive.

```
<%@ Page Language="C#" AutoEventWireup="true" CodeFile="TraceMe.aspx.cs"
Inherits="TraceMe" Trace="true" %>
```

As soon as you turn tracing on and surf to the page, you'll see tracing information appear at the end of the HTML stream. Listing 16-1 shows some code from the DebugORama example that came with the CD accompanying this book. The TraceMe.aspx page builds a table of strings as they're entered on the site. The list of strings is kept in session state and refreshes the table every time a new string is submitted.

Listing 16-1

```
public partial class TraceMe : System.Web.UI.Page
{
   ArrayList alTableEntries = null;

   protected void Page_Load(object sender, EventArgs e)
   {
     alTableEntries = (ArrayList)this.Session["TableEntries"];
     if (alTableEntries == null)
     {
        alTableEntries = new ArrayList();
     }
     AssembleTable();
   }
```

```
protected void AssembleTable()
{
   this.Table1.Rows.Clear();
   foreach (String s in alTableEntries)
   {
      TableRow row = new TableRow();
      TableCell cell = new TableCell();
      cell.Text = s;
      row.Cells.Add(cell);
      this.Table1.Rows.Add(row);
   }
}

protected void Button1_Click(object sender, EventArgs e)
{
   alTableEntries.Add(this.TextBox1.Text);
   this.Session["TableEntries"] = alTableEntries;
   AssembleTable();
}
}
```

Figure 16-1 shows how the page appears with tracing turned on.

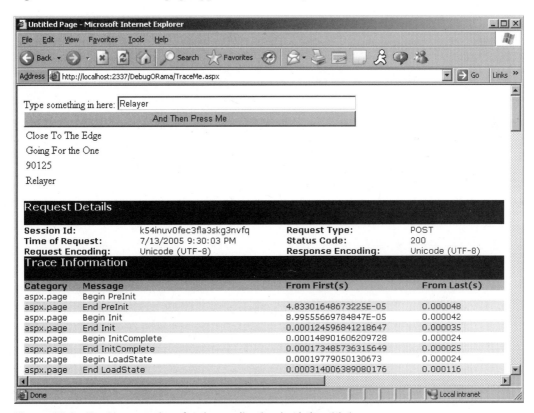

Figure 16-1 Tracing turned on for the application in Listing 16-1.

A bit further down the tracing output, you'll see the control tree (as we saw in Chapters 3, 4, and 5). The control tree for this page is shown in Figure 16-2.

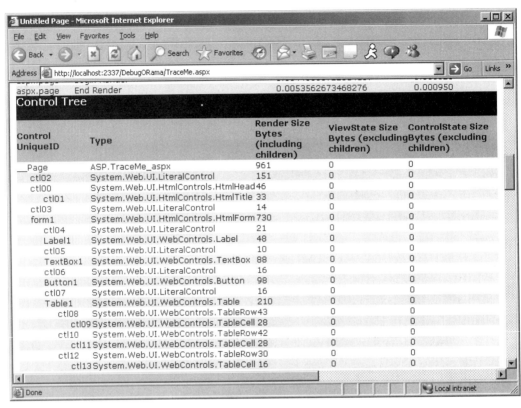

Figure 16-2   Tracing turned on for the application in Listing 16-1. Notice the control tree.

Finally, scroll down a teeny bit more, and you start seeing some of the context information associated with the request. Figure 16-3 shows this context information. This application uses session state to save the array of strings. Notice the session state tracing shows the contents of the session state dictionary. You also get to see other context information. For example, the tracing section shows the session ID and the URL used to surf to this page.

Of course, much of this information becomes more useful in cases where there's a problem with your Web site. For example, the table might stop building itself because you somehow removed the session state item holding the list of strings. You could detect that by examining the page trace. If users begin complaining about layout issues with your site, you may look at the user agent coming down with the request and learn that the client is using a browser not accommodated by your application.

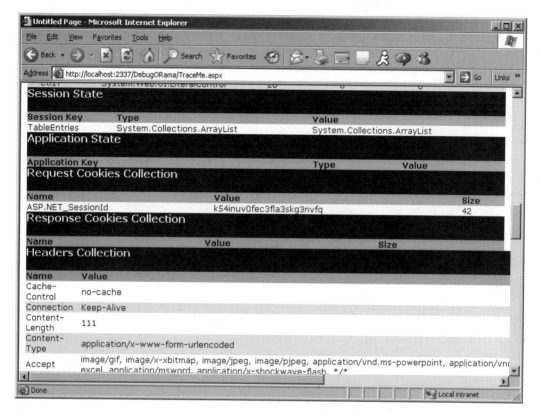

Figure 16-3   Tracing turned on for the application in Listing 16-1. Note the detailed information about the context of the request.

Trace Statements

In addition to all the request context information included with the HTML stream, the page trace also includes specific statements printed out during execution. If you scroll to the Trace Information block on the page, you can see these trace statements, shown in Figure 16-4.

The statements appearing in Figure 16-4 were produced by the ASP.NET framework. You can see the execution of the page progressing through the various events such as *PreInit*, *Init*, *LoadState*, and so forth.

Not only do you get tracing information from ASP.NET itself, but you may also insert your own tracing information. The *Page* class's *Trace* object provides a means of tracing page execution. Here's an exercise that shows you how to do this.

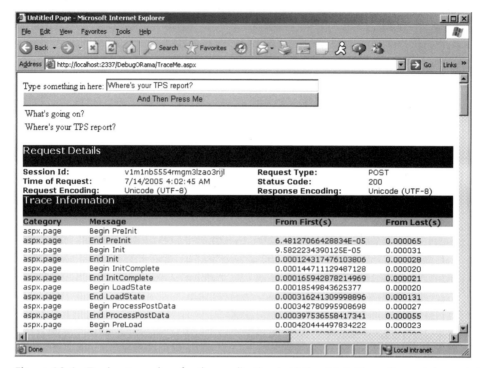

Figure 16-4   Tracing turned on for the application in Listing 16-1. These Trace statements track the execution of the page.

Adding Tracing Statements

1. Open the DebugORama Web site.

2. Open the TraceMe.aspx page and examine the code. Add tracing statements in strategic places through the page's *Trace* object. For example, you might want to monitor the table as it's being built. Do this by calling either *Trace.Write* or *Trace.Warn* within the page. *Trace.Write* renders the string in black, while *Trace.Warn* renders the tracing string in red. The first parameter is a category string you may use to help distinguish the statements you write when they finally render. You may add whatever you want to the category string.

```
public partial class TraceMe : System.Web.UI.Page
{
    ArrayList alTableEntries = null;

    protected void Page_Load(object sender, EventArgs e)
    {
        alTableEntries = (ArrayList)this.Session["TableEntries"];
        if (alTableEntries == null)
        {
            Trace.Warn("Page_Load", "alTableEntries is null");
            alTableEntries = new ArrayList();
        }
```

```
        AssembleTable();
    }

    protected void AssembleTable()
    {
        this.Table1.Rows.Clear();

        foreach (String s in alTableEntries)
        {
            Trace.Write("AssembleTable", "String found: " + s);
            TableRow row = new TableRow();
            TableCell cell = new TableCell();
            cell.Text = s;
            row.Cells.Add(cell);
            this.Table1.Rows.Add(row);
        }
    }

    protected void Button1_Click(object sender, EventArgs e)
    {
        Trace.Write("Button1_Click", "Adding string: " + this.TextBox1.Text);
        alTableEntries.Add(this.TextBox1.Text);
        this.Session["TableEntries"] = alTableEntries;
        AssembleTable();
    }
}
```

3. Compile the program and run the Web site. You should see your trace statements appearing in the output (as long as tracing is turned on).

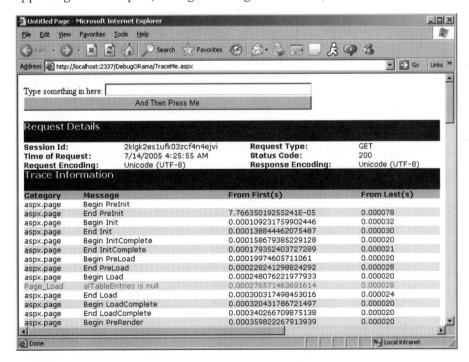

Application Tracing

While single page tracing is useful (especially for quick spot checks for problems), it has a major downside in that it litters the page with lots of garbage at the end. You can use application tracing to get around that. Application tracing shows you exactly the same details as page tracing, except they're held in memory and made available rendered as a different page and through a special handler.

To turn on tracing, you need to enable tracing in Web.Config like so:

```
<configuration>
   <system.web>
        <trace enabled='true'/>
   </system.web>
</configuration>
```

This simply turns tracing on. You can actually control several aspects of page tracing. For example, you could have tracing available on the host machine (in case you don't want clients getting to your trace information). You might also want to control the number of responses that are held in memory.

Table 16-1 shows the possible values that may go in the configuration file to support tracing.

Table 16-1   Web.Config settings supporting tracing.

Key	Possible Values	Meaning
enabled	true false	Enable or disable application-level tracing
localOnly	true false	Specify whether to show trace output only on local host or everywhere
pageOutput	true false	Specify whether to display trace output on individual pages in addition to caching application-level traces
mostRecent	true false	Specify whether to recycle traces once *requestLimit* is met or to keep the first *N* (up to the *requestLimit* threshold)
writeToDiagnosticsTrace	true false	Specify whether the trace data is also piped to *System.Diagnostics.Trace*
requestLimit	Decimal number	Specify how many traces to store in memory before removing earlier traces (default is 10)

The following exercise demonstrates how application-level tracing works and how to navigate around the results.

Application-level Tracing

1. Open the DebugORama project. Open the TraceMe.aspx page. Turn tracing off in the page by ensuring the *Page* class's *Trace* property is false.

2. Ensure that tracing is turned on in Web.Config. That is, open Web.Config and add a *trace* element, as shown above. If the application doesn't yet have a configuration file, you may add one by selecting **Add New Item** from the local project menu.

3. Surf to the page a few times.

4. In the URL appearing in the navigation bar, make the endpoint Trace.axd. Using this name in the URL redirects request processing through a special handler that will render the tracing results being kept in memory.

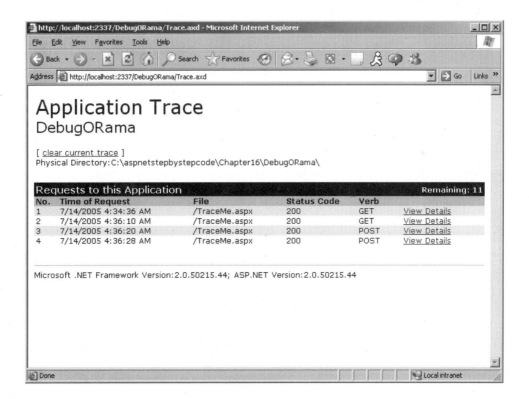

5. You should be able to see a list of requests. To see individual requests, get the request details by clicking on the link.

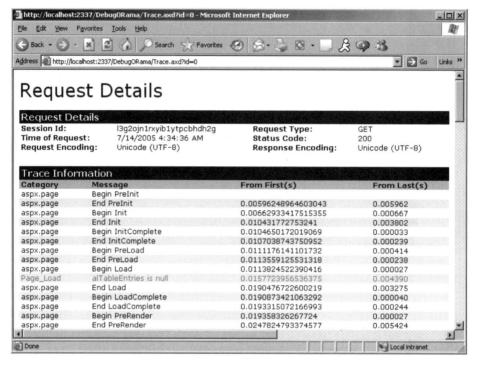

Notice how the output is exactly the same as the output on the earlier page tracing example. However, now the tracing information stands alone without cluttering up the Web page.

Enabling Tracing Programmatically

While much of the time you'll find yourself enabling tracing via the designer, there are times when it's useful to manage tracing during runtime (programmatically). For example, you might have regular clients receive normal content; however, when someone with specific credentials appears, you might want to enable tracing for that individual. You might also decide to modify tracing when a certain parameter comes through the request.

The DebugORama site includes a page named EnableTracing.aspx that illustrates how to control the tracing programmatically. If the user types the correct password, the tracing is turned on. The page also shows how to enable and disable tracing programmatically.

```
public partial class EnableTracing : System.Web.UI.Page
{
    protected void Page_Load(object sender, EventArgs e)
    {
    }
    protected void Button1_Click(object sender, EventArgs e)
    {
        if (this.TextBoxPassword.Text == "password")
```

```
        {
            this.Trace.IsEnabled = true;
        }
    }
    protected void Button2_Click(object sender, EventArgs e)
    {
        this.Trace.IsEnabled = false;
    }
}
```

The *TraceFinished* Event

The tracing context includes an interesting event named *TraceFinished* that gives you a last chance opportunity to log the tracing information or deal with it in some other way. The *TraceFinished* event is raised by the *Trace* object after all request information is gathered.

To subscribe to the event, simply set up the handler during the *Page_Load* event. The DebugORama example includes a page named TraceFinished.aspx that shows gathering the trace information and writing it to the debug console using *System.Diagnostics.Debug*.

```
public partial class TraceFinished : System.Web.UI.Page
{
    protected void Page_Load(object sender, EventArgs e)
    {
      Trace.TraceFinished +=
          new TraceContextEventHandler(TracingFinished);
    }
    void TracingFinished(object sender, TraceContextEventArgs e)
    {
        foreach (TraceContextRecord traceContextRecord in e.TraceRecords)
        {
            System.Diagnostics.Debug.WriteLine(
    traceContextRecord.Message);
        }
    }
}
```

Piping Other Trace Messages

In the last example, tracing messages were logged manually to the debug console by setting up the *TraceFinished* event handler in the *Trace* context. *System.Diagnostics.Debug* is a standard .NET type that's helpful for managing tracing and debugging information. ASP.NET 2.0 now has the ability to plug the *WebPageTraceListener* type so that calls to *System.Diagnostics.Trace* are also inserted into the ASP.NET trace. Setting it up is simply a matter of inserting a line into Web.Config. Notice this lies outside the normal *System.web* section of Web.Config.

```
<system.codedom>
    <compilers>
        <compiler compilerOptions="/d:TRACE" />
    </compilers>
</system.codedom>
```

Debugging with Visual Studio

The tracing support built into ASP.NET works really well and is a great way to debug your application–especially once it's deployed. However, when you're in development mode, having to plant tracing messages into your page and then run it to see what happened is old school, and sometimes not the most efficient way of debugging. Visual Studio provides excellent debugging support through the environment, and you may use it to watch your code execute and to step through the code one line at a time. In fact, you have access to all of Visual Studio's debugging facilities, even though you're developing Web applications.

Remember, ASP.NET and Visual Studio work in concert to make it feel like you're doing desktop application development, even though it's a Web application. That goes for the debugger, as well. The following exercise will familiarize you with the Visual Studio debugging environment.

Debug an Application

1. Open the DebugORama Web site. To support debugging, Web.Config needs to include the right settings. You may type it by hand if you wish; however, Visual Studio will insert it for you once you start debugging.

```
<system.web>
   <trace enabled="true"/>
   <compilation debug="true"/>
</system.web>
```

2. Open the TraceMe.aspx page and insert breakpoints in *Page_Load*, *AssembleTable*, *Button1_Click*. You may insert breakpoints by highlighting a line in the editor window and pressing the **F9** key. You may also select **Debug | Toggle Breakpoint** from the main menu. Visual Studio will show a big red dot to the left of the breakpoint lines.

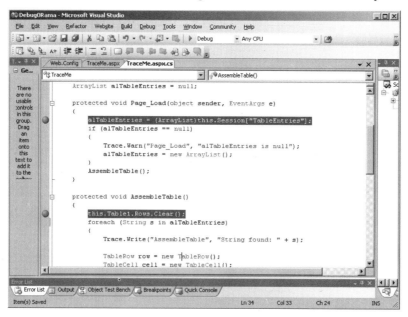

3. Start debugging by pressing the **F5** key. You may also debug by selecting **Debug | Start Debugging** from the main menu. If debugging is *not* turned on in the Web.Config file, Visual Studio will ask you before it turns on the debugging attribute. Visual Studio will start running the site. When it comes to your breakpoints, Visual Studio will stop execution and highlight the current line in yellow in the window.

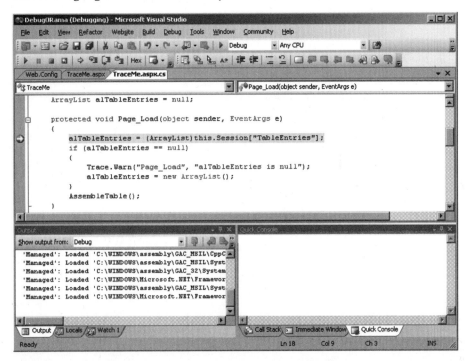

4. In this example, *Page_Load* is the first breakpoint Visual Studio encounters. At this point, you may start stepping through the code. **F10** steps over methods while **F11** steps *into* methods. Alternatively, you may use **Debug | Step Over** and **Debug | Step Into** from the main menu.

5. Hover your mouse cursor over any variables you see. Notice how Visual Studio displays the value of the variable in a ToolTip.

6. Hit **F5** to resume the program. Visual Studio will run until it hits another breakpoint. Run through all the breakpoints.

7. Next, post back to the server using the button. Notice the breakpoints are hit again. Also notice here that first the *Page_Load* is hit, and *then* the *Button_Click* handler. This highlights the ephemeral nature of a Web page. A new page is being created for each request that comes in.

8. Finally, try out a couple of the debug windows. You can monitor various aspects of your program by selecting **Debug | Window** from the main menu and choosing the window. Here's the Locals window, showing those variables within local scope.

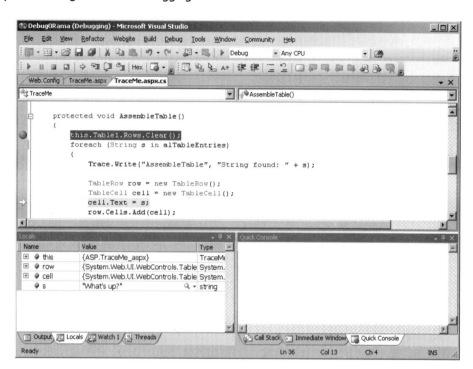

9. The Call Stack window shows how execution finally arrived at this spot. You may trace through and follow the entire program execution up to this point.

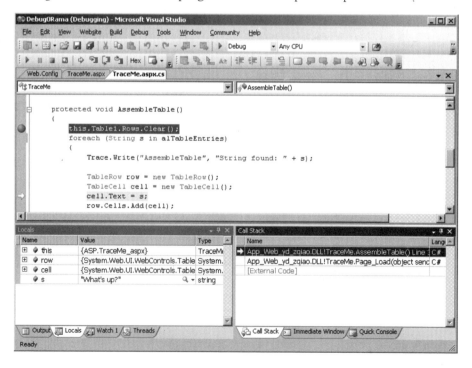

Other notable windows include the Watch window that lets you examine any variable you want. In addition, the Threads window will let you see how many threads are running, what their thread IDs are, and so forth.

Error Pages

As we've seen throughout the tour of ASP.NET, one of the main goals has always been to isolate as much of the Web development facility as possible into ASP.NET. At this point, IIS is really only a middle manager in the scheme of things. Many facilities previously handled by IIS are now handled by ASP.NET. One of those facilities is managing custom error pages. In ASP.NET, you may introduce custom error pages (instead of the client being bombarded with ASP.NET error messages).

To tell ASP.NET to display a particular page upon encountering errors anywhere within your application, just tweak the Web.Config file. Table 16-2 shows the custom error attributes for Web.Config.

Table 16-2   Web.Config values for setting error pages.

Attribute	Description
on/off	on == display custom pages
	off == display ASP.NET error pages
defaultRedirect	Direct users here in the event of an exception
remoteOnly	Display custom errors to client, display ASP.NET errors locally

The following example illustrates how to work with custom error pages.

Work with Error Pages

In this example, you'll add some error pages to your application and see what conditions cause them to show.

1. Open the DebugORama project.

2. Add a new Web form named ThrowErrors.aspx to the DebugORama application.

3. Add two buttons: one to throw 404 errors (the nearly ubiquitous "object not found" error) and one to throw other exceptions.

4. Add two HTML pages to your application to act as custom error pages. Name one page 404Error.html and the other SomethingBadHappened.html.

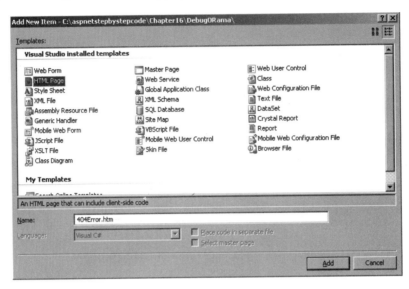

5. Tell ASP.NET to use the error pages by adding the *customErrors* section to Web.Config, like so:

```
<configuration>
  <system.web>
    <customErrors
        defaultRedirect='SomethingBadHappened.htm' mode='On'>
        <error statusCode='404'
            redirect='404Error.htm'/>
    <customErrors>
  </system.web>
</configuration>
```

This tells ASP.NET to show the 404Error.htm page when a file isn't found. ASP.NET will show SomethingBadHappened.htm for any other error.

6. Now add handlers to generate the errors. Handle the 404 error button by directing the client to a nonexistent page. Handle the second error generator by throwing a random exception.

```
public partial class ThrowErrors : System.Web.UI.Page
{
    protected void Page_Load(object sender, EventArgs e)
    {
    }
    protected void Throw404_Click(object sender, EventArgs e)
    {
        this.Response.Redirect("NotThere.aspx");
    }
    protected void ThrowOther_Click(object sender, EventArgs e)
    {
        throw new Exception();
    }
}
```

When you try to redirect to a nonexistent file, the "not found" error page shows:

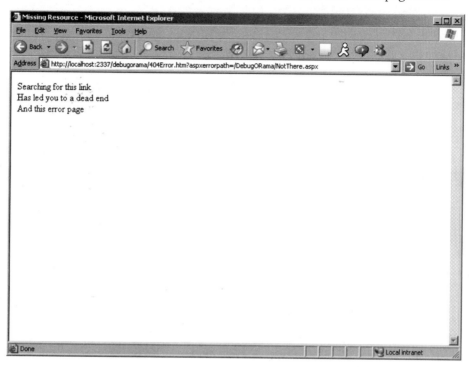

Throwing a generic exception will cause the other page to show.

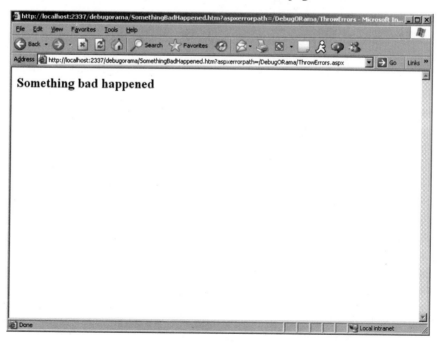

Before leaving debugging and diagnostics, let's take a look at trapping exceptions in a more graceful way.

Unhandled Exceptions

In the last example page that threw an exception, ASP.NET responded by redirecting to the default error page. ASP.NET also lets you trap exceptions by setting up a handler for *Error* events fired by *HttpApplication* so that you may handle them more appropriately.

The easiest way to accomplish this is to define a handler in your *HttpApplication*-derived class within Global.asax. With the handler connected to the event, your application will receive notifications whenever something bad happens, and you can deal with it gracefully. For example, you might log the error before redirecting the user to an error page.

```
<script runat="server">

    void Application_Start(Object sender, EventArgs e) {
     }

    void Application_End(Object sender, EventArgs e) {
     }

    void Application_Error(Object sender, EventArgs e) {
      Exception ex = Server.GetLastError();

      // display the exception before redirecting
      System.Diagnostics.Debug.WriteLine("Error in app: " + ex);

      if (ex is HttpUnhandledException)
      {
          Server.Transfer("somethingbadhappened.aspx");
      }
    }

    void Session_Start(Object sender, EventArgs e) {

    }

    void Session_End(Object sender, EventArgs e) {
    }

</script>
```

The code above traps the exception before the redirection happens. This gives you the opportunity to log the exception (or, as in the example above, to show it in the *System.Diagnosics.Debug* context). You may also redirect users to a different page, if you want to hijack the exception handling before ASP.NET redirects to the page specified in Web.Config. Be sure to call *Context.ClearError* first to clear the error so ASP.NET won't generate its standard error page.

Conclusion

Web development is difficult because an application's state can be all over the place. For example, the application holds some of the state, the browser holds some of the state, and some of the state is stuck in a session database. In addition, the executing portions of an application happen in multiple places—both on the server and on the client. That calls for debugging techniques different from what you'd require with a desktop application.

ASP.NET supports per-page tracing and application-level tracing. In both cases, ASP.NET displays the entire context of a request and response, including tracing statements. Visual Studio also supports debugging ASP.NET applications as though they were desktop applications. You simply set up breakpoints, fire up the debugger, and watch the fireworks. Debugging ASP.NET applications is very much like debugging desktop applications, thanks to Visual Studio.

Finally, ASP.NET takes over the custom error page handling process (which used to be managed by IIS in classic ASP). You may direct users to new pages depending upon the error that occurs. Finally, you can trap exceptions before they redirect and perform additional processing.

Chapter 16 Quick Reference

To	Do This
Prepare a Web site for debugging	Include the following in Web.Config: ``` <system.web> <compilation debug="true"/> </system.web> ```
Enable tracing for an entire application	Include the following in Web.Config: ``` <system.web> <trace enabled="true"/> </system.web> ```
Enable tracing for your page	Set the *Page* class's *trace* attribute to true using either the property page in Visual Studio or by declaring *trace=true* in the page directive
Debug a Web application in Visual Studio	Ensure that the debug attribute is turned on in Web.Config Start the program running in debug mode by 1. Selecting **Debug | Start Debugging** from the main menu OR 2. Hitting the F5 key
Set up breakpoints in an application in Visual Studio	Place the cursor on the line at which you'd like to stop execution and 1. Select **Debug | Toggle Breakpoint** OR 2. Hit the F9 key

To	Do This
Execute a line of source code in the Visual Studio debugger	While the debugger is running and execution has stopped at the line you'd like to execute 1. Select **Debug | Stop Over** from the main menu OR 2. Hit the F10 key
Step INTO a line of source code in the Visual Studio debugger	While the debugger is running and execution has stopped at the line you'd like to execute 1. Select **Debug | Stop Into** from the main menu OR 2. Hit the F11 key
Instruct ASP.NET to show a specific page when an error occurs	Assign the error handling page to the specfic error in the *<customErrors>* section of Web.Config
Trap specific errors in ASP.NET	Handle uncaught exceptions within the *Application_Error* handler in Global.ASAX. Usually, redirect to a specific page

The Application and HTTP Modules

After completing this chapter, you will be able to

- Use *HttpApplication* as a rendezvous point for your application

- Manage data within the *HttpApplication* object

- Manage events within the *HttpApplication* object

- Work with HTTP Modules

This chapter covers working with *application state* and *application-wide events* within your ASP.NET application. In normal desktop applications, the notion of a global meeting place for various parts of an application is well-understood. For example, MFC, a C++ class library supporting low-level Windows development, includes a class named *CWinApp* that holds state useful throughout the program. This state includes such items as a handle to the current instance of the application, a handle to the main window, and the parameters that were passed in when the application started. The *CWinApp* class also runs the message loop—something that can be done only within the global scope of a Windows application. A running Windows application contains one and only one instance of the *CWinApp* class, and it's perennially available from anywhere within the application.

Windows Forms—the .NET library supporting Windows forms—has a similar class named *Application*. It includes the same sort of state (command line parameters, a top-level window, other state required by the program). The Windows Forms *Application* class also runs the message loop.

Web development also requires the same sort of "global space" that a desktop application requires. Having a global space within a Web application makes implementing features such as caching data and session state possible. Let's take a look at how ASP.NET implements a global space for Web applications.

The Application: A Rendezvous Point

As we've seen so far, one of the most distinctive aspects of Web-based development is the requirement to be very mindful of the state of your application. By itself, raw Web application development includes no support for dealing with state. After all, Web requests are made over a disconnected protocol and the state of a request evaporates as soon as it hits an endpoint.

In Chapter 4 (all about server-side controls in depth), we took a look at the notion of view state within an ASP.NET application. ASP.NET server-side controls have the option of supporting view state. View state is embedded within the data going back and forth between the browser and the server and is used (most of the time) to keep the user interface appearing as though the browser and the server are connected continually. For example, without view state (or some special coding within the server), UI elements such as combo boxes lose their state between posts, causing the first item in the list to always show as the selected item—even if it wasn't really the item selected.

In Chapter 13, we looked at *session state*—or the data accompanying a specific session. Session state is useful for items such as shopping carts where the application has to associate data with a client.

Finally, in Chapter 14, we took a look at caching state so as to avoid unnecessary round-trips to a data source. Loading data from memory is usually much faster than loading it from a database or regenerating it. When it comes to storing data that all parts of your application can use, the data must be stored somewhere else besides view state and session state. We saw that the cache is available from virtually anywhere in the application via the *HttpContext* object. The *HttpContext* includes a reference to an instance of the *HttpApplication* object. In addition to being a holding place for the cache, the application object has its own dictionary that serves as a useful place to hold data. It works in very much the same way the *Cache* does. However, there are some subtle yet important differences between the *Cache* and the dictionary held by *HttpApplication*.

Keeping a dictionary and a data cache available for the rest of the application isn't the only good reason to implement a central application object. The other reason is to have a mechanism for handling application-wide events. We've seen that the *Page* class handles events for a request specifically. However, think about how the entire ASP.NET pipeline works. Some useful events aren't part of the page processing or request processing mechanism. Implementing those involves code working outside the normal page processing mechanism.

For example, we looked at session state in Chapter 13. When a request first comes through a site whose session state is enabled, when should the session object be set up? Certainly, you want it set up before the page-specific processing begins. In Chapter 10 we saw the ASP.NET security model. When should authentication and authorization be handled? You want those things to happen outside the context of the normal request processing, too. A final example is output caching, as we saw in Chapter 15. For output caching to work, ASP.NET needs to intercept the request when it first enters the pipeline so that it may bypass the whole page creation process and render the cached content instead.

ASP.NET's *HttpApplication* object can manage these sorts of things. When running, the *HttpApplication* object represents a rendezvous point for all the parts of your entire Web application. If you're looking for software patterns to identify within ASP.NET, the *HttpApplication* most closely represents the *singleton* pattern. You treat it as a single instance of an object within your application. A reference to it is accessible at any point in time through the *HttpContext* class via the *Current* property.

Overriding *HttpApplication*

Overriding the *HttpApplication* to include your own state and event handling is a matter of adding a file named Global.asax to your application. In fact, Visual Studio will add one to your application that is set up and ready to handle a few application-wide events. Remember from examining ASPX files that *Page* files include the *Page* directive at the top of the file. The Global.asax file includes a similar directive. The *Application* directive tells the runtime compiling machinery that this file is meant to serve as the application object.

Listing 17-1 shows an example of the *HttpApplication* expressed within a file named Global.asax. The Global.asax provided by Visual Studio overrides the *Application_Start*, *Application_End*, *Application_Error*, *Session_Start*, and *Session_End* events.

Listing 17-1
```
<%@ Application Language="C#" %>

<script runat="server">

    void Application_Start(Object sender, EventArgs e) {}
    void Application_End(Object sender, EventArgs e) {}
    void Application_Error(Object sender, EventArgs e) {}
    void Session_Start(Object sender, EventArgs e) {}
    void Session_End(Object sender, EventArgs e) {}

</script>
```

To get an idea as to how these events work, the following example illustrates placing a piece of data in the application's dictionary and retrieving it later when the page loads.

Managing Application State

1.   Start a new Web site named UseApplication.

2.   Drag a *GridView* onto the default page. Don't assign a data source to it yet. You'll populate it with a data that is stored with the application in later steps.

3. Add a Global.asax to the site. Right-click on the project in the Project Explorer (or select **Web Site | Add New Item** from the main menu). Choose the Global application template, as shown below.

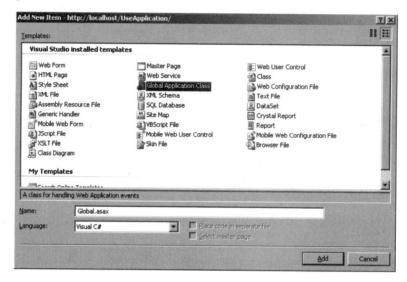

4. You've just added a file named Global.asax to your application. You can see that the *Application_Start* event is already handled (although it does nothing right now).

5. To have some data to store with the application object, import the *QuotesCollection* from Chapter 14. The project name is UseDataCaching. Select **Web Site | Add Existing Item** from the main menu and find the file QuotesCollection.cs. In addition to importing the QuotesCollection.cs file, grab the QuotesCollection.xml and QuotesCollection.xsd files from the UseDataCaching\App_Data directory.

6. Add some code to the *Application_Start* event to load the quotes data and place it in the application dictionary. *Server.MapPath* will give you the path from which the application is executing so you can load the XML and XSD files. Storing the data in the dictionary is very much like adding it to the cache.

```csharp
void Application_Start(Object sender, EventArgs e) {
    QuotesCollection quotesCollection = new QuotesCollection();

    String strAppPath = Server.MapPath("");

    String strFilePathXml =
            strAppPath  + "\\app_data\\QuotesCollection.xml";
    String strFilePathSchema = strAppPath +
            "\\app_data\\QuotesCollection.xsd";
    quotesCollection.ReadXmlSchema(strFilePathSchema);
    quotesCollection.ReadXml(strFilePathXml);

    Application["quotesCollection"] = quotesCollection;
}
```

7. Update *Page_Load* method in the Default.aspx page to load the data from the application's dictionary. The application state is available through the page's reference to the *Application* object. Accessing data within the dictionary is a matter of indexing it correctly. After loading the data from the dictionary, apply it to the *DataSource* property in the *GridView* and bind the *DataGrid*.

```
protected void Page_Load(object sender, EventArgs e)
{
  QuotesCollection quotesCollection =
    (QuotesCollection)Application["quotesCollection"];

  GridView1.DataSource = quotesCollection;
  GridView1.DataBind();
}
```

Application State Caveats

As you can see, the application state and the cache seem to overlap in their functionality. Indeed, they're both available from similar scopes (from any point in the application), and getting the data in and out involves using the right indexer. However, the application state and the cache vary in a couple of significant ways.

First, items that go into the application state stay in the cache until you remove them explicitly. The cache implements more flexibility in terms of setting expirations and other removal/refresh conditions.

In addition, putting many items into the application dictionary will inhibit the scalability of your application. To make the application state thread-safe, the *HttpApplicationState* class has a *Lock* method. While using the *Lock* method will ensure the data is not corrupted, locking the application frequently will greatly reduce the number of requests it can handle.

Ideally, data going into the application state should be read only once loaded—or changed very infrequently. As long as you're aware of these issues, the application state can be a useful place to store information required by all parts of your application.

Handling Events

The other useful aspect of the application object is its ability to handle application-wide events. As we saw in the previous example, the Global.asax file is a handy place to insert event handlers. Visual Studio will insert a few for you when you simply add one to your application. Some events are handled only in Global.asax, while others may be handled outside Global.asax. The events for which Visual Studio generates stub handlers inside Global.asax include *Application_Start*, *Application_End*, *Application_Error*, *Session_Start*, and *Session_End*. Following is a rundown of these events.

Application_Start

Application_Start happens when the application is first initialized, that is, when the first request comes through. Because *Application_Start* happens first (and only once) during the lifetime of an application, the most common response for the event is to load and initialize data at the start of the application (as with the example above).

Application_End

The ASP.NET runtime raises *Application_End* as the application is shutting down. This is a useful place to clean up any resources requiring special attention for disposal.

Application_Error

Unfortunately, bad things sometimes happen inside Web applications. If something bad has happened in one of your existing applications, you may already have seen the standard pale yellow and red ASP.NET error page. Once you deploy your application, you probably don't want clients to see this sort of page. Intercept this event (*Application_Error*) to handle the error.

Session_Start

The *Session_Start* event occurs when a user makes an initial request to the application, which initializes a new session. This is a good place to initialize session variables (if you want to initialize them before the page loads).

Session_End

This event occurs when a session is released. Sessions end when they time out or when the *Abandon* method is called explicitly. This event happens only for applications whose session state is being held in-process.

HttpApplication Events

The events listed above are implemented in Visual Studio's default Global.asax. The application object can fire a number of other events. Table 17-1 shows a summary of all the events pumped through the application object.

Table 17-1   Application-wide events.

Event	Reason	Order	Only in Global.asax
Application_Start	Application is spinning up.	Start of app	*
Application_End	Application is ending.	End of app	*
Session_Start	Session is starting.		*
Session_End	Session is ending.		*

Table 17-1 Application-wide events.   *(continued)*

Event	Reason	Order	Only in Global.asax
BeginRequest	A new request has been received.	1	
AuthenticateRequest/ *PostAuthenticateRequest*	The user has been authenticated, that is, the security identity of the user has been established.	2	
AuthorizeRequest/ *PostAuthorizeRequest*	The user has been authorized to use the requests resource.	3	
ResolveRequestCache/ *PostResolveRequestCache*	Occurs between authorizing the user and invoking handler. This is where the output caching is handled. If content is cached, the application can bypass the entire page rendering process.	4	
AcquireRequestState/ *PostAcquireRequestState*	Occurs when session state needs to be initialized.	5	
PreRequestHandlerExecute	Occurs immediately before request is sent to the handler. This is a last-minute chance to modify the output before it heads off to the client.	6	
PostRequestHandlerExecute	Occurs following the content being sent to the client.	7	
ReleaseRequestState/ *PostReleaseRequestState*	Occurs following request handling. This event occurs so the system may save state used if necessary.	8	
UpdateRequestCache/ *PostUpdateRequestCache*	Occurs following handler execution. This is used by caching modules to cache responses.	9	
EndRequest	Fires after request is processed.	10	
Disposed	Occurs before the application shuts down.	End of app	
Error	Fired when an unhandled application error occurs.	When an exception occurs	
PreSendRequestContent	Fired before content sent to client.		
PreSendRequestHeaders	Fired before HTTP headers sent to client.		

The following example shows how to time requests by intercepting the *BeginRequest* and the *EndRequest* events within Global.asax.

Timing Requests

1. Open up Global.asax within the UseApplication Web site.

2. Add handlers for *BeginRequest* and *EndRequest* as shown below.

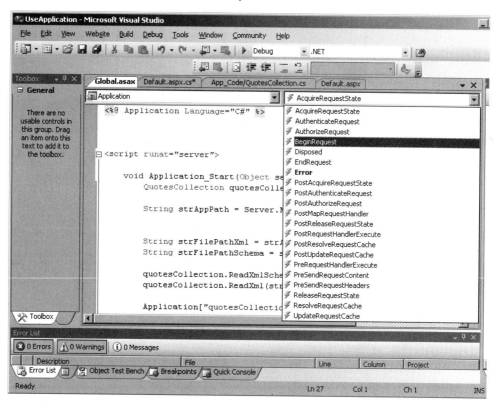

Visual Studio will insert the following stubs in Global.asax:

```
protected void Application_BeginRequest(object sender,
      EventArgs e)
{

}

protected void Application_EndRequest(object sender,
      EventArgs e)
{

}
```

3. Implement the *BeginRequest* handler by getting the current date and time and storing it within the *Items* property of the current *HttpContext*. The *Items* property is a name/value

collection that you may index in the same way you index the cache, the session state, and the *HttpApplication* dictionary. Implement the *EndRequest* handler by comparing the time stamp obtained from the beginning of the request and comparing it to the current date and time. Print out the amount of time taken to process the request using *Response.Write*.

```
protected void Application_BeginRequest(object sender, EventArgs e)
{
    DateTime dateTimeBeginRequest = DateTime.Now;

    HttpContext ctx = HttpContext.Current;
    ctx.Items["dateTimeBeginRequest"] = dateTimeBeginRequest;

}

protected void Application_EndRequest(object sender, EventArgs e)
{
    DateTime dateTimeEndRequest = DateTime.Now;

    HttpContext ctx = HttpContext.Current;
    DateTime dateTimeBeginRequest =
        (DateTime)ctx.Items["dateTimeBeginRequest"];

    TimeSpan duration = dateTimeEndRequest - dateTimeBeginRequest;

    Response.Write("<b> This request took " +
        duration.ToString() + "</b></br>");
}
```

You should see the duration printed near the top of the response returned to the browser:

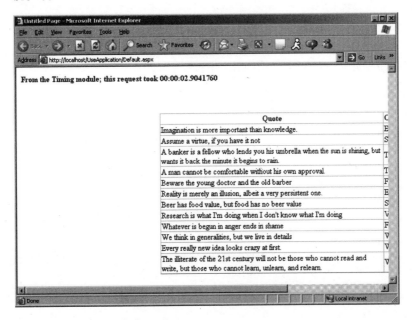

HttpModules

Overriding Global.asax is a very convenient way to manage data and events within an application. Visual Studio generates a Global.asax for you and even stubs out the more important events for you. However, overriding Global.asax isn't the only way to store state and handle application-wide events. The other way is to write an HTTP Module.

HTTP Modules serve very much the same role ISAPI filters served for classic ASP—as a place to insert functionality into the request processing. HTTP Modules plug into the ASP.NET processing chain to handle application-wide events in the same way that Global.asax handles application-wide events. In fact, many ASP.NET features are implemented through HTTP Modules.

Existing Modules

ASP.NET employs HTTP Modules to enable features such as output caching and session state. To get an idea of what features are implemented via HTTP Modules, take a look at the master configuration file for your machine (that is, go to the Windows directory, look in the Microsoft.NET directory, and drill down to the configuration directory for the most current release). The master Web.Config file mentions several modules in the *httpModules* section of the configuration, as shown in Listing 17-2. This list does not include entire strong names of the assemblies, but it gives you an idea as to what modules are already part of the ASP.NET pipeline.

Listing 17-2

```
<httpModules>
 <add name="OutputCache"
  type="System.Web.Caching.OutputCacheModule" />
 <add name="Session"
  type="System.Web.SessionState.SessionStateModule" />
 <add name="WindowsAuthentication"
  type="System.Web.Security.WindowsAuthenticationModule" />
 <add name="FormsAuthentication"
  type="System.Web.Security.FormsAuthenticationModule" />
 <add name="PassportAuthentication"
  type="System.Web.Security.PassportAuthenticationModule" />
<add name="RoleManager"
  type="System.Web.Security.RoleManagerModule" />
<add name="UrlAuthorization"
  type="System.Web.Security.UrlAuthorizationModule" />
<add name="FileAuthorization"
  type="System.Web.Security.FileAuthorizationModule" />
<add name="AnonymousIdentification"
  type="System.Web.Security.AnonymousIdentificationModule" />
<add name="Profile"
  type="System.Web.Profile.ProfileModule" />
<add name="ErrorHandlerModule"
type="System.Web.Mobile.ErrorHandlerModule " />
</httpModules>
```

The *<httpModules>* section mentions the name of a module, followed by a fully specified type that implements the feature. The following features are handled by modules:

- Output Caching
- Session State
- Windows Authentication
- Forms Authentication
- Passport Authentication
- Role Manager
- URL Authorization
- File Authorization
- Anonymous Identification
- Profile

Chapter 2 ("ASP.NET Application Fundamentals") includes a short summary of the ASP.NET pipeline. The Modules fit into the processing chain and take effect prior to being processed by the *HttpApplication* object. While the features themselves may require extensive code to implement (for example, imagine all the work that went into the session state manager), the basic formula for hooking a module into your application is pretty straightforward. Creating a module involves four steps:

1. Writing a class implementing *IHttpModule*
2. Writing handlers for the events you want handled
3. Subscribing to the events
4. Mentioning the module in Web.Config

Implementing a Module

Here's an example illustrating how HTTP Modules work. The earlier example in this chapter demonstrated how to time requests by handling events within Global.asax. The example showed time stamping the beginning of a request, storing the time stamp in the current *Http-Context*, and examining the time stamp as the request finished.

The following example performs the same functionality. However, the example uses an HTTP Module to handle the events.

A Timing Module

1. To implement a timing module, open the Web site solution file for this chapter—Use-Application. To work, the module needs to exist in an assembly. It's easiest to write a

completely separate assembly for the module. Add a project to the solution by selecting **File | Add | New Project** from the main menu. Make the project a Class Library and name the project *TimingModule*.

2. Visual Studio will add a class to the library named *Class1*. (The name of the file generated by Visual Studio is Class1.cs and the name of the class generated by Visual Studio is *Class1*). Change the name of the file to Timer.cs and the name of the class to *Timer*.

3. The module as generated by Visual Studio doesn't understand the ASP.NET types. Add a reference to *System.Web* to make the ASP.NET types available.

4. Add handlers for the beginning and ending of the request. You may borrow the code from Global.asax if you want to. The signatures for the event's handlers are such that the methods need to return void and accept two arguments: an *object* and *EventArgs*.

```csharp
using System;
using System.Data;
using System.Configuration;
using System.Web;
/// <summary>
/// Summary description for Timer
/// </summary>
public class Timer
{
    public Timer()
    {
    }

    public void OnBeginRequest(object o, EventArgs ea)
    {
        HttpApplication httpApp = (HttpApplication)o;

        DateTime dateTimeBeginRequest = DateTime.Now;

        HttpContext ctx;
        ctx = HttpContext.Current;
        ctx.Items["dateTimeBeginRequest"] = dateTimeBeginRequest;
    }

    public void OnEndRequest(object o, EventArgs ea)
    {
        HttpApplication httpApp = (HttpApplication)o;

        DateTime dateTimeEndRequest = DateTime.Now;

        HttpContext ctx;
        ctx = HttpContext.Current;
        DateTime dateTimeBeginRequest =
            (DateTime)ctx.Items["dateTimeBeginRequest"];
```

```
            TimeSpan duration = dateTimeEndRequest - dateTimeBeginRequest;

            ctx.Response.Write("<b> This request took " +
                duration.ToString() + "</b></br>");
        }
    }
```

5. Add *IHttpModule* to the class's inheritance list. Add implementations for the methods *Init* and *Dispose*. The job performed by *Init* is to subscribe to events. The job performed by *Dispose* is to release any resources used by the module (*Dispose* doesn't need to do anything in this example).

```
using System;
using System.Data;
using System.Configuration;
using System.Web;

/// <summary>
/// Summary description for Timer
/// </summary>
public class Timer :
        IHttpModule
{
    public Timer()
    {
    }

    public void Init(HttpApplication httpApp)
    {
        httpApp.BeginRequest +=
            new EventHandler(this.OnBeginRequest);

        httpApp.EndRequest +=
            new EventHandler(this.OnEndRequest);
    }
    public void Dispose() { }

// …
}
```

6. By default, the output produced by the compiler is directed to a separate binary and debug directory (that is, it doesn't go in a place where the Web site can use it). To make the assembly available to the Web site, you need to redirect the output of the compiler so it goes in the Web site's bin directory. To add a \Bin folder to the Web site project, right-click on the Web site project in Project Explorer and select **Add Folder**. Select **Bin folder**. Then right-click on the *Timer* project again and select **Properties**. On the property page, redirect the compiler output to the bin directory for the Web site. You can do this in the Build properties for the *TimerModule* project. If you created this as an IIS Web site, the bin directory will be directly under the project's IIS virtual directory. The following graphic shows the Visual Studio dialog for changing the target path.

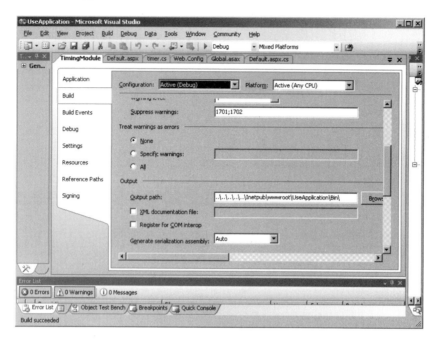

7. Finally, mention the *TimerModule* in the Web.Config file. It needs to appear within the *<httpModules>* section, nested within the *<system.web >* section, like so:

```
<configuration>
  <system.web>
      <httpModules>
        <add name="TimingModule"
            type="Timer, TimingModule" />
      </httpModules>
  </system.web>
</configuration>
```

As long as the *TimerModule* assembly is available to your application (that is, it's in the \bin subdirectory of your virtual directory), it will be linked into the processing chain.

See Active Modules

We saw above that many ASP.NET features are implemented through modules. While you can see the modules listed within the master configuration file, you can also see the list of available modules at runtime. They're available through the current application instance. The following exercise illustrates how to do this.

Listing the Modules

1. Add a button to the Default.aspx page of the UseApplication solution. This button will list the attached modules, so give it a *Text* property of *Show Modules*. Also add a list box to the page that will show the modules.

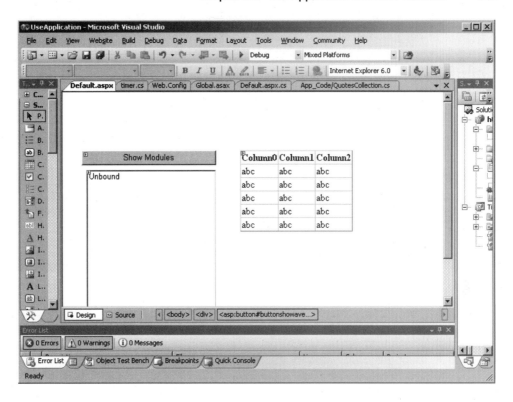

2. Double-click on the button to add a handler within the page.

3. Handle the button event by grabbing the list of modules from the application instance. The list comes back as a collection that you can apply to the list box's *Data-Source* property. Calling *DataBind* on the *ListBox* will put the names of all the modules in the *ListBox*.

```
protected void ButtonShowmodules_Click(object sender, EventArgs e)
{
    HttpApplication httpApp = HttpContext.Current.ApplicationInstance;
    HttpModuleCollection httpModuleColl = httpApp.Modules;

    Response.Write("<br>");
    String[] rgstrModuleNames;
    rgstrModuleNames = httpModuleColl.AllKeys;

    this.ListBox1.DataSource = rgstrModuleNames;
    this.ListBox1.DataBind();
}
```

Running the page and clicking the **Show Module** button will fill the list box with a list of modules plugged into the application (check out the *TimingModule* entry in the list).

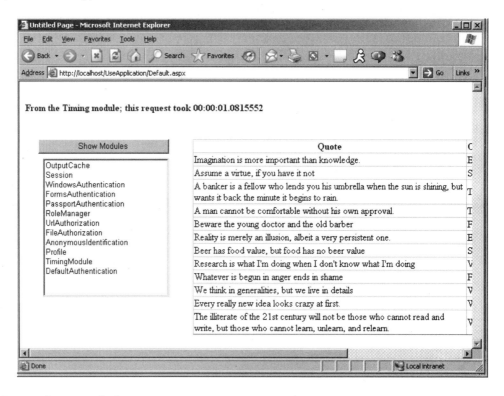

Storing State in Modules

HTTP Modules are also a very handy place to store global state for your application. The following example shows how to track the average request duration (which requires storing the duration of each request as part of application state).

Tracking Average Request Duration

1. Before inserting the functionality into the module, let's think a bit about how to use the information about the average request duration. You might use it to profile and to find bottlenecks in your application. While sending the information out to the client browser is always useful, there might be times when you want to use the information programmatically. To retrieve the information from the Module, you'll need to add one or more methods (above and beyond the *Init* and *Dispose* methods) to the *TimerModule*. The best way to do that is to define an interface that has functions you can use to talk to Module. The following listing defines an interface for retrieving the average request duration. Create a file named ITimerModule.cs and add it to the Timer Module subproject.

```
using System;
public interface ITimerModule
{
    TimeSpan GetAverageLengthOfRequest();
}
```

2. Implement the *ITimer* interface within the *Timer* class. Include a reference to the *Timer-Module* in the Default.aspx page so the page code has access to the interface. Include an *ArrayList* in the *Timer* class to hold on to durations of the requests. Store the duration of the request at the end of each request (in the *OnEndRequest* handler). Use clock ticks as the measurement to make it easier to compute the average duration. Finally, implement *GetAverageLengthOfRequest* (the method defined by the *ITimerModule* interface) by adding all the elements in the *ArrayList* and dividing that number by the size of the *Array-List*. Create a *TimeSpan* using the result of the calculation and return that to the client.

```
public class Timer : IHttpModule,
                                    ITimerModule{
   public Timer()
   {
   }

   protected ArrayList _alRequestDurations =
      new ArrayList();
   public void Init(HttpApplication httpApp)
   {
      httpApp.BeginRequest +=
         new EventHandler(this.OnBeginRequest);
      httpApp.EndRequest +=
         new EventHandler(this.OnEndRequest);
   }
   public void Dispose() { }

   public void OnBeginRequest(object o, EventArgs ea)
   {
      HttpApplication httpApp = (HttpApplication)o;

      DateTime dateTimeBeginRequest = DateTime.Now;

      HttpContext ctx;
      ctx = HttpContext.Current;
      ctx.Items["dateTimeBeginRequest"] = dateTimeBeginRequest;
   }

   public void OnEndRequest(object o, EventArgs ea)
   {
      HttpApplication httpApp = (HttpApplication)o;

      DateTime dateTimeEndRequest = DateTime.Now;

      HttpContext ctx;
      ctx = HttpContext.Current;
      DateTime dateTimeBeginRequest =
         (DateTime)ctx.Items["dateTimeBeginRequest"];

      TimeSpan duration =
               dateTimeEndRequest - dateTimeBeginRequest;

      ctx.Response.Write(
               "<b> From the Timing module; this request took " +
```

```
    duration.Duration().ToString() + "</b></br>");
    _alRequestDurations.Add(duration);
}
public TimeSpan GetAverageLengthOfRequest()
{
  long lTicks = 0;
  foreach (TimeSpan timespanDuration in this._alRequestDurations)
  {
    lTicks += timespanDuration.Ticks;
  }

  long lAverageTicks = lTicks / _alRequestDurations.Count;
  TimeSpan timespanAverageDuration = new TimeSpan(lAverageTicks);
  return timespanAverageDuration;
}
}
```

3. Now add some code in the Default.aspx page to examine the average time taken to process each request. Add a button to fetch the average duration, and a label to display the average duration. Give the button a caption something like "Show Average Duration Of Requests":

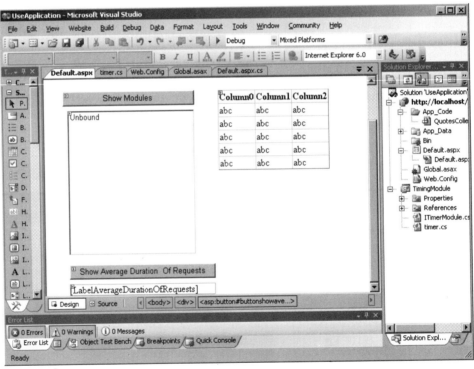

4. Double-click on the **Show Average Duration Of Requests** button to add a handler for it. Handle the event by fetching the *TimerModule* from the collection of Modules. You can fetch it by name because the collection is indexed on the module name (as specified in Web.Config).

```
protected void
    ButtonShowAverageDurationOfRequests_Click(
            object sender,
            EventArgs e)
{
   HttpApplication httpApp =
            HttpContext.Current.ApplicationInstance;

   HttpModuleCollection httpModuleColl = httpApp.Modules;
   IHttpModule httpModule =
            httpModuleColl.Get("TimingModule");
   ITimerModule timerModule =
            (ITimerModule)httpModule;

   TimeSpan timeSpanAverageDurationOfRequest =
      timerModule.GetAverageLengthOfRequest();
   LabelAverageDurationOfRequests.Text =
            timeSpanAverageDurationOfRequest.ToString();
}
```

The object you get back by accessing the module collection is an HTTP Module. To be able to talk to it using the *ITimerModule* interface, you need to cast the reference to the Module. Once you do that, you may call *GetAverageLengthOfRequest* and display it in the label:

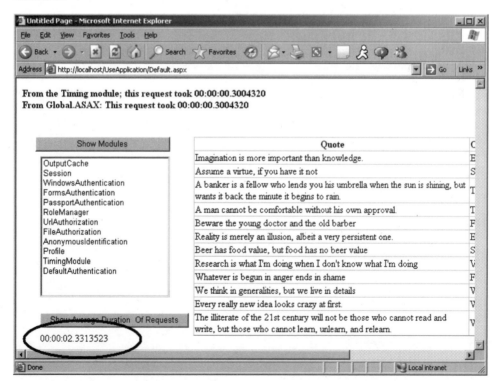

To see how the timing module might look in Visual Basic, see Listing 17-3.

Listing 17-3

```vb
Imports System
Imports System.Collections
Imports Timer
Imports System.Web
Public Class TimingModuleVB : Implements IHttpModule

    Protected _alRequestDurations As New ArrayList()

    Public Sub Init(ByVal httpApp As HttpApplication) _
     Implements IHttpModule.Init
        AddHandler httpApp.BeginRequest, _
          New EventHandler(AddressOf OnBeginRequest)

        AddHandler httpApp.EndRequest, _
          New EventHandler(AddressOf OnEndRequest)

    End Sub

    Public Sub Dispose() Implements IHttpModule.Dispose
    End Sub

    Private Sub OnBeginRequest(ByVal src As Object, _
      ByVal e As EventArgs)
        Dim httpApp As HttpApplication
        httpApp = CType(src, HttpApplication)

        Dim dateTimeBeginRequest As DateTime
        dateTimeBeginRequest = DateTime.Now

        Dim ctx As HttpContext
        ctx = HttpContext.Current
        ctx.Items("dateTimeBeginRequest") = dateTimeBeginRequest
    End Sub

    Private Sub OnEndRequest(ByVal src As Object, _
      ByVal e As EventArgs)
        Dim httpApp As HttpApplication
        httpApp = CType(src, HttpApplication)

        Dim dateTimeEndRequest As DateTime
        dateTimeEndRequest = DateTime.Now

        Dim ctx As HttpContext
        ctx = HttpContext.Current

        Dim dateTimeBeginRequest As DateTime

        dateTimeBeginRequest = _
          CType(ctx.Items("dateTimeBeginRequest"), DateTime)

        Dim duration As TimeSpan
        duration = dateTimeEndRequest - dateTimeBeginRequest
```

```
    ctx.Response.Write( _
     "<b> From the Timing module; this request took ")
    ctx.Response.Write( _
      duration.Duration().ToString() + "</b></br>")

    _alRequestDurations.Add(duration)
End Sub

Function GetAverageLengthOfRequest() As TimeSpan
    Dim lTicks As Long = 0

    Dim timespanDuration As TimeSpan

    For Each timespanDuration In _
      Me._alRequestDurations
        lTicks = lTicks + timespanDuration.Ticks
    Next

    Dim lAverageTicks As Long

    lAverageTicks = lTicks / _alRequestDurations.Count
    Dim timespanAverageDuration As TimeSpan
    timespanAverageDuration = _
      New TimeSpan(lAverageTicks)
    Return timespanAverageDuration

End Function

End Class
```

Global.asax versus *HttpModules*

Both the application object expressed through Global.asax and HTTP Modules offer a rendez-vous point for your application. You can use both of them to store global state between requests as well as respond to application-wide events. When choosing one over the other, remember that Global.asax really goes with your application. Global.asax is intended to manage state and events specific to your application. HTTP Modules exist as completely separate assemblies. They're not necessarily tied to a particular application, and may even be signed and deployed in the Global Assembly Cache. That makes Modules an ideal vehicle for implementing generic functionality that's useful between different applications.

Conclusion

In this chapter, we saw how the ASP.NET architecture includes a rendezvous point for all the requests passing through an application. This is especially important in Web applications composed of disparate components centered around a pipeline. While there are certain obvious places where a request context can show up (most notably in the end handler), it's clear that there are other points in the request chain where you need to have something to hold on to.

ASP.NET offers two broad choices in implementing such a "global space." Global.asax is a convenient representation of the *HttpApplication* object. ASP.NET applications have a singular instance of the *HttpApplication* class. The application object includes a handy dictionary in which to store data that needs to survive and be available from all points within the application. In addition, Global.asax offers a place to intercept various application-wide events.

HTTP Modules offer very much the same functionality, although in a different package. HTTP Modules implement the *IHttpModule* interface and are deployed with the application via the Web.Config file. When an application starts up, the ASP.NET runtime looks in the Web.Config file to see if any additional handlers need to be attached to the pipeline. (ASP.NET plugs in a number of Modules already—they implement such features as authentication and session state.) When ASP.NET sees a new Module within the Web.Config file, ASP.NET loads the Module and calls the *Init* method. Modules usually initialize by setting up handlers for various application-wide events.

Chapter 17 Quick Reference

To	Do This
Create a custom module assembly	Create a new class implementing *IHttpModule*
	Override *Init*
	Override *Disposet*
Insert the module into the processing chain	Mention the module in the *<httpModule>* node of the application's Web.Config file
Handle application events in the module	Write a handler (within the module) for every event you want to handle
	During the *Init* method, subscribe to the events by attaching the event handlers to the events
Override the application object in Global.asax file	Select **Web site	Add New Item**
	Select **Global Application Template** from the templates
	Insert your own code for responding to the application-wide events
Use the application's dictionary	Access the application object (it's always available from the current *HttpContext*). Use the indexer notation to access the dictionary

Chapter 18
Custom Handlers

After completing this chapter, you will be able to

■ Recognize the role of custom handlers in ASP.NET

■ Write custom binary handlers

■ Write just-in-time compiled custom handlers

■ Let IIS and ASP.NET know about your custom handler

This chapter covers writing custom HTTP handlers. In Chapter 2 we saw the ASP.NET pipeline. Remember that the endpoint of all requests handled by ASP.NET is always an implementation of *IHttpHandler*.

ASP.NET includes several classes capable of handling requests in the most common ways. For example, the *Page* class handles requests by interpreting the query strings and returning meaningful UI-oriented HTML. The *Service* class interprets incoming query strings as method calls and processes them accordingly. So far, we've been focusing on a single handler—*System.Web.UI.Page*. However, there are other times when it's appropriate to tweak the processing or even handle it in a completely different way. You may find yourself needing to handle a request in a way not already provided through the *System.Web.UI.Page* or the *System.Web.Services.Service* classes. What do you do then? ASP.NET supports custom HTTP handlers for just such occasions.

Handlers

So far, we've focused most attention upon the *Page* class. The *Page* class is responsible primarily for managing the UI aspects of an application. Because UI processing is very involved (and much of it is boilerplate-type code) the *Page* class has a great deal of functionality built into it. The *Page* class will solve the majority of user interface requiring UI processing.

Although we haven't come across Web services yet, the *WebService* class implements the details required to interpret HTTP requests as method calls. Clients call Web services by packaging method calls in an XML format formalized as the Simple Object Access Protocol (SOAP). Clients call Web services in the same way they make HTTP requests for Web pages—via HTTP GET and POST requests. When the request reaches the server, it becomes the server's job to unpack the parameters, place them on a call stack, and finally invoke the correct method. Most of the work required to make a method call via HTTP is well-understood and consistent and may be pushed down into the *Service* class.

As we saw in Chapter 2 on ASP.NET fundamentals, the endpoint for all HTTP requests destined for ASP.NET is a class implementing *IHttpHandler*. *IHttpHandler* is a simple interface, including a mere two methods. However, any class implementing that interface qualifies to participate in the HTTP pipeline as an HTTP handler. We'll see the interface in detail shortly.

HTTP handlers are simply classes implementing *IHttpHandler* (just as HTTP Modules are classes implementing *IHttpModule*). Handlers are listed inside Web.Config. As with the HTTP Modules, ASP.NET comes out of the box with several HTTP handlers already (for implementing features such as tracing and preventing access to sensitive files on the site). ASP.NET comes with these HTTP handlers already registered in the master Web.Config (which resides alongside Machine.Config in the main configuration directory) configuration file.

So far, ASPX, ASAX, and ASCX files have seemed to magically work within ASP.NET. For example, we saw earlier that simply surfing to an ASPX file causes ASP.NET to compile the file just-in-time and to synthesize a class based on *System.Web.UI.Page*. The reason the ASPX files work that way is because ASP.NET includes handlers for that functionality.

ASP.NET HTTP handlers are specified in Web.Config in much the same way as HTTP Modules. The format of the handler elements includes four items. First, they include a file name and/or extension to which the handler applies. This is done through the *add* attribute. Remember, all HTTP requests come to the server as resource requests—the HTTP protocol is built around the idea that requests contain file names. The second part of the handler specification, *verb*, is a list of verbs to which this handler applies. These verbs correspond to the HTTP specification. For example, you might want a handler to apply only to GET and not to POST requests. Or you may wish to have a handler apply to all requests. The third element, *type*, is the name of the .NET type assigned to handle the request. Finally, the last attribute, *validate*, specifies whether or not ASP.NET should load the class at startup immediately or wait until a matching request is received.

Listing 18-1 includes a smattering of the HTTP handlers already installed as part of ASP.NET's Web.Config file.

Listing 18-1

```
<httpHandlers>
    <add path="trace.axd" verb="*"
     type="System.Web.Handlers.TraceHandler" validate="True" />
    <add path="WebResource.axd" verb="GET"
     type="System.Web.Handlers.AssemblyResourceLoader" validate="True" />
    <add path="*.axd" verb="*"
     type="System.Web.HttpNotFoundHandler" validate="True" />
    <add path="*.aspx" verb="*"
     type="System.Web.UI.PageHandlerFactory" validate="True" />
    <add path="*.ashx" verb="*"
     type="System.Web.UI.SimpleHandlerFactory" validate="True" />
    <add path="*.asax" verb="*"
     type="System.Web.HttpForbiddenHandler" validate="True" />
    <add path="".ascx" verb="*"
     type="System.Web.HttpForbiddenHandler" validate="True" />
    <add path="*.master" verb="*"
     type="System.Web.HttpForbiddenHandler" validate="True" />
    <add path="*.config" verb="*"
     type="System.Web.HttpForbiddenHandler" validate="True" />
    <add path="*.cs" verb="*"
     type="System.Web.HttpForbiddenHandler" validate="True" />
<!--More handlers follow... -->
</httpHandlers>
```

Let's take a look at a couple of specific handlers—the *Trace* handler and the *Forbidden* handler—to get a good idea as to how having a separate request handling facility (i.e., one that is not tied specifically to UI or to Web services) can be useful.

Built-in Handlers

One of the best examples of custom handling is the *Trace* handler that is built into ASP.NET. We looked at tracing in Chapter 16. You turn tracing on within the Web.Config file by inserting the trace element *<trace enabled=true />*. This instructs the ASP.NET runtime to store summaries of the requests going through the site so they may be viewed for diagnostic purposes.

ASP.NET caches the tracing output in memory. To view the trace results, you surf to the virtual directory managing the site and ask for a specific file: Trace.axd. Take a look at Listing 18-1 and you'll see the first entry among all the standard HTTP handlers is for a resource named Trace.axd. The tracing functionality behind ASP.NET falls outside of normal UI processing, so it makes sense that tracing is handled by a custom handler.

When you surf to the Trace.axd resource, the handler renders HTML that looks like the output shown in Figure 18-1. The processing for this handler is very specific—the handler's job is to render the results of the last few requests. As you can see in Figure 18-2, selecting the View Details link resubmits the request with a parameter *id=3* in the query string. This causes the handler to render the details of the third request. Figure 18-3 shows the IIS file mapping for files with the .axd extension. The ISAPI extension DLL handling the request is aspnet_isapi.dll. That means IIS will pass requests for files with an extension of .axd on to ASP.NET. Once inside the ASP.NET pipeline, the Web.Config file tells ASP to handle the request with the *Trace* handler.

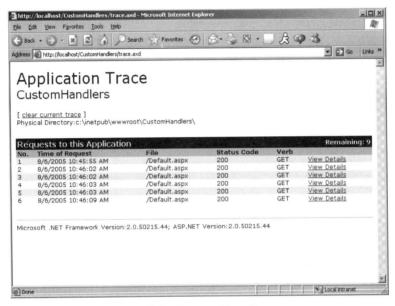

Figure 18-1   The output of the Trace.axd handler.

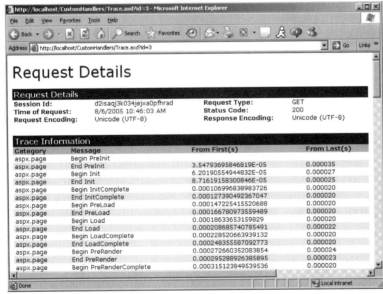

Figure 18-2   The output of the Trace.axd handler when drilling down into a request summary.

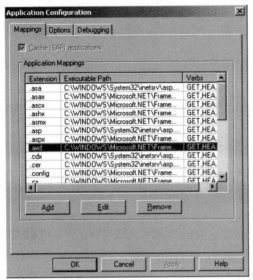

Figure 18-3   IIS understands files with the extension .axd.

If you look through the default Web.Config file a bit more, you'll see some other handlers. Source code is banned explicitly from normal clients by default. Notice files such as *.cs, *.config, and *.vb are handled by the *Forbidden* handler. If you try to look at source code via a Web browser, ASP.NET returns the page shown in Figure 18-4 by default:

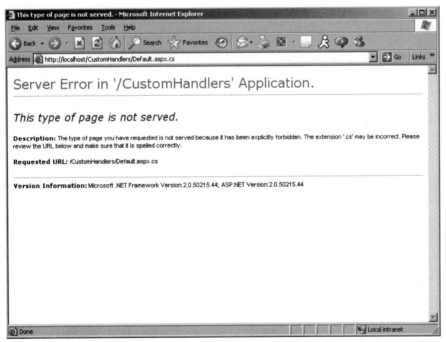

Figure 18-4   What happens when you try to view forbidden content.

Remember that ASP.NET's configuration is very malleable and that you may choose to let clients see your source code by one of two means. You may remove the source code extension to ASP.NET mappings within IIS. Alternatively, you may write your own source code viewer handlers and declare them in your application's Web.Config file.

These handlers plug into the pipeline by implementing *IHttpHandler*. Let's take a look at this key interface.

IHttpHandler

Here it is. Shield your eyes while you look at Listing 18-2.

Listing 18-2

```
public interface IHttpHandler
{
  void ProcessRequest(HttpContext ctx);
  bool IsReusable {get;}
}
```

There's really not much to it, is there? The interface includes a method named *ProcessRequest* and a property named *IsReusable*. If the handler instance can be used multiple times, then *IsReusable* should return true. The heart of the handler is the *ProcessRequest* method that includes a single parameter: the current *HttpContext*.

Once a request finally arrives at the handler (through the *ProcessRequest* method), *ProcessRequest* can literally do anything to respond to the request. The Trace.axd handler responds to a GET request by listing the requests being tracked by the runtime. The forbidden handler responds by throwing up a roadblock so the client can't see the source. A custom Web service might respond to the request by parsing the XML payload, constructing a call stack, and making a call to an internal method.

The following example illustrates how to handle forms processing in a custom handler.

Implementing IHttpHandler

Implementing *IHttpHandler* is simple—at least from the architectural point of view. The *ProcessRequest* method takes a single parameter—the current *HttpContext*. However, the code inside *ProcessRequest* is free to do just about anything possibly making the internal processing quite complex! The following example illustrates taking over the entire form-rendering process to display a list of choices within a combo box, allowing the end client to select from the choices, and finally rendering the chosen item.

Writing a Custom Handler

1. Create a project named CustomHandlers. Make it an HTTP site that uses IIS. This will be important because IIS will need to direct requests for a specific file extension to use aspnet_isapi.dll.

2. Add a new class library subproject to the CustomHandlers Web site (just as you did when you created an HTTP Module). Name the project CustomFormHandlerLib. The

name of the class it generates for you is *Class1*. Rename the file CustomFormHandler.cs and the class *CustomFormHandler*.

3. The library generated by Visual Studio comes without any knowledge of the ASP.NET classes. Add a reference to the System.Web assembly.

4. To turn the *CustomFormHandler* class into an eligible handler, add the *IHttpHandler* interface to the inheritance list.

```
using System;
using System.Collections.Generic;
using System.Text;
using System.Web;
public class CustomFormHandler :
    IHttpHandler
{
    public void ProcessRequest(HttpContext ctx)
    {
        ManageForm(ctx);
    }

    public void ManageForm(HttpContext context)
    {
        context.Response.Write("<html><body><form>");

        context.Response.Write(
            "<h2>Hello there. What's cool about .NET?</h2>");

        context.Response.Write(
            "<select name='Feature'>");
        context.Response.Write(
            "<option> Strong typing</option>");
        context.Response.Write(
            "<option> Managed code</option>");
        context.Response.Write(
            "<option> Language agnosticism</option>");
        context.Response.Write(
            "<option> Better security model</option>");
        context.Response.Write(
            "<option> Threading and async delegates</option>");
        context.Response.Write(
            "<option> XCOPY deployment</option>");
        context.Response.Write(
            "<option> Reasonable HTTP handling framework</option>");
        context.Response.Write("</select>");
        context.Response.Write("</br>");

        context.Response.Write(
            "<input type=submit name='Lookup'
        value='Lookup'></input>");
        context.Response.Write("</br>");

        if (context.Request.Params["Feature"] != null)
        {
            context.Response.Write("Hi, you picked: ");
```

```
            context.Response.Write(
                context.Request.Params["Feature"]);
            context.Response.Write(
                " as your favorite feature.</br>");
        }

        context.Response.Write("</form></body></html>");
    }

    public bool IsReusable {
        get
        {
            return true;
        }
    }
}
```

The code within the *ProcessRequest* will render a *<form>* tag and a *<selection>* tag that renders a form that can be submitted on the browser. When the form is submitted back to the server, the parameters collection will have a *Features* element in it. The code examines the parameter collection to see if it references a feature, and displays the feature if it's been selected.

5.   The class library you just created deposits its output in the project directory. In order for ASP.NET to use the page, the resulting executable needs to live in the virtual directory's \bin subdirectory. Right-click on the *CustomHandler* solution (in the Solution Explorer) and add a bin directory to the project. Then highlight the *CustomFormHandlerLib* project, select the project's build properties, and the compiled output to point to the bin directory. While you're in the configuration page, make sure the name of the target assembly is *CustomFormHandlerLib*.

6.   Now update Web.Config so that it uses the handler when clients request the *Custom-FormHandler* resource. If you don't already have a Web.Config in the project, add one. Then insert an *httpHandlers* section that points requests for the *CustomFormHandler* to the new *CustomFormHandler* class.

```
<configuration
xmlns="http://schemas.microsoft.com/.NetConfiguration/v2.0">
    <appSettings/>
    <connectionStrings/>
<system.web>
    <httpHandlers>
        <add path="customformhandler" verb="*"
        type="CustomFormHandlerLib, CustomFormHandler" validate="True" />
    </httpHandlers>
</system.web>
</configuration>
```

7.   You need to tell IIS about the new file types to be handled by the *CustomFormHandler*. Open IIS and drill down to the CustomHandler virtual directory. Right-click on the

directory and select **Properties**. Then click the **Configuration** button to show the file types and their mappings.

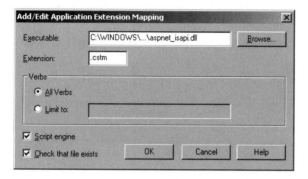

8. Click the **Add** button and create a mapping between files with the extension *.cstm and aspnet_isapi.dll. You can use the **Browse** button to search for the aspnet_isapi.dll assembly in the Windows directory on your machine.

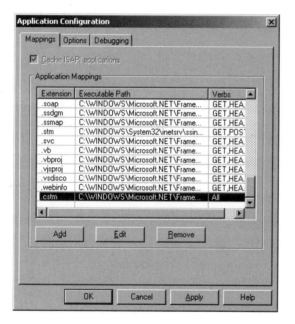

9. Finally, create a blank file named CustomHandler.cstm in the IIS virtual directory. The file with that extension needs to be there to work.

10. Surf to the customhandler.cstm file and ASP.NET will invoke the handler.

Of course, most of this processing could be handled more easily by setting up a Web form. However, this example shows the flexibility of the ASP.NET handler architecture. It should also give you more appreciation for the Web form and custom controls machinery within ASP.NET.

The *CustomFormHandler* Using VB

From the runtime's point of view, it doesn't matter how the handler was written—it just needs to fully implement the *IHttpHandler* interface. Listing 18-3 illustrates the same handler written in VB.NET.

Listing 18-3

```vb
Imports System.Web

Public Class CustomFormHandlerVB : Implements System.Web.IHttpHandler
    Public Sub ManageForm(ByVal context As HttpContext)

        context.Response.Write("<html><body><form>")

        context.Response.Write_
          ("<h2>Hello there. What's cool about .NET?</h2>")

        context.Response.Write("<select name='Feature'>")
        context.Response.Write_
          ("<option> Strong typing</option>")
        context.Response.Write_
          ("<option> Managed code</option>")
        context.Response.Write_
          ("<option> Language agnosticism</option>")
        context.Response.Write_
          ("<option> Better security model</option>")
        context.Response.Write_
          ("<option> Threading and async delegates</option>")
        context.Response.Write_
          ("<option> XCOPY deployment</option>")
        context.Response.Write_
          ("<option> Reasonable HTTP handling framework</option>")
        context.Response.Write("</select>")
        context.Response.Write("</br>")

        context.Response.Write_
           ("<input type=submit name='Lookup'value='Lookup'></input>")
        context.Response.Write("</br>")

        If (context.Request.Params("Feature")) <> Nothing Then
            context.Response.Write("Hi, you picked: ")
            context.Response.Write(context.Request.Params("Feature"))
            context.Response.Write(" as your favorite feature.</br>")
        End If
        context.Response.Write("</form></body></html>")
    End Sub

    Public ReadOnly Property IsReusable()_
      As Boolean Implements System.Web.IHttpHandler.IsReusable
        Get
            Return True
        End Get
    End Property
```

```
    Public Sub ProcessRequest_
        (ByVal context As System.Web.HttpContext) Implements
System.Web.IHttpHandler.ProcessRequest
        ManageForm(context)
    End Sub
End Class
```

The example accompanying this chapter includes the previous handler named *CustomForm-HandlerVB* in an assembly named *CustomFormHandlerLibVB*. Listing 18-4 shows how to refer to the second handler.

Listing 18-4

```
<httpHandlers>
    <add path="customhandler.cstm" verb="*"
        type="CustomFormHandler, CustomFormHandlerLib" validate="True"/>
    <add path="customhandlerVB.cstm" verb="*"
        type="CustomFormHandlerVB, CustomFormHandlerLibVB" validate="True"/>
</httpHandlers>
```

Handlers and Session State

In Chapter 13, we looked at session state. Session state works automatically within the context of *System.Web.UI.Page*. However, handlers need to turn on the ability to use session state deliberately.

The .NET architecture uses an interesting idiom known as *marker interfaces*. Marker interfaces are empty interfaces (without any methods or properties defined). Their sole purpose is to signal the runtime as to various aspects of the application. For example, ASP.NET runtime often uses them to turn on and off various features. When the runtime detects a marker interface as part of an object's class hierarchy, the runtime can bring into play certain features.

For a handler to use session state, it must have the *System.Web.SessionState.IRequiresSession-State* interface in its inheritance list. That way the runtime will know to load and store session state at the beginning and end of each request.

Listing 18-5 shows a handler with session state enabled.

Listing 18-5

```
using System;
using System.Collections.Generic;
using System.Text;
using System.Web.SessionState;

using System.Web;

public class HandlerWithSessionState :
    IHttpHandler, IRequiresSessionState
{
    public void ProcessRequest(HttpContext ctx)
    {
```

```
        String strData = (String)ctx.Session["SomeSessionData"];

        if (strData == null)
        {
            ctx.Session["SomeSessionData"] = "This goes in session state";
        }
        ctx.Response.Write("This was in session state: " + strData);
    }

    public bool IsReusable {
        get
        {
            return true;
        }
    }
}
}
```

Generic Handlers (ASHX Files)

Just as ASPX files can be compiled on the fly (just-in-time), so can handlers. Generic handlers have an extension of ASHX. They're equivalent to custom handlers written in C Sharp or Visual Basic.NET in that they contain classes that fully implement *IHttpHandler*. They're convenient in the same way ASPX files are convenient. You simply surf to them and they're compiled automatically.

The following example illustrates the *CustomFormHandler* implemented as a "generic handler."

Writing a Generic Handler

1. Add a "generic" handler to the Web site. Go to the Solution Explorer, right-click on the CustomHandler Web site node and select **Add New Item**. Select **Generic Handler** from the templates. Name the handler CustomFormHandler.ashx:

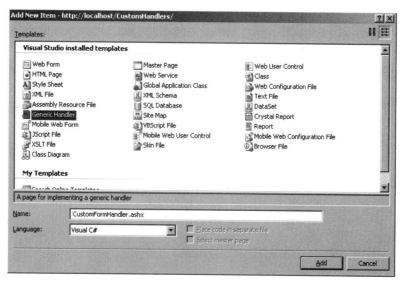

2. Visual Studio generates a handler that looks like this. It includes a stubbed-out *Process-Request* method and *IsReusable* property.

```
<%@ WebHandler Language="C#" Class="CustomFormHandler" %>

using System.Web;

public class CustomFormHandler : IHttpHandler {

    public void ProcessRequest (HttpContext context) {

        context.Response.ContentType = "text/plain";
        context.Response.Write("Hello World");
    }

    public bool IsReusable {
        get {
            return false;
        }
    }
}
```

3. Borrow the code from the earlier example to implement the handler. Replace the stubbed-out method and property with real implementations.

```
<%@ WebHandler Language="C#" Class="CustomFormHandler" %>
using System.Web;
public class CustomFormHandler : IHttpHandler {

    public void ProcessRequest (HttpContext context) {
        ManageForm(context);
    }

    public void ManageForm(HttpContext context)
    {
        context.Response.Write("<html><body><form>");

        context.Response.Write(
            "<h2>Hello there. What's cool about .NET?</h2>");
        context.Response.Write("<select name='Feature'>");
        context.Response.Write("<option> Strong typing</option>");
        context.Response.Write("<option> Managed code</option>");
        context.Response.Write("<option> Language agnosticism</option>");
        context.Response.Write("<option> Better security model</option>");
        context.Response.Write(
            "<option> Threading and async delegates</option>");
        context.Response.Write("<option> XCOPY deployment</option>");
        context.Response.Write(
            "<option> Reasonable HTTP handling framework</option>");
        context.Response.Write("</select>");
        context.Response.Write("</br>");
        context.Response.Write(
            "<input type=submit name='Lookup' value='Lookup'></input>");
        context.Response.Write("</br>");
```

```
        if (context.Request.Params["Feature"] != null)
        {
            context.Response.Write("Hi, you picked: ");
            context.Response.Write(context.Request.Params["Feature"]);
            context.Response.Write(" as your favorite feature.</br>");
        }

        context.Response.Write("</form></body></html>");
    }
    public bool IsReusable
    {
        get
        {
            return false;
        }
    }
}
```

4. Browse to the CustomFormHandler.ashx file. It should work in just the same way as the handlers implemented in CustomFormHandler.cs and CustomFormHandler.VB, as shown in the following graphic:

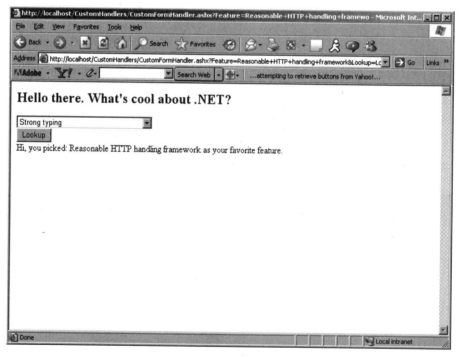

The advantage of using the generic handler is twofold. First, it's usually much more convenient to generate a simple handler than it is to create a whole new assembly to handle the request. Second, you don't need to run interference with either Web.Config or with IIS. That is, Web.Config and IIS already understand what to do about files with the extension of .ashx. Installing ASP.NET places those when mapping into IIS.

However, ASHX files have the same limitations as ASPX and ASCX files in terms of their place in an ASP.NET project. Simple generic handlers go with the project. That is, for the handler to work, it must accompany the whole project. Alternatively, custom handlers deployed as separate assemblies may be deployed and shared among the enterprise as Global Assembly assemblies (that is, strongly named assemblies placed in the Global Assembly Cache).

Conclusion

ASP.NET includes a number of built-in classes to handle most kinds of requests. For example, ASP.NET includes UI handlers (*System.Web.UI.Page* and *System.Web.UI.Control*). ASP.NET also includes a Web service handler (*System.Web.Services.Service*). These classes will probably solve most of the requirements you might come across. However, for those fringe cases requiring custom handling, ASP.NET supports the custom handler.

The endpoint for requests coming through ASP.NET is always a class implementing *IHttpHandler*. *IHttpHandler* has very little surface area. You simply override the *IsReusable* property and the *ProcessRequest* method. *ProcessRequest* can pretty much do anything you want it to. The example in this book included a handler that manages rendering a form and handling input.

For a custom handler assembly to work, it must be mapped to a file path or extension in the application's Web.Config file. The extension must also be mapped within the IIS metabase.

ASP.NET also supports handlers that may be compiled just-in-time. Simple handlers are easy to create and deploy because you don't need to modify the Web.Config file, nor do you need to modify the IIS metabase.

Chapter 18 Quick Reference

To	Do This
Create a custom handler assembly	Create a new class implementing *IHttpHandler*
	Override the *IsReusable* property
	Override *ProcessRequest*
Assign a file mapping to the handler in ASP.NET	Mention the handler in the < *httpHandler* > node of the application's Web.Config file
Assign a file mapping to the handler in IIS	Right-click on the virtual directory
	Select **Properties**
	Click the **Configure** button
	Click the **Add** button
	Add a new extension and map it to aspnet_isapi.dll
Create a simple handler	Select **Web site | Add New Item**
	Select **Generic Handler** from the templates
	Insert your own code for responding to the request

Chapter 19
Web Services

After completing this chapter, you will be able to

- Understand the importance of Web services
- Use the technologies underlying Web services
- Write Web services using ASP.NET
- Consume Web services

This chapter covers Web services from an ASP.NET perspective. Over the last few years "Web services" has emerged as a buzzword for enabling the next generation of computer connectivity. While networking a bunch of computers together isn't trivial, it's generally a solved problem these days. Most workplaces in the modern world depend upon an internal network of computers to allow the people staffing the enterprise to communicate and work effectively.

With the rise of the internal company network comes the desire to tie machines together programmatically as well. That is, a program on one machine should be able to call program methods on another machine without human intervention. Many enterprises spent nearly the entire final decade of the twentieth century trying to get their computers to talk to one another programmatically. On the Microsoft platform, this was usually done with Distributed COM (DCOM).

The next step in connecting computers is happening over the Internet. There's already a ubiquitous connection available (computers connected via HTTP) and a well-understood wire format (XML). Together, these two elements make up Web services.

Remoting

The desire to call software methods "over there" from "over here" has been around ever since the advent of distributed computing networks. Beginning in the days of Remote Procedure Calls all the way through the latest version of Distributed COM (DCOM), the promise of remoting has been to exercise a network of computers to solve computing problems rather than pinning the whole problem on a single computer.

Remoting involves several fundamental steps:

1. The caller flattens the call stack into a stream that may be sent over the wire.

2. The caller sends the serialized call stack across the wire.

3. The endpoint receives the serialized call stack and turns it into a usable call stack on the server.

4. The endpoint processes the method call.

5. The endpoint transmits the results back to the caller.

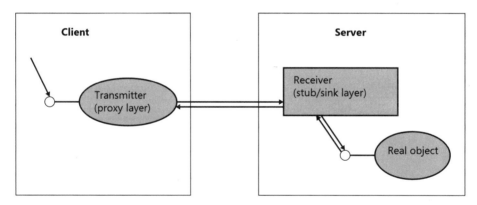

Figure 19-1   Illistrates the general remoting architecture employed by most remoting systems.

Several different network remoting technologies have emerged over the last decade, including DCOM and CORBA among others. (CORBA is an acronym for Common Object Request Broker Architecture—a remoting technology prevalent on other operating systems). It doesn't matter if the remoting framework is DCOM, CORBA, or even the .NET remoting services—the fundamental steps of remoting remain the same. For example, in DCOM the client talks to a component named the proxy, whose job it is to flatten the call stack and send it on its way. On the server side, a component named the stub receives the network packets and turns the incoming stream into a real call on the server. If the framework is .NET remoting, then the term for the proxy component is the "transparent proxy." The transparent proxy talks to the real proxy, which sends the bytes across the network. Once at the server, a component named the sink unpacks the bytes and turns them into a real call.

Web services work much the same way. The fundamental remoting steps are all there. However, this time around the wire format is an XML format formalized as SOAP and the connection protocol is HTTP.

Remoting Over the Web

Over the last 18 chapters we've looked primarily at how ASP.NET makes it easy to handle a wide variety of Web application scenarios. We've seen that ASP.NET handles GET and POST methods, redirecting the request to a handler. Up until now the job of the handler has been to process the incoming query string and render some output generally intended for human consumption. Developing a Web service is all about writing an application intended for consumption by another program.

Web services are Internet endpoints available most commonly through HTTP and HTTPS (Hypertext Transfer Protocol Secure). The job of a Web service is to consume HTTP requests containing XML payloads formatted as SOAP. The messages have a specific schema applied to them, which in effect may be thought of as a transportable type system. Web services are also responsible for providing metadata (Web Service Description Language) describing the messages they consume and produce.

Simple Object Access Protocol (SOAP)

While it seems obvious that the Web is an excellent medium for distributing a user interface–oriented application to the masses, it may not seem so obvious that the same technology might be used to make method calls. One of the main reasons Web services may exist now is because different enterprises can agree upon what a method call looks like, and they can all access it over already-existing HTTP connections.

Web service method calls are encoded using XML. The format that callers and services agree on is known as Simple Object Access Protocol (SOAP). The SOAP protocol is an XML formalization for message-based communication. SOAP defines how to format messages, how to bind messages over HTTP, and a standard error representation.

Transporting the Type System

The primary interoperability focus of Web services is to widen the audience of an application so that as many clients as possible can invoke methods of the service. Because the connective medium involved is the Internet, any computer that can invoke HTTP requests becomes a potential client. Paired with the ability to connect over HTTP and to format calls as XML SOAP messages, a client can make calls to any of your Web service's methods.

With the focus on interoperability between as many platforms as possible, it becomes very important that the caller and the service agree on the data types being passed back and forth. When a client calls a method containing parameters, the two endpoints might each have their own way of understanding the parameter types. For example, passing a character string between two .NET endpoints does *not* pose a big problem. However, passing a string between a client running a non-.NET platform and a service written using .NET *does* pose a problem because a character string type is almost certainly represented differently on each platform.

When calling methods between two computers using HTTP and XML, it's very important that a schema is provided on each end so that the parameter types are interpreted correctly. Fortunately, this detail has been pushed down into the Web service tools that are currently available now.

Web Service Description Language

Given a connection protocol (HTTP) and wire format (XML + SOAP), the final ingredient making Web services a viable technology is the notion of a service description. Even though two endpoints agree on the connection protocol and the wire format, the client still has to know how to set up the call to a service.

Services advertise their capabilities via another XML formalization named Web Service Description Language (or WSDL as it's commonly called). WSDL specifies the target URL of the service, the format in which the service expects to see methods packaged, and how the messages will be encoded.

If You Couldn't Use ASP.NET...

Just as there's nothing stopping you from writing code to handle HTTP requests from scratch, you could handle Web service requests from handwritten code. You could write a Web service armed with a only a decent XML parser and a socket library (for communicating over your server's communication ports). The work involved includes the following:

1.   Listening to port 80 to receive method calls

2.   Parsing the incoming XML stream, unpacking the parameters

3.   Setting up the incoming parameters and performing the work

4.   Packing a suitable XML SOAP response and sending it to the caller

5.   Advertising the service's capabilities via WSDL

After the second or third time implementing a service by hand, you'd probably come to the following conclusion. Much of the work involved in making a Web service work is repetitive and might as well be pushed into a library. That's exactly what ASP.NET does. ASP.NET will handle the details of making a Web service through the *System.Web.Services.Service* class.

A Web Service in ASP.NET

ASP.NET handles Web services with a limited amount of programming effort. Remember how the ASP.NET pipeline architecture works. Requests coming from clients end up at the server's port 80. ASP.NET Web services live in a file type named with the extension .asmx. If the server is running ASP.NET, IIS routes the request for files with the ASMX extension to ASP.NET, where they're handled like any other request.

ASP.NET includes an attribute named *[WebMethod]* that maps a SOAP request and its response to a real method in a class. To make the service work, you simply derive a class from *System.Web.Services.Service* and expose methods using the *[WebMethod]*. When the request comes through, the target class will be "bound" to the .asmx endpoint. As with normal page execution, the current *HttpContext* is always available. In addition, ASP.NET automates WSDL generation, and Microsoft provides tools to automate generating client-side proxies given the WSDL.

The following example illustrates a Web service that retrieves quotes from the quotes collection we saw in Chapter 11 ("Databinding"), Chapter 14 ("Application Data Caching"), and Chapter 17 ("The Application and HTTP Modules"). This example will expose the quotes collection via a set of methods expressed as a Web service.

Write an ASP.NET Web Service

1. Create a new Web site project. Name the project WebServicesORama. Make it an HTTP site that uses IIS.

2. Rename the class from *Service* to *QuoteService*. Rename the code file from Service.cs to QuoteService.cs. Rename the ASMX file from Service.asmx to QuoteService.asmx.

3. After Visual Studio is done, you'll get a stubbed-out Web service that looks like this:

```
using System;
using System.Web;
using System.Web.Services;
using System.Web.Services.Protocols;
[WebService(Namespace = "http://tempuri.org/"")]
[WebServiceBinding(ConformsTo = WsiProfiles.BasicProfile1_1)]
public class QuoteService : System.Web.Services.WebService
{
    public Service () {

    }

    [WebMethod]
    public string HelloWorld() {
        return "Hello World";
    }
}
```

You'll also get an ASMX file. The Web service handler (named ASMX, with "M" standing for method) works very much like the ASPX page handlers and the ASHX custom handlers. When clients surf to the ASMX page, IIS redirects the request to the ASP.NET ISAPI DLL. Once there, ASP.NET compiles the code associated with the ASMX file and runs it just as it would any other HTTP handler. Here's what the ASMX file looks like. There's not much here. Most of the code lies within the accompanying code file.

```
<%@ WebService Language="C#"
CodeBehind="~/App_Code/Service.cs" Class="QuoteService" %>
```

4.   Surf to the QuoteService.asmx file to see what a default GET renders:

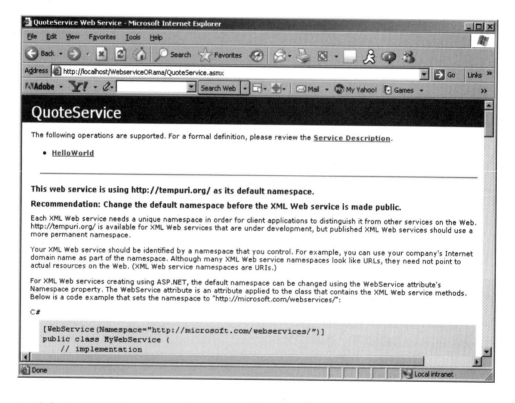

By default, ASP.NET renders the names of the available methods when you just GET the ASMX file. Notice that the *HelloWorld* method (provided by Visual Studio) is exposed. If you want to try running the *HelloWorld* method, you can click on the **HelloWorld** link, which renders a new page with a button you can click to invoke the method.

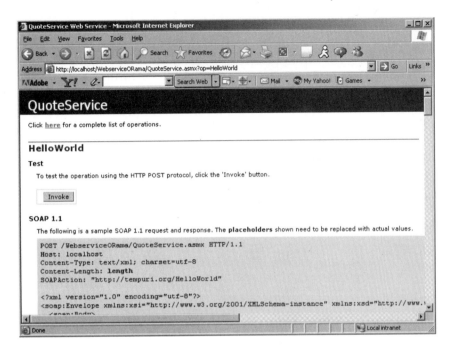

5. Before adding any code, click the **Service Description** link. The Web service will send back the WSDL for the site. You can page through it to see what WSDL looks like. This data is not meant for human consumption, but rather for client proxy generators (which we'll examine shortly).

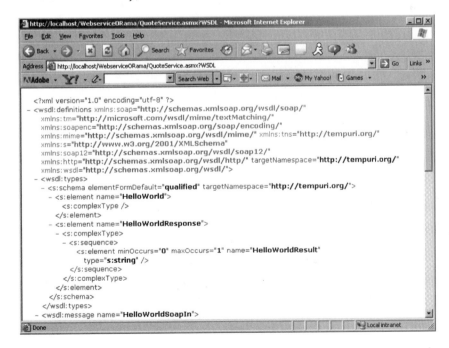

6. To have some quotes to expose as Web methods, import the *QuotesCollection* from Chapter 14. The project name is UseDataCaching. Highlight the **App_Code** node within the solution explorer. Select **Web Site | Add Existing Item** from the main menu and find the file QuotesCollection.cs. In addition to importing the QuotesCollection.cs file, grab the QuotesCollection.xml and QuotesCollection.xsd files from the UseDataCaching\App_Data directory and place them in the App_Data directory for this project.

7. Write a method to load the *QuotesCollection*. Check first to see if the *QuotesCollection* is in the cache. If not, create a *QuotesCollection* object and load it using the quotescollection.xml and quotescollection.xsd files. Load the quotes into the application cache during the construction of the *QuoteService* class. When you add the data to the cache, build a dependency upon the quotescollection.xml file. One of the Web methods we'll add will modify the XML file, so we'll want to flush it from the cache when it's updated.

```
using System;
using System.Web;
using System.Data;
using System.Web.Services;
using System.Web.Services.Protocols;
using System.Web.Caching;

[WebService(Namespace = "http://tempuri.org/")]
[WebServiceBinding(ConformsTo = WsiProfiles.BasicProfile1_1)]
public class QuoteService : System.Web.Services.WebService
{

    QuotesCollection LoadQuotes()
    {
      QuotesCollection quotesCollection;

      HttpContext ctx = HttpContext.Current;
      quotesCollection = (QuotesCollection)ctx.Cache["quotesCollection"];
      if (quotesCollection == null)
      {
        quotesCollection = new QuotesCollection();
        String strAppPath = Server.MapPath("");

        String strFilePathXml =
            strAppPath +
            "\\app_data\\QuotesCollection.xml";
        String strFilePathSchema =
            strAppPath +
            "\\app_data\\QuotesCollection.xsd";

        quotesCollection.ReadXmlSchema(strFilePathSchema);
        quotesCollection.ReadXml(strFilePathXml);

        CacheDependency cacheDependency =
            new CacheDependency(strFilePathXml);

        ctx.Cache.Insert("quotesCollection",
                quotesCollection,
```

```
                            cacheDependency,
                            Cache.NoAbsoluteExpiration,
                            Cache.NoSlidingExpiration,
                            CacheItemPriority.Default,
                            null);
        }
        return quotesCollection;
    }

    public QuoteService () {
    }

    [WebMethod]
    public string HelloWorld() {
        return "Hello World";
    }
}
```

8. Now write a method that gets a random quote from the table and send it back to the client. The *QuotesCollection* class inherits from the *DataTable* class, which is a collection of *DataRows*. Unfortunately, returning a *DataRow* from a Web method doesn't work because *DataRow* doesn't have a default constructor. So instead, add a new struct to the Web service that wraps the quote data. That is, a struct that contains strings for the quote, the originator's first name, and the originator's last name.

Name the method for fetching a quote *GetAQuote*. Have *GetAQuote* load the quotes using *LoadQuotes*. The *GetAQuote* method should generate a number between zero and the number of rows in the *QuotesCollection*, fetch that row from the table, wrap the data in a Quote structure, and return it to the client. Be sure to adorn the *GetAQuote* method with the [*WebMethod*] attribute.

```
using System;
using System.Web;
using System.Data;
using System.Web.Services;
using System.Web.Services.Protocols;
using System.Web.Caching;

public struct Quote
{
    public String _strQuote;
    public String _strOriginatorLastName;
    public String _strOriginatorFirstName;

    public Quote(String strQuote,
                 String strOriginatorLastName,
                 String strOriginatorFirstName)
    {
        _strQuote = strQuote;
        _strOriginatorLastName = strOriginatorLastName;
        _strOriginatorFirstName = strOriginatorFirstName;
    }
}
```

```
[WebService(Namespace = "http://tempuri.org/")]
[WebServiceBinding(ConformsTo = WsiProfiles.BasicProfile1_1)]
public class QuoteService : System.Web.Services.WebService
{

    QuotesCollection LoadQuotes()
    {
        QuotesCollection quotesCollection;

        HttpContext ctx = HttpContext.Current;
        quotesCollection = (QuotesCollection)ctx.Cache["quotesCollection"];
        if (quotesCollection == null)
        {
            quotesCollection = new QuotesCollection();
            String strAppPath = Server.MapPath("");

            String strFilePathXml =
                strAppPath + "\\app_data\\QuotesCollection.xml";
            String strFilePathSchema =
                strAppPath + "\\app_data\\QuotesCollection.xsd";
            quotesCollection.ReadXmlSchema(strFilePathSchema);
            quotesCollection.ReadXml(strFilePathXml);

            CacheDependency cacheDependency =
                new CacheDependency(strFilePathXml);

            ctx.Cache.Insert("quotesCollection",
                    quotesCollection,
                    cacheDependency,
                    Cache.NoAbsoluteExpiration,
                    Cache.NoSlidingExpiration,
                    CacheItemPriority.Default,
                    null);
        }
        return quotesCollection;
    }

    public QuoteService () {
    }
    [WebMethod]
    public string HelloWorld() {
        return "Hello World";
    }

    [WebMethod]
    public Quote GetAQuote()
    {
        QuotesCollection quotesCollection = this.LoadQuotes();
        int nNumQuotes = quotesCollection.Rows.Count;
        Random random = new Random();
        int nQuote = random.Next(nNumQuotes);
        DataRow dataRow = quotesCollection.Rows[nQuote];
        Quote quote = new Quote((String)dataRow["Quote"],
                        (String)dataRow["OriginatorLastName"],
```

```
                                 (String)dataRow["OriginatorFirstName"]);
               return quote;
           }


      }
```

9.   Finally, add two more methods: one to add a quote to the *QuotesCollection* and another
     to fetch all the quotes. Name the method for adding quotes *AddQuote*. *AddQuote* should
     take a *Quote* structure as a parameter and use it to create a new row in the *QuotesCollec-
     tion*. *AddQuote* should reserialize the XML and XSD files.

     GetAllQuotes should load the quotes from the cache, place the *QuotesCollection* in a
     DataSet, and return a *DataSet*. Use a *DataSet* because it marshals very cleanly back to the
     client. Be sure to adorn the methods with the [] attribute.

```csharp
using System;
using System.Web;
using System.Data;
using System.Web.Services;
using System.Web.Services.Protocols;
using System.Web.Caching;

public struct Quote
{
    public String _strQuote;
    public String _strOriginatorLastName;
    public String _strOriginatorFirstName;
    public Quote(String strQuote,
                 String strOriginatorLastName,
                 String strOriginatorFirstName)
    {
        _strQuote = strQuote;
        _strOriginatorLastName = strOriginatorLastName;
        _strOriginatorFirstName = strOriginatorFirstName;
    }
}

[WebService(Namespace = "http://tempuri.org/")]
[WebServiceBinding(ConformsTo = WsiProfiles.BasicProfile1_1)]
public class QuoteService : System.Web.Services.WebService
{

    QuotesCollection LoadQuotes()
    {
        QuotesCollection quotesCollection;

        HttpContext ctx = HttpContext.Current;
        quotesCollection = (QuotesCollection)ctx.Cache["quotesCollection"];
        if (quotesCollection == null)
        {
            quotesCollection = new QuotesCollection();
            String strAppPath = Server.MapPath("");
```

```
            String strFilePathXml =
                strAppPath + "\\app_data\\QuotesCollection.xml";
            String strFilePathSchema =
                strAppPath + "\\app_data\\QuotesCollection.xsd";

            quotesCollection.ReadXmlSchema(strFilePathSchema);
            quotesCollection.ReadXml(strFilePathXml);

            CacheDependency cacheDependency =
                new CacheDependency(strFilePathXml);

            ctx.Cache.Insert("quotesCollection",
                    quotesCollection,
                    cacheDependency,
                    Cache.NoAbsoluteExpiration,
                    Cache.NoSlidingExpiration,
                    CacheItemPriority.Default,
                    null);
        }
        return quotesCollection;
    }

    public QuoteService () {

    }

    [WebMethod]
    public string HelloWorld() {
        return "Hello World";
    }

[WebMethod]
public Quote GetAQuote()
{
    QuotesCollection quotesCollection = this.LoadQuotes();
    int nNumQuotes = quotesCollection.Rows.Count;

    Random random = new Random();
    int nQuote = random.Next(nNumQuotes);
    DataRow dataRow = quotesCollection.Rows[nQuote];
    Quote quote = new Quote((String)dataRow["Quote"],
                    (String)dataRow["OriginatorLastName"],
                    (String)dataRow["OriginatorFirstName"]);
    return quote;
}

    [WebMethod]
    public void AddQuote(Quote quote)
    {
        QuotesCollection quotesCollection = this.LoadQuotes();

        DataRow dr = quotesCollection.NewRow();
```

```
            dr[0] = quote._strQuote;
            dr[1] = quote._strOriginatorLastName;
            dr[2] = quote._strOriginatorFirstName;
            quotesCollection.Rows.Add(dr);

            String strAppPath = Server.MapPath("");
            String strFilePathXml =
                strAppPath + "\\app_data\\QuotesCollection.xml";
            String strFilePathSchema =
                strAppPath + "\\app_data\\QuotesCollection.xsd";

            quotesCollection.WriteXmlSchema(strFilePathSchema);
            quotesCollection.WriteXml(strFilePathXml);
        }

        [WebMethod]
        public DataSet GetAllQuotes()
        {
            QuotesCollection quotesCollection = LoadQuotes();
            DataSet dataSet = new DataSet();
            dataSet.Tables.Add(quotesCollection);
            return dataSet;
        }

    }
```

You now have a Web service that will deliver quotes to the client upon request. You can surf to the ASMX page and try out the methods if you want to see them work. However, the real power lies in writing clients against the Web service so the client can consume the Web Service programmatically.

Consuming Web Services

Note   Consuming a Web service is nearly as easy as writing one. The Microsoft .NET Framework and Visual Studio have handy utilities that generate proxies for Web services automatically. Visual Studio is not the only way to consume Web services. May modern applications have ways to consume Web services. Web services are meant to be platform independent, and most modern computing platforms support consuming Web services.

The following example illustrates consuming the QuoteService via a small command line program.

Use the QuoteService

1. Add a new subproject to the solution. Make the new project a console application by selecting the **Console Application** template. Name the project ConsumeWeb-Service.

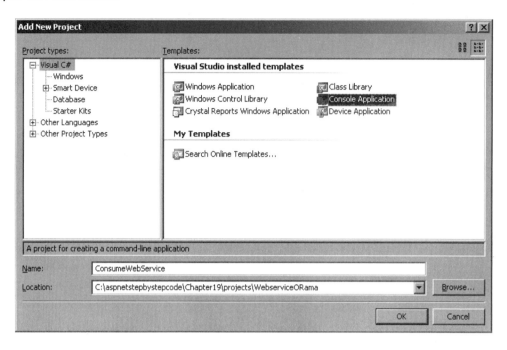

2. Highlight the ConsumeWebService project in the solution explorer and right-click. Select **Add Web Reference** from the local menu.

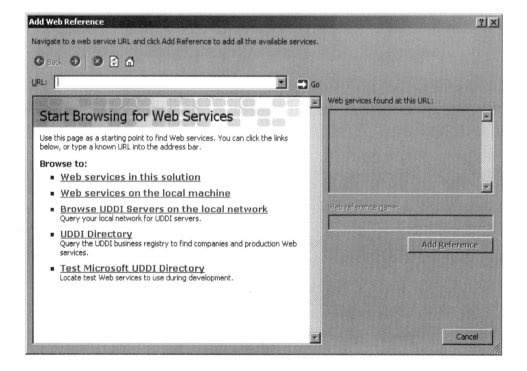

Click on the **Web services in this solution** link:

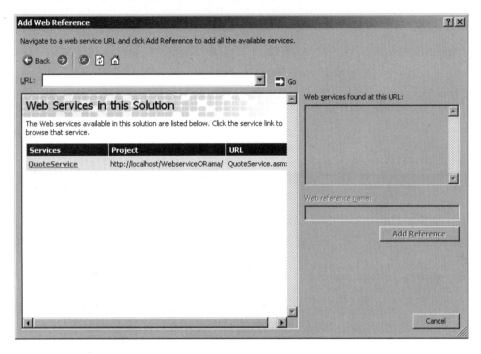

Select the **QuoteService** link. You should see all the available methods. Click the **Add Reference** button. Visual Studio will generate a proxy for you.

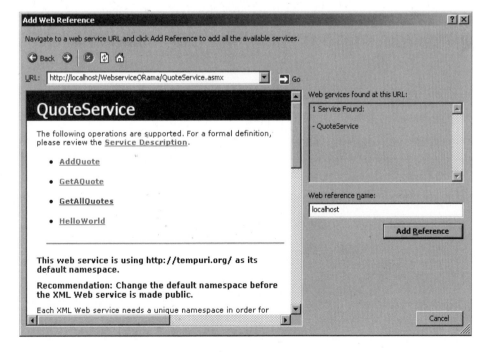

3. The namespace in which the new proxy lives reflects the origin of the Web service. Because this proxy came from a service on this machine, the namespace is *localhost*. To access types from the new service proxy, you must preface the types with *localhost*. You could also include the *localhost* in the using block where the other namespaces are imported into the project.

4. The name of the QuoteService proxy is (strangely enough) *QuoteService*. You instantiate it like you would any other class. When you call methods, the proxy will wrap the call in a SOAP envelope and send the request to the destination specified within the proxy. Try making calls to *GetAQuote*, *AddQuote*, and *GetAllQuotes*, as shown below.

```
using System;
using System.Collections.Generic;
using System.Text;
using System.Data;

namespace ConsumeWebService
{
    class Program
    {
        static void Main(string[] args)
        {
            localhost.Quote quote;
            localhost.QuoteService quoteService;

            quoteService = new localhost.QuoteService();

            for(int i = 0; i < 10; i++)
            {
```

```
        quote = quoteService.GetAQuote();
        System.Console.WriteLine("Quote: " + quote._strQuote);
        System.Console.WriteLine( "Originator: " +
                       quote._strOriginatorFirstName + " " +
                       quote._strOriginatorLastName);
        System.Console.WriteLine();
    }
  }
 }
}
```

When you run the application, you should see some output like this:

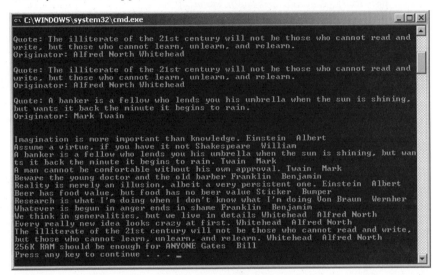

Remember, the beauty of Web services is that they're not tied to a particular platform. The previous example shows how to consume the QuoteService (which is an ASP.NET application). However, Visual Studio builds proxies for any normal Web service. You could easily have searched around for other sites implementing Web services for which Visual Studio will build you a suitable proxy.

Asynchronous Execution

The big advantage to using Web services is that they expose functionality literally worldwide. Because the Internet is so far reaching, you can call method between a client located in the United States and a service located in some place like Australia.

One of the downsides involved in making calls over such long distances is the latency. In addition to the expense of context switching, the speed of light is finite. Bits having to travel far distances make for long waits during Web method calls. For that reason, the proxies generated by Visual Studio include an asynchronous calling mechanism replete with completion callbacks.

If you look at the proxy generated by Visual Studio (Visual Studio includes it in the source code set. You may get to it using the Class View, or you may look for the file in the Web References\localhost subdirectory of the project), you'll see multiple versions of the methods exposed by the Web service. For example, there's a *GetAQuote* method *and* a *Get-AQuoteAsync* method. The proxy generated by Visual Studio also includes a number of delegates defined for subscribing to completion events.

For example, the callback delegate defined for being notified when the *GetAQuoteAsync* method is finished looks like this:

```
void GetAQuoteCompletedEventHandler(object sender,
        GetAQuoteCompletedEventArgs e);
```

The event callbacks are set up so that the second argument includes the results of calling the method (in this case, a *Quote* structure).

To make an asynchronous method call (and then be notified when it's done), you simply need to invent a callback method that matches the corresponding delegate and attach the callback to the instance of the Web service proxy you're working with.

Listing 19-1 augments the ConsumeWebService application to call the *GetAQuoteAsync* method.

Listing 19-1

```
using System;
using System.Collections.Generic;
using System.Text;
using System.Data;

namespace ConsumeWebService
{
    class Program
    {

        static void Main(string[] args)
        {
            localhost.Quote quote;
            localhost.QuoteService quoteService;

            quoteService = new localhost.QuoteService();

            for(int i = 0; i < 10; i++)
            {
                quote = quoteService.GetAQuote();
                System.Console.WriteLine("Quote: " + quote._strQuote);
                System.Console.WriteLine( "Originator: " +
                                quote._strOriginatorFirstName + " " +
                                quote._strOriginatorLastName);
                System.Console.WriteLine();
            }
```

```
System.Console.WriteLine();
localhost.Quote quoteToAdd =
    new localhost.Quote();
quoteToAdd._strQuote = "256K RAM should be enough for ANYONE";
quoteToAdd._strOriginatorLastName = "Gates";
quoteToAdd._strOriginatorFirstName = "Bill";

quoteService.AddQuote(quoteToAdd);

DataSet dataSetQuotes = quoteService.GetAllQuotes();

DataTable tableQuotes = dataSetQuotes.Tables[0];
foreach (DataRow dr in tableQuotes.Rows)
{
    System.Console.WriteLine(dr[0] + " " +
    dr[1] + "   " + dr[2]);
}


System.Console.WriteLine(
    "Press enter to fetch a quote using async");
System.Console.ReadLine();
quoteService.GetAQuoteCompleted += OnGetAQuoteCompleted;
quoteService.GetAQuoteAsync();
System.Console.WriteLine("Press return to end program ");
System.Console.ReadLine();


}


// from generated code  :
// public delegate
// void GetAQuoteCompletedEventHandler(object sender,
//     GetAQuoteCompletedEventArgs e);
public static void OnGetAQuoteCompleted(object sender,
    localhost.GetAQuoteCompletedEventArgs e)
{
    System.Console.WriteLine();
    System.Console.WriteLine("This is the callback for GetAQuote");
    System.Console.WriteLine("Quote: " + e.Result._strQuote);
    System.Console.WriteLine(e.Result._strOriginatorFirstName +
        "  " + e.Result._strOriginatorLastName);
}

}
}
```

After running the asynchronous version, you should see output like this. The callback should display two randomly selected quotes—the result of calling the *GetQuote* method twice:

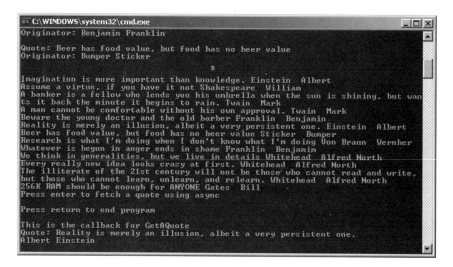

The screen shots look a bit odd here because of the order in which the code runs. The program fetches ten quotes synchronously. Then, waits for the enter key to be pressed (that's the "Press return to end program" line you see. Remember that the last Web method call is running asynchronously, so we see the result of the asynchronous call even as the main thread is waiting for the Enter keypress.

The callback mechanism is especially useful for application environments that cannot afford to stall. For example, if a Windows application takes too long to handle a message (the cardinal rule is 1/10 of a second or so), the entire application begins to suffer. Windows applications require a continuously running message pump. Calling a Web method within a Windows application is likely to stall the application for longer than you want. By calling the async versions of the Web methods, the calling thread returns immediately so it can continue doing whatever it's supposed to be doing (for example, running a message loop).

Web Services in Visual Basic

For completeness, this chapter includes a Visual Basic version of the QuoteService. It's in a separate project named QuoteServiceVB. The file name is QuoteServiceVB.asmx. Listing 19-2 shows the Visual Basic code for the service. Listing 19-3 shows the Visual Basic code for the QuotesCollection.VB utility class.

Listing 19-2

```vb
Imports System
Imports System.Data
Imports System.Configuration
Imports System.Web
Imports System.Web.Security
Imports System.Web.UI
Imports System.Web.UI.WebControls
Imports System.Web.UI.WebControls.WebParts
Imports System.Web.UI.HtmlControls
Imports System.IO

<Serializable()> _
Public Class QuotesCollection : Inherits DataTable

    Public Sub QuotesCollection()
    End Sub

    Public Sub Synthesize()

        Me.TableName = "Quotations"
        Dim dr As DataRow

        Columns.Add(New _
            DataColumn("Quote", GetType(String)))
        Columns.Add(New _
            DataColumn("OriginatorLastName", GetType(String)))
        Columns.Add(New _
            DataColumn("OriginatorFirstName", GetType(String)))

        dr = Me.NewRow()
        dr(0) = _
            "Imagination is more important than knowledge."
        dr(1) = "Einstein"
        dr(2) = "Albert"
        Rows.Add(dr)

        dr = Me.NewRow()
        dr(0) = _
            "Assume a virtue, if you have it not"
        dr(1) = "Shakespeare"
        dr(2) = "William"
        Me.Rows.Add(dr)

        dr = Me.NewRow()
            dr(0) = _
            "A banker is a fellow who lends you his " + _
```

```
            "umbrella when the sun is shining, but wants " + _
            "it back the minute it begins to rain."
    dr(1) = "Twain"
    dr(2) = "Mark"
    Me.Rows.Add(dr)

    dr = Me.NewRow()
    dr(0) = "A man cannot be comfortable without " + _
    "his own approval."
    dr(1) = "Twain"
    dr(2) = "Mark"
    Me.Rows.Add(dr)

    dr = Me.NewRow()
    dr(0) = "Beware the young doctor and the " + _
    "old barber"
    dr(1) = "Franklin"
    dr(2) = "Benjamin"
    Me.Rows.Add(dr)

    dr = Me.NewRow()
    dr(0) = "Reality is merely an illusion, " + _
    "albeit a very persistent one."
    dr(1) = "Einstein"
    dr(2) = "Albert"
    Me.Rows.Add(dr)

    dr = Me.NewRow()
    dr(0) = "Beer has food value, but food has " + _
    "no beer value"
    dr(1) = "Sticker"
    dr(2) = "Bumper"
    Me.Rows.Add(dr)

    dr = Me.NewRow()
    dr(0) = "Research is what I'm doing when I " + _
    "don() 't know what I'm doing"
    dr(1) = "Von Braun"
    dr(2) = "Wernher""
    Me.Rows.Add(dr)

    dr = Me.NewRow()
    dr(0) = "Whatever is begun in anger ends in shame"
    dr(1) = "Franklin"
    dr(2) = "Benjamim"
    Me.Rows.Add(dr)

    dr = Me.NewRow()
    dr(0) = "We think in generalities, but " + _
    "we live in details"
    dr(1) = "Whitehead"
    dr(2) = "Alfred North"
    Me.Rows.Add(dr)

    dr = Me.NewRow()
```

```
            dr(0) = "Every really new idea looks crazy " + _
            "at first."
            dr(1) = "Whitehead"
            dr(2) = "Alfred North"
            Me.Rows.Add(dr)

            dr = Me.NewRow()
            dr(0) = "The illiterate of the 21st century will " + _
            "not be those who cannot read and write, but those " + _
            "who cannot learn, unlearn, and relearn."
            dr(1) = "Whitehead"
            dr(2) = "Alfred North"
            Me.Rows.Add(dr)

    End Sub
End Class
```

Listing 19-3

```
Imports System
Imports System.Web
Imports System.Data
Imports System.Web.Services
Imports System.Web.Services.Protocols
Imports System.Web.Caching

Public Structure Quote

    Public _strQuote As String
    Public _strOriginatorLastName As String
    Public _strOriginatorFirstName As String

    Public Sub New(ByVal strQuote As String, _
            ByVal strOriginatorLastName As String, _
            ByVal strOriginatorFirstName As String)
        _strQuote = strQuote
        _strOriginatorLastName = strOriginatorLastName
        _strOriginatorFirstName = strOriginatorFirstName
    End Sub

End Structure

<WebService(Namespace:="http://tempuri.org/")> _
<WebServiceBinding(ConformsTo:=WsiProfiles.BasicProfile1_1)> _
Public Class QuoteServiceVB
    Inherits System.Web.Services.WebService

    Function LoadQuotes() As QuotesCollection

        Dim quotesCollection As QuotesCollection

        Dim ctx As HttpContext
        ctx = HttpContext.Current

        Dim o As Object
```

```vbnet
        o = ctx.Cache("quotesCollection")

        quotesCollection = CType(o, QuotesCollection)
        If quotesCollection Is Nothing Then
            quotesCollection = New QuotesCollection()
            Dim strAppPath As String

            strAppPath = Server.MapPath("")

            Dim strFilePathXml As String
            strFilePathXml = _
                strAppPath & _
                "\\app_data\\QuotesCollection.xml"

            Dim strFilePathSchema As String
            strFilePathSchema = _
                strAppPath & _
                "\\app_data\\QuotesCollection.xsd"

            quotesCollection.ReadXmlSchema(strFilePathSchema)
            quotesCollection.ReadXml(strFilePathXml)

            Dim cacheDependency As CacheDependency
            cacheDependency = New CacheDependency(strFilePathXml)

            ctx.Cache.Insert("quotesCollection", _
                quotesCollection, _
                cacheDependency, _
                Cache.NoAbsoluteExpiration, _
                Cache.NoSlidingExpiration, _
                CacheItemPriority.Default, _
                Nothing)
        End If
        Return quotesCollection
End Function


Public Sub QuoteService()

End Sub

<WebMethod()> _
Public Function HelloWorld() As String

    Return "Hello World"
End Function

<WebMethod()> _
Public Function GetAQuote() As Quote
    Dim quotesCollection As QuotesCollection
    quotesCollection = Me.LoadQuotes()
    Dim nNumQuotes As Integer
    nNumQuotes = quotesCollection.Rows.Count

    Dim random As Random
```

```vb
    random = New Random()

    Dim nQuote As Integer

    nQuote = random.Next(nNumQuotes)

    Dim dataRow As DataRow

    dataRow = quotesCollection.Rows(nQuote)

    Dim quote As Quote
    quote = New Quote(CType(dataRow("Quote"), String), _
        CType(dataRow("OriginatorLastName"), String), _
        CType(dataRow("OriginatorFirstName"), String))
    Return quote

End Function

<WebMethod()> _
Public Sub AddQuote(ByVal quote As Quote)

    Dim quotesCollection As QuotesCollection
    quotesCollection = Me.LoadQuotes()

    Dim dr As DataRow
    dr = quotesCollection.NewRow()
    dr(0) = quote._strQuote
    dr(1) = quote._strOriginatorLastName
    dr(2) = quote._strOriginatorFirstName
    quotesCollection.Rows.Add(dr)
    Dim strAppPath As String
    strAppPath = Server.MapPath("")
    Dim strFilePathXml As String
    strFilePathXml = _
        strAppPath + "\\app_data\\QuotesCollection.xml"
    Dim strFilePathSchema As String
    strFilePathSchema = _
        strAppPath + "\\app_data\\QuotesCollection.xsd"

    quotesCollection.WriteXmlSchema(strFilePathSchema)
    quotesCollection.WriteXml(strFilePathXml)
End Sub

<WebMethod()> _
Public Function GetAllQuotes() As DataSet
    Dim quotesCollection As QuotesCollection
    quotesCollection = LoadQuotes()
    Dim dataSet As DataSet
    dataSet = New DataSet()
    dataSet.Tables.Add(quotesCollection)
    Return dataSet
End Function

End Class
```

What Good Are Web Services?

So, it's pretty neat that you can call a method from one computer to the other. How is that useful? Web services represent the underpinnings of a whole new model for communicating between enterprises. Here are a couple of examples of how they are useful.

If you've ever gotten a package delivered to you via the United Parcel Service, you almost invariably need to scrawl your name on the big, brown, bulky tablet handed to you by the guy in the brown shirt. When you sign the tablet, UPS knows that you received the package and they can record that information. Tracking packages in real time is really useful for UPS's business. Recipients always want to know where their packages are at any time, and using this technology helps UPS provide this information to end customers.

UPS undoubtedly spent a great deal of money on their package tracking system. They developed the technology in the early 1990s—long before even Al Gore knew what the Internet was. With the advent of a worldwide connected network (the Internet), small and manageable wireless devices to connect to the Internet, and a commonly understood wire format (SOAP), enterprises can develop functionality similar to that used by UPS for a fraction of the cost.

A second way in which Web services will prove useful is in supply chain management. Back in the 1980s, Electronic Data Interchange (EDI for short) promised to allow companies to order supplies and services automatically with little or no human intervention. The idea was that different companies would subscribe to a data format and would be able to order supplies and services from other enterprises in a much more streamlined way.

Unfortunately, EDI turned out to be mostly a glorified e-mail system. The formats for data interchange were brittle and easily broken. Furthermore, when the format broke, it took a long time for the companies involved to reach another agreement on a new format.

Web services promise to help solve the problem of a brittle data interchange mechanism. Through more elaborate orchestration frameworks (like BizTalk from Microsoft), Web services promise to make automatic data interchange between enterprises much more doable and affordable than ever before.

Other Features

ASP.NET also implements a number of other features for enhancing Web services. For example, sometimes you want to include some metadata as part of a method call. For example, if you want to ensure only paying clients call your Web methods, you might issue them a token to prove they bought the service. The SOAP specification defines *SOAP headers* as a way to include such metadata in the method call.

In addition, it's sometimes useful to install pre- and post processing for Web methods. ASP.NET supports various SOAP extensions. For example, if you wanted to write your own encryption mechanism, you might write a client-side and a service-side extension that encrypts and unencrypts messages interacting with your server.

Conclusion

Web services represent the next generation of computer connectivity. Instead of relying upon a closed network protocol and wire format, Web services open up the availability of an application to the entire world. Web services are built upon an already existing network using a wire format that many enterprises agree upon for making method calls.

ASP.NET automates the detailed work necessary to unpack a SOAP request and turn it into a real method call. ASMX files are handlers in the same way as ASPX and ASHX files. ASMX files implement *IHttpHandler* by parsing the incoming XML, calling a method in the code-behind class, and returning a result. Simply adorning the method with the *[WebMethod]* attribute inserts the necessary functionality.

Visual Studio is also useful for consuming Web services. By adding a Web reference to your application, Visual Studio will consult the Web service for the WSDL code and use it to build a proxy. From there you simply instantiate the proxy and call methods. The proxy takes care of preparing the SOAP payload and sending it. The proxies generated by Visual Studio also support asynchronous method invocation so that the main calling thread doesn't block for too long.

Chapter 19 Quick Reference

To	Do This
Create a Web service	From an ASP.NET project, select **Web Site	Add New Item** from the main menu
	Select the **Web Service** template
Expose a class method as a Web method	Apply the *[WebMethod]* attribute immediately preceding the method signature
Consume a Web service	From within Visual Studio, select the project in solution explorer.
	Right-click on project
	Select **Add Web Reference**
	Surf to the Web service. Visual Studio will automatically ask for the WSDL and build a proxy

Chapter 20
Managing and Deploying Web Applications

After completing this chapter, you will be able to

- Recognize ways the Visual Studio project models affect deployment
- Build a Web setup utility

We've spent the last 19 chapters figuring out how the various features of ASP.NET work. A major theme within ASP.NET has always been to solve the most common use cases as far as developing Web sites is concerned. We saw ASP.NET's

- rendering model, which breaks down page rendering into small manageable pieces via server-side controls
- support for databinding, easing the task of rendering collections
- new login controls covering the most common login scenarios
- session state that makes tracking users manageable
- support for creating a common look and feel for an application through Master Pages and Skins

After building a feature-rich application that streamlines your company operations or drives customers to your business, you need to be able to manage it effectively, and deploy it. That's the topic of this chapter—how the various Visual Studio models affect your deployment strategy. In addition, we'll look at building a Web setup project.

Visual Studio Projects

Visual Studio 2005 gives you several options when building a Web site project (as opposed to earlier versions that depended upon IIS). These project models include the HTTP project, the FTP project, and the file project. Here's a summary of how each model works.

HTTP Project

The HTTP project is most like the model built into earlier versions of Visual Studio. Under the HTTP project model, Visual Studio creates a virtual directory under IIS and uses IIS to intercept requests during development time. Under this model, the solution file (the .sln file) resides in a directory specified under Visual Studio's project settings directory. The source code for the project is stored in the IIS virtual directory (that is, \Inetpub\wwwroot).

You may either have Visual Studio create a virtual directory for you, or you may create a virtual directory ahead of time. You may store the code for your Web site in any folder. The virtual directory just needs to point to that location.

Use this option if you want to work as closely as possible in the same mode as earlier versions of Visual Studio. In addition, using an IIS Web site during development lets you test the entire request path (not just the path through ASP.NET). This is important if you want to test an application that leverages IIS security, requires ISAPI filters, application pooling, or some other specific IIS features to run effectively. One reason to create a local Web site is to test your application against a local version of IIS. Using IIS as part of the development environment makes it easier to test these things. Of course, the downside to this approach is that you require IIS to be installed on your machine (it's not installed automatically—you have to take a deliberate step to install it). Having IIS on your machine may also compromise security.

FTP Project

The FTP project is meant for those projects you want to manage remotely through an FTP server. For example, this is a good option if you use a remote hosting service to host your Web site. The FTP site option represents a reasonable means of getting files from your development environment to the hosting site.

When creating this type of site, Visual Studio will connect to any FTP server for which you have reading and writing privileges. You then use Visual Studio to manage the content on the remote FTP server.

You might use this option to test the Web site on the live-deployed server where it will actually be deployed.

File System Project

The file project is probably the most developer-oriented project. File System projects rely upon the Web server inside Visual Studio instead of IIS. When you specify a file system Web site, you may tell Visual Studio to put it anywhere on your file system or in a shared folder on another computer.

If you don't have access to IIS, or you don't have administration rights to the system on which you're developing, then you'll want to create a file system-based Web site project. The site runs locally, but independently of IIS. The most common scenario in this case is to develop and test a Web site on the file system. Then when it comes time to expose your site, simply create an IIS virtual directory and point it to the pages in the file system Web site.

By default, Visual Studio does *not* precompile your Web application. Once you've developed a site using Visual Studio, you may decide to precompile it.

Precompiling

Earlier versions of Visual Studio (for example, Visual Studio 2003) automatically built ASP.NET applications when you hit the Build | Build Solution menu item. All the source code (the VB and the CS files) was compiled into a resulting assembly named the same as the project. This precompiled assembly went into the project's \bin directory and became part of the files used for deployment. ASP.NET will still precompile an application for you. However, now you have two choices as far as recompiling goes—using a virtual path (for applications already defined in IIS) and a physical path (for sites that live on the file system). In addition, you must be deliberate about precompiling. The two precompiling options include (1) precompiling for performance and (2) precompiling for deployment. Precompiling a Web site involves using command line tools.

Precompiling for Performance

The first option is also known as "precompiling in place." This is useful for existing sites for which you want to enhance performance. When you precompile the source code behind your site, the primary benefit is that ASP.NET doesn't have to run that first compilation when the site is hit for the first time. If your site requires frequent updates to the code base, you may see a small amount of performance improvement.

To precompile an IIS-based site in place, open a Visual Studio command window. Navigate to the .NET directory on your machine (probably Windows\Microsoft.Net\Framework\<versionnumber>). In that directory is a program named aspnet_compiler. Execute the aspnet_compiler program, with the name of the Web site as known by IIS following the −v switch. For example, if IIS has a virtual directory named MySite, the following command line will build it. The precompiled application ends up in the Temporary ASP.NET Files directory under your current .NET directory.

```
aspnet_compiler -v MySite
```

If the Web site is a file system Web site without an IIS virtual directory, use the −p command line parameter to specify the physical path.

This compilation option precompiles the code and places it in the bin directory for the application.

Precompiling for Deployment

Compiling for deployment involves compiling the code for a site and directing the output to a special directory from which it may be copied to the deployment machine or used in an install project (as we'll see momentarily). In this case, the compiler produces assemblies from all ASP.NET source files that are normally compiled at run time. That includes the code for the pages, source code within the App_Code directory, and resource files.

To precompile a site for deployment, open a Visual Studio command window. Navigate to the .NET directory. Run the aspnet_compiler command line program, specifying the source as either a virtual path or physical path. Provide the target folder following the input directory. For example, the following command builds the code in the MySite virtual directory and puts in c:\MySiteTarget.

```
aspnet_compiler -v MySite c:\MySiteTarget
```

If you add a –*u* command line parameter at the end of the command line, the compiler will compile some of the code and leave the page code files to be compiled just in time.

Once the code is compiled, one of the options you have is to build a Web setup program. The following example illustrates creating a Web setup program.

Creating a Web Site Installer

1. Start by creating a new site. Make it an HTTP site. Name the site DeployThis.
2. Create some content for the site. For example, add a few pages to the site, or borrow content from an earlier example.
3. Precompile the site for deployment. Tell the aspnet_compiler to use the Deploy this virtual directory as the source and to direct it to a target holding directory. The following graphic illustrates the command line. Use the –*u* option at the end of the command line to instruct the compiler to make an updateable Web site.

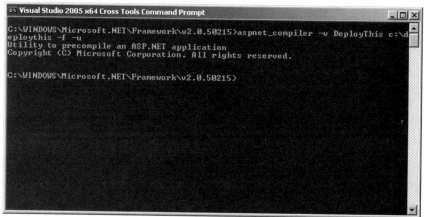

4. After the compiler runs, you'll have a target directory full of compiled code. The following graphic illustrates the results of the compilation.

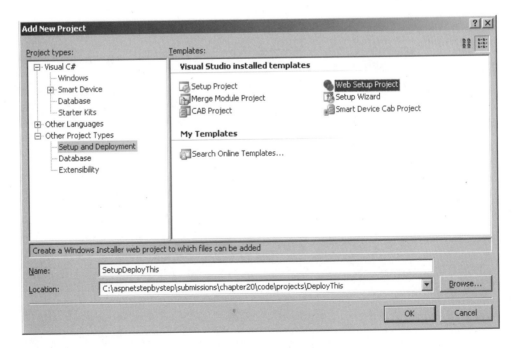

5. Add a second project to the solution. Make it a Web Setup Project, as shown in the following graphic. Name the project SetupDeployThis.

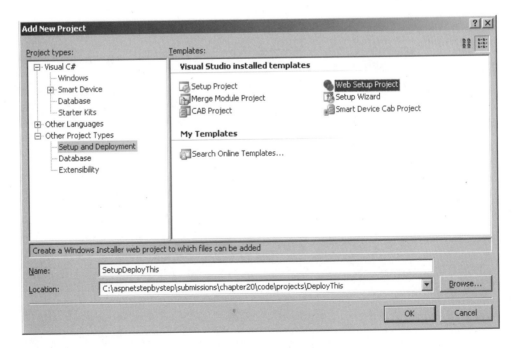

6. Visual Studio will generate a new setup project for you. You should see a screen like this after Visual Studio is done churning:

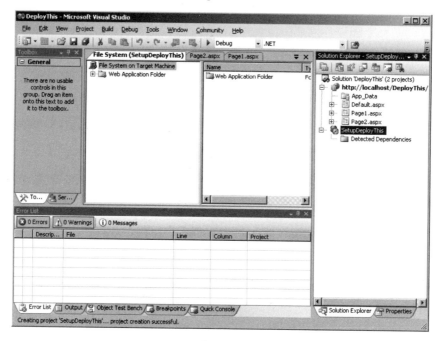

7. Right-click on the Web Application Folder to add the Web files. Navigate to the target directory containing the site code. This will be the precompile directory.

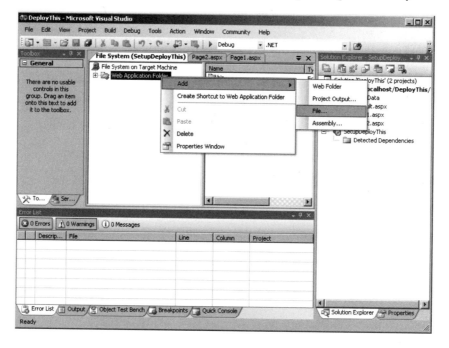

8. Add the Web files from the precompile directory.

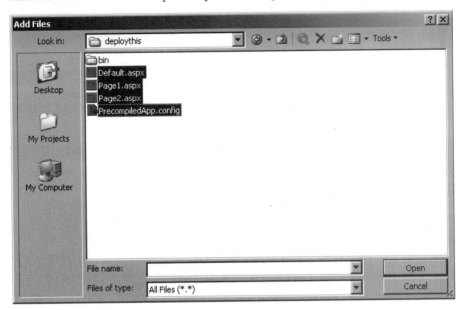

9. Add the dlls to the bin directory by right-clicking on the bin node to get the File Open dialog box. Then search for assemblies in the target directory's \bin directory.

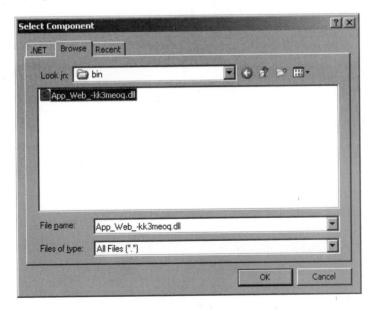

10. After adding all the files, the directory structure should look like this. The bin directory will have the site DLLs:

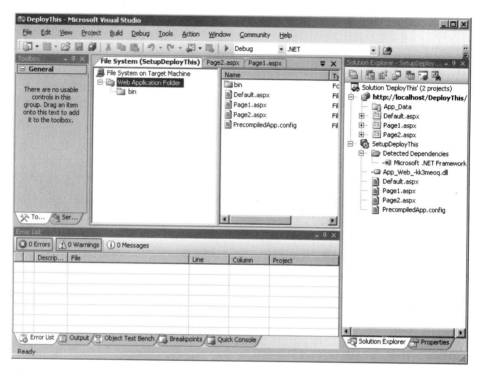

11. The Setup project properties include a prerequisite dialog box that you may review to ensure that certain prerequisites are installed on the end computer. The following graphic illustrates the prerequisites dialog box. Notice that the .NET Framework box is checked.

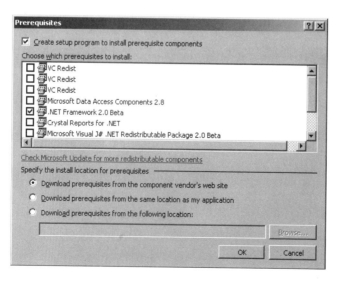

12. Right-click on the SetupDeployThis project and select **Build**. The resulting MSI file goes in the debug directory of the project.

13. Try running the Microsoft Installer file (the MSI file). The MSI file will guide you through several steps as it installs the Web site, as shown in the following graphics:

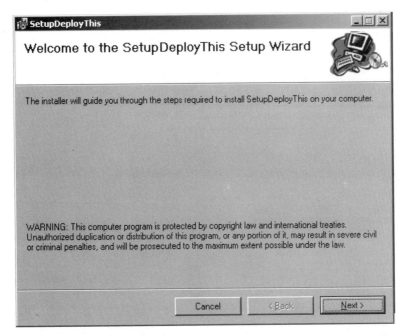

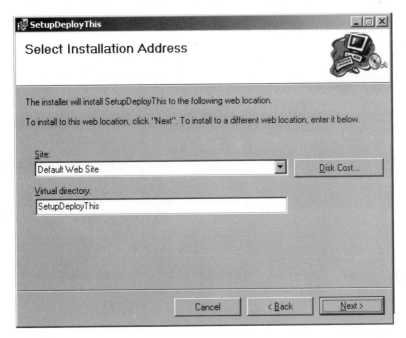

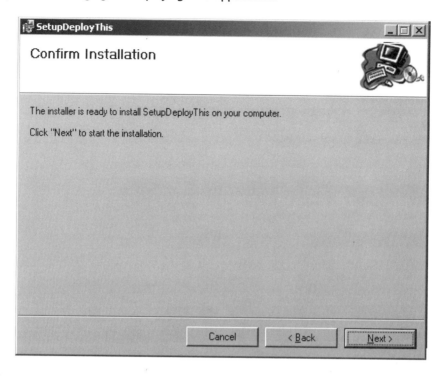

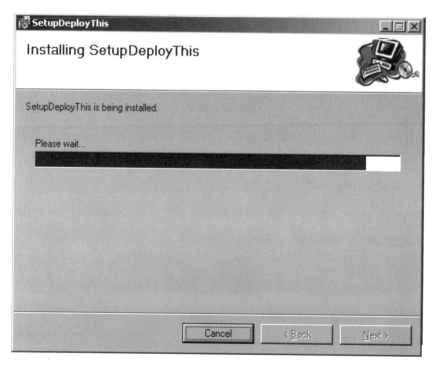

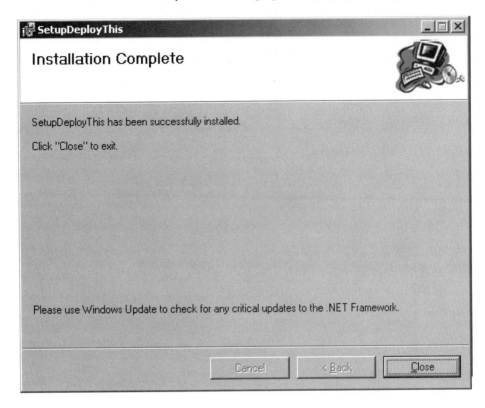

14. Now examine IIS. Refresh the Default Web Site node and look for the SetupDeployThis virtual directory (unless you named it something else during the install process). IIS will have the SetupDeployThis site:

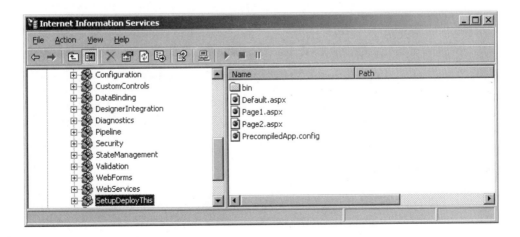

15.   After the site is installed, you can surf to it as you can any other site.

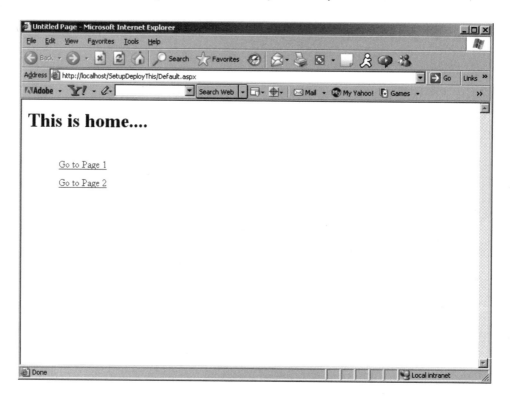

Setting up Install packages is a good way to distribute a Web application across the set of servers. You can push the MSI file out to the server as necessary and run it. However, using an Install package isn't the only way to distribute the application. You may also literally copy the entire directory from a development machine to the server (XCOPY deployment), or you may use some other file transfer mechanism to move the bits.

> **Note**   The term *XCOPY deployment* refers to the installation strategy available during the late 1980's when DOS 3.x - 5.x ran on most systems. The basic idea was to copy an entire directory structure and place it on the target machine. The directory structure in those days was pretty isolated and transferring entire directory structures was reasonable.

Conclusion

In this chapter, we looked at how the various Visual Studio projects affect the end deployment strategy for your Web site. Visual Studio provides several models, including

■   HTTP sites that use IIS on the development machine

- File system sites that exist in the development file system, using the Web server built into Visual Studio

- FTP sites, where the bits are transferred to the target server via FTP

In addition to copying the software directly to the deployment machine, you may also precompile the application before copying it. By precompiling, you save the first end user to hit your site the few seconds it takes to compile the site. Of course, the subsequent hits take a much shorter time. However, if you foresee the site churning a lot, it may be worthwhile to precompile for performance. In addition, you may precompile the application so as to deploy it using an installer or a copying technique.

Chapter 20 Quick Reference

To	Do This
Work on a Web site locally without going through IIS	Create a file system Web site
Work on a Web site using IIS	Create an HTTP Web site
Work on a Web site by copying files over to the server FTP	Create an FTP site
Precompile for performance or for deployment	Use the aspnet_compiler utility to precompile the code
Create an Installer for your Web application	Add a second project to your solution
	Make it a Web Setup Project
	Add the necessary files to the project to make it work
	Build the installer

Index

George Shepherd

As a Research Scientist at Rockwell Scientific, George investigates a variety of leading edge technologies for various industry and government-based programs, as well as participating in the development of multiple large software systems.

In addition, George is a DevelopMentor instructor, delivering short courses on various .NET topics worldwide.

As a contributing architect for Syncfusion's Essential .NET suites, George has provided insight into their Windows Forms and ASP.NET FAQs published at *http://www.syncfusion.com.*

George has authored and co-authored several other books on Microsoft technology including *MFC Internals* and *Applied .NET* from Addison-Wesley, *Inside Visual C++, Inside ATL*, and ***Programming Visual C++ .NET*** from Microsoft Press. He is a former columnist for *Dr. Dobb's Programming Journal*, and his articles appear frequently in *MSDN Magazine*, including "The ASP Column."

Additional Resources for Database Developers

Published and Forthcoming Titles from Microsoft Press

Microsoft® SQL Server™ 2005 Express Edition
Step by Step
Jackie Goldstein • ISBN 0-7356-2184-5

Teach yourself how to get database projects up and running quickly with SQL Server Express Edition—one step at a time! SQL Server Express is a free, easy-to-use database product that is based on SQL Server 2005 technology. It's designed for building simple, dynamic applications, with all the rich functionality of the SQL Server database engine and using the same data access APIs such as Microsoft ADO.NET, SQL Native Client, and T-SQL. With *Step by Step*, you work at your own pace through hands-on, learn-by-doing exercises. Whether you're new to database programming or new to SQL Server, you'll learn how, when, and why to use specific features of this simple but powerful database development environment. Each chapter puts you to work, building your knowledge of core capabilities and guiding you as you create actual components and working applications. You'll also discover how SQL Server Express works seamlessly with the Microsoft Visual Studio® 2005 environment, simplifying the design, development, and deployment of your applications.

Programming Microsoft ADO.NET 2.0
Applications: *Advanced Topics*
Glenn Johnson • ISBN 0-7356-2141-1

Get in-depth coverage and expert insights on advanced ADO.NET programming topics such as optimization, DataView, and large objects (BLOBs and CLOBs). Targeting experienced, professional software developers who design and develop enterprise applications, this book assumes that the reader knows and understands the basic functionality and concepts of ADO.NET 2.0 and that he or she is ready to move to mastering data-manipulation skills in Microsoft Windows. The book, complete with pragmatic and instructive code examples, is structured so that readers can jump in for reference on each topic as needed.

Microsoft ADO.NET 2.0
Step by Step
Rebecca Riordan • ISBN 0-7356-2164-0

In Microsoft .NET Framework 2.0, data access is enhanced not only through the addition of new data access controls, services, and the ability to integrate more seamlessly with SQL Server 2005, but also through improvements to the ADO.NET class libraries themselves. Now you can teach yourself the essentials of working with ADO.NET 2.0 in the Visual Studio environment—one step at a time. With *Step by Step*, you work at your own pace through hands-on, learn-by-doing exercises. Whether you're a beginning programmer or new to this version of the technology, you'll understand the core capabilities and fundamental techniques for ADO.NET 2.0. Each chapter puts you to work, showing you how, when, and why to use specific features of the ADO.NET 2.0 rapid application development environment and guiding as you create actual components and working applications for Microsoft Windows®.

Programming Microsoft ADO.NET 2.0
Core Reference
David Sceppa • ISBN 0-7356-2206-X

This *Core Reference* demonstrates how to use ADO.NET 2.0, a technology within Visual Studio 2005, to access, sort, and manipulate data in standalone, enterprise, and Web-enabled applications. Discover best practices for writing, testing, and debugging database application code using the new tools and wizards in Visual Studio 2005, and put them to work with extensive code samples, tutorials, and insider tips. The book describes the ADO.NET object model, its XML features for Web extensibility, integration with Microsoft SQL Server 2000 and SQL Server 2005, and other core topics.

Programming Microsoft Windows Forms
Charles Petzold • ISBN 0-7356-2153-5

Programming Microsoft Web Forms
Douglas J. Reilly • ISBN 0-7356-2179-9

Inside Microsoft SQL Server 2005: The Storage Engine (Volume 1)
Kalen Delaney • ISBN 0-7356-2105-5

Debugging, Tuning, and Testing Microsoft .NET 2.0 Applications
John Robbins • ISBN 0-7356-2202-7

Microsoft SQL Server 2005 Programming Step by Step
Fernando Guerrero • ISBN 0-7356-2207-8

Programming Microsoft SQL Server 2005
Andrew J. Brust, Stephen Forte, and William H. Zack
ISBN 0-7356-1923-9

For more information about Microsoft Press® books and other learning products,
visit: **www.microsoft.com/books** *and* **www.microsoft.com/learning**

Additional Resources for C# Developers
Published and Forthcoming Titles from Microsoft Press

Microsoft® Visual C#® 2005 Express Edition: Build a Program Now!
Patrice Pelland ● ISBN 0-7356-2229-9

In this lively, eye-opening, and hands-on book, all you need is a computer and the desire to learn how to program with Visual C# 2005 Express Edition. Featuring a full working edition of the software, this fun and highly visual guide walks you through a complete programming project—a desktop weather-reporting application—from start to finish. You'll get an unintimidating introduction to the Microsoft Visual Studio® development environment and learn how to put the lightweight, easy-to-use tools in Visual C# Express to work right away—creating, compiling, testing, and delivering your first, ready-to-use program. You'll get expert tips, coaching, and visual examples at each step of the way, along with pointers to additional learning resources.

Microsoft Visual C# 2005 *Step by Step*
John Sharp ● ISBN 0-7356-2129-2

Visual C#, a feature of Visual Studio 2005, is a modern programming language designed to deliver a productive environment for creating business frameworks and reusable object-oriented components. Now you can teach yourself essential techniques with Visual C#—and start building components and Microsoft Windows®–based applications—one step at a time. With *Step by Step*, you work at your own pace through hands-on, learn-by-doing exercises. Whether you're a beginning programmer or new to this particular language, you'll learn how, when, and why to use specific features of Visual C# 2005. Each chapter puts you to work, building your knowledge of core capabilities and guiding you as you create your first C#-based applications for Windows, data management, and the Web.

Programming Microsoft Visual C# 2005 Framework Reference
Francesco Balena ● ISBN 0-7356-2182-9

Complementing *Programming Microsoft Visual C# 2005 Core Reference*, this book covers a wide range of additional topics and information critical to Visual C# developers, including Windows Forms, working with Microsoft ADO.NET 2.0 and Microsoft ASP.NET 2.0, Web services, security, remoting, and much more. Packed with sample code and real-world examples, this book will help developers move from understanding to mastery.

Programming Microsoft Visual C# 2005 *Core Reference*
Donis Marshall ● ISBN 0-7356-2181-0

Get the in-depth reference and pragmatic, real-world insights you need to exploit the enhanced language features and core capabilities in Visual C# 2005. Programming expert Donis Marshall deftly builds your proficiency with classes, structs, and other fundamentals, and advances your expertise with more advanced topics such as debugging, threading, and memory management. Combining incisive reference with hands-on coding examples and best practices, this *Core Reference* focuses on mastering the C# skills you need to build innovative solutions for smart clients and the Web.

CLR via C#, Second Edition
Jeffrey Richter ● ISBN 0-7356-2163-2

In this new edition of Jeffrey Richter's popular book, you get focused, pragmatic guidance on how to exploit the common language runtime (CLR) functionality in Microsoft .NET Framework 2.0 for applications of all types—from Web Forms, Windows Forms, and Web services to solutions for Microsoft SQL Server™, Microsoft code names "Avalon" and "Indigo," consoles, Microsoft Windows NT® Service, and more. Targeted to advanced developers and software designers, this book takes you under the covers of .NET for an in-depth understanding of its structure, functions, and operational components, demonstrating the most practical ways to apply this knowledge to your own development efforts. You'll master fundamental design tenets for .NET and get hands-on insights for creating high-performance applications more easily and efficiently. The book features extensive code examples in Visual C# 2005.

Programming Microsoft Windows Forms
Charles Petzold ● ISBN 0-7356-2153-5

CLR via C++
Jeffrey Richter with Stanley B. Lippman
ISBN 0-7356-2248-5

Programming Microsoft Web Forms
Douglas J. Reilly ● ISBN 0-7356-2179-9

Debugging, Tuning, and Testing Microsoft .NET 2.0 Applications
John Robbins ● ISBN 0-7356-2202-7

For more information about Microsoft Press® books and other learning products, visit: **www.microsoft.com/books** *and* **www.microsoft.com/learning**

Additional Resources for Visual Basic Developers

Published and Forthcoming Titles from Microsoft Press

Microsoft® Visual Basic® 2005 Express Edition: Build a Program Now!
Patrice Pelland ● ISBN 0-7356-2213-2

Featuring a full working edition of the software, this fun and highly visual guide walks you through a complete programming project—a desktop weather-reporting application—from start to finish. You'll get an introduction to the Microsoft Visual Studio® development environment and learn how to put the lightweight, easy-to-use tools in Visual Basic Express to work right away—creating, compiling, testing, and delivering your first ready-to-use program. You'll get expert tips, coaching, and visual examples each step of the way, along with pointers to additional learning resources.

Microsoft Visual Basic 2005 *Step by Step*
Michael Halvorson ● ISBN 0-7356-2131-4

With enhancements across its visual designers, code editor, language, and debugger that help accelerate the development and deployment of robust, elegant applications across the Web, a business group, or an enterprise, Visual Basic 2005 focuses on enabling developers to rapidly build applications. Now you can teach yourself the essentials of working with Visual Studio 2005 and the new features of the Visual

Basic language—one step at a time. Each chapter puts you to work, showing you how, when, and why to use specific features of Visual Basic and guiding as you create actual components and working applications for Microsoft Windows®. You'll also explore data management and Web-based development topics.

Programming Microsoft Visual Basic 2005 *Core Reference*
Francesco Balena ● ISBN 0-7356-2183-7

Get the expert insights, indispensable reference, and practical instruction needed to exploit the core language features and capabilities in Visual Basic 2005. Well-known Visual Basic programming author Francesco Balena expertly guides you through the fundamentals, including modules, keywords, and inheritance, and builds your mastery of more advanced topics such as delegates, assemblies, and My Namespace. Combining

in-depth reference with extensive, hands-on code examples and best-practices advice, this *Core Reference* delivers the key resources that you need to develop professional-level programming skills for smart clients and the Web.

Programming Microsoft Visual Basic 2005 Framework Reference
Francesco Balena ● ISBN 0-7356-2175-6

Complementing *Programming Microsoft Visual Basic 2005 Core Reference*, this book covers a wide range of additional topics and information critical to Visual Basic developers, including Windows Forms, working with Microsoft ADO.NET 2.0 and ASP.NET 2.0, Web services, security, remoting, and much more. Packed with sample code and real-world examples, this book will help developers move from understanding to mastery.

Programming Microsoft Windows Forms
Charles Petzold ● ISBN 0-7356-2153-5

Programming Microsoft Web Forms
Douglas J. Reilly ● ISBN 0-7356-2179-9

Debugging, Tuning, and Testing Microsoft .NET 2.0 Applications
John Robbins ● ISBN 0-7356-2202-7

Microsoft ASP.NET 2.0 *Step by Step*
George Shepherd ● ISBN 0-7356-2201-9

Microsoft ADO.NET 2.0 *Step by Step*
Rebecca Riordan ● ISBN 0-7356-2164-0

Programming Microsoft ASP.NET 2.0 *Core Reference*
Dino Esposito ● ISBN 0-7356-2176-4

For more information about Microsoft Press® books and other learning products, visit: **www.microsoft.com/books** *and* **www.microsoft.com/learning**

Additional Resources for Web Developers

Published and Forthcoming Titles from Microsoft Press

Microsoft® Visual Web Developer™ 2005 Express Edition: Build a Web Site Now!
Jim Buyens ● ISBN 0-7356-2212-4

With this lively, eye-opening, and hands-on book, all you need is a computer and the desire to learn how to create Web pages now using Visual Web Developer Express Edition! Featuring a full working edition of the software, this fun and highly visual guide walks you through a complete Web page project from set-up to launch. You'll get an introduction to the Microsoft Visual Studio® environment and learn how to put the light-weight, easy-to-use tools in Visual Web Developer Express to work right away—building your first, dynamic Web pages with Microsoft ASP.NET 2.0. You'll get expert tips, coaching, and visual examples at each step of the way, along with pointers to additional learning resources.

Microsoft ASP.NET 2.0 Programming
Step by Step
George Shepherd ● ISBN 0-7356-2201-9

With dramatic improvements in performance, productivity, and security features, Visual Studio 2005 and ASP.NET 2.0 deliver a simplified, high-performance, and powerful Web development experience. ASP.NET 2.0 features a new set of controls and infrastructure that simplify Web-based data access and include functionality that facilitates code reuse, visual consistency, and aesthetic appeal. Now you can teach yourself the essentials of working with ASP.NET 2.0 in the Visual Studio environment—one step at a time. With *Step by Step*, you work at your own pace through hands-on, learn-by-doing exercises. Whether you're a beginning programmer or new to this version of the technology, you'll understand the core capabilities and fundamental techniques for ASP.NET 2.0. Each chapter puts you to work, showing you how, when, and why to use specific features of the ASP.NET 2.0 rapid application development environment and guiding you as you create actual components and working applications for the Web, including advanced features such as personalization.

Programming Microsoft ASP.NET 2.0
Core Reference
Dino Esposito ● ISBN 0-7356-2176-4

Delve into the core topics for ASP.NET 2.0 programming, mastering the essential skills and capabilities needed to build high-performance Web applications successfully. Well-known ASP.NET author Dino Esposito deftly builds your expertise with Web forms, Visual Studio, core controls, master pages, data access, data binding, state management, security services, and other must-know topics—combining definitive reference with practical, hands-on programming instruction. Packed with expert guidance and pragmatic examples, this *Core Reference* delivers the key resources that you need to develop professional-level Web programming skills.

Programming Microsoft ASP.NET 2.0
Applications: *Advanced Topics*
Dino Esposito ● ISBN 0-7356-2177-2

Master advanced topics in ASP.NET 2.0 programming—gaining the essential insights and in-depth understanding that you need to build sophisticated, highly functional Web applications successfully. Topics include Web forms, Visual Studio 2005, core controls, master pages, data access, data binding, state management, and security considerations. Developers often discover that the more they use ASP.NET, the more they need to know. With expert guidance from ASP.NET authority Dino Esposito, you get the in-depth, comprehensive information that leads to full mastery of the technology.

Programming Microsoft Windows® Forms
Charles Petzold ● ISBN 0-7356-2153-5

Programming Microsoft Web Forms
Douglas J. Reilly ● ISBN 0-7356-2179-9

CLR via C++
Jeffrey Richter with Stanley B. Lippman
ISBN 0-7356-2248-5

Debugging, Tuning, and Testing Microsoft .NET 2.0 Applications
John Robbins ● ISBN 0-7356-2202-7

CLR via C#, Second Edition
Jeffrey Richter ● ISBN 0-7356-2163-2

For more information about Microsoft Press® books and other learning products, visit: **www.microsoft.com/books** *and* **www.microsoft.com/learning**

What do you think of this book? We want to hear from you!

Do you have a few minutes to participate in a brief online survey? Microsoft is interested in hearing your feedback about this publication so that we can continually improve our books and learning resources for you.

To participate in our survey, please visit:

www.microsoft.com/learning/booksurvey

And enter this book's ISBN, 0-7356-2201-9. As a thank-you to survey participants in the United States and Canada, each month we'll randomly select five respondents to win one of five $100 gift certificates from a leading online merchant.* At the conclusion of the survey, you can enter the drawing by providing your e-mail address, which will be used for prize notification *only.*

Thanks in advance for your input. Your opinion counts!

Sincerely,

Microsoft Learning

Learn More. Go Further.

To see special offers on Microsoft Learning products for developers, IT professionals, and home and office users, visit: *www.microsoft.com/learning/booksurvey*